T0178325

Lecture Notes in Computer Science   13979

Founding Editors

Gerhard Goos
Juris Hartmanis

The series Lecture Notes in Computer Science (LNCS), including its subseries Lecture Notes in Artificial Intelligence (LNAI) and Lecture Notes in Bioinformatics (LNBI), has established itself as a medium for the publication of new developments in computer science and information technology research, teaching, and education.

LNCS enjoys close cooperation with the computer science R & D community, the series counts many renowned academics among its volume editors and paper authors, and collaborates with prestigious societies. Its mission is to serve this international community by providing an invaluable service, mainly focused on the publication of conference and workshop proceedings and postproceedings. LNCS commenced publication in 1973.

Elif Bilge Kavun · Michael Pehl
Editors

Constructive Side-Channel Analysis and Secure Design

14th International Workshop, COSADE 2023
Munich, Germany, April 3–4, 2023
Proceedings

Editors
Elif Bilge Kavun 🆔
University of Passau
Passau, Germany

Michael Pehl 🆔
Technical University of Munich
Munich, Germany

ISSN 0302-9743 ISSN 1611-3349 (electronic)
Lecture Notes in Computer Science
ISBN 978-3-031-29496-9 ISBN 978-3-031-29497-6 (eBook)
https://doi.org/10.1007/978-3-031-29497-6

This Springer imprint is published by the registered company Springer Nature Switzerland AG
The registered company address is: Gewerbestrasse 11, 6330 Cham, Switzerland

Preface

The 14th International Workshop on Constructive Side-Channel Analysis and Secure Design (COSADE 2023), was held in Garching near Munich, Germany, during April 3–4, 2023. The series of COSADE workshops started in 2010. COSADE provides a well-established international platform for researchers, academics, and industry participants to present current research topics in implementation attacks, efficient and secure HW/SW implementations, implementation attack-resilient architectures and schemes, hardware-intrinsic security, secure design and evaluation, practical attacks, test platforms, and open benchmarks.

COSADE 2023 was organized by the Technical University Munich and the Fraunhofer Institute for Applied and Integrated Security. This year, the workshop received 28 papers from authors of 15 countries. Each of the submissions was reviewed in an anonymous double-blind peer review process by three to four Program Committee members. Overall, the 40 Program Committee members and the 13 sub-reviewers provided 95 reviews. The Program Committee comprised of international experts from academia and industry with strong backgrounds in hardware-related attacks, secure implementations, and secure design, from 17 countries. From the 28 papers, 12 were accepted after the review process, which corresponds to an acceptance rate of approximately 43%. The selected works are contained within these proceedings and were presented as part of the program of COSADE 2023. We thank the Program Committee members as well as the sub-reviewers for their efforts in reviewing, assessing, and discussing the submissions.

In addition to the 12 presentations on regular papers, COSADE 2023 comprised two keynotes and three invited talks. The first keynote "Lightweight Authenticated Encryption" was given by Florian Mendel. It discussed countermeasures against side-channel attacks in the context of lightweight authenticated encryption using two examples: Ascon, an algorithm that – at the time of the conference – was recently selected by NIST for standardization for lightweight cryptography, and ISAP, an authenticated encryption scheme, which is based on the Ascon permutation and incorporates ideas from leakage-resilient cryptography to address certain side-channels attacks already on the model level. The second keynote "Recent Developments on Threshold Implementations" was given by Siemen Dhooghe. It discussed the application of threshold implementations from first to higher-order security in settings from software to hardware. The three invited talks highlighted the industrial perspective on real-world security. They were given by Wei Cheng from Secure-IC, Pierre-Yvan Liardet from eShard, and Marc Wittemann from Riscure. The first talk entitled "PQC-Ready Securyzr: A Full-Fledged Integrated Secure Element Complying with PQC Requirements in Terms of Firmware Management and Cryptographic Services" unveiled Secure-IC's PQC-ready Securyzr, an integrated secure element that provides platform security and user services that are 100% compliant with the CNSA 2.0 cipher suite. The second talk with the title "SOC: Spot the Odd Circuit" presented fault injection and side-channel attacks in the context of complex system-on-chip architectures. The third talk with the title "Riscure Vision on

Post Quantum Cryptography" discussed how to get security assurance given the complexity and variety of side channel and fault injection threats. We thank the speakers for their valuable contributions to COSADE 2023.

We would like to thank the Steering Committee, Jean-Luc Danger and Werner Schindler, and the General Chair, Georg Sigl. In particular, we want to thank the team members from the Fraunhofer Institute for Applied and Integrated Security and the Technical University of Munich, for the great preparation and implementation of the conference in Munich. We are very grateful for the financial support received from our generous sponsors eShard, Giesecke+Devrient, NewAE, Riscure, Secure-IC, ALPhANOV, Infineon, PQShield, and Siemens. Last but not least we want to thank the authors: Without your valuable research and submissions, COSADE 2023 would not have been possible.

April 2023   Elif Bilge Kavun
Michael Pehl

Organization

Steering Committee

Jean-Luc Danger	Télécom ParisTech, France
Werner Schindler	Bundesamt für Sicherheit in der Informationstechnik (BSI), Germany

General Chair

Georg Sigl	Technical University of Munich, Germany, and Fraunhofer Institute for Applied and Integrated Security, Germany

Program Committee Chairs

Elif Bilge Kavun	University of Passau, Germany
Michael Pehl	Technical University of Munich, Germany

Program Committee

Elham Amini	Technische Universität Berlin, Germany
Tolga Arul	University of Passau, Germany
Josep Balasch	KU Leuven, Belgium
Alessandro Barenghi	Politecnico di Milano, Italy
Shivam Bhasin	Nanyang Technological University, Singapore
Jakub Breier	Silicon Austria Labs, Austria
Olivier Bronchain	NXP Belgium, Belgium
Chitchanok Chuengsatiansup	University of Adelaide, Australia
Fabrizio De Santis	Siemens AG, Germany
Daniel Dinu	Intel Corporation, USA
Jean-Max Dutertre	Ecole des Mines de Saint-Étienne, France
Wieland Fischer	Infineon Technologies AG, Germany
Fatemeh Ganji	Worcester Polytechnic Institute, USA
Johann Heyszl	Google, Germany
Naofumi Homma	Tohoku University, Japan

Vincent Immler	Oregon State University, USA
Kimmo Järvinen	Xiphera Ltd., Finland
Jens-Peter Kaps	George Mason University, USA
Juliane Krämer	University of Regensburg, Germany
Victor Lomne	NinjaLab, France
Patrick Longa	Microsoft, USA
Roel Maes	Intrinsic-ID, The Netherlands
Dominik Merli	Augsburg University of Applied Sciences, Germany
Thorben Moos	Université catholique de Louvain, Belgium
Ralph Nyberg	Infineon Technologies AG, Germany
Colin O'Flynn	NewAE Technology Inc., Canada
Daniel Page	University of Bristol, UK
Samuel Pagliarini	Tallinn University of Technology, Estonia
Stjepan Picek	Radboud University, The Netherlands
Chester Rebeiro	Indian Institute of Technology Madras, India
Francesco Regazzoni	University of Amsterdam, The Netherlands, and Università della Svizzera italiana, Switzerland
Debapriya Basu Roy	Indian Institute of Technology Kanpur, India
Pascal Sasdrich	Ruhr University Bochum, Germany
Tobias Schneider	NXP Semiconductors, Austria
Sujoy Sinha Roy	Graz University of Technology, Austria
Marc Stöttinger	RheinMain University of Applied Sciences, Germany
Ruggero Susella	STMicroelectronics, Italy
Lennert Wouters	KU Leuven, Belgium
Tolga Yalçın	Qualcomm Technologies Inc., USA
Fan Zhang	Zhejiang University, China

Additional Reviewers

Luke Parkhurst Beckwith	Marina Krcek
Vinod CM	Gnanambikai Krishnakumar
Songqiao Cui	Michael X. Lyons
Samed Düzlü	Florian Stolz
Keerthi Kamalakshan	Patrick Struck
Felix Klement	Trevor Yap
Peter Knauer	

Contents

Analyses and Tools

Fault-Injection Analyses
and Countermeasures

SAMVA: Static Analysis for Multi-fault Attack Paths Determination

Antoine Gicquel[1]($\boxtimes$) (ID), Damien Hardy[1], Karine Heydemann[2,3] (ID),
and Erven Rohou[1] (ID)

[1] Univ Rennes, Inria, CNRS, IRISA, Rennes, France
{antoine.gicquel,damien.hardy,erven.rohou}@irisa.fr,
{antoine.gicquel,damien.hardy,erven.rohou}@inria.fr
[2] Sorbonne Université, CNRS, LIP6, 75005 Paris, France
karine.heydemann@lip6.fr
[3] Thales DIS, Meyreuil, France

Abstract. Multi-fault injection attacks are powerful since they allow
to bypass software security mechanisms of embedded devices. Assessing
the vulnerability of an application while considering multiple faults with
various effects is an open problem due to the size of the fault space to
explore. We propose SAMVA, a framework for efficiently searching vulnerabilities of applications in presence of multiple instruction-skip faults
with various widths. SAMVA relies solely on static analysis to determine
attack paths in a binary code. It is configurable with the fault injection
capacity of the attacker and the attacker's objective. We evaluate the
proposed approach on eight PIN verification programs containing various software countermeasures. Our framework finds numerous attack
paths, even for the most hardened version, in very limited time.

Keywords: Fault Injection Attack · Multi-fault · Static Analysis

1 Introduction

Fault injection attacks are a major concern for embedded systems since they
allow an attacker to overcome security mechanisms in order to retrieve secret
data or take over a device. To inject a fault, a physical perturbation must be
introduced in the circuit during the execution of the target program. Literature covers various means of injection [26], such as laser beams, electromagnetic
pulses, voltage or clock glitching. Throughout a fault propagation mechanism,
perturbations introduced at the hardware level impact the nominal execution of
the running program, corrupting variables, control-flow of the program, or both.

To protect against fault injections, several countermeasures have been proposed. At software level, they often rely on redundancy [23]: sensitive checks or
computations are duplicated; constant values are encoded such that it is difficult to change their value consistently. Also, some variables are added in order to
monitor the executed path and check its validity with respect to the original program [13]. As a consequence, attackers must inject multiple faults and/or faults

E. B. Kavun and M. Pehl (Eds.): COSADE 2023, LNCS 13979, pp. 3–22, 2023.
https://doi.org/10.1007/978-3-031-29497-6_1

that impact several consecutive instructions in order to bypass countermeasures and reach their objectives. Recent works have shown that it is possible to inject multiple faults [7] (i.e. at different instants) and to corrupt several consecutive instructions [5, 6, 8, 11, 15, 20]. Faults can have a width varying from a few up to more than one hundred consecutively executed instructions. Therefore, multiple and wide faults are now considered as a real threat and system security against fault attacks must be evaluated considering such attacker capacity.

Security assessment eventually relies on real fault injection campaigns. However, some analysis dedicated to the discovery of attack paths is often used as an early security evaluation process, i.e. before the final system is available. Moreover, concerning real fault injection campaigns, there is also a need to determine potential attack paths in order to reduce the time needed to prepare an attack. While there exist several approaches to help designers and evaluators to find attack paths, they are often limited by the combinatorial explosion that arises when considering either large applications, or multiple faults with variable widths or different effects. Existing approaches typically make use of fault simulation [22], symbolic execution [18] or model checking [4]. As a consequence, we believe there is a need for a new kind of approaches able to scale with the multiplicity and width of faults as well as the size of the target application.

In this paper, we go in this direction by proposing an approach only based on static analysis to determine the possible attack paths when considering multiple faults with various widths. Our framework named SAMVA implements this analysis, it quantifies the vulnerability of a binary code, for example, on the basis of the minimum number of faults necessary to perform an exploit or the characteristics of the required faults.

Our approach works at the binary-level. We currently supports Arm binaries and instruction-skip like faults. In addition to the binary, SAMVA takes as input the attacker's capacity as well as their goal. The goal is expressed with a list of code addresses – mandatory steps to reach their objective, that must be executed – and a set of code addresses that must never be executed – corresponding to attack detection. Attacker capacity describes the possible number of faults as well as their possible widths. The static analysis is based on a path search heuristic in a graph representing the program and the effect of potential faults. The found candidate paths are analyzed in order to determine when and which faults to inject in order to make the attack path feasible. The analysis outputs the set of paths that meet user-specified fault injection constraints. We evaluate SAMVA on eight variations of PIN verification from the FISSC suite [9] while considering different attacker capacities. We verify the validity of the attacks paths found by SAMVA with a fault simulator based on the gem5 [2]. We show that SAMVA is able to find in all implementations, even the most hardened, when and which faults to inject in order to reach an objective. Furthermore, we show that the required time to find attack paths is kept low even when considering hardened applications and a large set of potential effects of fault injections.

The threat model is introduced in Sect. 2. Section 3 depicts the core of our analysis for the search of attack paths. Our experimental setup and results are discussed in Sect. 4. We review related work in Sect. 5. Section 6 concludes.

2 Threat Model

Since the seminal paper of Boneh et al. in 1997 [3], a lot of research has been conducted around fault injection. While some research works demonstrate the feasibility to retrieve sensitive data or to take over a device, some others aim at characterizing fault injection effects in order to better harden target systems. Fault effects can be modeled at different levels (logical level, RTL, assembly code, source code) using a bottom-up approach. A lot of research works have focused on the modelling of fault injection effects at ISA-level. Fault injections can lead to several effects at this level such as an instruction replacement or the frequent special case of an instruction skip [1,16,25]. While these papers report single fault effects, recent works show that one fault injection or complex fault injection means can lead to the corruption of several consecutive instructions. Electromagnetic pulses can lead to the replay or the skip of several consecutive instructions, from two up to a dozen [5,15,19,20]. Laser-based fault injection techniques can also lead to the skip of few chosen instructions [8] or of a variable number of consecutive instructions, from 1 to 300 depending on the laser pulse duration [11]. Multiple instruction skips, from a few chosen ones up to almost one hundred, can also be achieved using cheaper injection means such as clock glitching [6]. Instruction skip is a fault model that encompasses many fault effects, such as instruction replacement with another one that does not alter the execution, the replay of idempotent instructions, the replacement of the destination register of an instruction with a dead register, etc. It is powerful as it allows to easily corrupt the control flow of the execution. Moreover, injecting multiple instruction-skip faults allows an adversary to combine their effects to realize even more powerful attacks: Péneau et al. [17] show that if precise and numerous instruction skips can be injected, a binary program can be attacked in many ways. They show that NOP-oriented programming is Turing-complete. In this paper, we consider an attacker able to inject multiple and precise faults that finally result in skipping the execution of one or several consecutive instructions. The distance between two fault injections, the minimal and maximal number of instructions that are skipped with one fault injection all depend on the injection mean. We then consider them as input of the proposed analysis.

3 Method

We first provide an overview of the approach implemented in SAMVA. Then, we detail the modeling of faults effects on the binary and finally the proposed static analysis to determine the location of faults to be injected at run-time.

3.1 Overview

Figure 1 gives an overview of the whole analysis dedicated to the search of attack paths. The analysis takes as inputs the binary, the objective of the attacker and the attacker's capacity. The output of SAMVA is a list of up to N attack paths,

N being defined by the user. An attack path contains the position of the required faults with their corresponding width (thereafter denoted fw) that need to be dynamically injected at run-time to achieve the attacker objective.

The objective of the attacker, denoted as *exploit specifications* in Fig. 1, are composed of (1) an ordered list of code locations that must all be reached during the execution in the specified order. This list composed of start addresses of straight-line code is referred to as the *targeted basic blocks*; (2) a set of code locations that must not be executed, for example it can correspond to code related to fault attack detection. This set is referred to as *forbidden basic blocks*.

The capacity of the attacker is expressed using three fault parameters (cf. Fig. 1): (1) fw_min indicates the minimal number of instructions skipped by one fault injection; (2) fw_max gives the maximal number of instructions skipped; (3) f_min_dist expresses the minimal number of instructions executed between two fault injections as imposed by the injection means. As an example, the setup of Dutertre et al. [11] (cf. Sect. 2) would be reflected by setting fw_min=1 and fw_max=300. The f_min_dist would be set according to the frequency of the targeted processor and the reloading time of the fault injection setup.

First, the analysis automatically generates the control-flow graph (CFG) of the binary. A CFG is composed of basic blocks (BB) defined as a maximal length sequence of straight-line (i.e. branch-free) code. Basic blocks are linked with oriented edges to represent all possible execution paths of the program. The CFG is extended and annotated to reflect the effects of possible fault injections, noted hereafter ECFG. Then, potential attack paths are computed using the ECFG as well as the attacker objective. Finally, the analysis infers a set of attack paths that meet the attacker capacity. Each output attack path takes the form of a list of BB with the faults to inject (location, width) in the instruction trace generated by the execution of all the instructions of the BB list.

3.2 Fault Effects Modeling

Our approach implemented in SAMVA starts with the CFG of the binary program which characterizes all the possible execution paths in the absence of attack. We call it the nominal CFG in the remainder. It can be obtained by static analysis or a combination of static and symbolic analysis. In SAMVA, we use the angr framework [21] to build it. The ability to skip the execution of chosen instructions allows an attacker to alter the control-flow of a program in a way to force an existing execution path, or to create a new one. We model such potential effects of instruction skips by generating an ECFG from the nominal CFG. This step is independent of the attacker as it models all potential fault effects without considering the attacker capacity. In the following, we detail the two transformations performed on the nominal CFG to generate the ECFG that is later used by our attack paths finding heuristic.

Hijacked Control-Flow Modeling. Being able to skip the execution of branch instructions enables an attacker to force the execution of the instructions which are located in memory right after these branch instructions.

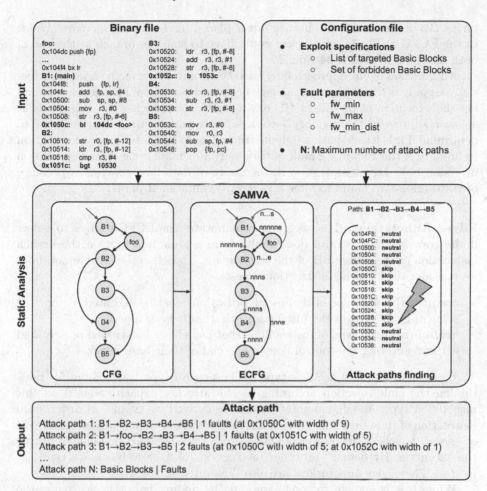

Fig. 1. Platform overview. In the code example, the targeted BB are [B1, B2, B5] and the set of forbidden BB is empty. Some found attack paths are given to illustrate the output format.

For the case of unconditional jump, we can choose to execute or to skip it. This allows an attacker to continue the execution with the instruction that comes after the jump instruction, according to the memory layout. The previously impossible control-flow is illustrated in Fig. 1 by the insertion of a new edge between B1 and B2 in the ECFG.

Concerning the skipping of a conditional branch, it forces the execution of the instruction that comes after the branch instruction, which corresponds to the case where the condition does not hold. As SAMVA currently does not rely on any dataflow analysis, and as each branch outcome must be statically known to compute feasible paths, the conditional jumps must always be skipped. As a consequence, the edges corresponding to the taken branches are removed of the ECFG. In the ECFG example in Fig. 1, the edge from B2 to B4 has been removed. Nonetheless, it is still possible, using several instruction skips, to execute the target BB of the conditional branch if it is placed further in the memory layout. In the ECFG in Fig. 1, an attacker would have to skip the branch at the end of both B2 and B3 to reach B4 from B2.

A limitation of our approach only based on control flow analysis and instruction skipping is that we cannot manage backward conditional branches, i.e. forcing the execution of the target BB of a conditional branch when this BB is at a lower address in the memory layout. This requires a data-flow analysis, to determine if it is feasible using only instruction-skip faults to force the condition to hold, or if this requires a fault outside our fault model (e.g. branch condition inversion). We keep as future work the study of data-flow analysis in presence of instruction-skip faults to force a backward conditional jump.

Edges Annotations. This second step annotates the ECFG's edges to reflect if the corresponding control flow results from a fault injection on the branch instruction of the source BB of the edge or not. To define the edge annotation, we consider the following instruction types:

- *execute* (e) is the type of the instructions that must be executed;
- *skip* (s) is the type of the instructions that must be skipped;
- *neutral* (n) is the type of instructions that can either be skipped or executed without affecting the control flow at the end of their basic block.

Every instruction of a BB is typed. The neutral type leaves room for positioning the fault injection according to the attacker capacity. Based on this instruction type, an edge annotation can be derived by typing, in order, each instruction of its source BB. Branch instructions are always typed as either *skip* or *execute* to reflect the condition under which the edge must be followed during the execution. By default, all other instructions of a basic block are typed as *neutral*. These edge annotations are also illustrated in Fig. 1.

While this is enough for our attack paths finding heuristic, we refine the typing strategy to avoid source of crashes when performing an attack. In fact, inconsistent stack pointer updates during the execution may lead to a crash of the attacked program. Moreover, inconsistent return address can make the execution deviate from the expected execution path. As a consequence, we add the two following typing rules:

- *R1: Execution of stack pointer updates.* Instructions writing into the stack pointer register (SP register), such as push and pop instructions, are always typed as *execute*. This guarantees that the memory allocated for the stack is subsequently deallocated. For Arm architectures, the return from a callee function to its caller uses a unique instruction, a pop pc instruction or equivalent, to retrieve the return address on the stack, to update the stack pointer and finally to return to the caller function. As the execution of pop instructions is forced by this typing rule, this ensures that a function call is either skipped or the return to the caller will be correctly executed.
- *R2: Execution of function-returns using the link register.* In case of leaf function, the link register lr, set by the call instruction bl, may be directly used

for returning to the caller, i.e. using a `bx lr` instruction or equivalent. This happens when the link register `lr` is not saved on the stack due to low register pressure. This additional rule types as *execute* all the `bx lr` instructions. As a consequence, a leaf function that does not save the link register on the stack is either skipped or the return to the caller will be correctly executed.

3.3   Attack Paths Finding

In this section, we present our heuristic for finding attack paths. We first explore the ECFG to generate a set of paths that are compliant with the attacker objective. These paths must contain the target basic blocks in the order specified by the user and must not contain any forbidden basic blocks. Edge annotations present on each path are then used to determine the position and the width of fault injections to perform while conforming with the instruction types. The position and the width of fault injections must be valid according to the attacker capacity given as input to the analysis.

Candidate Paths Generation. A set of candidate paths is generated by exploring the ECFG. Such paths must reach, in the correct order, the BB specified in the attacker objective and avoid the forbidden BB. Additionally, an ideal candidate path should allow an easy fault injection positioning by spacing out the *execute* and *skip* instructions, and reduce the number of fault injections by favoring *neutral* and *execute* instructions. Therefore, we associate to each edge of the ECFG a cost depending on its annotation.

- Cost = 1: if instructions are all typed as *neutral*;
- Cost = 2: if instructions are only typed as *neutral* or *execute*;
- Cost = 3: if instructions are only typed as *neutral* or *skip*;
- Cost = 4: if there are some instructions typed as *skip* and some other ones typed as *execute*.

This weighing policy hints the path search at finding more feasible attack paths. Thus, for each pair of successive basic blocks in the list of targeted basic blocks, a temporary set of paths is retrieved using the shortest paths algorithm [24] according to edge weights. The complexity to find the K first shortest paths in a CFG containing N_{BB} basic blocks is then $\mathcal{O}(KN_{BB}^3)$.

The final set of complete candidate paths $P_{candidate\_paths}$ passing through all the basic blocks specified in the attacker objective is then generated by making the Cartesian product of the temporary sets. We iteratively combine the sets corresponding to consecutive basic blocks and retain the K paths with the least costs. This final set is composed of candidate paths that do not ensure the possibility of the fault injection positioning according to the attacker capacity. The next step aims at finding a valid set of fault injections to perform to make a candidate path an attack path.

Fault Injection Positioning. The determination of fault injections to perform in order to make feasible a given candidate path is based on the instructions types retrieved on the edges annotations and the attacker capacity. For a given candidate path, we build a so-called "execution trace" which is a list of pairs ⟨*instruction address, instruction type*⟩. The fault injection positioning aims at finding the position and width of faults to inject such that instructions typed as *skip* are covered by a fault and instructions typed as *execute* are outside of any fault. Instructions typed as *neutral* can be covered by a fault or not.

The width of any injected fault must be included in [fw_min, fw_max]. As a consequence, there are potentially a lot of possibilities for the fault injection position and width as shown in Fig. 2. Nevertheless, the distance between two consecutive faults must be at least equal to the minimal distance f_min_dist. Computing the whole set of possible fault positions and widths is not realistic, as a consequence we use a two-step approach to determine a fixed-size set of solutions: (i) we first use simple rules to quickly determine when there is no valid solution for the fault positioning based on the distance between instructions (ii) then, the set of remaining fault configurations (i.e. position and width) is explored using a backtracking algorithm in order to find a valid configuration that make feasible a candidate path.

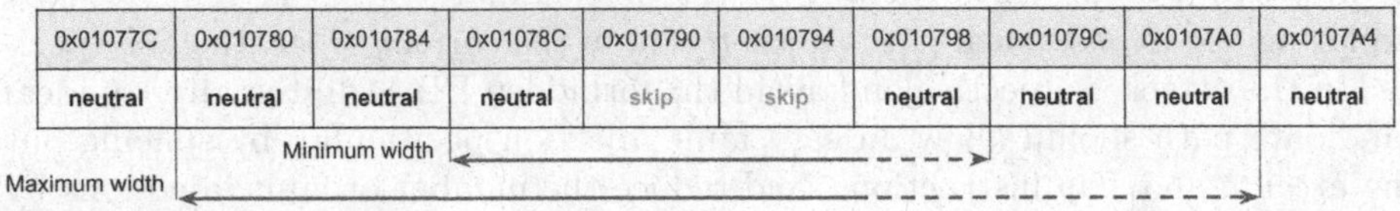

0x01077C	0x010780	0x010784	0x01078C	0x010790	0x010794	0x010798	0x01079C	0x0107A0	0x0107A4
neutral	neutral	neutral	neutral	skip	skip	neutral	neutral	neutral	neutral

Maximum width — Minimum width

Fig. 2. Example of fault positioning on trace with fw_min = 3, fw_max = 5

Unsolvability Verification. We use the following straightforward rules to quickly detect the unsolvability of the fault positioning problem on an execution trace:

- If there is at least one instruction typed as *skip* between two instructions i_0 and i_1 typed as *execute*, then the distance between i_0 and i_1 must be greater than or equal to fw_min the minimal width of a fault. Otherwise, any fault covering the instruction typed as *skip* would at least impact i_0 or i_1, and so the fault positioning problem is unsolvable;
- If there is at least one instruction typed as *execute* between two instructions i_0 and i_1 typed as *skip*, then the distance between i_0 and i_1 must be greater than or equal to f_min_dist the minimal distance between two faults. Otherwise, the fault positioning problem is unsolvable.

Backtracking Algorithm. The algorithm attempts to place faults in order to cover all the instructions typed as *skip* in a trace or to prove the invalidity of the attack path. Thus, we try to build a solution, consisting in a list of faults each having a position and a width. Additionally, these faults must respect the fault width constraints (fw_min, fw_max) and respect the distance between each other (i.e. meet the minimal distance requirement fw_min_dist).

A solution is built incrementally with a backtracking approach using recursion. Algorithm 1 gives an overview of our implementation. First, the position of

---

Algorithm 1. Fault positioning algorithm using backtracking

```
function FAULT_POSITIONING(trace, f_candidates, f_params)
    next_pos ← find_next_skip(trace, f_candidates)
    if next_pos = ∅ then
        return True
    for fw ∈ range(f_params.fw_max, f_params.fw_min, -1) do
        for pos ∈ range(next_pos, next_pos - fw, -1) do
            fault ← <pos, fw>
            if is_valid(fault, trace, f_candidates, f_params) then
                f_candidates.push(fault)
                if fault_positioning(trace, f_candidates, fault_params) then
                    return True
                else
                    candidate_faults.pop()
    return False
```

---

the next instruction typed as *skip* that is not yet covered by a fault is retrieved in the execution trace. Then, we vary the width and position of the fault in order to find a valid fault configuration.

To determine if a candidate fault configuration is valid, the following properties are verified:

- The fault position must fit in the trace, i.e. taking care of the trace bounds;
- The fault must not cover any instruction typed as *execute*;
- The fault must not overlap with the previous fault (if any) and their distance must be greater than the minimal distance between two faults.

The recursive calls stop when a final solution meeting all the constraints and covering all the instructions typed as *skip* is obtained. This happens when the function find_next_skip no longer finds any uncovered instruction typed as *skip*. During this process if we discover that the current solution will not be valid, we backtrack, i.e. we go back to the previous step by removing the last validated fault and try another fault configuration instead. Backtracking algorithms use the depth-first search method. In order to minimize the number of faults necessary to perform the attack, we first explore, as visible in the loops order, the possible positions starting from the one of the instruction to cover and then vary its width, starting with the widest one.

For the sake of performance, we do some optimizations to reduce the space of possible fault configurations. First, when validating a position of a fault, we also check if there is any instruction typed as *skip* further in the trace at a distance of less than fw_min_dist that would be covered by a conflicting fault. Consequently, even if the configuration of the fault is valid with the already chosen faults, it is rejected to avoid useless recursive calls.

Additionally, we decompose our execution trace into several sub-traces that are then handled independently. We apply a cut in the execution trace when (1) two instructions typed as *skip* are separated only by instructions typed as *neutral*, and (2) the distance between these two instructions is larger than twice the maximal fault width plus the minimal distance between two faults.

Fault Trimming. Our fault positioning algorithm tries to make the faults as large as possible in order to reduce their number. It can therefore find valid solutions that nonetheless cover unnecessarily instructions typed as *neutral*. For this reason, we apply a last pass that shortens the width of the faults when possible. It shifts the beginning and the end of a fault towards the first and the last instruction typed as *skip* while meeting the constraint of the minimal fault width (`fw_min`). We thus obtain smaller faults, potentially easier to achieve, and which reduce the risk of skipping critical instructions.

4   Experimentation

In this section, we evaluate the effectiveness of SAMVA. We first present the experimental setup comprising the targeted applications, the considered attacker capacity and our evaluation methodology. Then, we discuss the results.

4.1   Experimental Setup

Benchmarks. We evaluate our analysis on all PIN verification programs from the FISCC project [9]. This software collection contains eight implementations of `VerifyPIN`, one naive implementation, as illustrated in Lst. 1 and seven other implementations containing different set of countermeasures. The PIN code verification programs compare a user-provided PIN and the card PIN using the function `byteArrayCompare`. The variable `g_authenticated` is set according to its result. The number of tries is controlled by the variable `g_ptc`, initially set to 3 and decremented after each failed authentication attempt. Authentication is no longer permitted if `g_ptc` reaches zero, in order to avoid brute-forcing the PIN code. For protected implementations, i.e. version higher than V0, a fault handler is called when an attack is detected by a countermeasure. The fault handler sets to true a variable added to any protected version and named `g_countermeasure`. In the end, the evaluator is able to know afterward if the attack has been detected by the countermeasures. The implemented countermeasures are described below. Table 1 reports the countermeasures implemented in each `VerifyPIN` version as well as the number of instructions, BB and edges in the ECFG considered in the analysis at the binary level.

– Hardened Booleans (**HB**): Booleans are encoded with two constants, instead of 0 and 1, which are less sensitive to fault injection;
– Step counter (**SC**): some variables called step counters are added to the code in order to protect against attacks disrupting the control flow integrity. The number of loop iterations is checked at the loop exit in versions V2 to V5. All the statements and control flow constructs are protected using such variables in version V7;

- Inlined calls (**IC**): function calls are inlined in order to prevent the skip of the call. This also reduces the attack surface as there is no more instructions to pass parameters to the calls;
- Backup copy (**BC**): the number of remaining attempts is duplicated to prevent single fault attacks from targeting the attempt counter;
- Double test (**DT**): the call to the function verifying the PIN codes and all the tests are duplicated to prevent a single fault from bypassing them.

The objective of an attacker is to obtain an authentication without knowing the user PIN and without triggering any countermeasures. As a consequence, our analysis searches for the faults enabling to hijack the control-flow of the program in order to execute the authentication code (lines 4 and 5) without executing any attack detection. For the experiments, we manually retrieve the targeted and forbidden basic blocks for each implementation of `VerifyPIN`. The attacks start at the beginning of the verification function and then we define the targeted BBs as a list containing: the BB setting `g_authenticated` at true, possibly the BB setting `g_ptc` at 3 if this code is not included in the previous BB, and finally the BB in then `main` function that comes right after the call to `VerifyPIN`. The set of forbidden BB only includes the BB calling the detection function that sets the `g_countermeasure` variable.

The eight versions of `VerifyPIN` are compiled for Arm Thumb instruction set architecture (ARMv7-M). The cross-compiler used is GNU GCC gnueabi version 8.5.0. We deactivate all compiler optimizations (`-O0`) to avoid the alteration of the software countermeasures, as well as the use of predicated instructions that are not yet supported in SAMVA.

Listing 1. Source code of `Verify PIN` without countermeasures (V0)

```
1  g_authenticated = 0;
2  if(g_ptc > 0) {
3      if(byteArrayCompare(...))
        {
4          g_ptc = 3;
5          g_authenticated = 1;
6      } else {
7          g_ptc--;
8      }
9  }
```

Table 1. `VerifyPIN` suite description with the included countermeasures, their number of instructions, BB and ECFG edges (+ edges added to original CFG) at binary level

	HB	SC	IC	DT	BC	#Instr	#BB	#Edges
V0						142	24	46 (+12)
V1	✓					162	30	57 (+15)
V2	✓	✓				172	32	58 (+15)
V3	✓	✓	✓			158	30	54 (+13)
V4	✓	✓	✓	✓		221	41	79 (+20)
V5	✓	✓			✓	241	47	87 (+22)
V6	✓		✓		✓	177	36	68 (+17)
V7	✓	✓	✓		✓	306	66	140 (+38)

Fault Injection Parameters. For each implementation of `VerifyPIN`, we consider various fault injection parameters corresponding to various attacker capacities. We vary the width of the possible faults (using the fault parameters `fw_min` and `fw_max`) as well as the minimal distance between two consecutive faults (using the parameter named `fw_min_dist`). Our objective is to observe the sensitivity of the included countermeasures to the fault injection parameters required to perform an attack.

Let W be the set of possible fault width values measured in number of instructions. It is defined as: $W := \{1\} \bigcup \{2n : n \in \mathbb{N} \mid n \leq 32\}$. Thus, the minimum width varies over 1 and all even numbers between 2 to 64; the maximum width varies over the minimal width and all even numbers between 2 to 64 as well, such that: $\{(\texttt{fw\_min}, \texttt{fw\_max}) \in W \times W \mid \texttt{fw\_min} \leq \texttt{fw\_max}\}$. Finally, the minimal distance, in number of instructions, between two fault injections varies over all the power of 2, such that: $\texttt{fw\_min\_dist} \in \{2^n : n \in \mathbb{N} \mid n \leq 5\}$.

Moreover, we run SAMVA on all the versions of `VerifyPIN` considering instruction typing strategies (cf. Sect. 3.2). We pick three different strategies as follows: a first default one, denoted `default`, without any additional typing rule; a second one featuring the `R1` rule that forces the execution of stack pointer updates; a third one, denoted `R1 + R2`, that applies both `R1` and `R2` rules.

In summary, we test SAMVA on a total of 3366 distinct fault parameters, on each of the eight binary files, for each of the three instruction typing strategies, with fault trimming enabled and disabled.

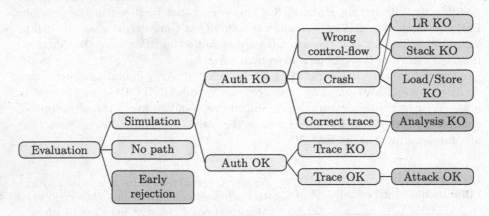

Fig. 3. Decision tree for attack results classification

Evaluation Methodology. We iterate through the possible fault parameters and binaries as described previously. For a given couple of binary and fault parameters, we strive to generate a set of N distinct attack paths. In our experiments, N equals 30, meaning that we expect to obtain up to 30 attacks paths, depending on the possibilities offered by the instructions used and the binary layout. The evaluation methodology followed to assess the results is depicted on Fig. 3. We classify the results as explained below.

The set of attack paths found by the analysis can be empty if our analysis does not find any candidate attack path for certain fault parameters (class "No path" □). Additionally, the fault parameters may not fit the binary if `fw_min`, the minimal fault width, is greater than the number of instructions distancing the starting point and the first targeted instruction of the attack (class "Early rejection" ■), since the execution of targeted BB is mandatory.

Otherwise, if the resulting set is not empty, the attack paths are validated by simulation of the instruction-skip fault model. The simulator used in our experiment is a modified version of gem5 [2] which is able to skip the execution of chosen instructions in a specified order of occurrence. It takes as input the binary program under analysis and the faults that must be injected for achieving an attack path. Once the simulation terminates, without reporting a crash, we first check the output containing the VerifyPIN variables. If the g_authenticated is set to true, g_ptc equals 3 and g_countermeasure stays at false, the authentication has been granted (node "Auth OK"). In this case, the execution trace resulting from the simulation and the one intended by the analysis are compared in order to make sure they match (class "Attack OK" ■). We stop iterating the set of attack paths after the first successful simulated attack. In the case of a simulation crash or if we did not get authenticated at the end of the simulation (node "Auth KO"), the simulated and expected execution traces are also analyzed. When they do not match, we determine the reason of the crash or of the divergence of control-flow respectively (classes "LR KO", "Stack KO" or "Load/Store KO"). The result is orange-colored (node "Crash" and "Wrong control-flow" ■). Finally, we also measure the failure of our analysis for two particular cases (class "Analysis KO" ■). The first one is when the authentication fails despite the matching of the execution traces and the expected authentication by the analysis. The second case is when we get authenticated but the traces do not match. These cases are sanity checks only, which should not happen. We did not encounter them in our experiments.

4.2   Experimental Results

Attack Path Evaluation Results. Experiments aim to measure the effectiveness of SAMVA in finding attack paths in the different benchmarks according to the different typing instruction strategies. We consider three strategies with and without fault trimming. Figure 4 shows the classification of the evaluation outcomes. The first row represents the results for the three strategies without the fault trimming and the second one with trimming.

First of all, we are able to find many attack paths in all cases. The main difference between the default strategy and the other ones preserving the execution of stack pointer updates is the higher number of crashes during the simulation using the default strategy. However, fault trimming seems to sensibly mitigate the number of crashes by reducing the number of instructions that must be skipped, meaning, it reduces the risk of skipping an instruction that is necessary for the execution of the program such as memory allocation for the stack. Nonetheless, fault trimming has only an impact when no instruction typing rule is enabled. Otherwise, the strategies guarantee the execution of some instructions reducing the number of crashes. Finally, the R1 + R2 strategy finds fewer attack paths. This reduced number of attack paths can be explained by the constraints induced by the instruction typing rules, resulting in a more difficult fault positioning. However, found attack paths lead to fewer crashes. This means that the few attack paths found are more prone to be effective. Remaining crashes are solely caused by invalid memory access due to instruction skips. To load or store a value, the address location is usually stored in a register that is defined before

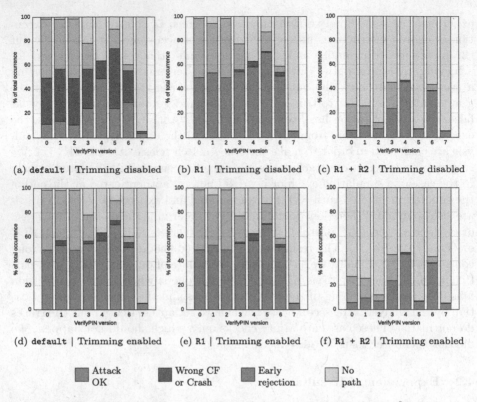

(a) default | Trimming disabled   (b) R1 | Trimming disabled   (c) R1 + Ṙ2 | Trimming disabled

(d) default | Trimming enabled   (e) R1 | Trimming enabled   (f) R1 + R2 | Trimming enabled

▆ Attack OK   ▆ Wrong CF or Crash   ▆ Early rejection   ▢ No path

Fig. 4. Results classification of attack path searches

by one or multiple instructions. If one of these instructions is skipped, then an illegal access can cause a crash. Future work will study data-flow analysis to handle these cases.

Fault Injection Parameters Study. An alternative manner of representing the results for the eight binaries is depicted on Fig. 5, which shows the classification of the analysis outcomes according to the considered three fault parameters (fw_min, fw_max, fw_min_dist). As expected, the general pattern that we can observe is that the smaller fw_min and fw_min_dist are, the larger the fw_max is, the more possibilities to find attack paths which result in successful attacks. We can see that versions V1, V2 and V5 have similar results to V0, meaning that the implemented countermeasures have only limited effect against multiple skips. We can also see that in V4 and V6, the distance between two faults is the main factor for the realization of the attack. This can be explained by the necessity to make several faults if fw_max does not allow to make a sufficiently large fault. Finally for V7, we only find few configurations that lead to successful attacks. The fine-grained control-flow integrity countermeasure included in this version forces to skip several small sets of instructions and thus require a higher precision to inject the faults.

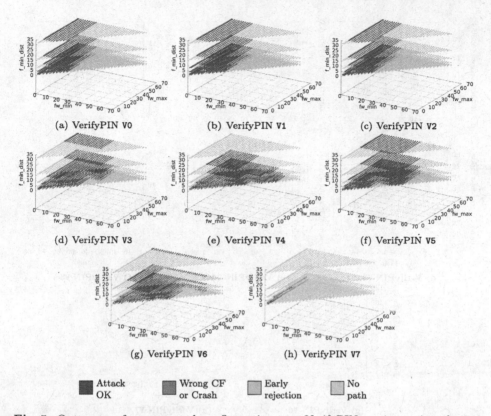

(a) VerifyPIN V0   (b) VerifyPIN V1   (c) VerifyPIN V2

(d) VerifyPIN V3   (e) VerifyPIN V4   (f) VerifyPIN V5

(g) VerifyPIN V6   (h) VerifyPIN V7

■ Attack   ■ Wrong CF   ■ Early   □ No
  OK   or Crash   rejection   path

Fig. 5. Outcomes of every tested configuration, per VerifyPIN version, using the R1 strategy and fault trimming enabled

Characteristics of Successful Fault Configurations. We now study the characteristic of the fault configurations that lead to successful attacks. Since the strategy featuring the additional typing rule R1 along with the fault trimming gives the highest number of successful attack paths, we base our study on its evaluation results. Figure 7 presents the number of faults required for each successful attacks. Our results show that versions from V0 to V3, V5 and V6 can be attacked with a single fault. Version V4 can be attacked with at least two faults and V7 requires at least three faults. The instruction typing obtained for a given attack path is responsible for the minimum number of faults. For instance, if two instructions are typed as *skip* with an instruction typed as *execute* in between, then two faults are necessary. Depending on the code layout and instructions induced by the countermeasures, the attack path may contain such constraints, resulting in a higher number of faults required for the V4 and V7.

To better understand the effects of instruction typing on the fault positioning, Fig. 6 represents the characteristic of the faults on an attack path. These different attack paths can report identical control-flow, although we can see some patterns. Taking the V0 as an example, we can notice that according to the fault injection parameters, SAMVA can choose to make one long fault to cover all the instructions typed *skip* or to make several smaller faults to cover them

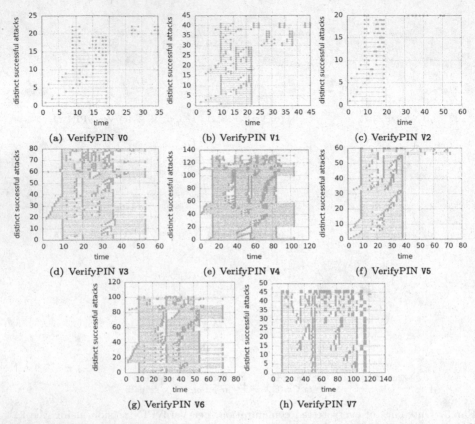

Fig. 6. Unique attacks found for each version of VerifyPIN. Each attack is represented horizontally. The x-axis represents time (more precisely consecutively executed instructions). Each segment denotes a fault whose width is the length. For example, V1 can be attacked with a single fault of width 12 (bottom segment ranging from x = 10 to x = 22); but also with four narrower faults shown at y = 41: a fault ranging from x = 10 to x = 15 followed by tree faults of width 3 at times x = 23, x = 33, and x = 43. Attacks are sorted vertically by their number of faults: fewer faults at the bottom, more towards the top.

individually. For some attacks, the BB restoring the variable g_ptc to its initial value and the BB turning g_authenticated to true may be different. As a result, we get mandatory checkpoints in the control-flow, which graphically manifests as a column in the figures, because no fault is allowed to cover this section of the attack path. Finally, we consider only fully predictable paths in our analysis. Since we do not use data-flow analysis, we hijack conditional jumps that do not necessarily require a fault. For instance, at the beginning of the VerifyPIN function the value of g_ptc is checked and must be greater than zero, as depicted in Lst. 1 (line 2). As we consider only one try, during the attack this condition always holds. In consequence, the branch instructions related to this check add unnecessary constraints by adding an instruction typed as *skip* and result in more faults than really required.

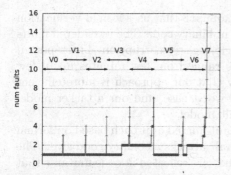

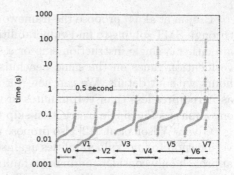

Fig. 7. Number of faults needed for each successful attack found for each version of VerifyPIN, using the strategy R1 with fault trimming enabled

Fig. 8. Time needed to generate the paths, for each considered fault parameter and per VerifyPIN, using the strategy R1 with fault trimming enabled

Execution Time. We measure the execution time of our framework in order to assess its performance. Figure 8 represents the time that our analysis took to find up to 30 distinct attack paths for each version of VerifyPIN and for each parameter configuration. These results do not include the simulation time. The strategy used for these measurements is the typing rule R1 with fault trimming enabled. We ran our benchmarks on a Xeon Gold 5218 CPU at 2.3 GHz featuring 32 physical cores, on which independent instances of SAMVA are launched. Each instance of SAMVA is sequential, hence the times reported are independent of the parallelism of the server. We obtain relatively short analysis times, most of the results are under the threshold of half a second. For the V4 and V7 versions, we can notice that the analysis times can rise significantly, up to 109 s and this can be explained by the usage of the fault positioning algorithm which uses backtracking. Indeed, the major part of the analysis time is actually spent in this algorithm and according to the typing of the instructions, we may need to backtrack a lot to prove the non-feasibility of an attack path.

5   Related Work

In order to help both security evaluators and countermeasure designers, different vulnerability and attack path search tools have been proposed.

Potet et al. [18] propose Lazart, a tool based on the modification of the CFG at LLVM-IR level to establish using symbolic execution the absence of attacks only based on multiple branch inversions. While convenient to early analyze the effectiveness of software countermeasures, this solution does not consider the binary layout and so requires a companion analysis at binary level. While the authors do not report the time required by the analysis, this approach is intrinsically limited by the symbolic execution engine that faces path or state explosion in case of complex applications with symbolic inputs which impact memory accesses or control flow.

Bréjon et al. [4] propose the framework RobustB that uses formal verification through SMT solving to find vulnerabilities in binary code. The considered faults are either a single instruction skip or a single register corruption. The reported verification times on the same benchmarks range from few minutes up to few hours without details. We can however say that our approach is more efficient as it requires less than two minutes in the worst case, and our attacker model encompasses the single instruction-skip fault model.

Given-Wilson et al. [12] also propose an automated approach based on formal verification to find vulnerabilities against fault attacks at binary code level. The approach only considers permanent faults that are reflected in code mutants that are then given to a model checker. This approach must then produce as many code mutants as the number of fault configurations to explore. This would not scale to multiple faults with various widths.

Werner et al. [22] extend the CELTIC simulation-based framework in order to search for attack paths considering up to two faults. Considered fault models are inferred from real experiments, as previously proposed by Dureuil et al. [10], and the whole approach enables to select fault injection parameters. As other simulation-based approach [14], it is however limited in the number of faults that can be injected. While simulation is better suited than formal approaches for analyzing large applications, the fault configurations space grows exponentially when considering multiple faults with variable width. The convergence towards successful fault configurations is dependent on the exploration strategy of the fault configurations space. To the best of our knowledge, there is currently no simulation-based approach able to consider a large number of such faults.

In summary, we believe that, even if only instruction-skip faults are supported yet, SAMVA, which is only based on static analysis, is the first tool able to search for multiple faults with variable width that leads to successful attacks.

6 Conclusion

In this paper, we propose SAMVA, a framework for assessing vulnerabilities of a program binary against multiple instruction-skip attacks. SAMVA is based on purely static analysis. We evaluate our approach by determining the required faults to attack eight versions of PIN code verification programs hardened by various countermeasures against faults. In our experiments, we explore numerous fault injection capabilities and the results show the capacities of SAMVA to find successful attack paths, even for the most hardened implementations. We also report that our approach scales well, making it an effective way to explore a wide range of fault configurations in limited time.

Future work will consider the extension of our threat model by integrating instruction-replay for our fault positioning. Additionally, we plan to link the attacks found by analysis with fault injection means to conduct physical attacks in order to validate experimentally the found attacks. This will make the bridge between our fault analysis and their realizations.

Acknowledgements. This study is partially funded by the ANR within the framework of the PIA EUR CyberSchool project (ANR-18-EURE-0004) and by Région Bretagne.

References

1. Balasch, J., Gierlichs, B., Verbauwhede, I.: An in-depth and black-box characterization of the effects of clock glitches on 8-bit MCUs. In: FDTC. IEEE Computer Society (2011)
2. Binkert, N.L., et al.: The gem5 simulator. SIGARCH Comput. Archit. News **39**(2), 1–7 (2011)
3. Boneh, D., DeMillo, R.A., Lipton, R.J.: On the importance of checking cryptographic protocols for faults. In: Fumy, W. (ed.) EUROCRYPT 1997. LNCS, vol. 1233, pp. 37–51. Springer, Heidelberg (1997). https://doi.org/10.1007/3-540-69053-0_4
4. Bréjon, J.B., Heydemann, K., Encrenaz, E., Meunier, Q., Vu, S.T.: Fault attack vulnerability assessment of binary code. In: CS2. ACM (2019)
5. Bukasa, S.K., Lashermes, R., Lanet, J.L., Legay, A.: Let's shock our IoT's heart: ARMv7-M under (fault) attacks. In: ARES 2018. ACM (2018)
6. Claudepierre, L., Péneau, P.Y., Hardy, D., Rohou, E.: TRAITOR: a low-cost evaluation platform for multifault injection. In: ASSS. ACM (2021)
7. Colombier, B., et al.: Multi-spot laser fault injection setup: new possibilities for fault injection attacks. In: Grosso, V. (eds.) Smart Card Research and Advanced Applications. CARDIS 2021. LNCS, vol. 13173. Springer, Cham (2021). https://doi.org/10.1007/978-3-030-97348-3_9
8. Colombier, B., Menu, A., Dutertre, J.M., Moëllic, P.A., Rigaud, J.B., Danger, J.L.: Laser-induced single-bit faults in flash memory: instructions corruption on a 32-bit microcontroller. In: IEEE HOST. IEEE (2019)
9. Dureuil, L., Petiot, G., Potet, M.-L., Le, T.-H., Crohen, A., de Choudens, P.: FISSC: a fault injection and simulation secure collection. In: Skavhaug, A., Guiochet, J., Bitsch, F. (eds.) SAFECOMP 2016. LNCS, vol. 9922, pp. 3–11. Springer, Cham (2016). https://doi.org/10.1007/978-3-319-45477-1_1
10. Dureuil, L., Potet, M.-L., de Choudens, P., Dumas, C., Clédière, J.: From code review to fault injection attacks: filling the gap using fault model inference. In: Homma, N., Medwed, M. (eds.) CARDIS 2015. LNCS, vol. 9514, pp. 107–124. Springer, Cham (2016). https://doi.org/10.1007/978-3-319-31271-2_7
11. Dutertre, J.-M., Riom, T., Potin, O., Rigaud, J.-B.: Experimental analysis of the laser-induced instruction skip fault model. In: Askarov, A., Hansen, R.R., Rafnsson, W. (eds.) NordSec 2019. LNCS, vol. 11875, pp. 221–237. Springer, Cham (2019). https://doi.org/10.1007/978-3-030-35055-0_14
12. Given-Wilson, T., Heuser, A., Jafri, N., Legay, A.: An automated and scalable formal process for detecting fault injection vulnerabilities in binaries. Concurr. Comput. Pract. Exp. **31**(23), e4794 (2019)
13. Heydemann, K., Lalande, J.F., Berthomé, P.: Formally verified software countermeasures for control-flow integrity of smart card C code. Comput. Secur. **85**, 202–224 (2019)
14. Hoffmann, M., Schellenberg, F., Paar, C.: ARMORY: fully automated and exhaustive fault simulation on ARM-M binaries. IEEE Trans. Inf. Forensics Secur. **16**, 1058–1073 (2021)

15. Menu, A., Dutertre, J.M., Potin, O., Rigaud, J.B., Danger, J.L.: Experimental analysis of the electromagnetic instruction skip fault model. In: DTIS. IEEE (2020)
16. Moro, N., Dehbaoui, A., Heydemann, K., Robisson, B., Encrenaz, E.: Electromagnetic fault injection: towards a fault model on a 32-bit microcontroller. In: FDTC. IEEE Computer Society (2013)
17. Péneau, P.Y., Claudepierre, L., Hardy, D., Rohou, E.: NOP-oriented programming: should we care? In: SILM EuroS&P Workshops. IEEE (2020)
18. Potet, M.L., Mounier, L., Puys, M., Dureuil, L.: Lazart: A symbolic approach for evaluation the robustness of secured codes against control flow injections. In: ICST. IEEE Computer Society (2014)
19. Proy, J., Heydemann, K., Berzati, A., Majéric, F., Cohen, A.: A first ISA-level characterization of EM pulse effects on superscalar microarchitectures: a secure software perspective. In: Proceedings of the 14th International Conference on Availability, Reliability and Security, ARES. ACM (2019)
20. Rivière, L., Najm, Z., Rauzy, P., Danger, J.L., Bringer, J., Sauvage, L.: High precision fault injections on the instruction cache of ARMv7-M architectures. In: HOST. IEEE Computer Society (2015)
21. Shoshitaishvili, Y., et al.: SOK: (state of) the art of war: offensive techniques in binary analysis. In: IEEE Symposium on Security and Privacy, SP. IEEE Computer Society (2016)
22. Werner, V., Maingault, L., Potet, M.L.: An end-to-end approach for multi-fault attack vulnerability assessment. In: FDTC 2020. IEEE (2020)
23. Witteman, M., Oostdijk, M.: Secure application programming in the presence of side channel attacks (2008). https://www.riscure.com/publication/secure-application-programming-presence-side-channel-attacks/
24. Yen, J.Y.: Finding the k shortest loopless paths in a network. Manage. Sci. **17**(11), 712–716 (1971)
25. Yuce, B., Ghalaty, N.F., Santapuri, H., Deshpande, C., Patrick, C., Schaumont, P.: Software fault resistance is futile: Effective single-glitch attacks. In: FDTC. IEEE Computer Society (2016)
26. Yuce, B., Schaumont, P., Witteman, M.: Fault attacks on secure embedded software: threats, design, and evaluation. J. Hardw. Syst. Secur. **2**(2), 111–130 (2018)

Efficient Attack-Surface Exploration for Electromagnetic Fault Injection

Daniele Antonio Emanuele Carta[3], Vittorio Zaccaria[2],
Gabriele Quagliarella[4], and Maria Chiara Molteni[1]

1 Security Pattern, Mazzano, Italy
m.molteni@securitypattern.com
2 Politecnico di Milano, Milan, Italy
vittorio.zaccaria@polimi.it
3 STMicroelectronics, Via Camillo Olivetti 2, 20864 Agrate Brianza, Italy
daniele.carta@st.com
4 Nozomi Networks, Via Maria Ghioldi-Schweizer 2, 6850 Mendrisio, Switzerland
gabriele.quagliarella@nozominetworks.com

Abstract. Electromagnetic Fault Injection is a physical attack that aims to disrupt the operation of hardware circuits to bypass existing confidentiality and integrity protections. The success probability of the attack depends, among other things, on many different variables such as the probe used to inject the pulse, its position, the pulse intensity, and duration. The number of such parameter combinations and the stochastic nature of the induced faults make a comprehensive search of the parameter space impractical. However, it is of utmost importance for hardware circuit manufacturers to identify these vulnerability points efficiently and introduce countermeasures to mitigate them.

This work presents a methodology to efficiently identify the subregion of the attack parameter space that maximizes the occurrence of a *informative* fault. The idea of this work consists in applying a multi-dimensional bisection method and exploiting the equilibrium between a pulse that is too strong and one that is too weak to produce a disruption on the circuit's operation. We show that such a methodology can outperform existing methods on a concrete, state-of-the-art embedded multicore platform.

Keywords: Electromagnetic Fault Injection · Parameters Search · Optimization · Methodology · Fault Model · System on Chip

1 Introduction

Today, System-on-Chips (SoCs) are increasingly used for sensitive tasks such as secure payments, critical infrastructure management, and other mission critical applications characterized by confidentiality and integrity constraints. However,

D. A. E. Carta and G. Quagliarella completed this work while at Security Pattern.

SoCs are complex architectures that might present a vast attack surface, which is difficult to protect. For this reason, they are increasingly equipped with Trusted Execution Environments (TEEs), which are small, isolated processing environments whose attack surface is more easily under control.

Ensuring a completely safe TEE is not a simple task, as the *boomerang* attack has shown [12]; However, even if the attack surface could be reduced to zero, fault injection (FI) could still be used to force the system to work outside its nominal conditions and expose otherwise absent vulnerabilities, perhaps justifying such an increase in research efforts.

Fault injection is all about disrupting the nominal operation of a circuit by invalidating design-time assumptions around the environment. A successful injection could be used to trigger instruction execution skips or corruption in working data with obvious consequences[1]; In fact, one of the most defining aspects of FI is the need to have physical access to the target[2]. Injection can be performed in several ways that vary in terms of equipment cost and robustness, e.g. altering the working temperature of the system, the clock signal, the power supply, and/or the system internal signals. The latter effect could be induced through either microprobing, a coherent light source (if the circuit has been decapped), or by injecting electromagnetic pulses (EMFI).

EMFI is particularly interesting because it represents a potentially cheaper alternative than other methods (see the ChipShouter project [17]). However, its cost vs. performance trade-off is characterized by less precise control over the fault injection position (with respect to optical or microprobing attacks) and the significant range of equipment configurations that can be used to perform it, such as the electromagnetic probe position, the voltage, the intensity, etc., which we call the *attack surface*.

This work stems from our efforts to overcome what we believe are the two limits of conventional approaches, i.e.,

- Using trial and error tests with the risk of leaving out interesting exploitable points [20], and
- Targeting the identification of a *single* (X, Y) faulty point by adopting some sort of occurrence ratio with the side effect of reducing fault differentiation [8].

This work proposes a target-agnostic methodology to efficiently search the EMFI attack surface for potentially exploitable configurations. We overcome the inherent limits of an exhaustive search (which is unfeasible) and a random search (which is suboptimal) by addressing, through a multidimensional bisection method, the probe position problem and the pulse configuration problem.

This paper is structured as follows. Section 2 introduces the state-of-the-art EMFI attacks to facilitate understanding of the motivation and problem statement of this work. Section 3 introduces the actual methodology, which is then validated by appropriate experimentation in Sect. 4. Section 5 concludes the paper with an outline of possible future work.

---

[1] Being able to skip a branch instruction could, for example, bypass security checks.
[2] This is not a requirement as some fault-injection attacks might work even remotely (e.g., *clkscrew* [22] and *rowhammer*).

2 State of the Art

Research efforts on EMFI have focused on understanding its effects (inference of the fault model), improving fault success rates, and building/validating attacks. The last two challenges are based on the tooling to perform the EMFI and the development of methodologies that integrate it with the fault model, a particular methodological issue being the exploration of the attack surface. When dealing with EMFI against programmable microcontrollers (MCU), we can identify a broad division between practical approaches, targeting FPGA or ASIC SoCs, and methodological contributions, summarized in Table 1.

Table 1. Summary of the state-of-the-art for EMFI .

Type	Year	Work	Target
MCU	2013	Moro et al. [16]	ARM Cortex-M3
	2017	Ordas et al. [19]	Xilinx Spartan 3-1000 ARM Cortex-M4
	2019	Menu et al. [15]	Atmel SAM3X8E ARM Cortex-M3
		Dumont et al. [4]	Custom designed
	2021	Dutertre et al. [6]	ATmega328P
SoC	2014	Hummel [10]	ARM Cortex-A8
	2017	Ang et al. [3]	Cisco 8861 IP Phone Broadcom BCM11123 SoC
	2019	Proy et al. [20]	ARM Cortex-A9
		Trouchkine et al. [23]	ARM BCM2837x86 Intel Core i3-6100T
	2020	Gaine et al. [8]	ARM Cortex-A53
	2022	Kuhnapfel et al. [11]	x86 AMD Ryzen 5 2600
Methods	2013	Omarouayache et al. [18]	Probes
		Carpi et al. [2]	Smartcards
	2019	Madau et al. [13]	ARM Cortex-M3 ARM Cortex-M4
		Maldini et al. [14]	ARM Cortex-M4
	2022	Gaine et al. [9]	Probes

2.1 EMFI on MCUs and FPGAs

FPGA technology, due to its lower clock frequency and hardware complexity, was a great starting point for white-box analysis of EMFI effects. For example, Moro et al. [16] have built an RTL model that predicted timing constraint violations on flash memory bus transfers. Their experiments (on a 56 MHz FPGA target) confirmed that an attacker could corrupt instructions fetched from memory. Similarly, Ordas et al. [19] have introduced a more refined model, which takes into account the corruption of internal registers' (flip-flop) data, essentially making it independent of the clock frequency. With a similar white-box approach, Menu et al. [15] derive a model that explains the corruption of data fetches from flash memory. Other researchers [4] have provided evidence and theoretical justification for a successful EMFI with pulses that are shorter than the target clock cycle. For example, Dutertre et al. [6] have introduced an instruction skip model that shows 100% repeatability on a single precise instruction that could be extended to deal with more than one instruction in different moments.

2.2 EMFI on ASIC SoCs

Commercial ASIC-based SoCs (generally based on application-class MPUs) introduce a whole new level of complexity in fault modeling. Researchers cannot apply white-box approaches anymore, as they do not control the underlying technology, and have to work with clock frequencies higher than their FPGA counterparts which makes synchronization difficult. Hummel et al. [10] is one of the first approaches in this field to successfully deal with a precise synchronization between raised exceptions and pulse timing. Ang et al. [3] try to overcome the synchronization problem by employing a second-order EMFI attack, which consists of attacking a secondary component to affect the primary target (by targeting an external DRAM running at a 40 MHz clock to disrupt the execution of the faster processor). This and other approaches, such as Kuhnapfel et al. [11], are characterized by relatively low-cost equipment ranging from $350 to $7000. Other works resorted to trial-and-error approaches to explain faults at higher levels. Proy et al. [20] (inspired by Dereuil et al. [5]) are among the first to define a CPU fault model based on the Instruction Set Architecture, while Trouchkine et al. [23] try to explain faults using architectural features such as register, pipeline, MMU, and caches. Finally, Gaine et al. [8] present an interesting hybrid approach consisting of privilege escalation in a Linux environment; here the target is a 1.2 GHz mobile SoC for which they have a white-box view. They are the first to introduce the concept of crash susceptibility, which we will exploit in the remainder of this work. However, they were unable to carry out the planned attack in a real-world scenario due to serious timing-synchronization issues with the fast target.

2.3 Existing Methodologies

Methodological approaches are more interested in maximizing the amount of information that can be obtained from an experimentation campaign than in a successful exploit. In fact, there is an overall underrated aspect of fault injection, that is, how and where to reliably reproduce a fault in the first place. The probe reliability and selection problem, originally addressed by Omarouayache et al. [18] is less difficult today than it was 10 years ago. Toolkit producers such as NewAE, eShard, Riscure and other vendors commercialize state-of-the-art probes with their offerings (whose accuracy obviously depends on the cost). However, identification and exploration of the configuration setup for fault injection is still in its infancy, although initial steps were proposed in 2013 by Carpi et al. [2] in the field of Voltage Fault Injection. They address the problem of identifying the subspace of the duration and intensity values of pulses that could produce an actual fault using a two-step process, that is, trying to optimize the parameters separately. Maldini et al. [14] bring this work to EMFI through an evolutionary algorithm that tries to find the optimal geometric and pulse intensity values that maximize *fault occurrence ratio* while keeping some of the configuration fixed (pulse duration). Madau et al. [13] offer an alternative methodology to locate the best areas to obtain unexpected behaviors on the surface of the chip; Each surface point, starting from a predefined grid, is rated using a *susceptibility criterion* that requires measuring electromagnetic emissions. In its testing environment, the criterion has efficiently led to the identification of 50% of the surface that produces a covering of 80% of the faulty surface. However, the susceptibility criterion requires expensive equipment to measure electromagnetic emissions. Furthermore, the criterion test is performed with a fixed pulse intensity and duration, while different durations and intensities could provide different results.

The current state of affairs is not satisfactory for several reasons. First of all, each of the above approaches has a set of setup variables which are fixed to some value perhaps identified through trial and error. This is done, of course, to limit the complexity of the analysis of the attack surface, but could leave some interesting exploitable points out of scope. Our work aims to provide a methodology that starts with instruments and setup capabilities and leaves nothing behind without an explanation.

Second, most of the existing approaches adopt some sort of *occurrence ratio* as a maximization objective to find a single (X, Y) chip surface coordinate. Instead, we aim to derive multiple points of the attack surface to enhance fault differentiation in the hope that non-frequent faults are more informative.

Third, as suggested by other authors [2], there are better strategies than random search [21] to improve both efficiency and efficacy. In fact, probe movement associated with random search introduces too much error and should be reduced as much as possible. However, so far, there has been no clear indication on how probe coordinates should be explored.

3   Methodology

We assume a *controller/target* evaluation setup such as the one represented in Fig. 1. The controller is responsible for guiding the injection probe on the target by modifying the coordinates (X, Y) of the probe, the intensity V and the duration d of the square pulse. Each injection of faults is modeled as a function $EMFI(X, Y, V, d)$ with three possible outcomes, similarly to [14]:

- OK: the target output is as expected.
- KO: the target locks up, freezes, resets, or does not produce a result.

28   D. A. E. Carta et al.

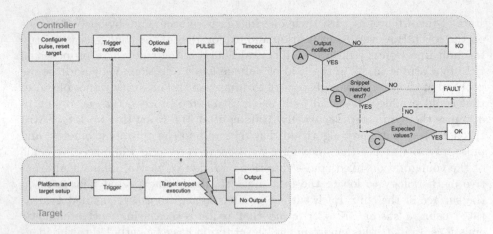

Fig. 1. Flowchart of evaluating the outcome of a single EMFI. A FAULT may be exploitable or not depending on the path that lead to it. Exploitable FAULTs follow the dotted arrow path, and Non-exploitable FAULTs follow the dashed arrow path.

– FAULT: anything else; this is the most rare behavior and is divided further into:
  • Informative: the FAULT that does not prevent the code under test from reaching its end, but does not show expected values.
  • Noninformative: any other FAULT such as processor *exceptions* of any kind.

Since EMFI is a probabilistic attack, we will need to work with statistics associated with n fault injections, which will provide, for each outcome $o \in \{\text{OK}, \text{KO}, \text{FAULT}\}$, its probability $P_o(X, Y, V, d, n)$. The problem is to efficiently identify the subregion of the attack space $X \times Y \times V \times d$ that maximizes probability P_{FAULT} for each coordinate that meets a susceptibility criterion, without resorting to a random search.

The proposed methodology is based on the idea that P_{FAULT} is non-negligible where P_{OK} and P_{KO} balance out. In fact, we rely on the idea that a pulse "too weak" ($P_{\text{OK}} \gg P_{\text{KO}}$) is not sufficient to cause the target fault. At the same time, a pulse that is "too strong" ($P_{\text{KO}} \gg P_{\text{OK}}$) may disturb execution too much. Our strategy is carried out in two steps: 1) reducing the physical surface of the target (X, Y) to only points susceptible to faults (*susceptible surface search*), and 2) identifying the intensity V and duration d of the pulse through a multidimensional bisection algorithm [1] (*coordinate search*). The methodology, shown in Fig. 2, is agnostic to the target architecture and relies only on the observability of an outcome, which could be a led lighting up or a log message from a debug console. The two methodological steps are outlined in the following two subsections.

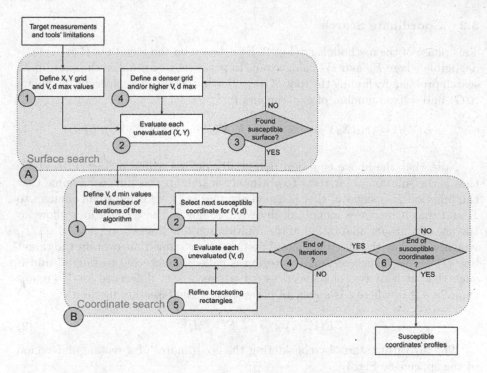

Fig. 2. Flowchart of the proposed search methodology.

3.1   Susceptible Surface Search

The search for the susceptible area (Fig. 2, A) consists of first defining a grid G of coordinates and the maximum intensity and duration of the pulse. This is done by measuring the spatial dimensions of the target $X_{min}, Y_{min}, X_{max}, Y_{max}$, choosing a grid *step* according to the precision of the probe positioning mechanism and defining the maximum value of intensity V_{max} and duration d_{max} exactly below the values that risk damaging the target.

Then, evaluate

$$\text{EMFI}(X_i, Y_j, V_{max}, d_{max})$$

on each point of the grid G and for a number of experiments $\bar{n}$ to derive the subset of "susceptible" surface points (S), i.e., those points that show at least some KO or FAULT result:

$$S(G) = \{(\bar{X}, \bar{Y}) | (\bar{X}, \bar{Y}) \in G \ \wedge$$
$$P_{\text{KO}}(\bar{X}, \bar{Y}, V_{max}, d_{max}, \bar{n}) + P_{\text{FAULT}}(\bar{X}, \bar{Y}, V_{max}, d_{max}, \bar{n}) > 0\}$$

If no susceptible points are found, run the procedure again on a grid with a smaller step, higher intensity, and/or duration of the pulse.

3.2   Coordinate Search

This phase of the methodology (Fig. 2, B) is based on the idea that P_{FAULT} is non-negligible where P_{OK} and P_{KO} balance out. In practice, we formalize the coordinate search problem by finding the root of the following equation for susceptible points $S(G)$ and a fixed number of experiments $\bar{n}$:

$$E(V,d) = \{P_{\text{KO}}(\bar{X},\bar{Y},V,d,\bar{n}) - P_{\text{OK}}(\bar{X},\bar{Y},V,d,\bar{n}) \simeq 0, (\bar{X},\bar{Y}) \in S(G)\} \tag{1}$$

Note that the above equation potentially defines a line in the (V,d) space that is the solution of interest. To optimally search for this line, we assume that the function E is smooth, that is, small changes in (V,d) bring small changes to E and that it increases monotonically with V and d. These conditions allow for the use of a proper adaptation of the multidimensional bisection[3] Algorithm [1], which will allow the identification of rectangular regions that contain the target line (V,d). Each such rectangular region is called "bracketing rectangle" and is such that at least two of its vertices i,j trigger a sign difference for E greater than $2\epsilon, \epsilon \geq 0$, where ϵ is a control parameter of the bisection method[4]:

$$E(V_i,d_i) < -\epsilon \wedge E(V_j,d_j) > \epsilon \tag{2}$$

The algorithm starts by considering the coordinates of a rectangular region of the space (see Fig. 3)

$$R = \{(V_{min},d_{min}),(V_{max},d_{min}),(V_{max},d_{max}),(V_{min},d_{max})\}$$

If the rectangle is bracketing, then it is divided into 4 equal subrectangles; the search is then repeated for those subrectangles that are bracketing until a maximum number of iterations is reached or there are no more bracketing rectangles.

The maximum number of iterations I_{max} is given by the discrete nature of the parameters V and d:

$$I_{max} = min\left(\left\lfloor \log_2\left(\frac{V_{max}-V_{min}}{V_{step}}\right)\right\rfloor, \left\lfloor \log_2\left(\frac{d_{max}-d_{min}}{d_{step}}\right)\right\rfloor\right) \tag{3}$$

where V_{step} and d_{step} are determined by the precision of the equipment / setup.

In the worst-case scenario (that is, a function with roots right above the bottom left perimeter of the initial bracketing rectangle) and at iteration I, the

---

[3] Conditions must be interpreted as sufficient as the bisection algorithm we are referring to can be applied to non-monotone functions as well by using a neighbor search.

[4] It is an indirect stop criterion for the bisection method. The higher ϵ, the lower the bar will be set to recognize the rectangles as bracketing rectangles, and thus continue the search.

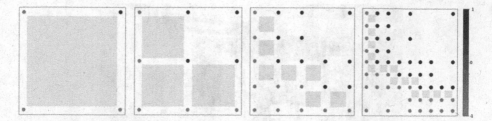

Fig. 3. Example iterations (0 to 3) of the Bi-dimensional bisection with $\epsilon = 0$. Vertices with $E > 0$ are highlighted in orange, those with $E < 0$ are highlighted in blue, while bracketing rectangles are highlighted in red. In iteration 1 the top right rectangle is not bracketing since it has no vertex V with $E(V, d) < 0$. (Color figure online)
Note that measurement units for X and Y axis are different (Volts vs nanoseconds).

bisection algorithm must evaluate $2^{I+2} - 3$ vertices $\bar{n}$ times; thus, we obtain the following bound for the number of experiments N:

$$N \leq 4\bar{n} + \left(\sum_{I=1}^{I_{max}} 2^{I+2} - 3 \right) \bar{n} \tag{4}$$

4   Experimental Validation

This section presents an experimental validation of the methodology presented in the previous section. We will introduce the setup of the injection platform and the target, as well as a qualitative and quantitative evaluation of the efficacy in identifying informative faults.

The hardware and software components of our setup are built around the ChipShouter platform for a comprehensive budget of less than 5K€ (excluding oscilloscope) and a standard laptop used to control the following parameters (see Fig. 4):

- Duration of d pulse injection to as low as 10 ns, through an Artix-7 35T Arty at 100 MHz
- (X, Y) position of the fault injection probe, through a 3d printer with a 0.1 mm resolution
- Intensity V of the pulse (directly on the ChipShouter).

The setting allows us to produce pulses with d ranging from 10 to 600 ns with a 10 ns resolution and V ranging from 150 to 500 V, with a 1 V resolution. To control the platform, we used the following software tools:

- Raiden [7], an open source FPGA project to handle the delay between the target and the pulse triggers. It also controls the duration of the trigger, allowing the pulse to last a fixed number of clock cycles. Finally, it resets the target to perform new experiments.

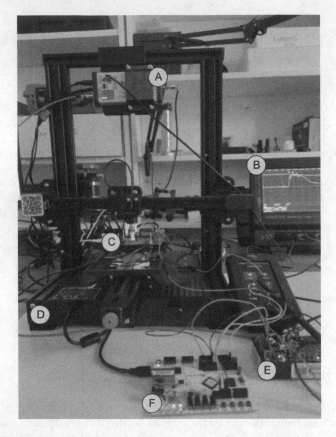

Fig. 4. Chipshouter (A), Oscilloscope (B), Target (C), 3D printer (D), Voltage translator (E) and FPGA (F).

- OctoPrint, a 3D-printer control application.
- A Python app that orchestrates Raiden, Octoprint, and the ChipShouter APIs to configure and collect the target output through a serial interface.

The target is an ARMv7 dual core, dual issue SoC that mounts a Cortex A7 with eight pipeline stages with data and instruction caches disabled. It runs at 600 MHz and does not perform any speculative execution. The chip has not been decapped, and we do not have information on the internal layout. The target has a serial port that is used by the central workstation to read the output of the experiments performed on it. The chosen target offers a standard procedure for building and deploying everything necessary for a robust and secure boot chain. We position our victim code in the First Stage Boot Loader (FSBL) of Trusted Firmware-A. Putting the victim code at this point in the boot-chain simplifies the collection and interpretation of the results; in particular, the code runs on a single core and allows us to minimize the time window for testing. We focus on the first core because it is the most interesting target for attackers;

indeed, it is responsible for the execution of security sensitive operations, such as authenticating boot-loader images. We expect that enabling the cache, MMU, and second core, along with other unutilized components, would increase the attack surface and the complexity of the analysis.

The victim code has a standard template; the initial part of the template triggers the pulse through a GPIO pin:

```
;Pulse trigger
        bl      set_gpio
        mov     r0, #89            ; 0x59
        bl      clk_enable
        ldr     r3, [pc, #124]     ; address for gpio high
        movs    r2, #128           ; 0x80
        str     r2, [r3, #0]       ; set gpio high
```

It then initializes each register from r0 to r12 to a unique value (r0=0x41414141, r1=0x42424242 ... r12=0x53535353) to recognize any unexpected/random change in its content:

```
;Register initialisation
        mov.w   r0, #1094795585    ; 0x41414141
        mov.w   r1, #1111638594    ; 0x42424242
        ...
        mov.w   ip, #1397969747    ; 0x53535353
```

The actual victim code (which belongs to a class of codes introduced in the following) is then executed, followed by a print, on the serial port, of the architectural state.

The code has a size limitation because it has to fit into the internal SRAM, according to the FSBL platform guidelines. The size of the FSBL image allows enough instructions to hit after accounting for the actual delay between the GPIO high instruction and the actual arrival of the electromagnetic pulse.

We designed the victim code snippets to stress the three main microarchitectural blocks of the processor: the arithmetic units, the memory subsystem (load/store unit), and the branching unit. The snippets have been designed to allow one to hit the same instruction independently of the time of arrival of the pulse. For this reason, they correspond to the repetition of the same instruction. In particular, we used:

- A sequence of NOPs; since NOPs do not change the architectural state, any observed change in the state itself could be attributed to an effect of EMFI.
- A sequence of ADDs which increment register r0 by one. Since NOPs could be optimized away by the core micro-architecture, we also try with instructions that update just a small portion of the architectural state and cannot be disregarded.
- A sequence of LDRs instructions to characterize the potential effects on the memory interface.

– A single bne instruction that jumps to itself. This snippet (called *Loop* in the following) does not produce any output, and its OK and KO behaviors are indistinguishable.

4.1   Trigger and Timing Synchronization

We achieve synchronization between the pulse and the victim code through a GPIO pin that is controlled directly by the victim. Figure 5 shows the view, captured via oscilloscope, of the timing of the signals involved.

First, the victim sets the GPIO to high (Fig. 5,A); in turn, this triggers the ChipShouter (Fig. 5,B), and finally the actual electromagnetic pulse is produced (Fig. 5,C). (Figure 5,D) is the actual amount of time that occurs between the victim's trigger instruction and the actual impact on the execution of the instructions (Fig. 5, F). The ChipShouter delay is less than 100 ns (Fig. 5, E).

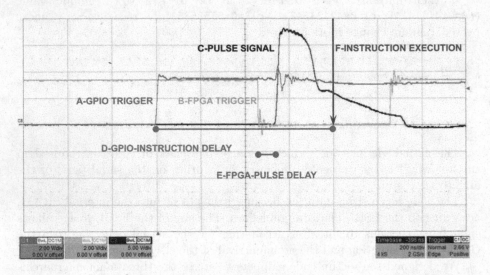

Fig. 5. Timing synchronization scheme from the oscilloscope perspective. The horizontal steps of the grid represent a period of 200 ns.

4.2   Surface Search

The surface mapping is performed using a 1 mm grid step. Given that the edge of the square chip surface is 13 mm, the resulting grid G corresponds to 169 points. According to the previous description, we used a V_{max} at 500 V, a duration of $d_{max} = 600$ ns (which is the maximum available on the ChipShouter as of 2022) and a number of experiments per point $\bar{n} = 8$.

First, we performed a surface search using the NOP victim code. The overall resulting dimension of the susceptible sub-grid $S(G)$ is 42, that is, 25.8% of the entire grid (see Fig. 6a). In this phase, we observed very few FAULTs, and the majority of experiments were KO. The victim code ADD behaves similarly (see Fig. 6b). Interestingly, the FAULTs are located on the perimeter of the KO subgrid and are essentially exceptions. We also found a case where a faulty behavior did not trigger an exception, i.e., the value of a register in the computation was modified and the computation reached the end. The victim code LDR behaves similarly (see Fig. 6c) to the other two with exceptions classified as link register abort (LRABT), and Data Abort. The Loop victim code is more difficult to characterize, as one can only observe either exceptions or sudden control changes that force the CPU out of the loop. Even in this case, we observed the FAULTs on the perimeter of the previous susceptible surface.

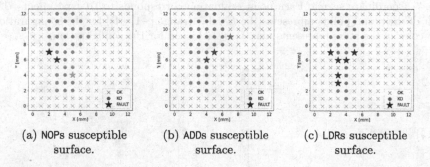

(a) NOPs susceptible surface.   (b) ADDs susceptible surface.   (c) LDRs susceptible surface.

Fig. 6. Surface search for different code snippets executions. Each point coordinate is evaluated 8 times at max intensity and duration of the pulse.

4.3   Coordinate Search

We sampled a few points within the subgrid $S(G)$ by using $\epsilon = 0$, thus forcing the maximum iterations of the bisection method to $I = 5$. The algorithm converged towards P_{FAULT} ranging from 30% to 80%. Once the bisection converged, some coordinates of $S(G)$ showed very different (V, d) profiles, which appeared even before reaching the maximum I, as Fig. 7 shows. In particular, some points produced a high probability of fault in the upper right quadrant (Fig. 7a), while some others were characterized by a very low maximum probability in the lower left quadrant (Fig. 7b), which incidentally goes against some results reported earlier [8]. We do not have conclusive explanations for this conflicting behavior, which, we think, could be better explained with a decapped chip.

Figure 8a shows all coordinates tested with the maximum P_{FAULT} obtained; By comparison, Fig. 8b shows the results obtained when both $S(G)$ and bisection are replaced by random sampling. Given the striking difference in precision, we

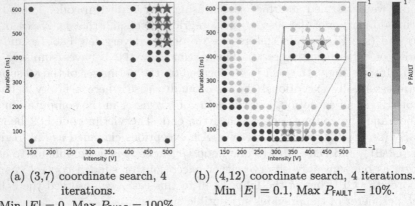

(a) (3,7) coordinate search, 4 iterations. Min $|E| = 0$, Max $P_{\text{FAULT}} = 100\%$.

(b) (4,12) coordinate search, 4 iterations. Min $|E| = 0.1$, Max $P_{\text{FAULT}} = 10\%$.

Fig. 7. Coordinate search. Each point evaluation corresponds to 10 experiments. The color of the round points represents the E value (range $[-1, +1]$) for the configuration. The color of the stars represents max P_{FAULT} achieved for the configuration.

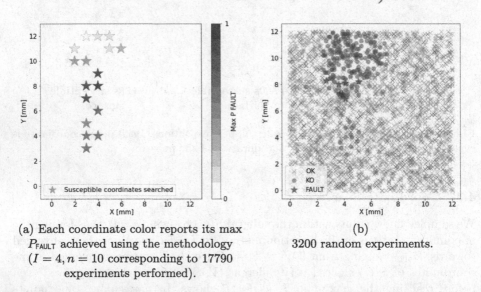

(a) Each coordinate color reports its max P_{FAULT} achieved using the methodology ($I = 4, n = 10$ corresponding to 17790 experiments performed).

(b) 3200 random experiments.

Fig. 8. Validation tests on susceptibility criterion.

further investigated the efficacy of the random search at some coordinates in $S(G)$ comparing it with the bisection method (Figs. 9 and 10), using as many random experiments as the amount needed for the four bisection iterations. The proposed bisection method obtained a number of faults that is almost triple the random one.

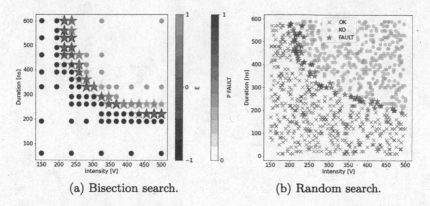

(a) Bisection search.   (b) Random search.

Fig. 9. Validation tests on coordinate (4,8). 960 experiments per Random and Bisection search.

On a selected subset of coordinates, we evaluated the importance of the threshold ϵ in Eq. 2. We expected that the lower the threshold, the closer we get to the roots of the E function in Eq. 1, and potentially the higher the probability of a fault. Figure 11 shows a perceived almost linear relationship between the two.

4.4 Testing a Fault Model

The previous methodology allowed us to identify some potential coordinates of interest to be further investigated. Although the following is outside the scope of the methodology, we report some results of this additional investigation. In particular, we focus on the ADD victim code. Recall that the ADD victim code is composed of an unrolled loop of ADD instructions that increment the r0 register by a deterministic amount. Inspecting some of the sensible coordinates, we found that the final value of the r0 register was off by a small margin relative to the expected value, indicating a potential *instruction skip*. These coordinates are characterized by a low P_{FAULT} (thus potentially discarded by other approaches); one of them, in particular, shows 166 total FAULTs, of which 154 are noninformative, 5 reflect the skip of two instructions, and 7 the skip of a single one. We tried, in the same coordinates, a different snippet (SUB) and we obtained a similar behavior.

It is well known that instruction skips, when applied to branch instructions, might be the most dangerous exploitable effect. In fact, you could skip complete security checks by skipping a branch. We thus tried a snippet consisting of a branch jumping on itself; after 59 experiments using random values over the (V, d) domain, we have obtained the result that the loop was effectively broken (for 455 V and 200 ns of duration). We were able to reproduce this fault with a probability of 2.2%. Even if these results might seem promising, we must underline that it is extremely difficult to target a single branch instruction in a realistic setting (i.e. one that does not jump to itself all the time).

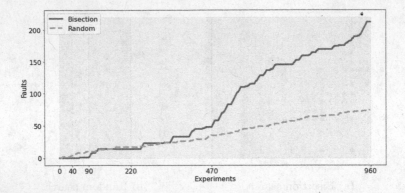

Fig. 10. Comparison between bisection and random search upon a fixed coordinate. Number of total Faults per experiments performed. Upon experiments intervals [0, 40], [40, 90], [90, 220], [220, 470] and [470, 960] execute iterations from 0 to 4.

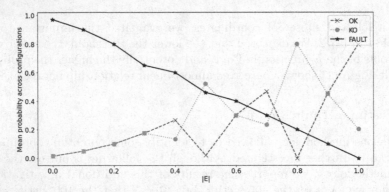

Fig. 11. Fault probability relationship with achieved $|E|$

What is thus the effectiveness of the equipment in targeting a single instruction on a 600 MHZ processor? To answer this question, we relied on a particular victim snippet of a single ADD and several NOPs surrounding it. We then observed the address reported by the LRABT exceptions that we have induced by varying the timing offset of the pulse (see Fig. 12). Some experiments allowed us to determine (by linear regression on the reported addresses) what was the most likely offset to skip the victim ADD. However, even concentrating on that offset, we have found that on average we were producing exceptions both before and after ADD and never ADD itself. Our conclusion is that the current equipment does not provide adequate accuracy when targeting a single instruction.

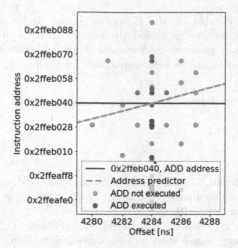

Fig. 12. Varying the timing offset allows to target a range of instruction addresses. The predicted address for the pulse offset 4284 ns was the victim ADD but we were not able to make it skip, almost all experiments impacting either before or after it.

5   Conclusion and Future Work

In this work, we presented a general methodology to identify possible EMFI attack coordinates in a large parameter space. The methodology does not discard any point that could produce a fault (i.e., it has high coverage) and has been proven to reduce the search space in a specific use case by five times. In particular, on configurations that balance P_{KO} and P_{OK}, we were able to produce faults with an average probability of 26.7% in all susceptible coordinates, some coordinates reaching 97.6%. The proposed bisection method has found a number of faults that is 3 times higher than a random search on selected coordinates and corroborates our idea that fault points lie at the equilibrium between OK and KO points. The present approach is slower than [14], but is applicable to a complex, high performance chip not intended for attack purposes. In contrast to [8], we have found that the most sensitive spots did not correspond to high occurrence ratios or informative faults. We acknowledge that there are still some additional parameters to be thoroughly examined, such as the probe's angle, type, size, and winding, which were fixed to conventional state-of-the-art values in the present study; we plan to address this issue in future work. Furthermore, the number of experiments was chosen taking into account the overall time budget assigned to the analysis, but there may be different methods. On a different note, we plan to address branch and load/store instructions more thoroughly. Lastly, the conclusions that were drawn from the analysis carried out on a single target board may be limited, yet the results obtained on a complex board are indicative of the potential of the methodology.

Acknowledgments. Funded by the European Union under grant agreement no. 101070008. Views and opinions expressed are however those of the author(s) only and do not necessarily reflect those of the European Union. Neither the European Union nor the granting authority can be held responsible for them.

Funded by
the European Union

References

1. Bachrathy, D., Stépán, G.: Bisection method in higher dimensions and the efficiency number. Periodica polytechnica. Mech. Eng. **56**, 81–86 (2012). https://doi.org/10.3311/pp.me.2012-2.01
2. Carpi, R.B., Picek, S., Batina, L., Menarini, F., Jakobovic, D., Golub, M.: Glitch it if you can: parameter search strategies for successful fault injection. In: Francillon, A., Rohatgi, P. (eds.) CARDIS 2013. LNCS, vol. 8419, pp. 236–252. Springer, Cham (2014). https://doi.org/10.1007/978-3-319-08302-5_16
3. Cui, A., Housley, R.: BADFET: defeating modern secure boot using Second-Order pulsed electromagnetic fault injection. In: 11th USENIX Workshop on Offensive Technologies (WOOT 17). USENIX Association, Vancouver, BC (2017). https://www.usenix.org/conference/woot17/workshop-program/presentation/cui
4. Dumont, M., Lisart, M., Maurine, P.: Modeling and simulating electromagnetic fault injection. IEEE Trans. Comput. Aided Des. Integr. Circuits Syst. **40**(4), 680–693 (2021). https://doi.org/10.1109/TCAD.2020.3003287
5. Dureuil, L., Potet, M.-L., de Choudens, P., Dumas, C., Clédière, J.: From code review to fault injection attacks: filling the gap using fault model inference. In: Homma, N., Medwed, M. (eds.) CARDIS 2015. LNCS, vol. 9514, pp. 107–124. Springer, Cham (2016). https://doi.org/10.1007/978-3-319-31271-2_7
6. Dutertre, J.M., Menu, A., Potin, O., Rigaud, J.B., Danger, J.L.: Experimental analysis of the electromagnetic instruction skip fault model and consequences for software countermeasures. Microelectron. Reliability **121**, 114133 (2021). https://doi.org/10.1016/j.microrel.2021.114133. https://www.sciencedirect.com/science/article/pii/S0026271421000998
7. Wypych, G., Laurie, A.: Raiden github repository. https://github.com/IBM/raiden (2020)
8. Gaine, C., Aboulkassimi, D., Pontié, S., Nikolovski, J.P., Dutertre, J.M.: Electromagnetic fault injection as a new forensic approach for SoCs. In: 2020 IEEE International Workshop on Information Forensics and Security (WIFS), pp. 1–6 (2020). https://doi.org/10.1109/WIFS49906.2020.9360902
9. Gaine, C., Nikolovski, J.P., Aboulkassimi, D., Dutertre, J.M.: New probe design for hardware characterization by electromagnetic fault injection. In: 2022 International Symposium on Electromagnetic Compatibility - EMC Europe, pp. 299–304 (2022). https://doi.org/10.1109/EMCEurope51680.2022.9901104
10. Hummel, T.: Exploring effects of electromagnetic fault injection on a 32-bit high speed embedded device microprocessor, Master's thesis, University of Twente (2014)
11. Kühnapfel, N., Buhren, R., Jacob, H.N., Krachenfels, T., Werling, C., Seifert, J.P.: EM-fault it yourself: Building a replicable EMFI setup for desktop and server hardware. arXiv preprint arXiv:2209.09835 (2022)

12. Machiry, A., et al.: BOOMERANG: exploiting the semantic gap in trusted execution environments. In: NDSS (2017)
13. Madau, M.: A methodology to localise EMFI areas on Microcontrollers, Theses, Université Montpellier (2019). https://tel.archives-ouvertes.fr/tel-02478873
14. Maldini, A., Samwel, N., Picek, S., Batina, L.: Optimizing electromagnetic fault injection with genetic algorithms. In: Breier, J., Hou, X., Bhasin, S. (eds.) Automated Methods in Cryptographic Fault Analysis, pp. 281–300. Springer, Cham (2019). https://doi.org/10.1007/978-3-030-11333-9_13
15. Menu, A., Bhasin, S., Dutertre, J.M., Rigaud, J.B., Danger, J.L.: Precise spatio-temporal electromagnetic fault injections on data transfers. In: 2019 Workshop on Fault Diagnosis and Tolerance in Cryptography (FDTC), pp. 1–8. IEEE (2019)
16. Moro, N., Dehbaoui, A., Heydemann, K., Robisson, B., Encrenaz, E.: Electromagnetic fault injection: towards a fault model on a 32-bit microcontroller. In: 2013 Workshop on Fault Diagnosis and Tolerance in Cryptography, pp. 77–88 (2013). https://doi.org/10.1109/FDTC.2013.9
17. NewAE: Chipshouter github repository. https://github.com/newaetech/ChipSHOUTER (2019)
18. Omarouayache, R., Raoult, J., Jarrix, S., Chusseau, L., Maurine, P.: Magnetic Microprobe design for EM fault attack. In: EMC EUROPE: Electromagnetic Compatibility. EMC EUROPE, Bruges, Belgium (2013). https://hal.archives-ouvertes.fr/hal-01893856
19. Ordas, S., Guillaume-Sage, L., Maurine, P.: Electromagnetic fault injection: the curse of flip-flops. J. Cryptogr. Eng. 7(3), 183–197 (2016). https://doi.org/10.1007/s13389-016-0128-3
20. Proy, J., Heydemann, K., Berzati, A., Majéric, F., Cohen, A.: A first ISA-level characterization of em pulse effects on superscalar microarchitectures: a secure software perspective. In: Proceedings of the 14th International Conference on Availability, Reliability and Security, pp. 1–10 (2019)
21. Raelize: Qualcomm IPQ40xx: Breaking into QSEE using fault injection. https://raelize.com/blog/qualcomm-ipq40xx-breaking-into-qsee-using-fault-injection (2021)
22. Tang, A., Sethumadhavan, S., Stolfo, S.: {CLKSCREW}: exposing the perils of {Security-Oblivious} energy management. In: 26th USENIX Security Symposium (USENIX Security 17), pp. 1057–1074 (2017)
23. Trouchkine, T., Bouffard, G., Clédière, J.: Fault injection characterization on modern CPUs. In: Laurent, M., Giannetsos, T. (eds.) WISTP 2019. LNCS, vol. 12024, pp. 123–138. Springer, Cham (2020). https://doi.org/10.1007/978-3-030-41702-4_8

A CCFI Verification Scheme Based on the RISC-V Trace Encoder

Anthony Zgheib[✉], Olivier Potin, Jean-Baptiste Rigaud,
and Jean-Max Dutertre

Mines Saint-Etienne, CEA, Leti, Centre CMP, 13541 Gardanne, France
{zgheib,olivier.potin,rigaud,dutertre}@emse.fr

Abstract. Control-Flow Integrity (CFI) is used to check at runtime that a program's execution path follows its corresponding Control-Flow Graph (CFG) and is not altered by software or physical attacks. In addition to the CFI's features, the Code and Control-Flow Integrity (CCFI) verifies the integrity of the executed program code. This paper presents a CCFI verification system for programs executed on RISC-V cores. Our solution is built upon the RISC-V Trace Encoder (TE) that provides information about the execution path of the user's program. An evolution of the TE specifications and additional logic have made it possible to monitor the integrity of a program control flow and of all the executed instructions. We implemented this approach on a RISC-V core and simulated its efficiency against Fault Injection Attacks. Its average hardware area and memory overheads are equal to 27.9% and 6.25% respectively. Compared to existing CCFI solutions, our methodology does not modify the user code, the RISC-V compiler or the core's pipeline.

Keywords: RISC-V · Trace Encoder · CFI · CCFI · FIA

1 Introduction

Fault Injection Attacks (FIA) are effective threats that can alter the intended behavior of a program running on a processor. The most common FIA techniques are described in [3]. These attacks could lead to skipping or corrupting a vulnerable instruction in the user application code, in order to bypass system security features [19] (e.g. bypassing a PIN code [12]). Against these attacks, Control-Flow Integrity (CFI) [1] verification schemes are used to verify that a program is correctly executed during runtime. It checks that its execution follows a path known to be correct in the application Control Flow Graph (CFG). This CFG can be drawn by statically analyzing the source code of the program (if all destinations can be computed during the compilation process). Note that indirect jump destinations in a program may not be predicted at compilation time, in this case the generation of the graph is difficult. The CFG represents the valid control flow changes in a normal program execution [8]. However, attacks made on instructions/operations within the user code are not always detected by CFI solutions, such as changing an addition of two values into a subtraction (if no violation of the CFG is induced).

E. B. Kavun and M. Pehl (Eds.): COSADE 2023, LNCS 13979, pp. 42–61, 2023.
https://doi.org/10.1007/978-3-031-29497-6_3

Code and Control-Flow Integrity (CCFI) countermeasures are designed to verify at runtime, in addition to CFI, the integrity of the executed user code. With this check, the entire code is protected against FIA not only the discontinuity instructions (monitored by CFI).

Contributions. Our work contributes to the CCFI state-of-the-art by adding a solution that does not require any code or compiler modification. In addition, no core nor Instruction Set Architecture (ISA) extension are made. Our solution consists in adding an additional verification system to the RISC-V core [2]. It detects software or physical attacks that derive the program CFG from its normal behavior. This graph is formed from all known destinations of the binary code. Therefore, our solution does not cover forward edge attacks (faults on indirect jump destinations that are not precisely known at binary level) nor attacks injected on data (register or memory). Our verification system is based on the RISC-V Trace Encoder (TE) [18]. To the best of our knowledge, this is the first solution that uses the RISC-V TE for CCFI verification.

Organization. Our paper is divided as follows: Sect. 2 provides insights on existing CCFI solutions. Sections 3 and 4 describe our CCFI methodology and countermeasure. Section 5 shows its effectiveness against simulated FIA. Sections 6 and 7 report the hardware requirements and the discussion about our solution. Finally, we conclude our paper in the last Section.

2   Related Work

In this section, the most relevant CCFI verification solutions are presented. Some countermeasures ensure both the integrity and confidentiality of the user code by encrypting the code instructions and deciphering it at runtime. From this category, we can cite SOFIA [7]. It is a hardware-based security architecture that protects the software integrity, performs CFI, prevents execution of tampered code and enforces copyright protection. This countermeasure is added by extending the processor. In another perspective, other countermeasures modify the user code and compiler to insert dedicated CCFI instructions. Werner et al. [21] designed SCFP, a solution that guarantees the confidentiality of a software IP and its authentic execution on a microcontroller. It covers code reuse, code injection and fault attacks on the code and control flow. The SCI-FI [4] solution belongs also to this category. It is designed for control signal, code and CFI verification. It protects against FIA. The verification process is triggered by dedicated and customized instructions added by extending the RISC-V ISA. Another approach is to connect external blocks to the processor without extending the ISA to verify the program CCFI like the solution presented in CCFI-Cache [6] and ATRIUM [22]. Danger et al., in [6], developed a hardware based solution that verifies code and CFG, ensures protection against cyber and physical attacks. It covers backward edges and forward edges in certain cases— when the indirect jump targets a destination address not pointing to a beginning of a Basic Block (BB), detected by checking the StartBB label—, code and fault injection. ATRIUM is a runtime attestation scheme targeting "bare metal" embedded systems software that works in parallel to the processor. It ensures CFI and instruction integrity. This solution covers code injection, code reuse, hardware fault attacks on instructions and TOCTOU (Time Of Check Time Of Use) attacks [20]. The previous countermeasures have an impact on the runtime of the programs. Except ATRIUM, these solutions require user code modification to ensure CCFI verification. Table 1 summarizes the average overhead costs of these countermeasures in terms of code size, performance and hardware area compared to our solution whose overhead is detailed in Sect. 6. In the following sections, we describe a new CCFI scheme that keeps unchanged the user code, compilation process and core design.

Table 1. State-of-the-art solutions average overhead costs.

Solution	SOFIA [7]	SCFP [21]	SCI-FI [4]	CCFI-Cache [6]	ATRIUM [22]	This Work
Code Size (%)	141	19.8	25.4	<30	0	0
Performance (%)	110	9.1	17.5	32	<22.7	0
Hardware Area (%)	28.2	N/A	<23.8	10	<20	**27.9**
TV BRAM Size (%)	0	0	0	0	0	**6.25**

3 CCFI Methodology

Our CCFI verification methodology is divided into 3 steps:

1. The static analysis of the binary code to obtain its CFG.
2. The generation of metadata related to the discontinuity instructions and Basic Blocks (BB, cf. Sect. 3.2 for definition).
3. The addition of an external hardware module - the Trace Verifier (TV) - to proceed to the CCFI verification.

Each step is described in detail in the next sections.

3.1 Static Analysis

A custom program has been developed to analyse statically the user's binary code in order to derive its CFG. This program is independent and is not part of the RISC-V toolchain backend. It only requires the binary file containing the program instructions. The CFG shows all the legitimate paths that a program could follow. From this analysis, all discontinuity instructions are reported. They refer to direct jumps—Jump (J) and Jump And Link (JAL) instructions—, branch and return instructions. Algorithm 1 illustrates the pseudo-code of the static analysis process used to build the program CFG. The application reports for each discontinuity instruction the address(es) of the next attempted discontinuity instruction(s). For a branch instruction, two addresses are reported: the first when the branch is taken and the second when the branch is not taken. In our

---

Algorithm 1. CFG Generation

Require: *Binary Code*
Ensure: *Discontinuity instructions with their Basic Blocks (cf. Sect. 3.2 for definition)*
  for $i \leftarrow program.begin$ to $program.end$ **do**
    #*Discontinuity on Branch, Jump, or Return*
    if *discontinuity instruction* **then**
      #*Default Report*
      report address at i;
      report instruction at i;
      if *branch instruction* **then**
        report next discontinuity's address when branch taken;
        report next discontinuity's address when branch non taken;
      else if *jump instruction* **then**
        report next discontinuity's address when call;
        report return address # equal to jump address + 4
      else if *return instruction* **then**
        report address and instruction;
      end if
    end if
  end for

---

strategy, indirect jumps represented by the Jump And Link Register (JALR) instructions are not considered. These instructions involve the code's program counter (PC) to jump to a destination whose address is calculated according to the content of a register and a value contained in its binary instruction. This register's content is not known at the time of the static analysis. However, the possible addresses can be guessed by parsing the code to form an array of possible destinations. This strategy complicates the control flow schemes to check for a correct destination. To allow easy and accurate extraction of the CFG, Gonzalvez et al. [11] proposed two modified ISAs by removing indirect jumps from a program. In our case, we dedicate our approach to cover the CCFI for programs that do not contain indirect jumps. We further discuss in Sect. 7 how these jumps could be treated as a further work.

3.2 Metadata Generation

From the discontinuity instructions of the CFG, metadata are generated constituting the CFG's map. Each data element contains the discontinuity instruction, its address and the index (address in the memory) of the following discontinuity. These instructions delimit a Basic Block (BB): a set of successive instructions for which execution is done consecutively and in order. A BB starts with the first instruction following a discontinuity instruction until the next discontinuity. In addition to the information stored in the data elements, hash signatures of BBs are calculated. A hash signature computation is made on the binary value of all the 32-bit length instructions of a BB using a Multiple-Input Signature Register (MISR) mechanism [9]. A 32-bit MISR module offers a better protection (a small aliasing probability [15]) than a 32-bit CRC module or a 32-bit hash function against collisions. The computation starts from the BB first instruction until the end of the BB for which the signature is generated. This signature is stored along with the discontinuity instruction pointing to the address of the BB first instruction. A runtime verification of this signature is bound to check the integrity of the executed instructions. Figure 1 illustrates an example of four BBs delimited by jump (j), branch if not equal to zero (bnez), jump and link (jal) and ret (return) instructions with their metadata. For example, the hash signature of "Basic Block 2", delimited by the addresses 0x374 and 0x380, is stored with the discontinuity instruction pointing to the starting address of this block - instruction j 374 at address 0x328. For a function call using JAL instruction, its return address reported by Algorithm 1 is used to delimit the BB formed by the instructions after its return till the next discontinuity. The instruction jal ra,308 at address 0x3a8 in Fig. 1 illustrates this case. Its corresponding metadata contains (see index 40), its address, the instruction and the index 3B of the next discontinuity instruction, the expected signature of "Basic Block 1" (BB starting with the instruction after the jump) and the expected signature of "Basic Block 4" (representing the BB after the return starting at address 0x3ac). A stored signature is a prediction of the correct BB signature when executed on core. A recalculation of the BB signature is done at runtime and an additional hardware module - the Trace Verifier (TV) - is in charge of comparing it with the metadata (stored in a memory).

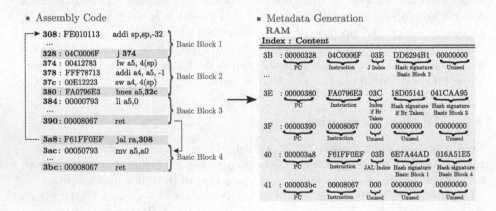

Fig. 1. Generated metadata content.

3.3   Trace Verifier

The TV is an additional hardware module (cf. Fig. 2, bottom). It receives, at runtime, information about the execution path followed by the program. These information are reported by the RISC-V Trace Encoder (TE) [18]. Based on the CFG metadata (cf. Sect. 3.2), the TV checks that the execution path of the program is included in its CFG. It also ensures the integrity of the user application code as a security propriety by verifying the BB signatures. An alarm is raised if a CFG derivation has been detected. The following section describes in more details our countermeasure.

4   Proposed CCFI Solution

4.1   Trace Encoder

Overview. The TE is a RISC-V hardware module [18]. It is an execution flow tracer that compresses at runtime the sequence of discontinuity instructions executed by the RISC-V core into trace packets. These packets sent to a debug tool allow developers to check the path followed by the program. By having access to the program binary, developers can reconstruct the program flow as depicted in Fig. 2 (top). This module alone is used for debugging purposes and allows neither CFI nor CCFI verification. The TE has a 3-stage pipeline to store the current (I), previous (I-1) and next (I+1) instructions [18]. Based on these three instructions, a packet defined by the TE standard [18] containing information about the path followed by the program since the last sent packet is emitted to an external debugging tool. It is emitted after fulfilling one of the seven conditions described in the TE specifications [18]. These conditions are related to the state of the core (context, privilege, exception) or to the instructions executed (first executed, discontinuity instructions, etc.). We briefly describe three of these conditions below that led in the verification of CCFI.

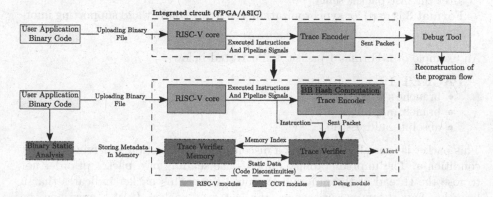

Fig. 2. A schematic of the RISC-V + TE (top), and its extension to ensure CCFI verification (bottom).

The other four conditions involve reporting the state of the core (as defined above), which does not cover the verification of CCFI but can be used to handle interruptions or core's exceptions. A packet is sent:

- Based on the previous instruction (I-1):
  a) An instruction with an unpredictable PC discontinuity is executed. This type refers to instructions applying a change to the PC whose offset could not be determined from the compiled code such as return instructions. To be able to follow the program path, the TE reports these discontinuities in form of trace packets. Hence, in its current configuration, it does not send a packet after each discontinuity instruction.
- Based on the current executed instruction (I):
  b) A first qualified instruction which refers to the first instruction executed in a program's code.
  c) The TE branch map is full (number of branches = 31, a packet is issued to clear its branch map) or it has a misprediction case (when branch predictor enabled).

Depending on these conditions, a packet is sent with a specific format identifier [18]. Referring to this standard, four packet formats are defined:

- **Format 0** is used to send optional efficiency extensions (such as the number of correctly predicted branches) when the core's branch prediction module is enabled. In our research, we based our CCFI solution while this module is disabled. A discussion about CCFI verification with this module active could be found in Sect. 7.
- **Format 1** reports a branch information when the TE branch counter reaches its maximum value (31 branches). Or, when an address needs to be reported and there has been at least one branch since the previous packet. This format only contains branch information.
- **Format 2** reports only the address of an instruction when no branch information need to be reported (for example, executing only a return instruction after the last packet sent).
- **Format 3** is used for synchronization, reporting context and supporting information.

An example of a Format 1 packet is illustrated below.

- **PACKET 1:**
  - branches: n
  - branch_map: n_map
  - absolute_address: PC

This packet is sent after executing a discontinuity instruction satisfying the first condition a. The unpredictability imposes the sending of a packet in order not to lose the thread of the program executed flow. This packet indicates that n branches have been executed since the last sent packet. It also mentions the branch_map (bit vector where taken/not taken status of each branch is stored chronologically) and address of the executed instruction after the discontinuity.

CFI. A prior work [23] exploits the TE in order to verify the CFI of a program executed on a RISC-V core. This design allows the detection of CFG integrity violations. Two CFI verification approaches were proposed. The first approach is consistent with the TE standard [18]. With this approach, only instruction skip on discontinuity instructions and backward edge attacks are detected. The second approach suggests an enrichment of the standard in order to detect more threat models. A packet is sent after each executed discontinuity instruction and not just after the unpredictable ones as in the first approach. This packet contains the address of the following executed instruction and more information depending on (I-1), (I) and (I+1) instructions. This permits to detect in addition to the previous threats, any corruption of a discontinuity instruction.

CCFI. Our paper contributes in extending the work of [23], by additionally adding a new functionality to the TE - thanks to its open-source specifications - to work in the CCFI verification mode. A hash signature computation is done on each BB in order to protect the entire code against FIA and not only the discontinuity instructions as in the CFI mode. The end of a BB is identified when a discontinuity instruction is executed. As for the CFI enhanced mode, a packet is sent after each discontinuity instruction. The BB generated signature is included in this packet with the information it sends originally. As an example, a Format 1 packet in CCFI configuration is enhanced as shown below.

- **PACKET 1:**
    - branches: n
    - branch_map: n_map
    - absolute_address: PC
    - **Signature_sent: Computed_Hash_Signature**

Figure 2 (bottom) illustrates the circuit for CCFI verification. It is composed of the TV, its memory containing the static metadata and the signature computation module (BB hash computation) in the TE.

4.2   Trace Verifier Hardware Description

As depicted in the bottom part of Fig. 2, our verification system is constituted by a memory (Trace Verifier Memory) and its core part (Trace Verifier).

TV Memory. The produced metadata are stored in a dedicated memory— Random Access Memory (RAM)—as illustrated in Fig. 2. Referring to Fig. 1, at index 3B, the **32-bit** jump instruction j 374 is stored with its **32-bit** address 0x328, the **12-bit** index of next discontinuity and the 32-bit signature 0xDD6294B1 of the following BB. In case of a branch instruction (e.g. at index 3E), **two 32-bit** hash signature values are stored referring to the two possible branches. In total, each discontinuity instruction requires **140-bit** of metadata.

TV Architecture. Figure 3 shows the architecture of our TV. It is composed of configurables modules (FIFO and LIFO), a Finite State Machine (FSM) and several processes. The verification process starts when it receives a packet from the TE that activates its FSM (1). Meanwhile, the packet is stored in a FIFO and will be acquired by the FSM (2). Subsequently, it is decoded in order to extract the reported address and signature (3). In case of a packet reporting the execution of a branch instruction, the branch and branch map are also extracted. Having the packet information, a navigation through the RAM metadata is done to constitute the path followed by the program and the expected hash signature (4). The last step of the FSM is to check the address stored in the packet against the static address computed from the navigation process and also compare the reported hash signature to the calculated signature (5). If the addresses and/or signatures are not equal, an error flag is raised. The process of resilience is not discussed here. This error could be treated as a software exception or hardware interruption with a dedicated process or as a message sent to the user.

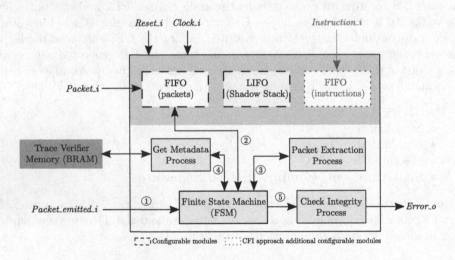

Fig. 3. Architecture of the TV.

TV FSM. The five steps listed in the **TV Architecture** are explicitly represented in Fig. 4. The TV is in an idle state until it receives a packet from the TE. Then, this packet is decoded to check its format—this refers to step 2 in Fig. 3. Step 3—`Packet extraction process`—is divided into 2 sequential FSM states (which requires 2 clock cycles). In the first state, the packet format is read. Then in the second state, the format-related fields are extracted (branch, address, signature). For instance, referring to Fig. 1 at index 3E and after the execution of the branch instruction `0xFA0796E3`, a Format 1 packet is reported indicating if the branch is taken or not. In case of a taken branch, the BRAM index will point to 3C and the branch address is extracted from the metadata binary instruction. In the other case, the index will be incremented by 1 to reach

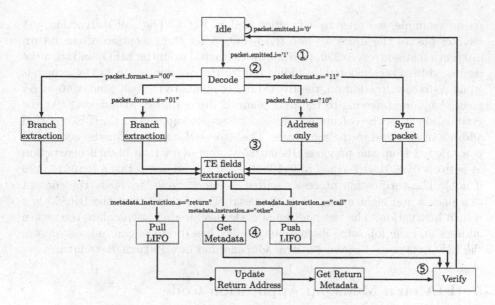

Fig. 4. FSM of the TV.

the index 3F which refers to the next planned discontinuity in the code. This corresponds to step 4. In the step 5, the TE content is verified by comparing the metadata extracted address to the TE reported address. The expected signature for the actual BB (contained within the previous metadata instruction) is also compared to the hash signature reported by the TE. The communication with the LIFO representing the "Shadow Stack" of our TV (cf. Fig. 3) is done when the BRAM navigation process points to a call or return instruction. After the FSM state TE fields extraction, the next state will depend on the type of the pointed instruction in the BRAM. We can distinguish 3 categories:

- **Function call (JAL instruction):** In this case, the next FSM state Push LIFO stores the instruction index in the LIFO module. Additionally, the call address and expected signature are extracted.
- **Return instruction:** The last call index stored in the LIFO is retrieved via the state Pull LIFO. The TV adds four to the retrieved call address in order to get the return address of the called function. It also increments the BRAM index by one to point to the discontinuity instruction following the call via steps Update Return Address and Get Return Metadata. The second signature stored at the call index corresponds to the expected signature for the BB executed after the return (as illustrated in Sect. 3.2). This signature is also extracted to be verified in the Verify state.
- **Branch or Jump (J) instruction:** The address and signature from the metadata are extracted in the state Get Metadata.

As an example, we refer to a function call in Fig. 1. The call instruction jal ra,308 pushes the index 40 into the LIFO. After the execution of the return instruction at address 0x390, the index is extracted from the LIFO, and then the return address is calculated by adding four to the call address 0x3a8+4, which is equal to 0x3ac. In addition, the BRAM index points to the call's index 40 incremented by one referring to the next planned discontinuity at index 41. At the verification step, the calculated address 0x3ac is compared to the TE reported address in addition to the signatures. The expected signature for the actual BB is extracted from the previous discontinuity metadata (the branch instruction at address 0x380). It is equal to 0x18D05141 if the branch is taken (0x041CAA95 if not). The verification process requires six clock cycles to verify the content of a packet and eight cycles when the instruction fetched from the BRAM is a return instruction. The two additional cycles are needed to calculate the return address and the following discontinuity index based on the call index stored in the LIFO via steps Update Return Address and Get Return Metadata.

5   FIA on a Memcmp Application Code

In this work, we address the protection of programs executed on a RISC-V core. Our CCFI solution detects attacks that divert the program CFG from its normal behavior. We consider that the attacker is able to alter the contents of the instruction memory by physical means (e.g. by laser injection at the reading of instructions from the memory [5]) as a single fault attack. We assume that the metadata stored in the memory of the TV cannot be modified by the attacker in order to defeat our countermeasure. Performing combined bit flips (multiple fault context) on the code execution and metadata content—contained in the TV—is a very complex fault hypothesis. This requires the attacker to:

- Know the MISR polynome to calculate a signature of the modified code.
- Inject multiple faults on the RISC-V architecture and the TV memory.

As illustration, this section demonstrates the detection of a FIA (physical attack) targeting a vulnerable instruction of a non protected comparison function Memcmp. It also outlines how our CCFI verification solution detects this attack.

Memcmp. It compares the values of two arrays. Its C function is shown in Fig. 5. The parameter n specifies the number of values to compare from src1 and src2 arrays. If no difference is reported between their elements, a value of 0 is returned. Otherwise, the difference of the first two different elements is returned.

FIA Scenario. An attacker might be interested in altering the result of this function. A fault could be injected to point that there is no difference while two different arrays are compared (e.g. a hash signature checking in an authentication

```
      int memcmp(const void *src1,
                 const void *src2,
                 unsigned int n) {
    · unsigned char *s1 = (unsigned char *)src1;
      unsigned char *s2 = (unsigned char *)src2;
      while (n--) {
        if (*s1 != *s2) {
          return *s1 - *s2; }
        s1++;
        s2++; }
      return 0; }
```

Fig. 5. Memcmp C Code.

process). This is possible by faulting the n value in the while condition (cf. Fig. 5). This condition checks that the number of values to compare n is greater than 0. It allows to enter the loop and to compare values from both arrays. Then, the value of n is decremented. The assembly code in charge of this operation is shown in Fig. 6. The instruction at address 0x374 retrieves the n value from the processor stack and store it in the a5 register. At address 0x380, a comparison of the a5 content with zero is done to decide if the program enters the while loop. If a5 content is different than zero, a comparison of array values is done.

FIA Setup. The code analysis of the unprotected Memcmp function leads to vulnerabilities, one of which is found at the instruction lw a5,4(sp) (cf. Fig. 6). A fault transforming this instruction to li a5,0 (0x00000793) writes in the a5 register the value 0. This is a complex fault that requires 4 bit flips. However, the FIA state-of-the-art proves that it is possible [5]. Based on this attack, the correct value of n is not retrieved from the stack. A comparison of the a5 content with zero is done at address 0x380. In this case, the branch if not equal to zero (bnez) condition is not fulfilled and the branch is not taken because n=0. Therefore, no comparison of values is done. The Memcmp function returns zero reporting that there are no differences between the two arrays even though they

```
  32c:   01c12783         lw      a5,28(sp)
          ........
  374:   00412783         lw      a5,4(sp)
  378:   fff78713         addi    a4,a5,-1
  37c:   00e12223         sw      a4,4(sp)
  380:   fa0796e3         bnez    a5,32c
  384:   00000793         li      a5,0
  388:   00078513         mv      a0,a5
  38c:   02010113         addi    sp,sp,32
  390:   00008067         ret
```

Fig. 6. Memcmp Assembly Code

are different. This attack could not be detected by pure CFI solutions, but rather by CCFI countermeasures checking the integrity of the code.

CCFI Verification. After executing the discontinuity instruction at address 0x380, a packet is sent by the TE. Figure 7 illustrates the faultless packet and the packet content if the FIA is done on the `lw` instruction. Referring to the attack scenario described in the **FIA setup**, corrupting the `lw` instruction generates a different hash signature at the end of the BB. We have simulated this fault attack by modifying the binary instruction at memory level. Figure 8 shows a simulation of the packet emission due to execution of the `bnez` instruction. The TE awaits the execution of two more instructions after the branch in order to have a visibility on the last three executed instructions to be able to generate a packet as discussed in Sect. 4.1. We present in Fig. 9 a simulation of the verification of the concerned packet. The enumerated FSM steps (as described in Fig. 4) lead to the integrity verification of the BB. As the signature of the faulted execution 0xDF6B9431 is different from the signature 0xDD6294B1 expected by the TV (cf. the correct one also in Fig. 1), the TV raises an error flag. Therefore, the FIA is detected. A comparison of our solution with the CCFI state-of-art solutions and the CFI solution of [23] could be found in Table 2. Compared to [23], our solution covers the integrity of the code. ATRIUM [22] has similar CCFI characteristics. However, it locks the processor if the hash of the current instruction block is not completed and a new block arrives (28 cycles are required to hash a block). The generated signature is sent at the end of the code region chosen by the trusted verifier `vrf` for remote CCFI verification. Our hash module requires only one cycle to compute the signature of an instruction and does not interfere with the core's activity. Compared to the CCFI related works, our solution does

▪ PACKET 1 Without FIA	▪ PACKET 1 With FIA
– branches: 1	– branches: **1**
– branch_map: 0	– branch_map: **1**
– absolute_address: 0x32C	– absolute_address: **0x384**
– Signature_sent: 0xDD6294B1	– Signature_sent: **0xDF6B9431**

Fig. 7. FIA impact on the sent packet content.

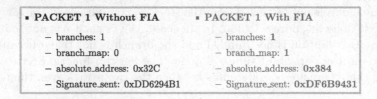

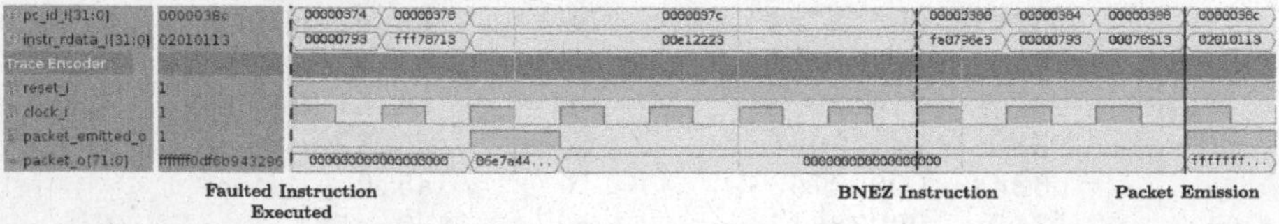

Faulted Instruction   BNEZ Instruction   Packet Emission
Executed

Fig. 8. Simulation of a packet emission due to the execution of the bnez instruction.

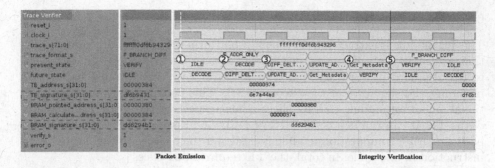

Fig. 9. Simulation of a packet's verification by the TV.

not impact the execution runtime of the user application code. Table 1 shows the overheads of these countermeasures compared to our solution which has no impact on the user code (size or execution time). It is a hardware verification method that neither modifies the RISC-V pipeline nor the compiler.

6   Hardware Metrics

All our simulations target the Artix-7 Field-Programmable Gate Array (FPGA) embedded on a Nexys video board. This FPGA contains 33,650 logic slices. Each slice is composed of four 6-input LUTs, 8 flip-flops, multiplexers and carry units. A description of the hardware requirements of our system in terms of slice is provided in the following parts.

Table 2. Comparison of our solution with related works

Solution	SOFIA [7]	SCFP [21]	SCI-FI [4]	CCFI-Cache [6]	ATRIUM [22]	TE-CFI [23]	This Work
No User Code Modification	✗	✗	✗	✗	✓	✓	✓
No Compiler Modification	✓	✗	✗	✗	✓	✓	✓
No Pipeline Modification	✗	✗	✗	✓	✓	✓	✓
No Performance Overhead	✗	✗	✗	✗	✗	✓	✓
Backward Edge Protection	✓	✓	✓	✓	✓	✓	✓
Forward Edge Protection	✗	✓	✗	(✗)	✗	✗	✗
Code Integrity	✓	✓	✓	✓	✓	✗	✓
Code Confidentiality	✓	✓	✗	✗	✗	✗	✗

6.1   Target Core

Our CCFI solution is implemented on an IBEX core [13]. It is a 32-bit open source RISC-V, low power core with a 2-stage pipeline suitable for IOT applications. Its area cost is equal to **645** slices. As our solution is independent of the chosen RISC-V core, it can be implemented on any core compatible with the TE. For instance, our TV could also be applied to the CV32E40P, a 32-bit 4-stage RISC-V core [14]. Its core implementation requires **1171** slices.

6.2   Trace Encoder

The TE module is extracted from the pulp-platform project [17]. Its implementation needs **239** slices. To verify the CCFI of a program, we made an enhancement to the standard in a way to send a packet after each discontinuity instruction including the signature of the executed BB. This enhancement and the additional signature module cost **62** slices while respecting the retro-compatibility of the TE. It can run in a normal [18] or CFI/CCFI mode. Note that, the 32-bit hash signature computation module is designed to compute the signature of an instruction in one cycle. In total, the TE requires **301** slices.

6.3   Trace Verifier Components

The TV is divided in 3 parts: its memory to store the static metadata—implemented as a Block Random Access Memory (BRAM) on FPGA, its core and its configurable block (FIFO and LIFO modules).

BRAM. Our CCFI solution was tested on several benchmarks from Pulpino project [16], Embench-IOT benchmarks [10] and some classic ones. These benchmarks were compiled with the RV32IM base instruction set and into 3 compilation optimizations level: **O1** for the basic level, **O2** for the advanced level and **O3** for the highest possible optimization level. As an illustration, Fig. 10 shows the ratio between the generated metadata and code size for the 3 optimization levels. The Metadata-Code size ratio ranges from 15% and 55%. The small benchmark codes have the highest ratio (e.g. the Memcpy and Memcmp codes). The BRAM is designed with a single read port model. The writing of the metadata is done upstream of the code execution. We have chosen the index width of the BRAM memory to be 12. This value delimit the depth of the metadata memory to $2^{12} = 4096$ lines. To give an order of magnitude, the "nshichneu" code from Embench-IOT [10] contained the most discontinuity instructions. In total, 1188 lines (discontinuities) were needed for a optimization in O1. With this configuration, the memory implementation requires only **16 BRAM blocks** without additional slices. This represents the maximum hardware utilization for the simulated benchmarks. Each benchmark code was loaded into a **256-block BRAM** memory connected to the IBEX. Our metadata were intentionally stored in an external RAM attached to the standalone TV to not modify the program code and its memory. Therefore, the BRAM metadata overhead is equal to 6.25% for a 12-bit BRAM TV index. This overhead could be considered as a code size overhead if the metadata were stored in the code memory. However, the TV area cost decreases by removing its BRAM.

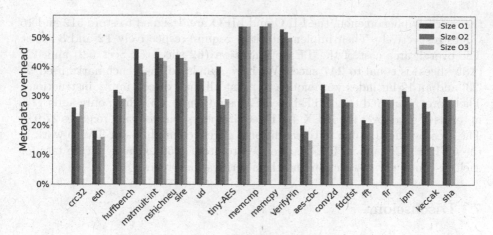

Fig. 10. Ratio between the metadata vs code size.

TV Core. It is composed of the FSM and processes. It requires **170** slices and could run in CFI or CCFI mode. A TE configuration packet initiates, at startup, the verification mode.

TV Configurable Block. It represents the LIFO (shadow stack) and FIFOs for storing the packets and discontinuity instructions. Their sizes are dependent of the running application and could be configured to a specific application. However, in the evaluation phase of our approach, we have chosen sufficiently large sizes to simulate all the targeted benchmarks for an FPGA or even ASIC implementation. Note that the instructions FIFO (cf. Fig. 3) is only used in the CFI mode. As a consequence, a comparison between discontinuity and meta-data instructions is performed for a given address to only check the integrity of the executed discontinuity instruction. In the CCFI mode, each identified BB containing a set of instructions ends with a discontinuity instruction. Therefore, a corruption of the discontinuity affects the computed hash signature. A FIA on the analyzed BB is detected by comparing the computed and metadata signatures. In this mode, the instruction FIFO is useless. As illustration of the configurable block requirements, Fig. 11 shows the FIFO and LIFO depths to store data for the compiled benchmarks with the O_2 optimization on a log scale. The maximum FIFO and LIFO depths are respectively **153** and **9**. Each application requires a different depth depending on the number of discontinuities/packets sent and the size of the BBs. The verification latency becomes important when packets are sent simultaneously and could not be verified by the TV on the fly. We discuss in Sect. 7 the reason behind this accumulation of packets. In order to have a generic solution compatible with more complex benchmarks and to avoid the overflow phenomenon, the FIFO and LIFO are designed to store 512 and 16 values respectively. Their implementations require respectively **12** and **3** slices. The overall area cost of the TE optimization (**62** slices, cf. Sect. 6.2) and TV (**185** slices) is equal to **247** slices. We have simulated the benchmarks used by [23] and an 12-bit index was enough to point all their discontinuity instructions. Therefore, compared to the TE-based CFI solution of [23] which only adds 17% in terms of slices over the IBEX + TE requirements, our solution requires 27.9%. The area overhead is due to the additional slices required by our TV to work in the CFI or CCFI mode. It is also related to store 2*32 extra signature bits for each discontinuity instruction and their verification process.

7 Discussion

Our TV does CCFI verification at runtime after receiving a packet from the TE. It needs 6 to 8 clock cycles to process a packet (cf. Sect. 4.2) concurrently to the program execution. The verification latency becomes significant when discontinuity instructions follow each other with fewer clock cycles than is required to process successive packets by the TV (6 clock cycles). Therefore, an increase in the FIFO depth is mandatory when a packet is issued after a BB execution containing less than 6 non-multi-cycle instructions. These executions send packets simultaneously. To process all of these packets, the FIFO is required to store them. Figure 11 illustrates the packet accumulations which induces a latency to verify all of them. The FIFO is used in order not to stall the processor while a packet is being verified. However, in order to reduce the hardware impact, it is possible to remove the FIFO. As a result, the processor will be stalled when the packet is received to complete its verification. Thus, performance overheads would be considered. The depth of the FIFO can be calculated statically by analyzing the binary code of an application. This can be done by counting the

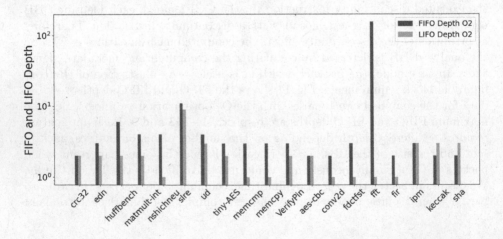

Fig. 11. FIFO and LIFO depths for programs compiled with O_2 optimization.

instructions formed by all BB and comparing the count to the number of FSM states. In the case of a parameter-conditioned loop containing fewer clock cycles than the FSM check cycles, the user can predict the number for that loop by analyzing the code to correctly increment the FIFO depth. Additionally, our verification is based on the static metadata. Indirect calls destinations are not known from the static analysis and then not covered in our solution. However, these calls emit a packet after their execution. To treat these instructions, we can wait for the packet sent after the one related to the indirect call. Having instruction and packet information, a navigation through the metadata could be done in order to find the discontinuity address and resume verification. Another perspective is to avoid these calls by modifying the user code or the compiler. In addition, our experiments covered the CCFI of all the user code. Referring to Sect. 5, an illustration of how the Memcmp code integrity has been protected against FIA. This code represents relatively simple control flows. For a complex firmware, the designer may need to cover just a sensitive section of the code (e.g. authentication function). It could be done by using the TE filter (cf. Chapter 5 of the TE standard [18]). It allows to specify the lower and higher addresses where packets need to be generated. Activating this functionality reduces drastically static data size and TV configurable modules area cost. This is due to the fact that there is less metadata in the TV's memory related just to this function. In our core implementation, the branch prediction feature was disabled. Enabling this option emits a specific packet after a discontinuity instruction with content defined by the TE standard. The TV could be enhanced to operate in this mode for CCFI verification. This is a perspective of our work.

8   Conclusion

In this paper, we propose a CCFI verification system based on the RISC-V Trace Encoder, a debug feature that allows to capture the execution path of a program. An additional feature is added to the TE mechanism in order to work in the CCFI mode. We demonstrate how discontinuity instructions and BB are protected against FIA. The comparison of a computed signature of a BB at runtime with a pre-calculated signature guarantees the integrity property of a program's code. Compared to state-of-the-art solutions, our countermeasure does not generate performance overheads. Only hardware overheads are reported. Its implementation modifies neither the RISC-V compiler nor the user code nor the core's architecture. It is a modular, non-invasive and does not depend of the RISC-V core. In our future work, we aim to verify that the executed BB instructions are also unaltered within the core's pipeline. This is known as verifying the Control Flow and Execution Integrity (CFEI) of the program.

References

1. Abadi, M., Budiu, M., Erlingsson, U., Ligatti, J.: Control-flow integrity principles, implementations, and applications. ACM Trans. Inf. Syst. Secur. (TISSEC) **13**(1), 1–40 (2009)
2. Asanović, K., Patterson, D.A.: Instruction sets should be free: the case for RISC-V. EECS Department, University of California, Berkeley, Tech. Rep. UCB/EECS-2014-146 (2014)
3. Barenghi, A., Breveglieri, L., Koren, I., Naccache, D.: Fault injection attacks on cryptographic devices: theory, practice, and countermeasures. Proc. IEEE **100**(11), 3056–3076 (2012)
4. Chamelot, T., Couroussé, D., Heydemann, K.: Sci-fi: control signal code and control flow integrity against fault injection attacks. In: 2022 Design, Automation & Test in Europe Conference & Exhibition, pp. 556–559. IEEE (2022)
5. Colombier, B., et al.: Multi-spot laser fault injection setup: new possibilities for fault injection attacks. In: Grosso, V. (eds.) Smart Card Research and Advanced Applications. CARDIS 2021. LNCS, vol. 13173, pp. 151–166. Springer, Cham (2021). https://doi.org/10.1007/978-3-030-97348-3_9
6. Danger, J.L., et al.: CCFI-Cache: a transparent and flexible hardware protection for code and control-flow integrity. In: 2018 21st Euromicro Conference on Digital System Design (DSD), pp. 529–536. IEEE (2018)
7. De Clercq, R., Götzfried, J., Übler, D., Maene, P., Verbauwhede, I.: Sofia: software and control flow integrity architecture. Comput. Security **68**, 16–35 (2017)
8. De Clercq, R., Verbauwhede, I.: A survey of hardware-based control flow integrity (CFI). arXiv preprint arXiv:1706.07257 (2017)
9. Elguibaly, F., El-Kharashi, M.W.: Multiple-input signature registers: an improved design. In: 1997 IEEE Pacific Rim Conference on Communications, Computers and Signal Processing, PACRIM. 10 Years Networking the Pacific Rim, 1987–1997, vol. 2, pp. 519–522. IEEE (1997)
10. Embench™: Open benchmarks for embedded platforms (2021). https://github.com/embench/embench-iot
11. Gonzalvez, A., Lashermes, R.: A case against indirect jumps for secure programs. In: Proceedings of the 9th Workshop on Software Security, Protection, and Reverse Engineering, pp. 1–10 (2019)
12. Kiaei, P., Breunesse, C.B., Ahmadi, M., Schaumont, P., Van Woudenberg, J.: Rewrite to reinforce: rewriting the binary to apply countermeasures against fault injection. In: 2021 58th ACM/IEEE Design Automation Conference (DAC), pp. 319–324. IEEE (2021)
13. Lowrisc: Ibex documentation (2021). https://ibex-core.readthedocs.io/en/latest
14. OpenHW Group: Cv32e40p (2022). https://github.com/openhwgroup/cv32e40p
15. Pradhan, D.K., Gupta, S.K., Karpovsky, M.G.: Aliasing probability for multiple input signature analyzer. IEEE Trans. Comput. **39**(4), 586–591 (1990)
16. PULP-platform: PULPino: A small single-core RISC-V SOC (2019). https://github.com/pulp-platform/pulpino
17. PULP-platform: Trace debugger for RISC-V core (2020). https://github.com/pulp-platform/trace_debugger
18. RISC-V International: efficient trace for RISC-V (2020). https://github.com/riscv/riscv-trace-spec
19. Timmers, N., Spruyt, A., Witteman, M.: Controlling pc on arm using fault injection. In: 2016 Workshop on Fault Diagnosis and Tolerance in Cryptography (FDTC), pp. 25–35. IEEE (2016)

20. Wei, J., Pu, C.: Tocttou vulnerabilities in unix-style file systems: an anatomical study. FAST **5**, 12 (2005)
21. Werner, M., Unterluggauer, T., Schaffenrath, D., Mangard, S.: Sponge-based control-flow protection for IoT devices. In: 2018 IEEE European Symposium on Security and Privacy (EuroS&P), pp. 214–226. IEEE (2018)
22. Zeitouni, S., et al.: Atrium: Runtime attestation resilient under memory attacks. In: 2017 IEEE/ACM International Conference on Computer-Aided Design (ICCAD), pp. 384–391. IEEE (2017)
23. Zgheib, A., Potin, O., Rigaud, J.B., Dutertre, J.M.: A CFI verification system based on the RISC-V instruction trace encoder. In: 2022 25th Euromicro Conference on Digital System Design (DSD). IEEE (2022)

Side-Channel Analyses
and Countermeasures

ASCA vs. SASCA

A Closer Look at the AES Key Schedule

Emanuele Strieder[1]($\boxtimes$)(iD), Manuel Ilg[1], Johann Heyszl[1,3],
Florian Unterstein[2](iD), and Silvan Streit[1](iD)

[1] Fraunhofer Institute for Applied and Integrated Security (AISEC),
Lichtenbergstraße 11, 85748 Garching near by Munich, Germany
{emanuele.strieder,manuel.ilg,johann.heyszl,
silvan.streit}@aisec.fraunhofer.de
[2] Infineon Technologies AG, Munich, Germany
florian.unterstein@infineon.com
[3] Google GmbH, Munich, Germany
johannheyszl@google.com

Abstract. We compare two key recovery methods for single trace attacks on the AES key schedule. The 2018 CHES capture-the-flag (CTF) challenge which includes an unprotected key schedule raises the question, which method performs best during key recovery: Soft Analytical Side-Channel Attacks (SASCAs) or Algebraic Side-Channel Attacks (ASCAs). SASCAs as well as ASCAs exploit knowledge about the attacked algorithm by leakage recombination and allow for a computationally efficient key recovery based on e.g. Hamming Weight (HW) leakage. We use Belief Propagation (BP), which is the most popular choice for SASCA and a SAT solver as an ASCA algorithm. In this work we attack real traces of the CTF challenge to demonstrate the limitations of SASCAs while handling the XOR operation. We exemplify that SASCAs may not always be the most favorable solution. The comparison is solidified by evaluating the success rate of SASCAs and ASCAs with simulated HW leakage on varying noise levels. During attacks on the AES key schedule the convergence of BP is not only graph dependent but data dependent. Further, we discuss possible graph clusters and adaptations of the input distributions to mitigate the influence of the XOR operations and increase the success rate of BP. All experiments are compared against equivalent SAT solver approaches. Based on our results we propose a combination of brute-force and BP to level the performance of the SAT solver and BP. Apart from this, we address unsolved questions regarding the benefit of an early break of BP and point out implementation details which lead to a better success rate.

Keywords: SASCA · ASCA · Belief propagation · SAT · AES · Key schedule · Key expansion

J. Heyszl and F. Unterstein—Work was done while the author was at Fraunhofer AISEC.

1   Introduction

Algebraic Side-Channel Attacks (ASCAs) as published by Renauld et al. [25] as well as Soft Analytical Side-Channel Attacks (SASCAs) as published by Veyrat-Charvillon et al. [30] are key recovery methods. ASCA as well as SASCA can be seen as a bridge between cryptanalysis and side-channel analysis (SCA). They utilize the knowledge about an attacked algorithm to recombine noisy leakage samples taken from different intermediate values of one attack trace. Noisy leakage can have many reasons like countermeasures, imprecise leakage models, technology architectures or the algorithm itself.

One example is the AES key schedule, which derives round keys during an AES encryption or decryption. For a given key, the key schedule only computes a fixed set of intermediate values. Therefore, the data complexity during an attack is inherently one and dedicated attacks are difficult as no differential leakage with varying inputs can be exploited. Profiled SCAs can exploit such leakages. Typically, profiled SCAs use leakage models like the HW model to closely match the physical processes causing the leakage. Most of the time, this results in information loss and the extractable information is insufficient to recover the key without additional measures, e.g. brute-force. Hence, it is beneficial to target as many intermediate values as possible during an attack on the AES key schedule, i.e. not only the original key or one single round key. The challenge then remains in combining those multiple results in a meaningful way.

The 2018 CHES CTF challenge contains an AES implementation that includes a reasonably protected main data-path and an unprotected key schedule that ultimately allows successful key recovery. The challenge led to multiple contributions proposing different solving strategies. Damm et al. [8] use Gaussian Template Attacks (TAs) to recover the HWs of the round key bytes. To recover the master key they implement a smart brute-force algorithm introduced by VanLaven et al. [29], which is specially tailored to HW leakage. However, this algorithm can only tolerate a very limited amount of faulty results, i.e. results where HWs are not determined correctly, which is a major drawback. Gohr et al. [10] propose a different approach employing a Residual Neural Network (ResNet) to extract the HWs. They then use a SAT solver to combine the HW leakages of the intermediate values to recover the master key.

Apart from the CTF challenge, Bouder et al. [5] employ for the first time a factor graph of the AES key schedule and BP to recombine leakage of key bytes extracted from the AES data path. The proposed attack exploits differential leakage between the output of the mix-column operation and the sub-byte output. They claim this intermediate leakage can be extracted using a non-profiled SCA. They additionally simulate the performance of BP using HW leakage in a multi-trace setting starting with 100 attack traces. Bouder et al. [5] do not mention any possible alterations of the factor graph or adaptations of the input data to enhance the convergence of BP. Their results lack information about single-trace attacks and the noise levels may not be representative for real-world attacks. Further, they do not discuss any data dependency and use the average rank as success metric which merely yields any interpretable information in this context.

These examples raise the question, which key recovery method performs best for single-trace attacks on the AES key schedule: SASCAs versus ASCAs. Both methods are contrasted by Grosso et al. [12] in a general way. Grosso et al. specifically discusses the problem of XOR operations which are a major problem for all mentioned key recovery methods. The XOR operation has two inputs and if one is close to uniform information from the second input cannot propagate (cf. [11]). Nevertheless, Grosso et al. concluded that SASCA is the favorable solution. Our contribution reevaluates this question in the specific setting of the AES key schedule which is build mainly from XOR operations. This work demonstrates, that SASCA is not always the most favorable choice.

Green et al. [11] investigates different graphs for the AES data path and circumvents the key schedule because of the mass of XOR operations. They note, that the convergence of BP is mainly graph and less data dependent. We show, that this is not always the case. Guo et al. [13] investigate SASCA in-depth and show the close connection of SASCA with coding theory.

There are several recent applications of BP: Kannwischer et al. as well as You et al. [18, 31] successfully attack software implementations of Keccak. Primas et al. and Pessl et al. [20, 23] attack a software implementation of the Number Theoretic Transform (NTT) using BP with a single trace. Pessl et al. [20] combine factor nodes avoiding short loops to improve the performance of their attack. Hamburg et al. [14] use BP in combination with a chosen-ciphertext attack (CCA) on the NTT used in multiple PQ algorithms. Hermelink et al. [17] introduce a shuffle node which increases the performance of BP against shuffled input. Hermelink et al. [16] introduce a fault attack on the Fujisaka-Okamoto transform which is possible by solving a system of inequalities using BP.

For a more thorough discussion about ASCA we refer to Carlet et al. [6] and Renauld et al. [26]. Applications of ASCA can be found in Bettale et al. [4] and Adomnicai et al. [2].

Contribution. We investigate the performance of SASCA and ASCA in the specific setting of the AES key schedule. The AES key schedule is of special interest as it poses a major challenge due to many XOR operations (cf. [11, 12]). Each XOR operation has two input distributions and hinders the information flow. The contribution has two major parts: We first analyze the 2018 CHES CTF challenge which includes an unprotected AES-128 key schedule. We perform TAs with and without linear discriminant analysis (LDA) on the provided traces and compare these results with the state-of-the-art which uses a Machine Learning (ML)-based approach. Afterwards, we apply BP and a SAT solver to reduce HW leakage to value leakage during the key recovery phase. This case study exemplifies, that SASCA may not be the most favorable solution if only key byte leakage is present.

Therefore, we secondly evaluate the success rates of SASCA and ASCA while exploiting simulated HW leakage of an AES key schedule in single trace attacks.

We demonstrate that BP's convergence is more data dependent than graph dependent in this setting. Further, we discuss different graph clustering possibilities to mitigate the influence of the data dependency and increase the success rate of BP. Dropouts as well as constraining the input distribution to the top-2 results are investigated. All experiménts are contrasted with comparable SAT solver approaches. The contribution addresses unsolved questions regarding the benefit of an early break, sub-graph convergence and implementation details. Finally, we propose a new solving strategy that extends BP using a brute-force step, leveling the success rates of SAT solving and BP.

2   Preliminaries

2.1   AES Key Schedule

AES is a symmetric block cipher with a number of security levels. The 2018 CHES CTF challenge uses a 128-bit version, which we focus on in this contribution. However, all findings are transferable because the key schedules of the different variants use mainly the same operations but a different number of rounds. AES-128 uses a key schedule with 10 rounds. In each round, a 16-byte round-key is generated based on the master key. Therefore, in total, there are 176 key bytes for a full key schedule. Each round consists of one rotation operation, XOR and sub-byte operations and the addition of fixed round constants defined in the standard [28]. A graph-based representation of one AES key schedule round is given in Fig. 1.

2.2   2018 CHES CTF Challenge

One part of the 2018 CHES CTF contest is an attack on an AES-128 implementation using ML. The challenge includes three training datasets, each containing 10k power traces with random plaintext and random key from three different devices. A fourth dataset with random plaintext and a fixed key is intended for validation during the profiling phase. The challenge is to extract a correct key candidate from two additional attack datasets, 5 and 6, with 1000 traces each. Dataset 5 was captured from a device also used during the creation of one training dataset and dataset 6 was captured from an unseen device. We concentrate on dataset 6 because it was identified as the harder challenge and can be considered the worst-case scenario for an attacker (cf. [8–10]).

2.3   Profiled Side-Channel Attacks

Profiled SCAs derive a profile that models the data dependency of traces as closely as possible. These profiles allow for attacks with a very low number of side-channel traces. Profiled SCAs are considered the most powerful attacks because noise as well as data are modeled at the same time. In extreme cases, only a single trace is sufficient to extract enough information to compromise a device. Two different profiling methods have been used while attacking the 2018 CHES CTF contest:

Gaussian Template Attacks. One of the most frequently used profiled SCA method are Gaussian TAs. As all profiling attacks TAs consist of at least two stages: profiling and attack. The profiling step, in most cases, requires either the full control of an adversary over the target device or a copy of the target device. During profiling, a large number of side-channel traces are captured while the algorithm is executed with random input. The traces are grouped using a leakage model of the target intermediate value - e.g. the HW of a key byte of the AES key schedule or the HW of the output of a sub-byte operation. For each group g, a mean vector $\boldsymbol{\mu}_g$ and a covariance matrix $\boldsymbol{\Sigma}_g$ are derived. The mean vector and the covariance matrix parametrize the Gaussian leakage distribution for the respective group, the chosen intermediate value and leakage model. During the attack phase the likelihood is computed with which n traces $\boldsymbol{t}_i$ are fitting each of the groups:

$$s_g = \prod_{i=1}^{n} \mathcal{N}(\boldsymbol{t}_i, \boldsymbol{\mu}_g, \boldsymbol{\Sigma}_g),$$

where s_g is called score value. In this work, the groups are all possible HWs of an 8-bit value: $g \in \{0, 1, \ldots, 8\}$ and the number of traces is $n = 1$ since the data complexity of the AES key schedule is inherently one (cf. Sect. 2.1). For a more in-depth description of TAs, we refer to Chari et al. [7] or Rechberger et al. [24].

Machine Learning Attacks. In recent years many Deep Neural Network (DNN)-based approaches have been investigated for leakage extraction (cf. [10,21]). The variety of ML-based approaches is manifold, but CNN-based approaches are dominating because of their benefits with respect to shift invariance. Gohr et al. [10] were one of the first to use a ResNet to guess all key bytes of the AES key schedule. ResNets have the advantage of mitigating the vanishing gradient problem [15]. For a detailed explanation of Gohr et al.'s approach, we refer to the original publication [10]. Instead of treating the leakage as a classification task, Gohr et al. are handling it as a regression problem. Therefore, the network returns a real-valued number $x_k \in [0, 8]$ rather than probabilities for each HW of each key byte. In order to use the outputs in SASCA methods like BP we transform the outputs as follows: Let $\boldsymbol{s}$ be a vector that holds a score value for each possible HW and let x_k be the output of the ResNet for a key byte k. We set all values of the vector to 0 except for $\boldsymbol{s}_{\lfloor x \rfloor}$ and $\boldsymbol{s}_{\lceil x \rceil}$, because the network does not output any information except for the adjacent HWs. The probabilities for the adjacent HWs $\boldsymbol{s}_{\lfloor x \rfloor}$ and $\boldsymbol{s}_{\lceil x \rceil}$ evaluate to:

$$\boldsymbol{s}_{\lfloor x \rfloor} = \begin{cases} x \bmod 1 & \text{if } (x \bmod 1) \geq 0.5 \\ 1 - (x \bmod 1) & \text{if } (x \bmod 1) < 0.5 \end{cases}$$

and

$$\boldsymbol{s}_{\lceil x \rceil} = \begin{cases} x \bmod 1 & \text{if } (x \bmod 1) < 0.5 \\ 1 - (x \bmod 1) & \text{if } (x \bmod 1) \geq 0.5. \end{cases}$$

Dimensionality Reduction. Each trace in the CTF datasets has 650k samples. It is impractical to use all sample points because of the limited number of traces in the training sets and the *curse of dimensionality*, which has a negative effect on the learnability of a dataset during the training of a Neural Network (NN) and on the size of the covariance matrix for TAs. Therefore, Gohr et al. use only every 100th sample point [10]. In case of TAs, we employ the correlation-based approach of Durvaux et al. [9] with a threshold of $\rho = 0.04$. We additionally performed TAs with the prior application of LDA. We kept all eigenvalues, which explained 99% of the data.

2.4 ASCA and SAT

ASCA is a combination of SCA and cryptanalysis. The coarse idea of ASCA is the creation of a system of equations that models the target algorithm while constraining the solution space with side-channel information (cf. Bard et al. [3]). SAT solvers are one type of possible solver. However, other solver strategies could be employed in ASCA, too. Following the approach of Gohr et al. [10] we use CryptoMiniSat for the SAT solving step. It performs superiorly over other SAT solvers in the context of cryptographic algorithms. It was developed by Soos et al. [27] and uses e.g. Gaussian elimination, conflict-driven solving, backtracking-based and depth-first search algorithms to mitigate the problems of classical SAT solvers with huge numbers of XOR equations.

Transformation and Dropout. The SAT solver uses clauses in conjunctive normal norm (CNF) to model and constrain the AES key schedule. Each variable in a clause is called literate (e.g. for an 8-bit value there are 8 literates). The number of clauses and literates is a limiting factor in SAT solving, because it increases the computational costs (cf. [27]). A CNF is a conjunction of disjunctions and each algorithm can be transformed as such. For example, a XOR operation in CNF is given by:

$$(\neg x_0 \vee x_1 \vee x_2) \wedge (x_0 \vee \neg x_1 \vee x_2) \wedge$$
$$(x_0 \vee x_1 \vee \neg x_2) \wedge (\neg x_0 \vee \neg x_1 \vee \neg x_2).$$

Constraining clauses are created by adding all CNFs of an intermediate value that do not result in the expected HW. If, for example, HWs 0 and 8 are to be excluded and the byte value constraints literates are x_{0-7}, the constraining clauses are as follows:

$$(x_0 \vee x_1 \vee x_2 \vee x_3 \vee x_4 \vee x_5 \vee x_6 \vee x_7) \wedge$$
$$(\neg x_0 \vee \neg x_1 \vee \neg x_2 \vee \neg x_3 \vee \neg x_4 \vee \neg x_5 \vee \neg x_6 \vee \neg x_7).$$

Gohr et al.'s SAT solver approach drops a number of constraint clauses randomly to mitigate the influence of errors in the input distribution. We decided on 100 tries for each SAT experiment and a dropout rate of 10%. The influence of the dropout rate will be discussed in Sect. 3.3. Since the number of clauses is a limiting factor in SAT solving, only the top-x results of the marginal probability distributions are used. The transformation of HW into constraining clauses is performed as: Let s be a vector which holds a score or probability value for each possible HW of an intermediate value. The top-x HW values with the highest score or probability are chosen from s.

2.5 SASCA and Belief Propagation

BP is a message-passing algorithm that infers information about marginal probability distributions using a bipartite factor graph. The marginals are computed efficiently by exchanging messages. Let $P(\mathbf{x})$ be a function of $\mathbf{x}$, where $\mathbf{x}$ is a set of N random variables $\mathbf{x} \equiv \{x_n\}_{n=1}^{N}$. We define $P(\mathbf{x})$ as a product of M functions $f_m(\mathbf{x}_m)$ where each function uses a subset $\mathbf{x}_m$ of $\mathbf{x}$. In the case of SASCA, the initial prior distributions for each $\mathbf{x}_m$ are the score values extracted from attack traces. The goal of BP is to calculate the marginals

$$Z_n(x_n) = \sum_{\{x_{n'}\},n' \neq n} P(\mathbf{x})$$

or the normalized version. Variables are modeled as variable nodes and their pair-wise relations as factor nodes. These nodes are structured in a factor graph reflecting the attacked algorithm. BP performs the inference of the marginals efficiently by iteratively exchanging messages between the nodes. BP defines two types of messages. The variable-to-factor message is defined as:

$$u_{n \to m}(x_n) = \prod_{m' \in \mathcal{M}(n) \backslash \{m\}} v_{m' \to n}(x_n),$$

and the factor-to-variable messages as:

$$v_{m \to n}(x_n) = \sum_{x_m \backslash n} \left(f_m(\mathbf{x}_m) \prod_{n' \in \mathcal{N}(m) \backslash m} u_{n' \to m}(x_{n'}) \right).$$

The algorithm exchanges messages until the algorithm is converged or another break condition is reached. The belief or marginal distributions Z_n at each variable node can be calculated by

$$Z_n(x_n) = \prod_{m \in \mathcal{M}(n)} v_{m \to n}(x_n).$$

All factor graphs in this contribution are based on the AES Furious implementation [1] which was also used in the 2018 CHES CTF contest. Each variable node holds a prior distribution, which contains 256 probabilities for each possible value of an 8-bit value. Hence, each factor node operates with input vectors of the same dimensions. In the following, the basic graph is described and possible graph reductions are illustrated.

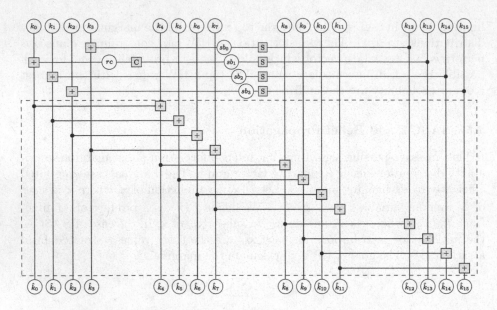

Fig. 1. Basic factor graph of one round of the AES key schedule.

Basic Graph. The basic factor graph of one round of the AES key schedule is shown in Fig. 1. Circles represent variable nodes and rectangles factor nodes. There are three basic factor types: XOR (⊞), Sub-Byte (⑤) and the addition of the round-dependent RCon value (©). Each variable node represents a marginal distribution of an intermediate value, derived by e.g. a profiled SCA. The AES-128 key schedule expands the master key to round keys using 10 rounds.

Reduced Graphs. Figure 1 illustrates the optimal leakage situation: For each key byte as well as for each intermediate value, a marginal distribution could be extracted from the side-channel traces. In general, this is rarely the case. Depending on the extracted marginals, variable nodes can be removed and factor nodes can be combined. Figure 2 shows the first reduction. The distribution of the intermediate value after the RCon operation is removed and the factor node is concatenated with the XOR operation. This graph implies that an estimate e.g. HW leakage of the output of the sub-byte operations is known. Figure 3 presents the second reduction. By concatenation of the sub-byte with the RCon and the XOR operation included in the mix column path the variable node of the sub-byte output is excluded. This graph would be used if only key byte leakage could be extracted. The choice of which factor graph is used, depends on the ability to extract an estimate of the intermediate values. Therefore, these representations show only two basic alterations. Many other alterations could be devised.

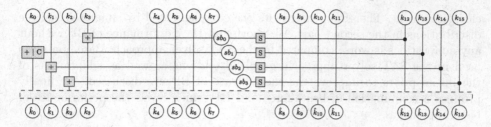

Fig. 2. Reduced factor graph of one round of the AES key schedule. The reduction is achieved by concatenation the SubBytes and the RCon operation.

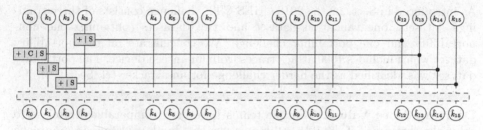

Fig. 3. Reduced factor graph of one round of the AES key schedule. The reduction is achieved by concatenation of the SubBytes, RCon and XOR operations.

2.6 Leakage Model and Simulation

We used simulations to investigate the key recovery algorithms in the specific use case of a single trace attack against the AES key schedule for different noise levels and multiple keys. If not stated differently, all simulations assume an 8-bit HW leakage. Most simulations are testing different normally distributed noise levels which we control by the standard deviation σ. Following [14,17] and [20] we derive a noisy HW by:

$$h' \xleftarrow{\$} HW(\boldsymbol{v}) + \mathcal{N}(0, \sigma), \tag{1}$$

where the function $HW(\cdot)$ sums the number of bits in $\boldsymbol{v}$'s binary representation which are non-zero. We then create a Gaussian distribution around h', $\mathcal{N}(h', \sigma)$ and derive noisy samples for each possible HW emulating a template attack. The resulting probability vector was additionally multiplied by the probability of observing the respective HW to mitigate the bias of a HW distribution.

3 Results

The result section is divided into two parts: We first analyze the results of two profiled attack paths on the 2018 CHES CTF challenge. The score values are utilized to create a preliminary understanding of how well BP and the SAT solver perform in this setting. The results are indecisive and do not allow a clear statement. Therefore, the results are complemented by simulated leakage distributions in the second part. We show that the performance of BP without any adaptations is worse compared to the SAT solver approach. Based on ideas used in the SAT solver approach, graph alterations as well as adaptations of the initial priors to improve the success rate of BP are discussed. We finally propose a combination of brute-force and BP which levels the performance of both approaches.

3.1   Case Study: 2018 CHES CTF

As introduced in Sect. 2.2 the 2018 CHES CTF challenge consists of three trainings datasets, one validation dataset and two datasets containing one non-portability and one portability challenge. We concentrate on the portability dataset which includes 1000 attack traces from an unseen device. The portability dataset was identified as the harder challenge for an attacker (cf. Sect. 2.2).

Deriving Score Values. Multiple teams have used comparable strategies to solve the challenge (cf. [8–10]). All teams use the divide-and-conquer approach by extracting HW leakages for every key byte using profiled SCA attacks. The resulting score values are used in the key recovery phase to find the value of the correct master key. Gohr et al. [10] use a ResNet and Damm et al. [8] use TAs in combination with LDA for dimensional reduction. We re-generated the HWs of the 176 key bytes using the published and already trained ResNet of Gohr et al. [10] for all 1000 attack traces. Additionally, we performed our own TAs with and without LDA on the 1000 traces. All attacks are using first order leakage.

Table 1. Cumulative distributions of the number of traces which had none or less-or-equal than 1, 2, 3 or 4 false top-2 HW guesses after each respective attack path. The absolute number of traces contained in attack set 6 is 1000 and the total number of key bytes which have been guessed 176. Only single-trace attacks are considered.

Number of false top-2 guesses					
	0	≤1	≤2	≤3	≤4
ResNet [10]	7.4%	24.3%	43.0%	61.9%	76.0%
Template [8]	0.0%	0.1%	0.6%	2.1%	4.7%
Template (this work)	0.0%	0.3%	0.6%	1.8%	3.3%

Following the evaluation of Damm et al. as well as Gohr et al., Table 1 shows the cumulative distribution of the number of traces that had none or less-or-equal than 1, 2, 3 or 4 false top-2 HW guesses after each respective attack path. A top-2 error is the event that the correct HW guess has neither the highest nor the second-highest likelihood. Table 1 indicates that our TAs reach comparable results as Damm et al. [8]. Slight differences could be a result from numerical variations. Based on TAs not a single set of score values could be created that has no top-2 error. The ResNet approach reaches superior results, yielding 74 out of 1000 score sets with no top-2 error. We further analyzed this behavior by plotting the standard deviation from the correct value for all 176 key bytes. Figure 4 shows the standard deviation for the three profiling methods: ResNet, LDA combined with TA and TA without LDA. The results indicate that the ResNet is out-performing TAs and LDA-TA with an average standard deviation of $\bar{\sigma}_{\text{ResNet}} = 0.58$ compared to $\bar{\sigma}_{\text{TA}} = 0.83$ and $\bar{\sigma}_{\text{LDA-TA}} = 0.82$. Yet, there is no explanation for this discrepancy and we consider this as future research.

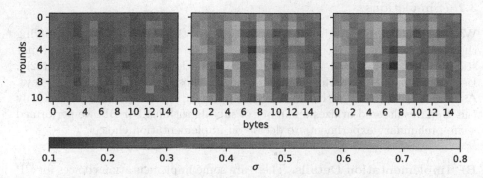

Fig. 4. Standard deviation of all 176 key bytes based on 1000 attacked traces using three profiling methods. Left: ResNet by Gohr et al., middle: LDA combined with TA, right: and only TA.

Key Recovery. We performed key recovery attacks on the extracted score sets using a SAT solver and BP with the factor graph presented in Fig. 3. Table 2 shows the success rates of both methods using the HW results of Gohr's ResNet ($\bar{\sigma}_{\text{ResNet}} = 0.58$) and our TAs ($\bar{\sigma}_{\text{TA}} = 0.83$). The results of the TAs with LDA did not yield better results than the TAs alone. Table 2 indicates that the SAT solver leads more often to the correct key than BP while using the HW results of the ResNet. When using the HW results of the TA, BP's performance is slightly better than the performance of the SAT solver. This is interesting and one explanation could be the respective concrete distributions of bad HW guesses and good HW guesses (cf. Fig. 4). Although the success rates are very low, each combination has a non-zero probability of successfully recovering the correct key candidate when using all 1000 independent traces. All in all, the results on the real traces yield no decisive answer to the question of which method performs better. We attacked only two unevenly distributed noise levels and only one fixed master key. Therefore, we continued with simulations.

Table 2. Success rate of recovering the correct key based on HW leakage using 1000 attack traces. The HWs have been generated by Gohr's ResNet [10] and own TAs. The SAT solver leads more often to the correct key than BP using the HW results of the ResNet. When using the HW results of the TA, BP's performance is slightly better.

	SAT	BP
ResNet ($\bar{\sigma}_{ResNet} = 0.58$) [10]	0.270	0.002
Template ($\bar{\sigma}_{TA} = 0.83$)	0.001	0.016

3.2   Simulations

We used simulations to substantiate the results of the case study by diversifying the master keys and investigating multiple noise levels instead of only two. If not stated otherwise, we used the HW leakage simulations as presented in Sect. 2.6. Each experiment was performed on randomly chosen but fixed AES-128 keys. As discussed in Sect. 2.4 the SAT solver approach uses dropouts, includes only the top-2 results and utilizes a number of sub-algorithms. For BP, we performed some preliminary experiments to decide on implementation choices.

BP Implementation Details. There are some implementation choices for BP that cannot be answered generally. This includes the number of iterations and the choice of a number space in which all mathematical operations are performed. The AES key schedule has a cyclic graph. BP is not guaranteed to converge for cyclic graphs (cf. [19]). Therefore, and to reduce the run time of BP an iteration limit has to be found. We performed preliminary experiments using samples of random AES keys with perfect HW leakage and a graph that relies only on key byte leakage. Perfect HW leakage is defined by a probability of 1 divided by the number of occurrences of the HW for the values with the correct HW at each variable node. To determine the optimal number of iterations, we run each experiment 1000 times. More than 95% of keys that converged did so within 100 iterations. In rare cases, BP took 800 iterations until it converged, which could of course be even higher. If this behavior occurs, BP oscillates until it converges within 20 to 50 iterations without any noticeable linear decline beforehand. There was no experiment in which BP converged to a wrong key. Hence, we used 100 iterations as an upper bound for all further experiments. We evaluated all BP experiments using the histogram-based key rank estimation of Poussier et al. [22]. This algorithm estimates a rank for the master key based on the rank of the 16 key bytes, which is faster than key enumeration. The key rank estimate is calculated after each iteration and is used to introduce an early break condition, allowing for faster simulation cycles. If the differences between the estimated key ranks is smaller than $\epsilon = 0.01$ for 10 successive iterations, BP is stopped early. Key rank estimation is only applicable if the target key is known and hence is not usable for an actual attacker. Additional experiments showed a more stable convergence if all calculations were performed in log space. Therefore all mathematical operations are performed in this spaces which is not always the best choice with regard to computational performance. All experiments were implemented in Python 3.

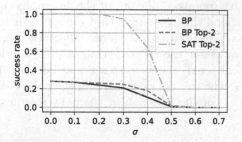

Fig. 5. Comparison of the success rates of inferring the correct AES-128 key bytes using the SAT solver approach with top-2 results or BP while inserting the full probability distributions or also with the limitation to the top-2 results. Each success rate is calculated by using 100 randomly chosen keys and noise sampled as described in Sect. 2.6.

Baseline Simulation Results. Figure 5 depicts a comparison of the success rates of a SAT solver experiment set and two BP experiment sets. Each data point is based on 100 randomly chosen master keys. The SAT solver approach uses only the top-2 HW results of each score vector while ignoring the likelihood. Each of the top-2 HWs will be factored in equally by constrain clauses. There are two reasons why the SAT solver is only using top-2 results: First, the computational complexity increases with a larger number of constrain clauses. Second, a system of equations that is constrained by more equally likely constrain clauses could result in more conflicts and the system of equations could finally be unsolvable. BP however, allows for a more inbound representation because each value has a probability according to its HW likelihood in the respective score vector. This fits with the output of a TA. Hence, BP could be perceived as the best solution without information loss. Figure 5 shows however, that this is not the case. In this setting, the SAT solver outperforms BP, achieving ≈100% success rate in the noise-free case and better performance for higher noise levels. We compare this with two BP experiment sets. One uses the full probability distribution as prior information and the second uses only the top-2 results. In the noise-free case, BP has a success rate of ≈30% of converging to the correct master key. BP achieves a slightly better performance from $\sigma \geq 0.2$ onwards when using the top-2 HWs. However, the influence is minor compared to the SAT solver results. In the following, different adaptations of the BP approach are presented to mitigate the discrepancy between the SAT solver and BP.

Round Sub-graphs. The round function of the AES key schedule is invertible, i.e., every round key can be transferred back into the master key. Therefore, it is enough to infer one of the 10 round keys to recalculated the master key.

We ran preliminary BP experiments on successful keys and discovered that a minimum of 4 AES key schedule rounds are required to successfully converge to a correct value. If the HW prior distributions of all 176 key bytes can be extracted using a SCA, it is possible to create 36 sub-graphs with a minimum distance of 4 successive rounds. If one out of the 36 graphs converges, a solution is found. The idea behind this method is that any prior distribution that could be wrong or noisy is taken out, so it cannot affect the convergence. Figure 6 shows on the left results for the BP experiments and on the right results for the SAT solver. As expected, the success rates of both methods are increased by inferring sub keys. The success rate of BP in the noise-free case increased by ≈50% reaching ≈45%. For the SAT solver, the noise tolerance increased by 0.1.

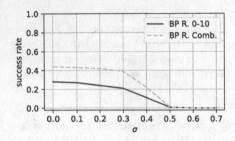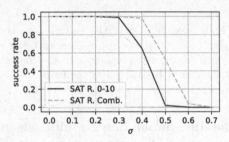

Fig. 6. Comparison of the success rates of inferring the correct AES-128 key bytes using a graph which uses all 176 key bytes at once (Round 0–10) and the success rate when using 36 possible sub-graphs that only use a subset of the 176 once at a time (Round Combination). Each success rate is calculated by using 100 random chosen keys. Left: BP results, right: SAT solver results.

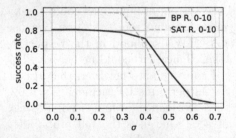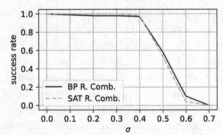

Fig. 7. Comparison between the success rates of the SAT solver approach and BP while using additional leakage of the output of the sub-byte operation. Each data point includes 100 different AES keys. Left: All HWs are used at once (Rounds 0–10). Right: All round combinations are evaluated separately (cf. Sect. 3.2).

Adding Sub-byte Leakage. We have shown that a graph-dependent adaptation of the factor graph increased the performance of BP by ≈50%. Nevertheless, the performance of the SAT solver is still superior. Therefore, the next step was an adaptation of the input data. The SAT solver uses a system of equations for modeling the AES key schedule, including the sub-byte operations. The used factor graph shown in Fig. 3, which was used during the preceding experiments, includes the sub-byte operation only in combination with the RCon and the XOR operations. We changed the graph according to Fig. 2, which implies leakage of the output of the sub-byte operations. To have a fair comparison, we added constraining clauses for the sub-byte output values to the SAT solver. Figure 7 shows results that compare the success rates of the SAT solver approach and BP while exploiting the additional leakage of the output of the sub-byte operations. On the left side of Fig. 7, experiments that only included rounds 0–10 are shown. The SAT solver approach still extracts the correct AES key with a probability $\approx100\%$ up to a sigma level of 0.3. From 0.3 on, the success rate declines to 2% at $\sigma = 0.5$. BP starts with an overall success rate of 81% and reaches its minimum success rate of 5% at $\sigma = 0.6$. On the right side of Fig. 7 experiments are depicted that employ round combinations as discussed in Sect. 3.2 in combination with the addition of sub-byte output leakage. In this setting, the simulated results of BP are performing slightly better than the results of the SAT solver.

Table 3. Success rate of recovering the correct key based on HW leakage of 1000 single trace attacks utilizing TAs.

	SAT	BP
Key byte	0.001	0.016
Key byte + Sub-byte	0.000	0.193

Sub-byte Leakage - 2018 CHES CTF. Encouraged by these results, we performed an additional point-of-interest search on the traces of the CTF challenge and could detect leakage of the outputs of the sub-byte operations. Indeed, we could extract the leakage by using additional TAs for all of the 40 sub-byte outputs. Table 3 shows the results of recovering the correct key based on the HW leakage of 1000 single trace attacks utilizing TAs with solely key byte leakage and key byte leakage plus sub-byte output leakage. Although the SAT solver could derive one master key from 1000 score sets with only key byte leakage, it could not derive any when sub-byte output leakage was added. On the other side, the performance of BP is heavily improved by adding the sub-byte output leakage, with 193 key recoveries out of 1000 score sets. This indicates that, given the sub-byte output leakage is present, BP is more noise-tolerant. The reason for this behavior could be that if the HW of the input and the HW of the output of a sub-byte operation are known, on average 70% of the 256 possible values can be ruled out. Compared to that, if the correct HWs of the two inputs and the output of a XOR operation are known, only 53% of the 256 possible values of the output can be ruled out.

Combining BP and Brute-Force. It was shown that sub-byte output leakage improves the performance of BP for attacks on the AES key schedule. However, this implies that this leakage has to be present and exploitable by a SCA. If this leakage is not present, we propose to brute-force the HWs of the sub-byte output based on the adjacent key byte leakages. We have discussed that the information contained in the sub-graphs of the AES key schedule is enough to converge to the correct solution. The minimum number of key schedule rounds that still show convergence is 4. A 4-round sub-graph contains 12 sub byte outputs (cf. Fig. 2). Each of these sub-byte nodes has 9 possible HW solutions. This would result in 9^{12} possible combinations. However, the 9 HWs can be constrained by using the priors of adjacent variable nodes. On the left side of Fig. 8 the message flow to estimate the HWs at the artificial sub-byte node (dashed) is shown. The initial priors of the adjacent key bytes are transmitted through the factor nodes. The resulting probability vector at the sub-byte node contains probabilities for each of the 256 possible values. These values have to be transformed back to HW leakage. The values are ranked based on their probability and unlikely values are dropped. The remaining values are translated to HW and the likelihood for each HW is calculated based on the number of occurrences. The result is a HW distribution that ranks each HW for the artificially introduced sub-byte operation and excludes unlikely HWs based on adjacent variable nodes. This is done for each of the 12 artificial sub-byte variable nodes. A correct set of sub-byte output HWs will lead to a better convergence (cf. Sect. 3.2). We estimated the remaining brute-force complexity shown in Fig. 8 using the rank estimation algorithm of Poussier et al. [22]. The remaining key rank lies between 19 and 25 keys for all tested noise levels, which can be brute-forced.

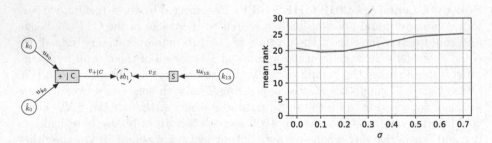

Fig. 8. Left: Message flow to estimate artificially estimated sub-byte leakage. Right: Remaining mean rank for 12 artificially added sub-byte output nodes based on 100 keys.

3.3   Dropouts and Early Break

The Influence of Dropouts. The SAT solver approach uses dropouts to mitigate the influence of erroneous top-2 guesses. Each experiment consists of 100 tries while randomly dropping constraining clauses. The left side of Fig. 9 shows the influence of this approach. It compares the success rates for the SAT solver

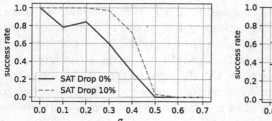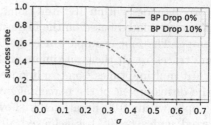

Fig. 9. Comparison approaches with a dropout rate of 0% and 10%. The experiments have been performed without key bytes leakage.

approach with a dropout rate of 0% and 10% of the HW side-channel information. The results indicate that the success rate of the SAT solver is generally better, with a dropout rate of 10%. We transferred this approach to BP by assigning uniformly distributed priors to 10% randomly chosen variable nodes and performing 100 tries. Figure 9 shows a comparison of the success rates using solely key byte leakage and a dropout rate of 0% and 10%. Also for BP, this improves the success rate to 60%.

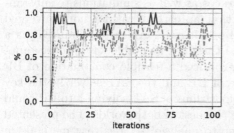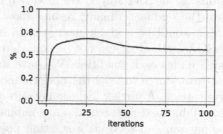

Fig. 10. Left: Four example traces showing the development of the percentage of correctly inferred variable nodes within 100 iterations for non-converging BP runs. The percentage is calculated based on the maximum number of correctly inferred nodes for each attempt. Right: Mean trace of the percentage of correct inferred variable nodes within 100 iterations for 30000 non-converging BP runs.

Number of Correct Nodes. BP is not guaranteed to converge for cyclic graphs. An open research question is whether it is possible to stop a non-converging BP run and use the probabilities (cf. Kannwischer et al. [18]). Finding such a fixed iteration implies the existence of a sweet spot where the number of correctly inferred nodes reaches a maximum. We investigated this by tracking the number of correctly inferred variable nodes in all BP runs. *Correctly inferred* means that the correct value has the highest probability at the respective variable node. On the left of Fig. 10, four examples of the development of the number of correct nodes within 100 iterations are depicted. The percentage of correct nodes is calculated based on the highest number of correct nodes reached in this attempt. The four example traces indicate that there might be no sweet spot. Some traces reach their maximum in the first 10 iterations, some later, some reach it multiple times, some only once. On the right of Fig. 10, the mean trace of the development of the percentage of correct nodes for 30000 non-converged attempts within 100 iterations is shown. The highest percentage of correctly inferred nodes ($\approx$70%) is achieved after 25 iterations on average. This could be considered a sweet spot for this implementation. For now we cannot answer the question how to use these non-converged probability distributions and will consider this as future work.

4   Conclusion

We have analyzed SASCA as well as ASCA in the specific setting of the AES key schedule. The AES key schedule consists mainly of XOR operations, which hinder the flow of information. It was shown that, given only key byte leakage, SAT solving is the better choice. BP, however, outperforms the SAT solver if the output of the sub-byte operation leaks HWs. We discussed multiple possible graph-related as well as prior-related adaptations for BP to reach similar results as the SAT solver. We used real traces as well as simulations to substantiate the findings. Finally, results show that an early break for non-converged graphs could be a viable next step in improving BP. All in all, plain BP as a SASCA method should not be considered the most favorable key recovery approach under each condition. We have introduced a feasible combination of BP and brute-force to level the performance of BP and the SAT solver in the key byte setting. A further inclusion of sub-algorithms of SAT-solving into BP could be a viable next research step to combine the best of both worlds. The presented comparison can serve as a starting point to analyze key recovery methods in the broader context of other block ciphers, including substitution-permutation networks, Feistel and LS-based ciphers. The success of these methods depends on a variety of parameters, such as the leakage distribution, graph clustering possibilities, implementation details like the construction of confusion layers or register width and many others. We therefore consider the question of predicting which method works best for other ciphers an open research question.

Acknowledgements. This work was supported by the German Ministry of Education, Research and Technology in the context of the project Aquorypt (reference numbers 16KIS1018).

References

1. AES Furious. http://point-at-infinity.org/avraes/
2. Adomnicai, A., Masson, L., Fournier, J.J.A.: Practical algebraic side-channel attacks against ACORN. In: Lee, K. (ed.) ICISC 2018. LNCS, vol. 11396, pp. 325–340. Springer, Cham (2019). https://doi.org/10.1007/978-3-030-12146-4_20

3. Bard, G.V., Courtois, N.T., Jefferson, C.: Efficient methods for conversion and solution of sparse systems of low-degree multivariate polynomials over GF(2) via sat-solvers. IACR Cryptology ePrint Archive, p. 24 (2007). http://eprint.iacr.org/2007/024

4. Bettale, L., Dottax, E., Ramphort, M.: Algebraic side-channel attacks on masked implementations of AES. In: Samarati, P., Obaidat, M.S. (eds.) Proceedings of the 15th International Joint Conference on e-Business and Telecommunications, ICETE 2018 - Volume 2: SECRYPT, Porto, Portugal, 26-28 July 2018, pp. 424–435. SciTePress (2018). https://doi.org/10.5220/0006869504240435

5. Le Bouder, H., Lashermes, R., Linge, Y., Thomas, G., Zie, J.-Y.: A multi-round side channel attack on AES using belief propagation. In: Cuppens, F., Wang, L., Cuppens-Boulahia, N., Tawbi, N., Garcia-Alfaro, J. (eds.) FPS 2016. LNCS, vol. 10128, pp. 199–213. Springer, Cham (2017). https://doi.org/10.1007/978-3-319-51966-1_13

6. Carlet, C., Faugère, J., Goyet, C., Renault, G.: Analysis of the algebraic side channel attack. J. Cryptogr. Eng. 2(1), 45–62 (2012). https://doi.org/10.1007/s13389-012-0028-0

7. Chari, S., Rao, J.R., Rohatgi, P.: Template attacks. In: Kaliski, B.S., Koç, K., Paar, C. (eds.) CHES 2002. LNCS, vol. 2523, pp. 13–28. Springer, Heidelberg (2003). https://doi.org/10.1007/3-540-36400-5_3

8. Damm, T., Freud, S., Klein, D.: Dissecting the CHES 2018 AES challenge. IACR Cryptol. ePrint Arch. p. 783 (2019), https://eprint.iacr.org/2019/783

9. Gohr, A., Jacob, S., Schindler, W.: CHES 2018 side channel contest CTF - solution of the AES challenges. IACR Cryptology ePrint Archive, vol. 2019, p. 94 (2019). https://eprint.iacr.org/2019/094

10. Gohr, A., Jacob, S., Schindler, W.: Efficient solutions of the CHES 2018 AES challenge using deep residual neural networks and knowledge distillation on adversarial examples. IACR Cryptology ePrint Archive, vol. 2020, p. 165 (2020). https://eprint.iacr.org/2020/165

11. Green, J., Roy, A., Oswald, E.: A systematic study of the impact of graphical models on inference-based attacks on AES. In: Bilgin, B., Fischer, J.-B. (eds.) CARDIS 2018. LNCS, vol. 11389, pp. 18–34. Springer, Cham (2019). https://doi.org/10.1007/978-3-030-15462-2_2

12. Grosso, V., Standaert, F.-X.: ASCA, SASCA and DPA with enumeration: which one beats the other and when? In: Iwata, T., Cheon, J.H. (eds.) ASIACRYPT 2015. LNCS, vol. 9453, pp. 291–312. Springer, Heidelberg (2015). https://doi.org/10.1007/978-3-662-48800-3_12

13. Guo, Q., Grosso, V., Standaert, F., Bronchain, O.: Modeling soft analytical side-channel attacks from a coding theory viewpoint. IACR Trans. Cryptogr. Hardw. Embed. Syst. 2020(4), 209–238 (2020). https://doi.org/10.13154/tches.v2020.i4.209-238

14. Hamburg, M., et al.: Chosen ciphertext k-trace attacks on masked CCA2 secure kyber. IACR Trans. Cryptogr. Hardw. Embed. Syst. 2021(4), 88–113 (2021). https://doi.org/10.46586/tches.v2021.i4.88-113

15. He, K., Zhang, X., Ren, S., Sun, J.: Deep residual learning for image recognition. In: 2016 IEEE Conference on Computer Vision and Pattern Recognition, CVPR 2016, Las Vegas, NV, USA, 27–30 June 2016, pp. 770–778. IEEE Computer Society (2016). https://doi.org/10.1109/CVPR.2016.90

16. Hermelink, J., Pessl, P., Pöppelmann, T.: Fault-enabled chosen-ciphertext attacks on Kyber. In: Adhikari, A., Küsters, R., Preneel, B. (eds.) INDOCRYPT 2021. LNCS, vol. 13143, pp. 311–334. Springer, Cham (2021). https://doi.org/10.1007/978-3-030-92518-5_15

17. Hermelink, J., Streit, S., Strieder, E., Thieme, K.: Adapting belief propagation to counter shuffling of NTTs. IACR Cryptology ePrint Archive, p. 555 (2022). https://eprint.iacr.org/2022/555

18. Kannwischer, M.J., Pessl, P., Primas, R.: Single-trace attacks on keccak. IACR Trans. Cryptogr. Hardw. Embed. Syst. **2020**(3), 243–268 (2020). https://doi.org/10.13154/tches.v2020.i3.243-268

19. MacKay, D.J.C.: Information Theory, Inference, and Learning Algorithms. Cambridge University Press, Cambridge (2003)

20. Pessl, P., Primas, R.: More practical single-trace attacks on the number theoretic transform. In: Schwabe, P., Thériault, N. (eds.) LATINCRYPT 2019. LNCS, vol. 11774, pp. 130–149. Springer, Cham (2019). https://doi.org/10.1007/978-3-030-30530-7_7

21. Picek, S., Perin, G., Mariot, L., Wu, L., Batina, L.: Sok: deep learning-based physical side-channel analysis. IACR Cryptology ePrint Archive, p. 1092 (2021). https://eprint.iacr.org/2021/1092

22. Poussier, R., Standaert, F.-X., Grosso, V.: Simple key enumeration (and rank estimation) using histograms: an integrated approach. In: Gierlichs, B., Poschmann, A.Y. (eds.) CHES 2016. LNCS, vol. 9813, pp. 61–81. Springer, Heidelberg (2016). https://doi.org/10.1007/978-3-662-53140-2_4

23. Primas, R., Pessl, P., Mangard, S.: Single-trace side-channel attacks on masked lattice-based encryption. In: Fischer, W., Homma, N. (eds.) CHES 2017. LNCS, vol. 10529, pp. 513–533. Springer, Cham (2017). https://doi.org/10.1007/978-3-319-66787-4_25

24. Rechberger, C., Oswald, E.: Practical template attacks. In: Lim, C.H., Yung, M. (eds.) WISA 2004. LNCS, vol. 3325, pp. 440–456. Springer, Heidelberg (2005). https://doi.org/10.1007/978-3-540-31815-6_35

25. Renauld, M., Standaert, F.-X.: Algebraic side-channel attacks. In: Bao, F., Yung, M., Lin, D., Jing, J. (eds.) Inscrypt 2009. LNCS, vol. 6151, pp. 393–410. Springer, Heidelberg (2010). https://doi.org/10.1007/978-3-642-16342-5_29

26. Renauld, M., Standaert, F.-X., Veyrat-Charvillon, N.: Algebraic side-channel attacks on the AES: why time also matters in DPA. In: Clavier, C., Gaj, K. (eds.) CHES 2009. LNCS, vol. 5747, pp. 97–111. Springer, Heidelberg (2009). https://doi.org/10.1007/978-3-642-04138-9_8

27. Soos, M., Nohl, K., Castelluccia, C.: Extending SAT solvers to cryptographic problems. In: Kullmann, O. (ed.) SAT 2009. LNCS, vol. 5584, pp. 244–257. Springer, Heidelberg (2009). https://doi.org/10.1007/978-3-642-02777-2_24

28. of Standards, N.I., Technology: advanced encryption standard. Technical report, Department of Commerce, Federal Information Processing Standards Publications (FIPS PUBS) 197, 2001, U.S., Washington, D.C. (2001). https://doi.org/10.6028/nist.fips.197

29. VanLaven, J., Brehob, M., Compton, K.J.: Side channel analysis, fault injection and applications - a computationally feasible SPA attack on AES VIA optimized search. In: Sasaki, R., Qing, S., Okamoto, E., Yoshiura, H. (eds.) SEC 2005. IAICT, vol. 181, pp. 577–588. Springer, Boston, MA (2005). https://doi.org/10.1007/0-387-25660-1_38

30. Veyrat-Charvillon, N., Gérard, B., Standaert, F.-X.: Soft analytical side-channel attacks. In: Sarkar, P., Iwata, T. (eds.) ASIACRYPT 2014. LNCS, vol. 8873, pp. 282–296. Springer, Heidelberg (2014). https://doi.org/10.1007/978-3-662-45611-8_15

31. You, S., Kuhn, M.G.: Single-trace fragment template attack on a 32-bit implementation of keccak. In: Grosso, V., Pöppelmann, T. (eds.) CARDIS 2021. LNCS, vol. 13173, pp. 3–23. Springer, Cham (2021). https://doi.org/10.1007/978-3-030-97348-3_1

Removing the Field Size Loss
from Duc et al.'s Conjectured Bound
for Masked Encodings

Julien Béguinot[1], Wei Cheng[1,2], Sylvain Guilley[1,2], Yi Liu[1], Loïc Masure[3(✉)],
Olivier Rioul[1], and François-Xavier Standaert[3]

[1] LTCI, Télécom Paris, Institut Polytechnique de Paris, Palaiseau, France
[2] Secure-IC, Paris, France
[3] ICTEAM Institute, Université catholique de Louvain, Louvain-la-Neuve, Belgium
`loic.masure@uclouvain.be`

Abstract. At EUROCRYPT 2015, Duc *et al.* conjectured that the success rate of a side-channel attack targeting an intermediate computation encoded in a linear secret-sharing, a.k.a. *masking* with $d+1$ shares, could be inferred by measuring the mutual information between the leakage and each share separately. This way, security bounds can be derived without having to mount the complete attack. So far, the best proven bounds for masked encodings were *nearly* tight with the conjecture, up to a constant factor overhead equal to the field size, which may still give loose security guarantees compared to actual attacks. In this paper, we improve upon the state-of-the-art bounds by removing the field size loss, in the cases of Boolean masking and arithmetic masking modulo a power of two. As an example, when masking in the AES field, our new bound outperforms the former ones by a factor 256. Moreover, we provide theoretical hints that similar results could hold for masking in other fields as well.

1 Introduction

If Side-Chanel Analysis (SCA) may be considered as a critical threat against the security of cryptography on embedded devices, it is no longer a fatality. Over the past decades, the *masking* counter-measure [4,13] has gained more and more success among designers and developers, both from an implementation and from a theoretical point of view. Masking can be seen as a linear secret sharing applied on each intermediate computation in the implementation of a cryptographic primitive that depends on some secret. In a nutshell, masking increases the attack complexity of any SCA adversary exponentially fast with the number of shares — provided that the leakages are sufficiently *noisy* and *independent* — while increasing the runtime and memory overhead at most quadratically [14]. This makes masking a theoretically *sound* counter-measure.

The Evaluation Challenge. Despite these achievements, the evaluation of a protected implementation remains cluttered by various technical and even conceptual difficulties. One way for evaluators to assess the security level of an implementation is to mount some known end-to-end attacks and to infer some security level based on the outcomes of these attacks. Nevertheless, this relies on the assumption that the attacks mounted by the evaluators could depict well the optimal attacks that any adversary could realize. As an example, if for masking with two shares, end-to-end attacks using Deep Learning (DL) depict well optimal attacks [2,19], it is no longer true when masking uses more shares [3, 21]. This could result in a false sense of security, and leaves the developers in an uncomfortable situation where implementations become increasingly hard to evaluate as their security level increases.

The Paradigm of Worst-Case Attacks. One way to circumvent this issue is to consider attacks in a so-called *worst-case* evaluation setting [1]. The core idea is to apply Kerckhoff's principles to side-channel security, by granting all the knowledge of the target to the adversary, *e.g.*, the random nonces used during the encryption, except the knowledge of the secret to guess. This way, the evaluator can efficiently profile the target implementation in order to (more) easily mount online attacks that approach the optimal ones. She can also analyze the leakage of the shares independently, in order to take advantage of masking security proofs to bound the security level under some assumptions.

Indeed, a series of theoretical works on masking allow to bound the amount of information leaked by a masked secret, depending on the amount of information leaked by each share separately, under the assumption that the shares' leakages are independent. Such bounds can be expressed, *e.g.*, in terms of the Mutual Information (MI), and then in turn be translated in terms of the Success Rate (SR) of any attack, as shown by Duc *et al.* at EUROCRYPT 2015 [9]. Nevertheless, most of the current masking security proofs provide conservative bounds, possibly due to technical artifacts. In particular, they generally require more noise and more shares than expected by the best known attacks in order to reach a given security level [8,11,23,24].

Duc *et al.*'s Conjecture. Confronting this observation with empirical evidences, Duc *et al.* conjectured that the required number of queries to the target device needed to recover the target secret of a SCA is inversely proportional to the product of the MIs of each share [9]:

$$N_a(\mathsf{SR}) \approx \frac{f(\mathsf{SR})}{\prod_{i=0}^{d} \mathsf{MI}(Y_i; L_i)} \ ,$$

where d stands for the masking *order*,[1] and f is a "small constant depending on the target SR" [10, p. 1279]. Later at CHES 2019, Chérisey *et al.* bounded this constant based on the entropy of the target secret [7].

Due to its practical relevance, this conjecture recently gained attraction with two independent and simultaneous works by Ito *et al.* [16] at CCS 2022 and by Masure *et al.* [22] at CARDIS 2022. Using different approaches, both works

---

[1] *i.e.*, the number of shares is $d + 1$ if the independence assumption is met.

prove a *nearly*-tight version of Duc *et al.*'s conjecture for masked encodings, up to a constant factor equal to the field size M of the encoding.

This represents a significant improvement with respect to the previous proved bounds — *e.g.*, $\mathcal{O}(M^d)$ in Duc *et al.*'s proof [9], which additionally suffers from a reduced noise amplification rate. But it remains loose compared to empirical attacks performed against implementations of concrete ciphers like the Advanced Encryption Standard (AES). At a high level, Ito *et al.* and Masure *et al.*'s approaches used some back and forth between the MI and other metrics, such as the Total Variation (TV) [22] or the Euclidean Norm (EN) [16], in order to state noise amplification lemmata.[2] If these conversions taken separately are tight, their combination introduces an $\mathcal{O}(M)$ overhead, leading to the question whether tighter bounds could be proved, on which we focus.

Our Contribution. In this paper, we positively address the latter question, by removing this field size loss for masked encodings. At a high level, we do that by working directly with noisy leakages, without relying on reductions to more abstract (e.g., random probing) leakage models. Technically, our approach consists in stating the amplification lemma *directly* in terms of the MI, without any lossy conversion to other statistical distances. This idea is implemented using a result from Information Theory called Mrs. Gerber's Lemma (MGL) [5,17]. The MGL allows us to bound the MI between the secret and the whole leakage by a function of the MIs between each share and their corresponding leakage. Moreover, the bound given by the MGL is proved to be *tight*, in the sense that there exists some leakage distributions for which the inequality from the MGL is actually an equality. The only limitation compared to the previous works is that our bound only works for fields whose size is a power of 2. Thankfully, this limitation is not prohibitive, since our result covers, *e.g.*, Boolean masking or arithmetic masking modulo 2^n. Nevertheless, we argue at the end of this paper that similar results could also be obtained in different fields, whose size is not necessarily a power of 2. More generally, and since our results are for now specialized to masked encodings, it remains a natural question whether they generalize to computation, as also conjectured by Duc. et al. [9].

2   Statement of the Problem

We start the paper by stating the problem under consideration, before providing the solution in Sect. 3, and discussing some perspectives in Sect. 4.

2.1   Notations and Background

Side-Channel Attack. Let $(\mathcal{Y}, \oplus)$ be a group of finite order, denoted by M. Let $\mathrm{K} \in \mathcal{Y}$ be the secret key chunk to guess. To this end, we consider that

---

[2] *e.g.*, Young-Minkowski's convolution inequality for the TV [22] or Plancherel's formula combined with the convolution theorem for the EN [16].

the adversary knows a sequence of N_a plaintexts $\{P\}_{N_a}$, and can observe the sequence of leakages $\{\mathbf{L}\}_{N_a}$ associated to the corresponding intermediate computations $\{Y = \mathbf{C}(K, P)\}_{N_a}$. Based on this side-channel information, the adversary returns a key guess $\widehat{K}$. We define the Success Rate (SR) as $\mathsf{SR} = \Pr\left(K = \widehat{K}\right)$. Since the SR increases when the number of observed traces N_a increases as well, we next define the quantity $N_a(\mathsf{SR}, \mathcal{Y})$ as the minimal number of leakage traces required for any adversary to reach a success rate at least SR.

Masking. In order to protect cryptographic secrets against side-channel leakage, we consider the intermediate computation Y — assumed to be uniformly distributed — to be masked.[3] Let $Y_0, \ldots, Y_d$ be $d + 1$ random variables out of which d are uniformly drawn from $\mathcal{Y}$, that we call the *shares*, and denote by $Y = Y_0 \oplus \ldots \oplus Y_d$ the random variable to protect, that we call the *secret*. Concretely, for each trace $\mathbf{L} = (L_0, \ldots, L_d)$, the adversary observes a *leakage* L_i, whose distribution conditionally to Y_i is independent of all the other random variables. In our setting, we assume that an evaluator has been able to characterize the amount of uncertainty about Y_i that has been removed by observing L_i, measured in terms of the MI, whose definition is recalled hereafter.

Definition 1 (Mutual Information). *Let* p, m *be two Probability Mass Function (p.m.f.) over the finite set* $\mathcal{Y}$.[4] *We denote by* $\mathsf{D}_{\mathsf{KL}}(\mathsf{p} \parallel \mathsf{m})$ *the Kullback - Leibler (KL) divergence between* p *and* m:

$$\mathsf{D}_{\mathsf{KL}}(\mathsf{p} \parallel \mathsf{m}) = \sum_{y \in \mathcal{Y}} \mathsf{p}(y) \log_2\left(\frac{\mathsf{p}(y)}{\mathsf{m}(y)}\right) \ . \tag{1}$$

Then, we define the Mutual Information (MI) between a discrete random variable Y *and a continuous random vector* $\mathbf{L}$ *as follows:*

$$\mathsf{MI}(Y; \mathbf{L}) = \mathop{\mathbb{E}}_{\mathbf{L}}\left[\mathsf{D}_{\mathsf{KL}}\left(\mathsf{p}_{Y \mid \mathbf{L}} \parallel \mathsf{p}_Y\right)\right] \ , \tag{2}$$

where p_Y *and* $\mathsf{p}_{Y \mid \mathbf{L}}$ *respectively denote the Probability Mass Function (p.m.f.) of* Y *and the p.m.f. of* Y *given a realization* $\mathbf{l}$ *of the random vector* $\mathbf{L}$, *with the expectation taken over* $\mathbf{L}$.

In the remaining of this paper, we will assume that for each share Y_i and its corresponding sub-leakage L_i, we have a bound $\mathsf{MI}(Y_i; L_i) \leq \delta_i$. Intuitively, the lower the δ_i, the less informative the leakages, and the lower the SR. Moreover, we do not focus on the potential implementation overhead of masking in this paper — that could grow quadratically in memory and runtime [15] — to only focus on the security aspect of the counter-measure.

---

[3] For cryptographic reasons, the vast majority of the intermediate computations are uniformly distributed, including the inputs and outputs of Sbox — provided that the plaintext and the key are uniformly distributed as well. The only non-uniform intermediate computations of a block cipher may be the potential intermediate calculations of an Sbox.

[4] We assume without loss of generality that m has full support over $\mathcal{Y}$.

2.2 Problem and Conjecture

The problem that we consider here is to obtain upper bounds of the shape:

$$N_a(\mathsf{SR}, \mathcal{Y}) \geq \frac{f(\mathsf{SR}, \mathcal{Y})}{\prod_{i=0}^{d}(\delta_i/\tau)^r} \ , \tag{3}$$

where $f(\mathsf{SR}, \mathcal{Y})$ is a constant, τ is the so-called *noise threshold*, *i.e.*, the maximum amount of leakage that can leak such that the masking counter-measure remains sound and r is the *amplification rate*. Duc *et al.* [9] conjectured that N_a satisfies an upper bound of the shape of Eq. 3, where $\tau \approx 1$ and $r = 1$.

A Reduction to Mutual Information Maximization. At CHES 2019, Chérisey *et al.* have shown that N_a can be linked to the MI as follows:

$$N_a(\mathsf{SR}, \mathcal{Y}) \geq \frac{f(\mathsf{SR}, \mathcal{Y})}{\mathsf{MI}(Y; \mathbf{L})} \ , \tag{4}$$

where f is a known, computable function of SR that can be bounded based on the entropy of Y so that $f(\mathsf{SR}, \mathcal{Y}) = \mathcal{O}(\log(M))$ [7]. In other words, it is possible to reduce the problem of bounding the security level of masked implementation to the problem of bounding the MI:

$$\begin{aligned} \max_{\Pr(\mathbf{L}_i \mid Y_i), i \in [\![0,d]\!]} & \quad \mathsf{MI}(Y; \mathbf{L}) \\ \text{s.t.} & \quad \mathsf{MI}(Y_i; \mathbf{L}_i) \leq \delta_i \end{aligned} \tag{5}$$

Following the previous conjecture, we expect that $\mathsf{MI}(Y; \mathbf{L}) \approx \prod_{i=0}^{d}(\delta_i/\tau)^r$ is a valid upper bound for this problem, where $\tau \approx 1$, and $r = 1$, whereas it could so far only be proven that $\mathsf{MI}(Y; \mathbf{L}) \approx M \prod_{i=0}^{d}(\delta_i/\tau)$.

We note that the optimization defined in Eq. 5 is convex, with convex constraints, as stated hereafter.[5]

Proposition 1. *The optimization problem defined in Eq. 5 is convex.*

Proof. Let $\mathbf{l}$ be fixed. The mapping

$$\Pr(Y_0 \mid \mathbf{L}_0 = l_0), \ldots, \Pr(Y_d \mid \mathbf{L}_d = l_d) \mapsto \Pr(Y \mid \mathbf{L} = \mathbf{l})$$

is a convolution product [21, Prop. 1] so it is $(d+1)$-linear, and thereby convex. Hence, since the mapping $\Pr(Y \mid \mathbf{L} = \mathbf{l}) \mapsto -H(Y \mid \mathbf{L} = \mathbf{l})$ is also convex, the composition of both mappings remains convex. Since $\Pr(Y \mid \mathbf{L}) \mapsto -H(Y \mid \mathbf{L})$ is the expectation of the latter composed mappings, it remains convex. Adding $H(Y) = \log_2(M)$ keeps the convexity property unchanged.   □

As a result of this convexity, the optimal solution to the optimization of Eq. 5 is necessarily such that for each $i \in [\![0, d]\!]$, we have $\mathsf{MI}(Y_i; \mathbf{L}_i) = \delta_i$.

---

[5] The interested reader may find a similar convexity result, stated in terms of statistical distance, in the works of Dziembowski *et al.* [12, Cor. 2].

Serial vs. Parallel Leakages. In this section, we have implicitly assumed that the leakages occured in serial, which mostly depicts what could happen in a software implementation. We stress that our results may also extend without loss of generality to leakages occuring in parallel, *e.g.*, leakages of the form $\mathbf{L} = \mathbf{L}_0 + \ldots + \mathbf{L}_d$, provided that the independence assumption remains verified. It suffices to reduce to the serial case, thanks to the Data Processing Inequality (DPI):

$$\mathsf{MI}(\mathrm{Y}; \mathbf{L}_0 + \ldots + \mathbf{L}_d) \leq \mathsf{MI}(\mathrm{Y}; \mathbf{L}_0, \ldots, \mathbf{L}_d) \ .$$

3 A Proof Without Field Size Loss

We now provide our main result, namely we give a solution to the optimization problem stated in Eq. 5. Compared to previous works, we introduce a mild additional assumption on the group $\mathcal{Y}$, namely that its order is a power of two. Nevertheless, this assumption covers Boolean masking and arithmetic masking modulo 2^n. To this end, we need to introduce some definitions.

3.1 Introducing Mrs. Gerber's Lemma

We first recall the definition of the entropy for a binary random variable.

Definition 2 (Binary Entropy). *Let*

$$H_b : \begin{vmatrix} [0,1] \longrightarrow [0,1] \\ p \longmapsto -p\log_2(p) - (1-p)\log_2(1-p) \end{vmatrix}$$

be the binary entropy function. Let $H_b^{-1} : [0,1] \mapsto [0,\frac{1}{2}]$ be the inverse of H_b restricted to $[0,\frac{1}{2}]$.

Likewise, we introduce the convolution for a binary random variable.

Definition 3 (Binary Convolution $\star$). *Let*

$$\star : \begin{vmatrix} [0,1]^2 \longrightarrow [0,1] \\ x,y \longmapsto (1-x)y + x(1-y). \end{vmatrix}$$

Note that when $\star$ is iterated, it can be replaced by a product, as stated next.

Proposition 2 (Iterated Star for Bias). *For $x_0, \ldots, x_d \in [0,1]$, the $\star$ operations can be mapped into a product for operands in the form of a bias as follows*

$$\overset{d}{\underset{i=0}{\star}} \left(\frac{1}{2} - x_i \right) = \frac{1}{2} - 2^d \prod_{i=0}^{d} x_i.$$

Proof. This is proved by induction on d. $\qquad\square$

Definition 4 (Mrs. Gerber's functions). *For any positive integers n, p, let* $f_{H,2^n} : [0,1]^{p+1} \to [0,1]$ *be the function defined by*

$$f_{H,2^n}(x_0, \ldots, x_p) = H_b\left(\overset{p}{\underset{i=0}{\star}} H_b^{-1}(x_i)\right) .$$

Moreover, we also define the function $f_{MI,2^n} : [0,1]^{p+1} \to [0,1]$ *as*

$$f_{MI,2^n}(\delta_0, \ldots, \delta_p) = 1 - f_{H,2^n}(1 - \delta_0, \ldots, 1 - \delta_p).$$

Remark 1. The function f_{MI} is decreasing with respect to each of its inputs, and is equal to 0 when every $\delta_i = 0$.

We are now equipped to introduce the technical lemma that will set the ground for our result, namely the so-called MGL. MGL has been first established by Wyner and Ziv [30] for a two-element group $\mathcal{Y}$, but it has been extended to any Abelian group whose order is a power of two by Jog and Anantharam [17].

Theorem 1 (Mrs. Gerber's Lemma [17, Thm. V.1, Claim V.1]). *Let* $(\mathcal{Y}, \oplus)$ *be any Abelian group of order* $M = 2^n$. *Let* $Y_0, \ldots, Y_d$ *be* $d+1$ *independent* $\mathcal{Y}$*-valued random variables with side information* $L_0, \ldots, L_d$. *We assume that conditionally to* Y_i, L_i *is independent of any other random variable. Define* $x_i = H(Y_i \mid L_i)$, *and without loss of generality assume that* $x_0 \geq \ldots \geq x_d$. *Let* $k = \lfloor x_0 \rfloor$ *and* $p = \max\{i \mid \lfloor x_i \rfloor \geq k\}$, *then*

$$k + f_{H,2^n}(x_0 - k, \ldots, x_p - k) \leq H(Y_0 \oplus \ldots \oplus Y_d \mid L_0, \ldots, L_d). \quad (6)$$

Proof. Let us denote $Y = Y_0 \oplus \ldots \oplus Y_d$ for short, and for any $i \in [\![0, d]\!]$, let $X_i(l) = H(Y_i \mid L_i = l)$, such that $\underset{L_i}{\mathbb{E}}[X_i(L_i)] = x_i$. Moreover, notice that by assumption, all the $X_i(L_i)$ are mutually independent.

Jog and Anantharam claim [17, Thm. V.1] that for a fixed leakage $l = (l_0, \ldots, l_d)$, we have

$$\varphi(X_0(l_0) \ldots, X_d(l_d)) \leq H(Y \mid \mathbf{L} = l) ,$$

for some function φ that is convex with respect to each variable, when the remaining are kept fixed [17, Cor. V.1]. Combining this property with the independence of the $X_i(L_i)$, we may apply Jensen's inequality $d + 1$ times:

$$\varphi(x_0, \ldots, x_d) \leq \underset{l}{\mathbb{E}}[\varphi(X_0(l_0) \ldots, X_d(l_d))] \leq \underset{l}{\mathbb{E}}[H(Y \mid \mathbf{L} = l)] = H(Y \mid \mathbf{L}) .$$

Finally, replacing φ by its expression from [17, Thm. 5.1] results in Eq. 6. $\quad\square$

Remark 2. In this paper, for better readability, all the logarithms are taken in base 2, but all the results we rely on have been established with logarithms in natural base. Thankfully, the proof of the MGL for $M = 2$ can be straightforwardly extended to logarithms in any base [5, Thm. 1]. Likewise, all the technical results used in Jog and Anantharam's proof remain insensitive to the base, as they essentially involve computing ratios of logarithms [17, Sec. 2].

3.2 Application of Mrs. Gerber's Lemma to Masking

Using the MGL, we prove the following upper bound on the side-channel information leaked by a masked encoding.

Corollary 1 (Security of Masking). *Let $M = 2^n$ and d be a positive integer. Let $Y_0, \ldots, Y_d$ be a $(d+1)$-sharing of the uniform random variable Y and $\mathbf{L} = (L_0, \ldots, L_d)$ be such that, conditionally to Y_i, the variable L_i is independent of the others. For all $i \in [\![0, d]\!]$, define $\mathsf{MI}(Y_i; L_i) = \delta_i$, and assume without loss of generality that there is a positive integer p such that for all $i \le p$, $\delta_i \le 1$ and for all $i > p$, $\delta_i \ge 1$. Then*

$$\mathsf{MI}(Y; \mathbf{L}) \le \mathsf{f}_{\mathsf{MI}, 2^n}(\delta_0, \ldots, \delta_p) \ . \tag{7}$$

Proof. We upper-bound $\mathsf{MI}(Y; \mathbf{L}) = \mathsf{H}(Y) - \mathsf{H}(Y \mid \mathbf{L}) = n - \mathsf{H}(Y \mid \mathbf{L})$ by lower-bounding $\mathsf{H}(Y \mid \mathbf{L})$, using Theorem 1.

$$\mathsf{H}(Y \mid \mathbf{L}) = \mathsf{H}(Y_0 \oplus \ldots \oplus Y_d \mid \mathbf{L})$$
$$\ge n - 1 + \mathsf{f}_{\mathsf{H}, 2^n}(\mathsf{H}(Y_0 \mid L_0) - (n-1), \ldots, \mathsf{H}(Y_p \mid L_p) - (n-1))$$
$$= n - 1 + \mathsf{f}_{\mathsf{H}, 2^n}(1 - \mathsf{MI}(Y_0; L_0), \ldots, 1 - \mathsf{MI}(Y_p; L_p))$$
$$= n - \mathsf{f}_{\mathsf{MI}, 2^n}(\mathsf{MI}(Y_0; L_0), \ldots, \mathsf{MI}(Y_p; L_p))$$

$\square$

3.3 Comparison with Former Upper Bounds

The removal of the field size loss in Theorem 1 is illustrated by Fig. 1. The graph depicts the upper bounds on $\mathsf{MI}(Y; L)$ (in bits) with respect to the noise parameter δ — assuming that the δ_i are all equal. The dotted curves correspond to the bounds given by Masure et al. [22][6] for different masking orders, whereas the dashed curves are obtained with our new bound. It can for example be noticed that for $d = 1$ and $\delta_i = 2^{-7}$, the bound from Ito et al. and Masure et al. [22] is roughly equal to 2^{-5}, whereas our upper bound is less than 2^{-12}, meaning that the gain is roughly 2^{12-5} which corresponds to half the field size. A similar factor is observed for larger d values.

We also add the following proposition (proven in Appendix) that gives a more intuitive view of our results and makes the removal of the field size loss explicit.

Proposition 3 (Approximation in 0). *The Taylor expansion of the MGL function is the following:*

$$\mathsf{f}_{\mathsf{MI}, 2^n}(\delta_0, \ldots, \delta_d) = \eta \prod_{i=0}^{d} \frac{\delta_i}{\eta} + o\left(\prod_{i=0}^{d} \delta_i\right) , \tag{8}$$

where $\eta = (2 \ln 2)^{-1} \approx 0.72$.

---

[6] We have afterwards noticed that the proof of Masure et al.'s bound [22, Prop. 2, Thm. 3] was suboptimal, so the bound of Masure et al. is actually slightly better than Ito et al.'s one by a factor $\frac{1}{2}$. That is why in the remaining of this paper, we mainly compare against the bound of Masure et al..

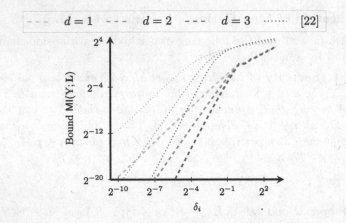

Fig. 1. Illustration of Eq. 1 for $M = 256$ (e.g., the AES S-box).

We note that the η parameter does not exactly correspond to the noise rate τ of Subsect. 2.2, since it depends on the noise level. But for high noise levels, where the first-order Taylor expansion is accurate, its value of 0.72 corresponds to the noise threshold in the CCS 2022 and the CARDIS 2022 papers.[7]

3.4 The MGL: Tighter or Tight?

We have shown in Subsect. 3.3 that our upper bound obtained from the MGL is tighter than the one achieved by Ito *et al.* [16] and Masure *et al.* [22]. We may therefore wonder to what extent the new MI upper bound is *tight*. In other words, are there some leakage models such that the MI between the secret and the leakage of all shares equals the MGL function. In this respect, Jog and Anantharam's results could be interpreted as the fact that the bound given by the MGL is at least *locally* tight, as stated hereafter.

Proposition 4 ([17, Thm. 5.1]). *For all $(x_0, \ldots, x_d) \in [0, n]^{d+1}$, there exists a leakage distribution $(\mathbf{L} \mid Y)$ such that:*

1. For all $i \in [\![0, d]\!]$, we have $\mathsf{H}(Y_i \mid L_i = l_i) = \delta_i$ and
2. $\mathsf{H}(Y \mid \mathbf{L} = (l_0, \ldots, l_d)) = k + \mathsf{f}_{\mathsf{H}, 2^n}(x_0 - k, \ldots, x_p - k)$,

where k and p are the parameters defined in Theorem 1.

In other words, without further assumption on the leakage model, the bound given by the MGL is the best possible. We next investigate whether it is actually tight for practically-relevant leakage functions by confronting the bounds from

---

[7] For low noise levels, it gets gradually closer to one, but this gain has limited practical relevance since masking only provides high security with sufficient noise.

the MGL to the direct computation of the MI for a shared secret. For this purpose, we assume that each share leaks a deterministic function of its value with an additive Gaussian noise, similarly to the experiments conducted by Ito *et al.* [16, Sect. 7.1] and Masure *et al.* [22, Sect. 3.1]. In particular, we consider two deterministic leakages, namely the Least Significant Bit (l.s.b.) of the share, or its Hamming weight. The MI is estimated with Monte-Carlo methods by sampling $N_v = 10,000$ leakages. Then, for each simulated leakage, the conditional p.m.f. can be exactly computed using a Soft-Analytical SCA (SASCA) [28].[8]

The results are depicted in Fig. 2, for Boolean sharings with 2 shares and 3 shares, and for l.s.b. (Figs. 2a, 2b) and Hamming weight leakages (Figs. 2a, 2b). Each plot depicts the MI of the secret, depending on the variance σ^2 of the additive Gaussian noise. As one can observe on Fig. 2a and Fig. 2b, the bounds obtained by the MGL, depicted in dashed curves, are tight with the plain curves computed from the SASCA for the l.s.b. leakage model. However, for the Hamming weight leakage model, we observe a gap between our upper bound and the ground truth. Moreover, the gap between the dashed curve and the plain curve in Fig. 2d seems wider than the one in Fig. 2c. This shows that the Hamming weight leakage model does not verify Proposition 4. The combination of these observations confirms that no significant improvements of the bound can be obtained without making additional assumptions on the leakage function.

3.5 Linking the MI with the Success Rate

Having upper bounded the MI between the secret and *one* side-channel trace, we may then lower bound the required number of queries for any SCA adversary, by leveraging Chérisey *et al.*'s $f(\mathsf{SR}, \mathcal{Y})$ function, as stated hereafter.

Corollary 2. *In the same setting as in Corollary 1,*

$$N_a(\mathsf{SR}) \geq \frac{f(\mathsf{SR}, \mathcal{Y})}{\mathsf{f}_{\mathsf{MI},2^n}(\delta_0, \ldots, \delta_p)} \ . \tag{9}$$

Proof. Combining Corollary 1 with Eq. 4.   □

We compare this approach with a simulated SASCA attack on Fig. 3, for the two leakage models investigated in Subsect. 3.4. The plain curves denote the attack complexity obtained from a key recovery. There, the success rate is estimated with *re-sampling* from a validation set of $N_v = 10,000$ traces. More precisely, the N_v validations traces are re-shuffled between 100 and 1,000 times to emulate different attack sets. While this method is prone to be biased when N_a is close to N_v, the method remains sound if the success rate converged towards 1 within N_v traces, as it cancels the bias.[9] The dotted green curves correspond to Eq. 4 where the direct estimation of the MI between the shared secret and the leakage of the shares (from Fig. 2) is used. The dashed red curves correspond to the bound

---

[8] https://scalib.readthedocs.io/en/latest/index.html.
[9] This condition is verified retrospectively on Fig. 3.

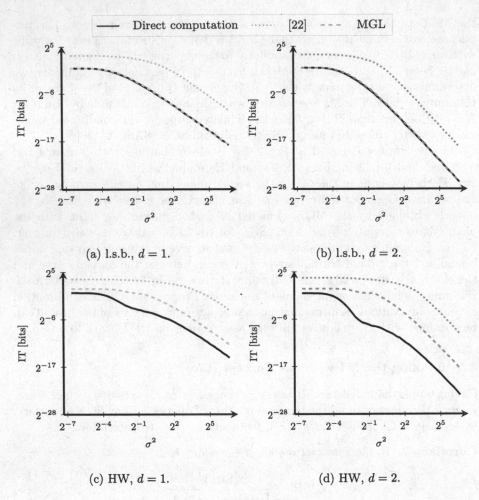

Fig. 2. MI in function of the Gaussian noise variance σ^2, for $n = 8$ bits.

given by Eq. 9. One can notice that the plain curves and the dotted curves are always close to each other, meaning that Chérisey *et al.*'s function is reasonably tight in our context. Moreover, similarly to what was noticed in Subsect. 3.4, the bound provided by Eq. 9 is tight for the l.s.b. leakage model, but remains non-tight for the HW leakage model.

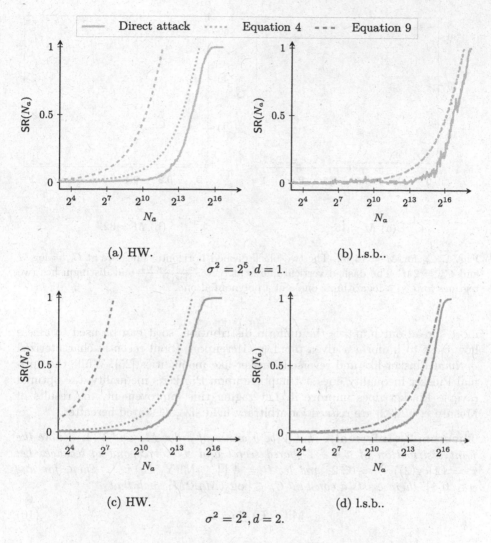

Fig. 3. Extending MI bounds to concrete security bounds.

4   On the Dependence of the Group Structure

In our previous derivations, we assume that the field in which masking is applied is a power of two. Since this is the only limitation compared to the results of Ito *et al.* [16] and Masure *et al.* [22], we finally discuss whether this additional assumption is crucial. To this end, we show that Masure *et al.*'s approach using Pinsker [6, Lemma 11.6.1] and reverse Pinsker [26, Theorem 1] inequalities can be improved using the theory of *majorization* [20].

In a nutshell, majorization can be seen as a partial order relationship on p.m.f.'s quantifying "how spread out" a p.m.f. is, compared to another. The

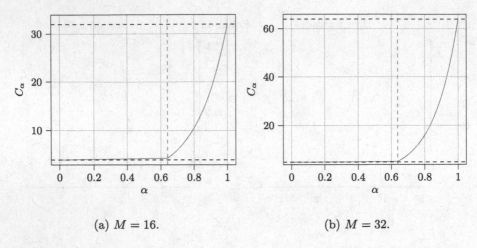

(a) $M = 16$.   (b) $M = 32$.

Fig. 4. C_α for $M = 16, 32$. The two black dashed horizontal lines are at $C_\alpha = \log M$ and $C_\alpha = 2M$. The dashed vertical line is at $\alpha = \frac{\log(M \log M)}{2 \log(M-1)}$ and distinguishes two regimes for C_α, a logarithmic one and a polynomial one.

most spread out p.m.f. is the uniform distribution, so it can be used to assess how close to uniform a given p.m.f. is. Hereupon, Rioul recently characterized *optimal* Pinsker-like and reversed Pinsker-like inequalities [25]. While the optimal Pinsker inequality does not improve upon Pinsker's inequality, the optimal reverse Pinsker does improve it. Leveraging this improvement, the results of Masure *et al.* [22] are refined for arbitrary field size, as stated hereafter.

Theorem 2 (Informal). *Let $\mathcal{Y}$ be a group of order M, and $Y, \mathbf{L}$ denote the joint distribution of a $d + 1$-shared secret and its corresponding leakage. Let $\tau = (2 \log(2))^{-1} \approx 0.72$, and let $P = \frac{1}{4} \prod_{i=0}^{d} \mathsf{MI}(Y_i; L_i) \tau^{-1}$. Then, for any $\alpha \in [0, 1]$, there exists a constant $C_\alpha \in [\log_2(M), 2M]$ such that*

$$\mathsf{MI}(Y; \mathbf{L}) \leq C_\alpha P^\alpha \ . \tag{10}$$

In particular, for $\alpha = \frac{1}{2}$, we have

$$\mathsf{MI}(Y; \mathbf{L}) \leq \log(M) \left(1 + \frac{1}{M}\right) P^{1/2} \ . \tag{11}$$

The bounds in Theorem 2 — whose formal statement is given and proven in Appendix — are not as tight as the ones from Corollary 1 but hold for any field size M, which makes them interesting when M is not a power of two.

Figure 4 depicts the range of C_α depending on α. It illustrates that there is a trade-off between the constant factor overhead C_α and the effective number of shares $\alpha \cdot (d + 1)$. Overall, this provides good hints towards the conjectured absence of constant factor overhead in non-binary fields, and opens some perspectives towards a formal proof of the masked encoding bound in this context.

5   Conclusion and Perspectives

From a practical perspective, our work contributes to formalizing the soundness of so-called shortcut evaluations, where the security level of an implementation protected with higher-order masking is assessed based on the security of its individual shares. By performing our proofs directly with noisy leakages, we show that such shortcuts are actually tight for masked encodings.

As mentioned in introduction, a natural extension of this work is to explore the tightness of bounds for masked computations (e.g., multiplications) and not only encodings. Besides, our results of Subsect. 3.4 show that while the bound we provide is locally tight (i.e., tight for some leakage functions), it is not tight for other practically-relevant leakage functions like the Hamming weight one (and, in general, for leakage functions having preimages of different sizes). It could therefore be interesting to study whether a mild characterization of the leakages could be used to improve the shortcut evaluation of masking for these functions. Another possible track of research is to study whether improved connections between the mutual information and the success rate can be obtained: despite the bounds of Subsect. 3.5 already give good evaluations, there remains a small gap that could possibly be removed (e.g., taking advantage of other information theoretic metrics like the Alpha-Information [18]). Eventually, yet another question is whether these bounds, for now studied in a known (random) plaintext context cover adaptive chosen-plaintext side-channel attacks [29]?

Acknowledgments. François-Xavier Standaert is a Senior Research Associate of the Belgian Fund for Scientific Research (FNRS-F.R.S.). This work has been funded in part by the ERC project number 724725 (acronym SWORD). This work has also partly benefited from the bilateral MESRI-BMBF project "APRIORI" from the ANR cybersecurity 2020 call. The authors also acknowledge financial support from the French national Bank (BPI) under Securyzr-V grant (Contract DOS0144216/00), a RISC-V centric platform integrating security co-processors.

A   Proof of Proposition 3

$$\mathsf{MI}(Y;\mathbf{L}) \leq 1 - H_b\left(\frac{1}{2} - 2^d \prod_{i=0}^{d}\left(\frac{1}{2} - H_b^{-1}(1 - \mathsf{MI}(Y_i;\mathbf{L}))\right)\right)$$

$$= \frac{2\log(e)}{4}\prod_{i=0}^{d}4(\frac{1}{2} - H_b^{-1}(1 - \mathsf{MI}(L_i;Y_i)))^2$$

$$+ o\left(\prod_{i=0}^{d}4(\frac{1}{2} - H_b^{-1}(1 - \mathsf{MI}(L_i;Y_i)))^2\right)$$

$$= \frac{2\log(e)}{4}\prod_{i=0}^{d}4\frac{\mathsf{MI}(L_i;Y_i)}{2\log e} + o\left(\prod_{i=0}^{d}4\frac{\mathsf{MI}(L_i;Y_i)}{2\log e}\right)$$

That it under normalized form

$$\mathsf{MI}(Y;\mathbf{L}) \leq \frac{\log(e)}{2} \prod_{i=0}^{d} \mathsf{MI}(L_i;Y_i) \frac{2}{\log e} + o\left(\prod_{i=0}^{d} \mathsf{MI}(L_i;Y_i)\right)$$

$$= \eta \prod_{i=0}^{d} \frac{\mathsf{MI}(L_i;Y_i)}{\eta} + o\left(\prod_{i=0}^{d} \mathsf{MI}(L_i;Y_i)\right).$$

B   Technical Statements and Proofs from Sect. 4

Proposition 5 (Optimal Reversed Pinsker). *Let f_{opt} be the optimal reverse Pinsker inequality, i.e.,*

$$f_{\mathsf{opt}} : \left|\begin{array}{l} [0, \frac{1}{M}] \longrightarrow \mathbb{R}_+ \\ \Delta \longmapsto \frac{1}{M}((1 + M\Delta)\log(1 + M\Delta) \end{array}\right.$$
$$+ ((1 - \Delta)M - L)\log((1 - \Delta)M - L)) \quad (12)$$

where $L = \lfloor M(1 - \Delta) \rfloor$. For all p.m.f. P we have $\mathsf{D_{KL}}(P \parallel U) \leq f_{opt}(\Delta(P, U))$.

Proof. By applying the entropy which is Schur-concave to Eqn. 51 in [25]. We factor $-\log M$ in each term of the inequality to obtain Prop. 5. □

Theorem 3 (Formal version of Theorem 2). *Let $\mathcal{H}$ be the class of function that is lower bounded by f_{opt}, concave when composed with a square root and increasing. Let $P = \frac{1}{4} \prod_{i=0}^{d} C\,\mathsf{MI}(Y_i; L_i)$, we have*

$$\mathsf{MI}(Y;\mathbf{L}) \leq \inf_{f \in \mathcal{H}} (f \circ \sqrt{\cdot})(P). \quad (13)$$

Let $C_\alpha = \sup_{\Delta \in]0, 1-\frac{1}{M}]} f^*(\Delta)\Delta^{-2\alpha} = \max_{\Delta = k/M, k \in \{1, \dots M-1\}} f^*(\Delta)\Delta^{-2\alpha}$. We have

$$\mathsf{MI}(Y;\mathbf{L}) \leq \min\left(\log(1 + M^2(4^{\frac{1}{M}} - 1)P), (\frac{1}{M} + \sqrt{P})\log(1 + M\sqrt{P})\right) \quad (14)$$

$$\leq \inf_{\alpha \in [0,1]} C_\alpha \cdot P^\alpha \quad (15)$$

$$\leq \log(M)(1 + \frac{1}{M}) \cdot P^{\frac{1}{2}}. \quad (16)$$

Remark 3. The infinum in Eqn. 13 can be computed with the Legendre-Fenchel transform $f \mapsto f^*$ (i.e. $f^*(p) = \sup_x \{px - f(x)\}$). Indeed, it is given by $\Delta \mapsto -(-f_{\mathsf{opt}} \circ \sqrt{\cdot})^{**}(\Delta^2)$ by applying Thm. 10 in [27].

The different inequalities are shown in Fig. 5. f_1 is the best for $\Delta \leq 1/M$ and else f_2 is the best. Eqn. 16 shows that if we reduce the security exponent to $\frac{1}{2}$ we can obtain a mild (logarithmic) dependency in the field size.

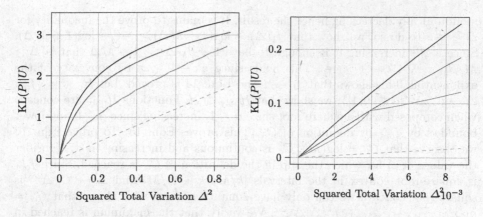

Fig. 5. Illustration of the inequalities for $M = 16$. Pinsker is the dashed blue line. The classical reverse Pinsker is the orange line. The optimal reverse Pinsker f_{opt} is the green curve. The dotted curve is f_2 and the red curve f_1. (Color figure online)

Proof. All derivations of [22] hold for $f \in \mathcal{H}$ which shows Eqn. 13. Indeed,

$$\text{KL}(Y|\mathbf{L}\|U) \leq f_{\text{opt}}(\Delta) \qquad\qquad\qquad Prop.\ 5$$

$$\leq f(\Delta) \qquad\qquad\qquad f_{\text{opt}} \leq f$$

$$\leq f\Big(\frac{1}{2} \prod_{i=0}^{d} 2\Delta((Y_i|L_i); U)\Big) \qquad\qquad \text{XOR Lemma}$$

$$= (f \circ \sqrt{\cdot})\Big(\frac{1}{4} \prod_{i=0}^{d} 4\Delta((Y_i|L_i); U))^2$$

$$\leq (f \circ \sqrt{\cdot})\Big(\frac{1}{4} \prod_{i=0}^{d} C\,\text{KL}(Y_i|L_i\|U)\Big) \qquad \text{Pinsker}$$

Since $(f \circ \sqrt{\cdot})$ is concave, we apply Jensen inequality and take the expectation to obtain the desired inequality. The expectation of the product is simplified to the product of the expectations by independence of the terms. Let $f_1 : \Delta \mapsto \log(1 + M^2(4^{\frac{1}{M}} - 1)\Delta^2) \approx MC\Delta^2$ and $f_2 : \Delta \mapsto (\Delta + \frac{1}{M})\log(1 + M\Delta)$. We show that f_1 and f_2 are in $\mathcal{H}$. For f_2 it is clear since f_2 is f^* where we removed the negative $1/M$ periodic term. f_1 is clearly concave in Δ^2 and increasing. To ensure that $f_1 \geq f_{\text{opt}}$ we consider the case of equality in $\frac{1}{M}$. This imposes $\log(1 + \beta_M M^{-2}) = \frac{2}{M}$ where $\beta_M = M^2(4^{\frac{1}{M}} - 1)$. For $\Delta \leq \frac{1}{M}$, $Mf_{\text{opt}}(\Delta) = (1 + M\Delta)\log(1 + M\Delta) + (1 - M\Delta)\log(1 - M\Delta) \leq \frac{2}{M}\log(1 + M^2\Delta^2)$ by Jensen in equality. This upper bound of f_{opt} is a lower bound of f_1. Since log is increasing the inequality holds if and only if $1 + \beta_M\Delta^2 \geq (1 + M^2\Delta^2)^{\frac{2}{M}}$. Equality holds in 0 and $1/M$ and we show that the derivative of the difference is increasing then decreasing. The derivative is given by $2\Delta(\beta_M - 2M(1 + M^2\Delta^2)^{\frac{2}{M}-1})$ and its sign is given by $\beta_M - 2M(1 + M^2\Delta^2)^{\frac{2}{M}-1}$. This quantity is positive in 0 and monotonically decreasing hence the result. It remains to prove the inequality for $\Delta \geq \frac{1}{M}$. To do so, we show that $f_1(\Delta) \geq \log(1 + M\Delta) \geq \frac{1+M\Delta}{M}\log(1 + M\Delta)$. Since log is increasing it is enough to have $1 + \beta_M \Delta^2 \geq 1 + M\Delta$ that is $\Delta \geq M/\beta_M$ i.e., $4^{\frac{1}{M}} - 1 \geq \frac{1}{M}$. This holds since $e^x - 1 \geq x$ by convexity of the exponential. This shows that $f_1 \in \mathcal{H}$ and Eqn. 14 is proved. Let $\mathcal{H}_{\mathrm{poly}} = \{f_\alpha : \Delta \mapsto C_\alpha \Delta^{2\alpha} | \alpha \in [0, 1]\}$, we show that $\mathcal{H}_{\mathrm{poly}} \subset \mathcal{H}$. Functions $\mathcal{H}_{\mathrm{poly}}$ are concave when composed with a square root since $\alpha \leq 1$, increasing since $\alpha \geq 0$ and lower bounded by f_{opt} by definition of C_α. This proves Eqn. 15. To prove Eqn. 16 we observe that $C_0 = \log(M)$, C_α is continuous and increasing in α. Consider the values of Δ for which the sup in the definition of C_α is reached. Since f_{opt} is square-root convex in the intervals $[k/M, (k+1)/M]$ and $\Delta \mapsto C_\alpha \Delta^{2\alpha}$ is square-root concave we can only have equality in $\frac{k+1}{M}$. This shows that $C_\alpha = \max_{\Delta = k/M, k \in \{1, \ldots M-1\}} f^*(\Delta)\Delta^{-2\alpha}$. We verify that the maximum is reached in $1 - 1/M$ when $\alpha = \frac{1}{2}$. The ratio of the sequence $f^*(k/M)(\frac{k}{M})^{-2\alpha}$ is larger than 1 which proves Eqn. 16. $\qquad\Box$

References

1. Azouaoui, M., et al.: A systematic appraisal of side channel evaluation strategies. In: van der Merwe, T., Mitchell, C., Mehrnezhad, M. (eds.) SSR 2020. LNCS, vol. 12529, pp. 46–66. Springer, Cham (2020). https://doi.org/10.1007/978-3-030-64357-7_3

2. Benadjila, R., Prouff, E., Strullu, R., Cagli, E., Dumas, C.: Deep learning for side-channel analysis and introduction to ASCAD database. J. Crypt. Eng. **10**(2), 163–188 (2019). https://doi.org/10.1007/s13389-019-00220-8

3. Bronchain, O., Standaert, F.X.: Side-channel countermeasures' dissection. IACR Transactions on Cryptographic Hardware and Embedded Systems **2020**(2), 1–25 (2020). https://doi.org/10.13154/tches.v2020.i2.1-25, https://tches.iacr.org/index.php/TCHES/article/view/8542

4. Chari, S., Jutla, C.S., Rao, J.R., Rohatgi, P.: Towards sound approaches to counteract power-analysis attacks. In: Wiener, M. (ed.) CRYPTO 1999. LNCS, vol. 1666, pp. 398–412. Springer, Heidelberg (1999). https://doi.org/10.1007/3-540-48405-1_26

5. Cheng, F.: Generalization of Mrs. Gerber's lemma. Commun. Inf. Syst. **14**(2), 79–86 (2014). https://doi.org/10.4310/cis.2014.v14.n2.a1

6. Cover, T.M., Thomas, J.A.: Elements of information theory (2 ed.). Wiley (2006)

7. de Chérisey, E., Guilley, S., Rioul, O., Piantanida, P.: Best information is most successful. IACR Transactions on Cryptographic Hardware and Embedded Systems **2019**(2), 49–79 (2019). https://doi.org/10.13154/tches.v2019.i2.49-79, https://tches.iacr.org/index.php/TCHES/article/view/7385

8. Duc, A., Dziembowski, S., Faust, S.: Unifying leakage models: from probing attacks to noisy leakage. In: Nguyen, P.Q., Oswald, E. (eds.) EUROCRYPT 2014. LNCS, vol. 8441, pp. 423–440. Springer, Heidelberg (2014). https://doi.org/10.1007/978-3-642-55220-5_24

9. Duc, A., Faust, S., Standaert, F.-X.: Making masking security proofs concrete. In: Oswald, E., Fischlin, M. (eds.) EUROCRYPT 2015. LNCS, vol. 9056, pp. 401–429. Springer, Heidelberg (2015). https://doi.org/10.1007/978-3-662-46800-5_16

10. Duc, A., Faust, S., Standaert, F.-X.: Making masking security proofs concrete (or how to evaluate the security of any leaking device), extended version. J. Crypt. **32**(4), 1263–1297 (2018). https://doi.org/10.1007/s00145-018-9277-0

11. Dziembowski, S., Faust, S., Skorski, M.: Noisy leakage revisited. In: Oswald, E., Fischlin, M. (eds.) EUROCRYPT 2015. LNCS, vol. 9057, pp. 159–188. Springer, Heidelberg (2015). https://doi.org/10.1007/978-3-662-46803-6_6

12. Dziembowski, S., Faust, S., Skórski, M.: Optimal amplification of noisy leakages. In: Kushilevitz, E., Malkin, T. (eds.) TCC 2016. LNCS, vol. 9563, pp. 291–318. Springer, Heidelberg (2016). https://doi.org/10.1007/978-3-662-49099-0_11

13. Goubin, L., Patarin, J.: DES and differential power analysis the "duplication" method. In: Koç, Ç.K., Paar, C. (eds.) CHES 1999. LNCS, vol. 1717, pp. 158–172. Springer, Heidelberg (1999). https://doi.org/10.1007/3-540-48059-5_15

14. Ishai, Y., Sahai, A., Wagner, D.: Private circuits: securing hardware against probing attacks. In: Boneh, D. (ed.) CRYPTO 2003. LNCS, vol. 2729, pp. 463–481. Springer, Heidelberg (2003). https://doi.org/10.1007/978-3-540-45146-4_27

15. Ishai, Y., Sahai, A., Wagner, D.: Private circuits: securing hardware against probing attacks. In: Boneh, D. (ed.) CRYPTO 2003. LNCS, vol. 2729, pp. 463–481. Springer, Heidelberg (2003). https://doi.org/10.1007/978-3-540-45146-4_27

16. Ito, A., Ueno, R., Homma, N.: On the success rate of side-channel attacks on masked implementations: information-theoretical bounds and their practical usage. In: Yin, H., Stavrou, A., Cremers, C., Shi, E. (eds.) Proceedings of the 2022 ACM SIGSAC Conference on Computer and Communications Security, CCS 2022, Los Angeles, CA, USA, November 7–11, 2022. pp. 1521–1535. ACM (2022). https://doi.org/10.1145/3548606.3560579

17. Jog, V.S.: The entropy power inequality and Mrs. gerber's lemma for groups of order 2^n. IEEE Trans. Inf. Theory **60**(7), 3773–3786 (2014). https://doi.org/10.1109/TIT.2014.2317692

18. Liu, Y., Cheng, W., Guilley, S., Rioul, O.: On conditional alpha-information and its application to side-channel analysis. In: ITW, pp. 1–6. IEEE (2021)

19. Maghrebi, H., Portigliatti, T., Prouff, E.: Breaking cryptographic implementations using deep learning techniques. In: Carlet, C., Hasan, M.A., Saraswat, V. (eds.) SPACE 2016. LNCS, vol. 10076, pp. 3–26. Springer, Cham (2016). https://doi.org/10.1007/978-3-319-49445-6_1

20. Marshall, A.W., Olkin, I., Arnold, B.C.: Inequalities: theory of majorization and its applications. Springer Series in Statistics (1980)

21. Masure, L., Cristiani, V., Lecomte, M., Standaert, F.: Don't learn what you already know scheme-aware modeling for profiling side-channel analysis against masking. IACR Trans. Cryptogr. Hardw. Embed. Syst. **2023**(1), 32–59 (2023). https://doi.org/10.46586/tches.v2023.i1.32-59

22. Masure, L., Rioul, O., Standaert, F.X.: A nearly tight proof of Duc et al'.s conjectured security bound for masked implementations. In: Buhan, I., Schneider, T. (eds.) Smart Card Research and Advanced Applications, pp. 69–81. Springer International Publishing, Cham (2023). https://doi.org/10.1007/978-3-031-25319-5_4

23. Prest, T., Goudarzi, D., Martinelli, A., Passelègue, A.: Unifying leakage models on a rényi day. In: Boldyreva, A., Micciancio, D. (eds.) CRYPTO 2019. LNCS, vol. 11692, pp. 683–712. Springer, Cham (2019). https://doi.org/10.1007/978-3-030-26948-7_24

24. Prouff, E., Rivain, M.: Masking against side-channel attacks: a formal security proof. In: Johansson, T., Nguyen, P.Q. (eds.) EUROCRYPT 2013. LNCS, vol. 7881, pp. 142–159. Springer, Heidelberg (2013). https://doi.org/10.1007/978-3-642-38348-9_9

25. Rioul, O.: What is randomness? The interplay between alpha entropies, total variation and guessing. Phys. Sci. Forum **5**(1) (2022). https://doi.org/10.3390/psf2022005030, https://www.mdpi.com/2673-9984/5/1/30
26. Sason, I., Verdú, S.: Upper bounds on the relative entropy and Rényi divergence as a function of total variation distance for finite alphabets. In: 2015 IEEE Information Theory Workshop - Fall (ITW), Jeju Island, South Korea, October 11–15, 2015, pp. 214–218. IEEE (2015). https://doi.org/10.1109/ITWF.2015.7360766
27. Touchette, H.: Legendre-Fenchel transforms in a nutshell (2005). https://www.ise.ncsu.edu/fuzzy-neural/wp-content/uploads/sites/9/2019/01/or706-LF-transform-1.pdf
28. Veyrat-Charvillon, N., Gérard, B., Standaert, F.-X.: Soft analytical side-channel attacks. In: Sarkar, P., Iwata, T. (eds.) ASIACRYPT 2014. LNCS, vol. 8873, pp. 282–296. Springer, Heidelberg (2014). https://doi.org/10.1007/978-3-662-45611-8_15
29. Veyrat-Charvillon, N., Standaert, F.-X.: Adaptive chosen-message side-channel attacks. In: Zhou, J., Yung, M. (eds.) ACNS 2010. LNCS, vol. 6123, pp. 186–199. Springer, Heidelberg (2010). https://doi.org/10.1007/978-3-642-13708-2_12
30. Wyner, A.D., Ziv, J.: A theorem on the entropy of certain binary sequences and applications-I. IEEE Trans. Inf. Theory **19**, 769–772 (1973)

Improving Side-channel Leakage Assessment Using Pre-silicon Leakage Models

Dillibabu Shanmugam[✉] and Patrick Schaumont

Worcester Polytechnic Institute, Worcester, MA 01609, USA
{dshanmugam,pschaumont}@wpi.edu

Abstract. Side-channel leakage assessment is an essential tool in the security evaluation of new chip designs. Pre-silicon side-channel analysis tools have made significant progress in delivering assessment results early in the chip design flow. However, a gap remains with actual implementations where measurements are affected by noise and distortions. These measurement imperfections degrade the assessment of the physical prototype and may lead to false negatives. In this contribution, we present a transfer learning technique to improve the assessment of physical prototypes using pre-silicon side-channel leakage simulation of the same implementation. The noiseless simulation traces are used for initial profiling to train a convolutional neural network (CNN). The trained CNN is then used in the assessment of measured traces. We apply this idea to ASCON and XOODYAK, two different sponge-based cryptographic primitives proposed in the NIST Lightweight Crypto competition. The target platform is a software implementation on a RISC-V (RV32IMC) microcontroller realized using 180 nm CMOS technology. Side-channel leakage is first captured using gate-level power simulation and then measured from a chip prototype of the same design. We investigate different side-channel analysis strategies under simulated and measured scenarios and demonstrate that, in each case, machine-learning-based side-channel leakage assessment outperforms other profiled and non-profiled analysis. However, using the proposed transfer learning technique, we can improve the side-channel leakage assessment even further. With the proposed transfer learning technique, we need approximately 2.87 less measured traces compared to the previous best profiled attack. We conclude that the proposed transfer learning using pre-silicon leakage models can improve the side channel leakage assessment of post-silicon implementations.

Keywords: Transfer learning · ASCON · XOODYAK

1 Introduction

Side-channel leakage assessment, a critical step in the security evaluation of an IC, quantifies the amount of side-channel leakage from the implementation. There are multiple methodologies to characterize side-channel leakage of a cryptographic implementation [15]. However, all of them rely on data measurements.

E. B. Kavun and M. Pehl (Eds.): COSADE 2023, LNCS 13979, pp. 105–124, 2023.
https://doi.org/10.1007/978-3-031-29497-6_6

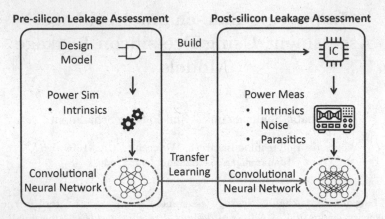

Fig. 1. Post-silicon leakage assessment can be improved with transfer learning from a pre-silicon leakage model.

This practical aspect of measurement requires engineering skills as well as insight into the cipher design, the target hardware technology, and the methodology of trace measurement. Practical side-channel measurement also faces challenges of reproducibility, because IC performance characteristics and power consumption are affected by voltage and temperature. For example, a side-channel campaign that gathers millions of traces takes days or even weeks to complete, requiring environmental controls on the test setup.

Pre-Silicon Side-Channel Leakage Assessment. During the design of a new IC, side-channel leakage assessment (SLA) can be directly implemented on the design descriptions of the hardware or the firmware [5]. A designer then uses simulation to create power traces for a design. Pre-silicon power simulation is noiseless and does not suffer from the imperfections suffered by physical measurement. In contrast to traditional SLA pre-silicon SLA is implemented in a white-box scenario with full knowledge of the design implementation details. Thus, pre-silicon SLA helps a designer to understand the weak parts of a design before committing it to silicon. In addition, pre-silicon SLA is able to support root-cause analysis of side-channel leakage to the single gate or the single instruction [12].

Improving Post-Silicon Side-Channel Leakage Assessment. In this contribution, we investigate how pre-silicon design knowledge can be applied to improve post-silicon SLA. We want to use the knowledge of simulated side-channel leakage properties on the evaluation of measured side-channel leakage. So far, this problem was studied only as a cross-device attack between different *physical* implementations [8,22]. Instead, we are using a portability threat model [16] from simulation to implementation. Architectural abstracts as a predictive leakage model were explored in PARAM [1] and ROSITA [19].

Figure 1 shows our strategy which makes use of deep learning. A pre-silicon leakage assessment uses simulated power traces to map design-intrinsic leakage properties into a CNN. The simulated traces are noiseless and without distortion. A post-silicon leakage assessment of the same design uses measured power traces to map design-intrinsic leakage properties to a threat model. Measured power traces may be corrupted by noise and measurement parasitics. Because of these distortions, the post-silicon CNN has a harder time to learn the intrinsic leakage properties of the design. To improve the post-silicon training, we apply a *transfer learning* technique, which carries over some of the properties of the pre-silicon CNN to the post-silicon CNN. Earlier work in transfer learning to support the portability threat model was presented by Thapar *et al.* for the case of cross-FPGA analysis [21], and by Paguada *et al.* as a generic toolbox for deep-learning based side-channel analysis [14]. We believe our work is the first to demonstrate the use of transfer learning techniques for SLA between the pre-silicon (simulated) and post-silicon (measured) environment.

Use Scenario. Since our proposed transfer learning for SLA assumes that both the design files and the physical implementation of a design are available, we motivate the practical meaning of this assumption. First, we observe that for new designs, the pre-silicon design phase always transitions into a post-silicon phase after tape-out. Hence, it is helpful to transfer the pre-silicon SLA results to the chip prototype evaluation, for the same reason pre-silicon test vectors are beneficial to test the prototype's functionality.

Second, intellectual property modules for cryptography can benefit from a mechanism to transfer side-channel leakage properties from design to implementation. In current practice, only high-level (algorithmic) leakage models, such as the Hamming Distance on a specific intermediate variable, capture the side-channel leakage properties of an intellectual property (IP) module. In contrast, our pre-silicon CNN is developed from gate-level power simulation and reflects the specific leakage characteristics in much greater detail. This model is, therefore, of practical use to the system integrator of the IP module.

Hence, we see the practical use of the proposed SLA for both in-house IC design and external IP modules. Finally, we emphasize that the proposed technique is an SLA method and *not* an attack method; the assumption that an attacker needs access to detailed design information is too impractical.

Analysis Targets. In our experiments with side-channel leakage assessment, we target Ascon [9] and Xoodyak [7], two sponge-based ciphers that have been proposed as part of the NIST Lightweight Crypto competition. In contrast to standard block-ciphers, only a limited number of side-channel analysis have been published on sponge-based ciphers.

- A Differential Power Analysis (DPA) on Ascon was demonstrated by Samwel on a Spartan-6 FPGA and required around 40K traces [18]. A machine-learning based attack by Ramazanpour on Ascon required around 24K traces on a Artix-7 FPGA [17].
- A simulated CPA on Xoodyak was demonstrated by Batina *et al.* using 30K traces [2].

In our work we substantially improve upon these earlier results and find a correct key *within a few hundred traces*. The authors of Xoodyak argue that the design has several built-in features against DPA, including slow absorption of the nonce, key rolling, and ratchetting of the internal state [7]. Our assessment only assumes that the XOODYAK design can be restarted, each time with a different controlled nonce.

We use a software implementation of ASCON and XOODYAK on RISC-V (RV32IMC) processor implemented in 180nm CMOS standard cells with on-chip memory. Because this chip is an in-house design, we have access to the netlist of the chip and we can establish a precise cycle-by-cycle correspondence between gate-level simulated (pre-silicon) and measured (post-silicon) power traces.

To evaluate the SLA on our ASCON and XOODYAK implementations, we use a combination of non-profiled and profiled techniques [15]. In addition to the proposed transfer-learning technique, we use signal-to-noise ratio (SNR) analysis, correlation power analysis (CPA), template attack (TA) and standard deep learning analysis with a CNN. We measure the efficiency of the SLA through the key rank or the measurements to disclosure (MTD) for a known key. We acknowledge that test vector leakage assessment (TVLA) is a popular side-channel leakage assessment technique, but we use an assessment that also shows how efficiently the key can be recovered (which is not possible using TVLA alone).

Contributions of the Paper. We perform side-channel leakage trace collection for ASCON and XOODYAK using power simulation (pre-silicon) and measurement (post-silicon). We then present a side-channel leakage assessment using SNR, CPA, TA and CNN. For each case, we compare the pre-silicon simulation result to the post-silicon measurement result. We present a novel transfer learning technique from the pre-silicon threat model to the post-silicon threat model to improve the deep learning assessment. We analyze the assessment complexity and time complexity for all of the above cases.

Organization of the Paper. In Sect. 2 we summarize the implementation details of ASCON and XOODYAK for the RISC-V processor. Section 3 presents a traditional side-channel vulnerability analysis of ASCON and XOODYAK in terms of SNR, CPA and TA. Section 4 describes the CNN assessment and our new transfer learning technique. Section 5 summarizes and analysis the experimental results. We then conclude the paper in Sect. 6.

2   Preliminaries

In this section, we define the metrics used for SLA, and we describe to test setup of pre- and post-silicon SLA.

2.1   Side-channel Leakage Assessment Metrics

We rely on the following well known metrics [15].

- The SNR for simulated SLA is defined as the ratio of the data variance to the algorithmic noise variance, whereas the SNR for measured SLA is defined as the ratio of the data variance to the algorithmic and measurement noise variance.

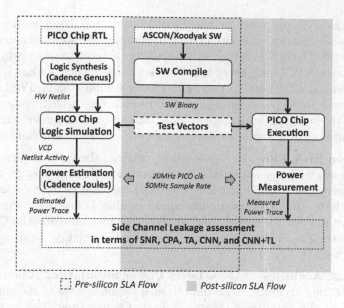

Fig. 2. Implementation flow and test set-up for Pre- and Post Silicon side channel leakage assessment.

- The *key rank* of a key $k \in K^m$ is defined as the number of keys with a probability greater than k [13]. In SLA, the key rank of the known key k_0 reflects how much information is disclosed under a given assessment method.
- MTD denotes the number of traces required to reduce the key rank of a known key k_0 to 1.
- Pearson's Correlation coefficient is used to correlate measured and hypothetically modelled power consumption (P_{msd} and P_{hyp}) and compute a correlation for each key k. In SLA, the MTD is reached when the known key k_0's correlation coefficient becomes maximal among all $k \in K^m$.

2.2   Target Platform for SLA

The transfer learning is based on the combination of pre-silicon simulation results with post-silicon measurements of the same design. The target is a small SoC based on the open-source PicoRV RISC-V core. The chip uses 180nm TSMC standard cells and includes 64 KB of on-chip RAM to hold variables. The instructions are fetched from an off-chip serial flash chip (QSPI). For this implementation, we have created an SLA flow that can analyze the implementation either in pre-silicon context starting from the design files, or else in post-silicon context starting from a prototype chip implementation (Fig. 2). Both flows lead to traces that can be compared regardless of their origin. The simulation and measurement setup use a common chip clock (20 MHz) and a common power sample rate clock (50 MHz).

Pre-Silicon SLA Flow. In a pre-silicon setting, power-based side-channel leakage is simulated on a post-synthesis netlist of the design. Initially, we write the target as a C program for the PicoRV core, and compile the program using `riscv32-unknown-elf-gcc` (v 10.2.0) compiler without optimization into a binary image. The design is then simulated at gate-level accuracy while collecting toggle traces (VCD) for every net. We then use Cadence Joules (RTL Power Solution, Version v20.11-s001_1) and a Skywater 130nm standard cell library to compute frame-based power estimation for the complete netlist using the toggle traces and the post-synthesis netlist. This simulation and power estimation is repeated for every test vector in the side-channel measurement campaign.

Post-Silicon SLA Flow. In a post-silicon setting, the same binary is run on the actual chip while we captured power-based side-channel leakage through a Lecroy Waverunner 7 oscilloscope. We filtered the side channel leakage signal using a 100 KHz - 30 MHz minicircuits bandpass filter before digitizing. To mark the region of interest for side-channel analysis, we instrumented the C program with GPIO triggers. The same method is used for simulation so that all traces can be aligned.

On the SLA Accuracy of Gate-Level Power Simulation. A power simulation is never fully accurate, so an important question relates to the similarity of simulated and measured power traces. Indeed, a power simulation must make a trade-off between the simulation accuracy and the simulation speed of a model. By increasing modeling detail, the estimated power consumption will be a better approximation of the physical power consumption, while the power simulation speed will drastically decrease. Side-channel leakage originates from *any* data-dependency in the power consumption. As we go down in abstraction level from RTL to transistor, each new abstraction level uncovers additional dependencies. For example, gate-level power models can capture gate drive strength, static power leakage, and IR-drop effects, all of which are invisible at the RTL power model yet contribute data-dependent power dissipation. We rely on gate-level power modeling but accept that some power details, such as parasitic coupling, will be ignored by the simulation. At the time of writing, transistor-level power simulation of a complete cryptographic side-channel assessment cannot yet be completed using a reasonable amount of design power [20].

3   Traditional Side-Channel Vulnerability Analysis

In this section, we capture the SLA of Ascon and Xoodyak using common side-channel leakage assessment tools. We use the analysis of the SNR to establish the leakage point of interest for each target. Then, we perform a CPA and a TA.

3.1   Results Summary

Table 1 summarizes the results for *all* assessment techniques investigated in this contribution, including a non-profiled technique (CPA) and several profiled techniques (TA, CNN). For each of Ascon and Xoodyak, we analyze three cases: SLA using simulated traces, SLA using measured traces, and SLA with the proposed transfer learning technique (TL). We will elaborate on individual result entries in the following subsections.

Table 1. Assessment using MTD metric for all targets. The number of traces shown is the *average* needed to retrieve a key byte. For profiled attacks, the number of traces used for profiling are listed separately.

Primitive	SLA flow	**CPA**	**TA**		**CNN**	
		MTD	Profiling (x 1,000)	MTD	Profiling (x 1,000)	MTD
ASCON	Simulated	8	9	2	9	2
	Measured	2,000	90	573	90	500
	TL	–	–	–	19	176
Xoodyak	Simulated	91	19	84	19	60
	Measured	700k	90	520	90	490
	TL	–	–	–	60	170

3.2   Traditional SLA on ASCON

Ascon ASCON-128 is an authenticated-encryption with associated-data primitive which is selected as a finalist in the NIST Lightweight Cryptography competition [10]. ASCON-128 is a duplex-sponge-based construction with four phases of operation: initialization, associated data, plaintext/ciphertext, and finalization. All phases use the same permutation function which includes a constant addition, a substitution layer, and a linear layer. ASCON-128 has 320 bits of state, divided into five double words that hold the 64-bit initialization vector (X_0), the 128-bit key (X_1, X_2) and the 128-bit nonce (X_3, X_4) respectively.

In ASCON's SLA we aim to demonstrate that the 128-bit key can be recovered at a given number of traces. The controlled variable, required to drive differential power analysis, is the nonce (X_3, X_4). We focus on the non-linear operations in the S-box of ASCON that compute X_1 and X_4, as expressed in the following Boolean equations. In these equations, the nonce is loaded in (X_3, X_4) and the key is loaded in (X_1, X_2).

$$X_4 = (X_4 \oplus X_3) \oplus ((255 \oplus (X_0 \oplus X_4)) \& X_1)$$
$$X_1 = ((X_1 \oplus ((255 \oplus (X_2 \oplus X_1)) \& X_3)) \qquad (1)$$
$$\oplus ((X_0 \oplus X_4) \oplus ((255 \oplus X_1) \& (X_2 \oplus X_1))))$$

The target implementation of ASCON is an 8-bit reference implementation in software. Listing 1.1 shows the assembly code to compute X_4 as a byte-wise operation. The point where key and control inputs merge is sensitive to side-channel leakage. The **and** operation on line 16 is the first line where that happens. Subsequent operations, such as on line 18 and 20, are potential targets as well. To understand which of these operations is the best candidate to mount a CPA, we perform SNR analysis on 500 simulated traces (Fig. 3, top) [15]. This analysis shows that the store instruction contributes a greater data-dependent power variation and, therefore, is the proper target for the side-channel leakage assessment.

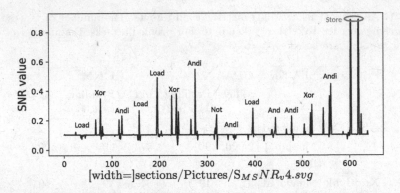

[width=]sections/Pictures/S$_{MS}NR_v$4.svg

Fig. 3. SNR Analysis of X_4: (top) SNR on 500 simulated traces to identify leaky instructions (bottom) SNR on 2K simulated traces (black) and 200K measured traces (grey) to estimate illustrate by practical measurement. (Color figure online)

Ascon SNR Analysis. The SNR analysis of Fig. 3, top, demonstrates an important major advantage of simulation-based traces, namely the absence of measurement noise. Figure 3, bottom, compares the SNR of 2K simulated traces to the SNR of 200K measured traces. Both the measured and simulated traces are aligned by making use of a GPIO trigger in the real and simulated Ascon software. The range of the X axis is roughly equivalent to the execution of Listing 1. The X axis spans 640 sample points, which corresponds to 12.8 μs or 256 cycles. The simulated SNR shows two sharp peaks corresponding to the memory-store operation (Fig. 3, top). However, the SNR on measured traces is much noisier and shows leakage over the last 64 samples of the curve. We attribute these extra leaky points to measurement noise, trigger signal jitter, and possibly an unexplained effect from the off-chip QSPI flash.

Ascon Correlation Power Analysis. Fig. 4 shows the outcome of CPA on Ascon for both a simulated assessment (black) and a measured assessment (grey). Both cases converge at the same key value, although the simulated CPA requires only 8 traces while the measured CPA needs 2,000 traces (Table 1).

The power model of the CPA is the Hamming Weight of X_4, whose update depends on both the lower half of the secret key $K1$ and the controlled nonce. Specifically, with i representing the test vector index, and j denoting the key byte index 0 to 7, we find the following power model.

$$X_k^{i,j} = (N2^{i,j} \oplus N1^{i,j}) \oplus ((255 \oplus (IV^{i,j} \oplus N2^{i,j}))\&K1_k^{i,j})$$
$$P_{hyp} = HW[(X_k^{i,j})] \tag{2}$$

The correlation of the power model with the power traces then leads to the value of $K1$. After $K1$ is found, its value is used to mount a CPA on the value of X_1 which combines both the upper half $K2$ and the lower half $K1$ of the secret key. This leads to the value of $K2$.

Listing 1.1. Portion of the SBOX computation of ASCON. Instructions highlighted in blue are potential targets for CPA.

```
1   lui     a5,0x30005
2   addi    a5,a5,8
3   li      a4,1
4   sw      a4,0(a5)        // GPIO trigger up
5   lbu     a4,-52(s0)
6   lbu     a5,-60(s0)
7   xor     a5,a5,a4        // a4 <- X3^X4
8   andi    a4,a5,255
9   lbu     a3,-28(s0)
10  lbu     a5,-52(s0)
11  xor     a5,a5,a3        // a5 <- (X4^X0)
12  andi    a5,a5,255
13  not     a5,a5           // a5 <- (255^(X4^X0))
14  andi    a3,a5,25
15  lbu     a5,-36(s0)
16  and     a5,a5,a3        // a5 <- (255^(X4^X0))&X1
17  andi    a5,a5,255
18  xor     a5,a5,a4        // a5 <- (X3^X4)^(255^(X4^X0))&X1
19  andi    a5,a5,255
20  sb      a5,-52(s0)      // store X4
21  lui     a5,0x3000
22  addi    a5,a5,8
23  sw      zero,0(a5)      // GPIO trigger down
```

Ascon Template Attack. A template attack is a well known profiled attack [6]. It uses a profiling phase to compute a template, a set of probability distributions that describe how the power traces vary for many different keys. Then, in the testing phase, it estimates the probability distribution of the target and finds the best matching distribution from the template. This leads to the unknown key. The template is computed over a limited number of point of interest (POI) in the trace. In our ASCON Template Attack, we select 15 POIs among 640 possible trace points. We build the profile on the Hamming Weight of X_4, computing the mean and covariance matrix for each Hamming Weight Value. Because of the profiling phase, a template attack can outperform a CPA. Table 1 demonstrates that the ASCON key is extracted using just 2 simulated power traces, or 573 measured power traces.

3.3   Traditional SLA on XOODYAK

XOODYAK is an authenticated-encryption with associated-data primitive which is also selected as a finalist in the NIST Lightweight Cryptography Competition [7]. Like ASCON, XOODYAK is based on duplex-sponge construction which allows its use in multiple symmetric-key applications. The XOODYAK design is inspired by the KECCAK round permutation. The assessment target in XOODYAK is the θ function which adds the key K, the nonce N and a counter C as $X = K \oplus N \oplus C$. In this expression, the nonce and the counter are the controlled variables. The assessment of XOODYAK is harder than that of ASCON for two reasons. First, the

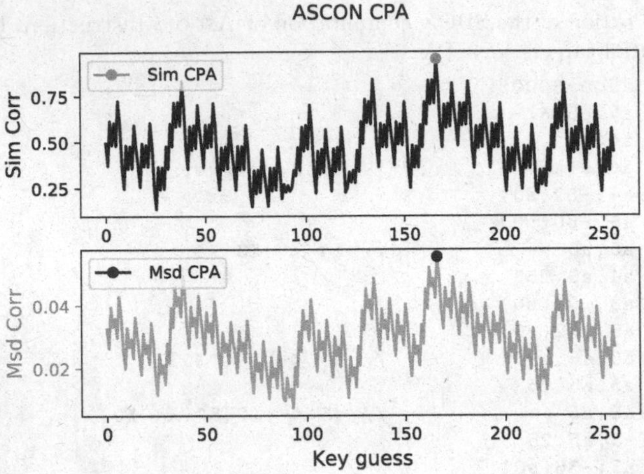

Fig. 4. Ascon: Correlation Power Analysis on simulated (black) and measured (grey) traces. (Color figure online)

XOR operation which combines the controlled variables with the key is linear. Since $A \oplus B = \bar{A} \oplus \bar{B}$, this leads to so-called ghost-peaks of equally-likely keys in the assessment [4]. Second, our specific implementation of Xoodyak is implemented on a 32-bit wordlength which combines 4 different key bytes in a single 32-bit RISCV instruction. Hence, the Xoodyak traces will have a higher level of algorithmic noise. Listing 2 shows the relevant portion of the Xoodyak implementation under consideration for SLA. The xor operation on line 7 is a potential target, as well as the dependent xor on line 9 and the store-word instruction on line 10.

Xoodyak SNR Analysis. Because a single execution of Listing 2 computes on four different key bytes, one can compute four different SNR curves for a single set of power traces. Figure 5a shows the SNR on 10K simulated traces. Its X-axis corresponds roughly to the execution of Listing 2, and we find that leakage is concentrated in a few power samples. Similar to the analysis on Ascon, we find the store-word instruction to be a dominant contributor to data-dependent power dissipation. The same SNR curve is also computed on 1500K measured traces as shown in Fig. 5b. Using a common GPIO trigger, we are able to align the SNR analysis of the simulated traces to the measured traces. Because of the high level of algorithmic noise, the resulting SNR is extremely noisy. We mark the last 100 samples of the measurement window as containing leaky samples in SLA.

Xoodyak Correlation Power Analysis. Xoodyak's CPA uses a Hamming Weight power model on $P_x^{i,j}$, where x denotes a word index range from 0 to 3, i represents the test vector, and j denotes the key byte index range from 0 to 3. $P_x^{i,j}$, depends on the lower half of the secret key $K_x^{i,j}$, the controlled nonce $N_x^{i,j}$ and counter value $C_x^{i,j}$. We find the following power model.

Listing 1.2. Portion of the θ computation of XOODYAK. Instructions highlighted in blue are potential targets for CPA.

```
1   lui    a5,0x3000
2   addi   a5,a5,8
3   li     a4,1
4   sw     a4,0(a5)          // GPIO trigger up
5   lw     a4,-24(s0)
6   lw     a5,-20(s0)
7   xor    a5,a5,a4          // a5 <- K[0:3]^N[0:3]
8   lw     a4,-28(s0)
9   xor    a5,a5,a4          // a5 <- K[0:3]^N[0:3]^C[0:3]
10  sw     a5,-24(s0)        // store X
11  lui    a5,0x3000
12  addi   a5,a5,8
13  sw     zero,0(a5)        // GPIO trigger down
```

$$HW[P_x^{i,j}] = HW[K_x^{i,j} \oplus N_x^{i,j} \oplus C_x^{i,j}] \tag{3}$$

Correlating the power model and the power traces yields the subkey of K_0. Figure 6 shows a correlation plot of the XOODYAK CPA. Two peaks are found, one on the true key byte (253) and one on the complementary key byte (2). Both the simulated and measured correlation plot are similar, even though the measured plot requires 700K traces due to the noisy SNR.

Xoodyak Template Attack. The template attack on XOODYAK proceeds as on ASCON, and builds the template on the Hamming Weight of the θ function output. Table 1 shows that the key is extracted on 84 simulated power traces or 520 measured power traces.

4 Deep Learning Assisted Side Channel Analysis

We now develop the transfer learning technique as an extension of deep learning based side-channel vulnerability analysis.

4.1 Deep Learning SLA on ASCON

Ascon CNN Development. The network architecture and hyperparameter selection play an important role in successful adversarial threat modeling [16]. The CNN for a single ASCON keybyte consists of a feature extractor and a 256-class classifier. The input to the CNN is a window of 64 power samples, selected through the SNR analysis of Fig. 3, bottom. A convolutional layer extracts specific features, similar to POIs, from the power samples. Next, the dense layers map the variation within and across different traces into a set of 256 probabilities. Batch normalization transforms the output of a previous layer by subtracting the batch mean and dividing by the batch standard deviation. Dropouts are used to randomly turn off a percentage of the network's neurons in order to

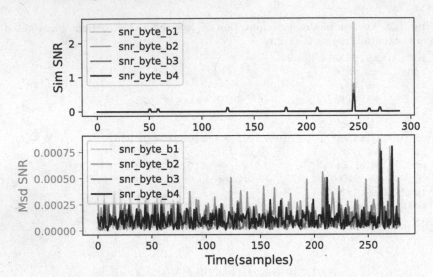

Fig. 5. XOODYAK: (a) SNR on 10K simulated traces (b) SNR on 1500K measured traces

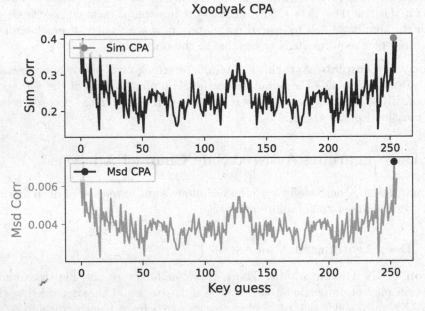

Fig. 6. XOODYAK: Correlation Power Analysis on simulated (black) and measured (grey) traces. (Color figure online)

improve the model's learning. Figure 7 shows our network and its hyperparameters. We adopted the ASCAD network [3] and optimized it for ASCON using random search over the hyperparameters provided in Table 2. The resulting sim-

Table 2. Hyperparameter search space for ASCON CNN. We selected the best hyperparameter (fit) through exhaustive search of the search space.

Hyperparameter	Ranges		
	Min	Max	Fit
Batch size	50	200	50
Convolution layers	1	5	1
Kernel size	1	11	3
Stride	1	4	1
Dense layers	1	3	2
Neurons	10	256	64
Learning rate	0.00001	0.001	0.001
Epochs	50	500	200
Drop out	10%	30%	30%
	Options		Fit
Pooling type	(Average,Max)		Average
Optimizer	(Adam, RMSprop)		Adam
Activation function	(ReLU,SeLU)		ReLU

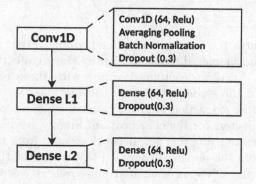

Fig. 7. ASCON: Convolutional Neural Network architecture for adversarial threat model of simulated and measured traces

ulated model has an accuracy of 94%, whereas the measured model and transfer learning model are close to each other (82% and 81% respectively).

Ascon Transfer Learning. We now apply transfer learning and demonstrate a reduction in learning time as well as in assessment effort. The idea is to transfer a part of the pre-silicon threat model to the post-silicon threat model. Post-silicon traces are noisy, which means that a large amount of traces are needed to learn the threat model at a high learning cost. Pre-silicon simulations are slow, but the pre-silicon traces are noiseless and a threat model can be learned from them quickly using much fewer traces.

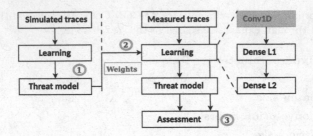

Fig. 8. Transfer Learning: (1) training from simulated traces, (2) transfer learning on measured traces keeping the convolutional layer frozen, and (3) assessment using the transfer-learned CNN.

Table 3. Three test cases are investigated over simulated and transfer learning models. For each test case, corresponding simulated model weights are used for transfer learning

Primitive	SLA of Sbox X_4	Simulated			Transfer		
		Profiling (x 1,000)	MTD	Accuracy	Profiling (x 1,000)	MTD	Accuracy
ASCON	Test case_1	5	11	94%	19	191	80%
	Test case_2	10	2	94%	40	176	81%
	Test case_3	20	2	94%	60	162	82%

Figure 8 illustrates the proposed transfer learning. First, we perform deep learning SCA on the simulated traces to identify the architecture, hyperparameters and weights. Next, we continue learning with these parameters on the measured traces. In the second phase, the convolutional layer remains frozen. This keeps the feature extraction layer unchanged, while the other layers maintain trainable parameters for the classification. Finally, we perform assessment on the measured traces using this new network created from transfer learning.

Table 3 represents the number of profiled traces against the number of test traces (MTD) for the CNN on simulated and transfer learning on measured traces. Here, three test cases are used to demonstrate different trade-offs between profile learning and testing. In the Table 4, we calculated the number of test traces against the number of profiled traces for measured traces. Using transfer

Table 4. On average, transfer learning model requires 1.97 times less profiling traces and 2.85 times less testing traces compare to measured learning model

Primitive	SLA of Sbox X_4	Measured		
		Profiling (x 1,000)	MTD	Accuracy
ASCON	Test case_1	45	521	80%
	Test case_2	90	491	82%
	Test case_3	100	490	82%

Table 5. Two test cases are investigated over simulated and transfer learning models. For each test case, corresponding simulated model weights are used for transfer learning

Primitive	SLA of Linear(θ)	Simulated			Transfer		
		Profiling (x 1,000)	MTD	Accuracy	Profiling (x 1,000)	MTD	Accuracy
Xoodyak	Test case_1	18	56	93%	45	160	80%
	Test case_2	19	60	94%	60	170	81%

Table 6. On average, transfer learning model requires 2.87 times less testing traces compare to measured learning model

Primitive	SLA of Linear (θ)	Measured		
		Profiling (x 1,000)	MTD	Accuracy
Xoodyak	Test case_1	80	486	81%
	Test case_2	90	494	83%

learning, we obtain faster learning because we need to process fewer traces. Moreover, we need fewer test traces to assess the design. Overall, the accuracy for simulated, transfer and measured are 94%, 81% and 82% respectively.

Figure 9 displays 16 subplots corresponding to the 16 key bytes of ASCON. Each subplot represents convergence of the key rank of the measured and transfer learning model. A major rank comparison between the transfer and the measured learning model in the convergence region shows that the model on measured traces lags by 42 ranks on average. This indicates that transfer learning models provide a gain of 5 to 6 bits in guessing entropy.

4.2 Deep Learning SLA on Xoodyak

Xoodyak CNN development We adopted the same architecture as in Fig. 7 with the following changes. First, all layers use batch normalization and dropout (0.3). Second, the learning rate is fine-tuned to 0.0001.

Xoodyak Transfer Learning. Table 5 compares the CNN performance for simulated and transfer learning on measured traces. From Table 6, it is clear that, transfer learning model (TL) requires 1.61 and 2.88 times less profile and test traces compare to measured model (CNN). Once again, transfer learning achieves faster learning and shorter evaluation.

Similar to ASCON, transfer learning model of Xoodyak converge 68 rank faster compare to measured model as given in Fig. 10.

5 Analysis of Results

Finally, we compare the performance of the proposed transfer learning technique to classic SLA as well as deep learning SLA.

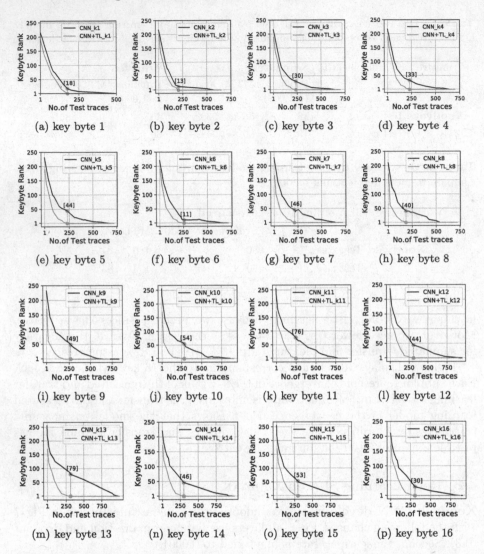

Fig. 9. The red color highlighted in the subplots indicates that there is a difference in key byte rank between measured(CNN) and transfer(CNN+TL), when CNN+TL converges to rank zero. (Color figure online)

Assessment Complexity. We summarize the experiments on transfer learning with simulated traces as follows. First, it is clear that the proposed transfer learning method outperforms all other assessment we tried. Table 7 expresses the relative assessment gain over CPA. This is the ratio of the number of traces required to reveal a key byte using a chosen assessment over the number of traces required using CPA. For the transfer learning method, the gain goes up to 4,100x for a *noisy* target. This is not unexpected since noisy traces are a

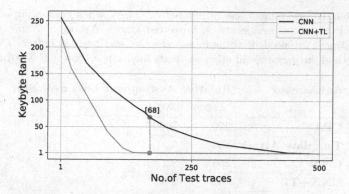

Fig. 10. XOODYAK : Key rank converge of transfer learning (CNN+TL) is 68 ranks faster than measured (CNN)

Table 7. Relative Assessment gain in number of traces, using Correlation Power Analysis as the reference. A Gain of N means that N times more traces are needed in CPA, so higher is better. The transfer learning method outperforms the best template attack as well as the measurement-only deep learning method.

Assessment	Relative Assessment Gain on CPA	
	ASCON	XOODYAK
CPA	1	1
Template Attack	3.4	1,300
CNN	4	1,400
CNN+TL	11.4	4,100

harder training target for the deep learning threat model. Second, it is clear that the proposed transfer learning method is much less sensitive to distortions from the measurement setup than any other attack. Table 8 expresses the relative assessment loss for each assessment, which is measured as the increase in number of traces for an attack when moving from simulated traces to measured traces. The transfer learning method shows the lowest relative assessment loss among all assessments.

Time Complexity. There are two dimensions in the analysis of time complexity of the proposed technique. One dimension quantifies the difference between simulating a power trace, versus capturing a power trace from a real chip. The second dimension quantifies the cost of SLA on the collected power traces. We perform all simulation and SLA experiments on an Intel Xeon Gold 6248 server. The power simulation for one power trace of ASCON took approximately 5 min, which can be shortened to 30 s per simulated trace by running 10 parallel simulation threads. In contrast, capturing a trace took form a real chip took 0.15 s, so that the measurement of traces is 200 times faster than their gate-level simulation. Hence, we confirm that power simulation time remains a dominant portion

Table 8. Relative assessment loss in number of traces, when comparing assessments on simulated traces to assessments on measured traces. A Loss of N means that N times more traces are needed on the measurements, and lower is better. The transfer learning method outperforms all other methods for both ASCON and XOODYAK.

Assessment	Relative Assessment Loss over Sim	
	ASCON	XOODYAK
CPA	250	7600
Template Attack	136	6.2
CNN	250	8.2
CNN+TL	88	2.8

Table 9. Time complexity of all side-channel vulnerability analysis for ASCON. # = number of traces needed, AT = Attack Time, LT = Learning Time.

Primitive	SLA flow	CPA		TA			CNN		
		#	AT	#	LT	AT	#	LT	AT
ASCON	Simulated	8	< 1m	9K	10m	5m	9K	50m	10m
	Measured	2k	< 10m	90K	30m	20m	90K	6hr	20m
	TL	–	–	–	–	–	19K	60m	15m

in data collection. Table 9 shows the time complexity of CPA, TA and CNN. Each experiment lists the number of traces required and the associated learning time and attack time. The assessment part of the transfer learning method is competitive with traditional (measurement-based) CNN, as it completes the task in 60+50 min as opposed to 6 h. XOODYAK has a similar pattern of time complexity. Our machine learning experiments are running on a traditional CPU configuration (without GPU), which makes them relatively slow compared to some published results [11].

6   Conclusion

This work shows that transfer learning based side channel analysis on post-silicon using a pre-silicon threat model. The proposed technique evaluates the design by 2.87 times fewer traces compared to the Naive CNN technique. We are considering further improvements to our method, such as using techniques to understand and eliminate noise and distortions on measured traces. This material is based upon work supported by the National Science Foundation under Grant No. 1931639.

References

1. Arsath K F, M., Ganesan, V., Bodduna, R., Rebeiro, C.: PARAM: a microprocessor hardened for power side-channel attack resistance. In: 2020 IEEE International Symposium on Hardware Oriented Security and Trust (HOST), pp. 23–34 (2020). https://doi.org/10.1109/HOST45689.2020.9300263
2. Batina, L., et al.: Side-Channel evaluation report on implementations of several NIST LWC finalists (August 2022). https://hdl.handle.net/2066/253567
3. Benadjila, R., Prouff, E., Strullu, R., Cagli, E., Dumas, C.: Deep learning for side-channel analysis and introduction to ASCAD database. J. Crypt. Eng. **10**(2), 163–188 (2020)
4. Brier, E., Clavier, C., Olivier, F.: Correlation power analysis with a leakage model. In: Joye, M., Quisquater, J.-J. (eds.) CHES 2004. LNCS, vol. 3156, pp. 16–29. Springer, Heidelberg (2004). https://doi.org/10.1007/978-3-540-28632-5_2
5. Buhan, I., Batina, L., Yarom, Y., Schaumont, P.: SoK: design tools for side-channel-aware implementations. In: Suga, Y., Sakurai, K., Ding, X., Sako, K. (eds.) ASIA CCS 2022: ACM Asia Conference on Computer and Communications Security, Nagasaki, Japan, 30 May 2022–3 June 2022, pp. 756–770. ACM (2022). https://doi.org/10.1145/3488932.3517415
6. Chari, S., Rao, J.R., Rohatgi, P.: Template attacks. In: Kaliski, B.S., Koç, K., Paar, C. (eds.) CHES 2002. LNCS, vol. 2523, pp. 13–28. Springer, Heidelberg (2003). https://doi.org/10.1007/3-540-36400-5_3
7. Daemen, J., Hoffert, S., Peeters, M., Van Assche, G., Van Keer, R.: Xoodyak, a Lightweight Cryptographic Scheme. IACR Transactions on Symmetric Cryptology, pp. 60–87 (2020)
8. Das, D., Golder, A., Danial, J., Ghosh, S., Raychowdhury, A., Sen, S.: X-DeepSCA: cross-device deep learning side channel attack. In: Proceedings of the 56th Annual Design Automation Conference 2019, DAC 2019, Las Vegas, NV, USA, June 02–06, 2019, p. 134. ACM (2019). https://doi.org/10.1145/3316781.3317934
9. Dobraunig, C., Eichlseder, M., Mendel, F., Schläffer, M.: Ascon v1.2. Submission to Round 1 of the NIST lightweight cryptography project (2019). https://csrc.nist.gov/CSRC/media/Projects/Lightweight-Cryptography/documents/round-1/spec-doc/ascon-spec.pdf
10. Gross, H., Wenger, E., Dobraunig, C., Ehrenhöfer, C.: Suit up!-made-to-measure hardware implementations of ASCON. In: 2015 Euromicro Conference on Digital System Design, pp. 645–652. IEEE (2015)
11. Ito, A., Saito, K., Ueno, R., Homma, N.: Imbalanced data problems in deep learning-based side-channel attacks: analysis and solution. IEEE Trans. Inf. Forensics Secur. **16**, 3790–3802 (2021)
12. Kiaei, P., Schaumont, P.: SoC Root Canal! Root cause analysis of power side-channel leakage in system-on-chip designs. IACR Trans. Cryptogr. Hardw. Embed. Syst. **2022**(4), 751–773 (2022). https://doi.org/10.46586/tches.v2022.i4.751-773
13. Martin, D.P., Martinoli, M.: A note on key rank. Cryptology ePrint Archive, Paper 2018/614 (2018). https://eprint.iacr.org/2018/614
14. Paguada, S., Batina, L., Buhan, I., Armendariz, I.: Playing with blocks: toward re-usable deep learning models for side-channel profiled attacks. IEEE Trans. Inf. Forensics Secur. **17**, 2835–2847 (2022). https://doi.org/10.1109/TIFS.2022.3196273
15. Papagiannopoulos, K., Glamocanin, O., Azouaoui, M., Ros, D., Regazzoni, F., Stojilovic, M.: The side-channel metric cheat sheet. IACR Cryptol. ePrint Arch, p. 253 (2022). https://eprint.iacr.org/2022/253

16. Picek, S., Perin, G., Mariot, L., Wu, L., Batina, L.: SoK: deep learning-based physical side-channel analysis. IACR Cryptol. ePrint Arch, p. 1092 (2021). https://eprint.iacr.org/2021/1092

17. Ramezanpour, K., Abdulgadir, A., Diehl, W., Kaps, J.P., Ampadu, P.: Active and passive side-channel key recovery attacks on ASCON. In: Proceedings of the NIST Lightweight Cryptogr. Workshop, pp. 1–27 (2020)

18. Samwel, N., Daemen, J.: DPA on hardware implementations of Ascon and Keyak. In: Proceedings of the Computing Frontiers Conference, pp. 415–424 (2017)

19. Shelton, M.A., Chmielewski, L., Samwel, N., Wagner, M., Batina, L., Yarom, Y.: Rosita++: automatic higher-order leakage elimination from cryptographic code. In: Proceedings of the 2021 ACM SIGSAC Conference on Computer and Communications Security, pp. 685–699. CCS 2021, Association for Computing Machinery, New York, NY, USA (2021). https://doi.org/10.1145/3460120.3485380

20. Šijačić, D., Balasch, J., Yang, B., Ghosh, S., Verbauwhede, I.: Towards efficient and automated side-channel evaluations at design time. J. Crypt. Eng. **10**(4), 305–319 (2020). https://doi.org/10.1007/s13389-020-00233-8

21. Thapar, D., Alam, M., Mukhopadhyay, D.: Deep learning assisted cross-family profiled side-channel attacks using transfer learning. In: 22nd International Symposium on Quality Electronic Design, ISQED 2021, Santa Clara, CA, USA, April 7–9, 2021, pp. 178–185. IEEE (2021). https://doi.org/10.1109/ISQED51717.2021.9424254

22. Wang, H., Brisfors, M., Forsmark, S., Dubrova, E.: How diversity affects deep-learning side-channel attacks. In: Nurmi, J., Ellervee, P., Halonen, K., Röning, J. (eds.) 2019 IEEE Nordic Circuits and Systems Conference, NORCAS 2019: NORCHIP and International Symposium of System-on-Chip (SoC), Helsinki, Finland, October 29–30, 2019, pp. 1–7. IEEE (2019). https://doi.org/10.1109/NORCHIP.2019.8906945

Attacks on PQC and Countermeasures

Fast First-Order Masked NTTRU

Daniel Heinz[1,2]([✉]) and Gabi Dreo Rodosek[1]

[1] Research Institute CODE, Universität der Bundeswehr München,
85577 Neubiberg, Germany
{Daniel.Heinz,Gabi.Dreo}@unibw.de
[2] Infineon Technologies AG, Am Campeon 1-15, 85579 Neubiberg, Germany

Abstract. Even though Kyber is the lattice-based KEM selected for standardization by NIST, NTRU and its variants are still of great relevance to several practical applications. This is why we want to shed light on the side-channel resilience of NTTRU, which is a very fast variant of NTRU designed to use the Number-Theoretic Transform. It outperforms NTRU-HRSS significantly in an unprotected context, which raises the question of whether this performance advantage holds when side-channel attacks have to be considered.

To answer that, we present the first masked implementation of NTTRU optimized for first-order. To achieve a fast performance, we present a table-based approach for the masked sampler and the modulus conversion, similar to the A2B conversion proposed by Debraize in 2012. The modulus conversion is also applicable to other NTRU variants. Due to its usage in NTTRU, we present a fully first-order masked SHA512 implementation based on A2B and B2A conversions. We come to the conclusion that performance is heavily impacted by the SHA2 family in masked implementations and strongly encourage the employment of SHA3 in these cases. This result is also of relevance for the 90s/AES variants of the NIST standardization candidates Kyber and Dilithium.

We achieve a performance of the NTTRU-SHA3 of around 3.1 million cycles on the ARM Cortex M4. Finally, we show that our proposed methods provide side-channel security in practice by employing the well established TVLA methodology.

Keywords: Lattice-based cryptography · NTRU · NTTRU · DPA · Countermeasure · Masking · ARM Cortex M4

1 Introduction

In recent years, post-quantum cryptography has seen increased research attention as classic public-key cryptographic solutions could be broken by advanced quantum computers using Shor's algorithm [1]. During the NIST standardization process [2], several quantum-resistant schemes have been proposed to make secured key exchanges possible even when large-scale quantum computers become available. The schemes are based on different mathematical problems. Among the lattice-based candidates, Kyber [3], Saber [4], and NTRU [5,6] were

E. B. Kavun and M. Pehl (Eds.): COSADE 2023, LNCS 13979, pp. 127–148, 2023.
https://doi.org/10.1007/978-3-031-29497-6_7

part of the final round of the NIST standardization process. For instance, NTRU is a cryptosystem that makes use of structured lattices to exchange keys in a 'quantum secure' way. An advantage of schemes based on structured lattices are their comparatively small key sizes. Additionally, encryption and decryption can often be performed faster than in traditional RSA or EC-based schemes [7].

Despite ciphertext, public key, and secret key being almost of the same size as in Kyber, in general, NTRU-based schemes perform better in terms of speed during encryption and decryption. Additionally, NTRU-based ciphertexts only consist of one element which is of advantage when a zero-knowledge proof of the honest generation of the ciphertext is needed [7]. Even though NTRU and its variants were not standardized, NTRU is still a very important cryptosystem. An important example is the OpenSSH [8] program that includes an implementation of NTRUprime since April 2022. Additionally, Google has recently announced to use NTRU-HRSS for their internal encryption-in-transit protocol ALTS [9]. This shows that alternatives to the NIST competition are of great relevance for practical applications.

In lattice-based algorithms, the speed of polynomial multiplication is one of the bottlenecks. Depending on the modulus of the underlying algebraic ring, various schemes tackle this issue differently. The key encapsulation mechanism (KEM) Saber [4], for instance, makes use of a combination of Toom-Cook, school-book, and Karatsuba multiplication whereas Kyber's parameter set [3] allows fast multiplication using the Number-Theoretic Transform (NTT).

The NTT approach for polynomial multiplication is especially fast in dimensions that are a power of two. Kyber solves this issue by using a matrix/vector structure with multiple polynomials of dimension 2^8. To obtain a security level of 128 bits, the dimension of the ring is, according to current security analysis, required to be around 700 to 800 [10]. NTRU-based schemes do not use a matrix/vector structure and, thus, secret key, public key and ciphertext only consist of one polynomial. As there exists no power of two in the 128 bit security range between 700 and 800, the most efficient NTT technique is not applicable for NTRU with this security parameter. This might be the reason why an NTRU-based scheme that makes use of NTTs was not part of the NIST standardization process. The authors of [7] propose a specific parameter set to use the NTT approach in the NTRU scheme to gain additional performance gains and call their scheme NTTRU. The authors consider it at least as secure as the corresponding NTRU-HRSS variant that was part of the third round of the NIST competition. Therefore, it is worth taking a closer look at the so-called NTTRU.

Due to its good performance, NTTRU is a potential candidate to be used on embedded devices. Naturally, embedded devices are exposed to a large number of physical attacks such as fault attacks or side-channel attacks as first demonstrated by Kocher et al. [11]. Thus, it is crucial to secure cryptographic schemes against these threats. Correlation between power consumption or electromagnetic radiation and secret intermediate values can be counteracted by the so-called masking countermeasure where each sensitive variable is split into several randomized shares. Each share is then processed separately from a secret intermediate value. Some of the PQC lattice-based candidates have already seen increased research attention in this regard. For Kyber [12–14] and Saber [15, 16] first- and higher-order masked implementations exist. Recently, a masked higher-order implementation of NTRU-HRSS has been proposed [17]. However, no first-order optimized version of NTRU has been published. We aim at closing the gap with our work.

Contributions. In this work, we present the first first-order masked implementation of NTTRU. We employ the first-order masking technique in the complete scheme. Hereby, we propose a new table-based method for a first-order secured modulus conversion. We emphasize that this technique is potentially applicable to all other NTRU variants. Subsequently, we present a first-order masked implementation of the SHA2-512 algorithm based on fast table-based conversions, because it is an important building block of NTTRU, and a new table-based sampling technique. We provide detailed performance numbers on the different components and conclude that the SHA2 family is significantly more expensive to protect with masking compared to the SHA3 family. This result is also of great interest when taking a look at the 90s/AES versions of the NIST selected algorithms Kyber and Dilithium. We verify the results using the state-of-the-art TVLA methodology for our newly proposed components. Finally, we propose a slightly adapted version of NTTRU that achieves a cycle count for decapsulation of around 3.1 million cycles on the ARM Cortex-M4 even without assembler optimized code for the ARM Cortex-M4. This is about a factor of ten faster than the first-order cycle count for NTRU-HRSS on the ARM Cortex M3 [17].

2 Preliminaries

In this section, we present the preliminaries of masking the NTTRU scheme.

2.1 Notation

For any prime q and a polynomial f, we denote R_q as the polynomial ring $\mathbb{Z}_q[X]/(f)$ where $\mathbb{Z}_q$ denotes the quotient ring $\mathbb{Z}/q\mathbb{Z}$. Polynomials in R_q are denoted as lowercase letters. The NTT transform of a polynomial a is represented as $\hat{a}$ and the base multiplication in the NTT domain (not necessarily coefficientwise) is denoted as $\circ$. The i-th coefficient of a polynomial p is denoted as $p[i]$. Given a distribution χ, we use $x \leftarrow \chi$ to mean x is sampled according to the distribution χ. For a polynomial, this is adjusted such that $p \leftarrow \chi^n$ where $n - 1$ is the degree of the polynomial. We denote the modular reduction of x to the domain $[-(q-1)/2, (q-1)/2]$ as $x \bmod {}^{\pm}q$.

We denote the j-th share of a shared variable $x^{(\cdot)}$ as $x^{(j)}$, whereas the unshared variable itself is denoted as x. Concatenation is represented as $\|$.

2.2 The Number-Theoretic Transform

A common solution to make fast arithmetic in lattice-based solutions possible is the usage of the Number-Theoretic Transform (NTT). It is based on the Chinese Remainder Theorem For a prime q and a polynomial f that factors into the product $f = gh$ with g and h relatively prime, the isomorphism

$$\mathbb{Z}_q[X]/(f) \cong \mathbb{Z}_q[X]/(g) \times \mathbb{Z}_q[X]/(h) \tag{1}$$

is valid. Apparently, it is possible to compute a linear operation in the two factor rings and invert the result back to the original ring. If the map and inverse map to the smaller factor rings can be computed efficiently, it is possible that this approach is more efficient than the simple computation in the main ring $\mathbb{Z}_q[X]/(f)$.

2.3 NTTRU

In the final round of the NIST standardization process [2] two NTRU-based schemes were present. Both, NTRU [6] and NTRUprime [18] make use of polynomial arithmetic. The discerning feature of NTRUprime is that it deliberately avoids cyclotomic rings. In [7], Lyubashevsky and Seiler propose a specific parameter set to optimize NTRU for NTT-based multiplication. In contrast to both finalists, a decryption error can occur when using this parameter set. However, in [7], it is proven that the resulting IND-CCA2 KEM is still appropriately secure. The authors additionally state that their scheme is at least as secure as NTRU-HRSS as they use the same error distribution while increasing the ring dimension and decreasing the modulus. It is not possible to give a formal security reduction because of the different rings. According to their findings, this results in a major speed-up of the scheme. We give an overview of the underlying OW-CPA secure encryption scheme in Algorithms 1–3.

Algorithm 1: NTTRU.KeyGen	**Algorithm 2:** NTTRU.Encrypt
Output: Key Pair (sk, pk)	**Input:** message m, randomness r, public key $\hat{h}$
1 $f' \leftarrow \beta_2^{768}$	**Output:** ciphertext $\hat{c}$
2 $f \leftarrow 3f' + 1$	1 $\hat{r} \leftarrow NTT(r)$
3 $\hat{f} \leftarrow NTT(f)$	2 $\hat{m} \leftarrow NTT(m)$
4 $g \leftarrow \beta_2^{768}$	3 $\hat{v} \leftarrow \hat{r} \circ \hat{h}$
5 $\widehat{3g} \leftarrow NTT(3g)$	4 **return** $\hat{c} := \hat{v} + \hat{m}$
6 if f is not invertible: restart	
7 $\hat{h} \leftarrow \widehat{3g} \circ \hat{f}^{-1}$	
8 **return** $(sk = \hat{f}, pk = \hat{h})$	

The FO-Transform. The direct usage of these algorithms results in a scheme that is not resilient against chosen-ciphertext attacks. To counter these attacks the NTTRU scheme introduces a re-encryption step. The decrypted message is

---

Algorithm 3: NTTRU.Decrypt

Input: ciphertext $\hat{c}$, secret key $\hat{f}$
Output: message m
1 $\hat{m} \leftarrow \hat{c} \circ \hat{f}$
2 **return** $m := INTT(\hat{m}) \bmod {}^{\pm}3$

---

re-encrypted and the resulting ciphertext is compared with the input ciphertext. The approach was first proposed at Crypto '99 by Fujisaki and Okamoto [19]. The transformed algorithm is shown in Algorithm 4. In contrast to the OW-CPA version, the randomness for (re-)encrypting is not sampled completely at random but derived deterministically from the message to encrypt. This way, any wrongly decrypted message results in different randomness and consequently completely randomizes the re-encrypted ciphertext. The comparison at the end will fail and the wrongly decrypted message will not be the output. The algorithm will return 0. In this context, we write $\mathcal{H}_{D_{\mathcal{R}}}$ to denote a cryptographic hash function that generates elements according to the distribution $D_{\mathcal{R}}$ with an input seed m. The hash $\mathcal{H}_{\mathcal{R}}$ produces elements uniformly at random in $\mathcal{R}$. In the context of NTTRU, $\mathcal{H}_{D_{\mathcal{R}}}$ is initialized as

$$\mathcal{H}_{D_{\mathcal{R}}} = (AES256ctr(SHA512(m), nonce)) \tag{2}$$

where *AES256ctr* is the AES256 in counter mode with a key derived from the hash SHA512 [20] of m and a nonce. We describe the symmetric algorithms and the sampling algorithm in the next sections.

Algorithm 4: CCA.NTTRU.Decrypt

Input: ciphertext c, secret key f
Output: shared key k
1 $m \leftarrow NTTRU.Decrypt(c, sk)$
2 $seed \leftarrow \mathcal{H}_{D_{\mathcal{R}}}(m)$
3 $r \leftarrow Sampler(seed)$
4 **if** $c \neq NTTRU.Encrypt(m, r, pk)$ **then**
5 $\quad|\quad$ **return** $k \leftarrow 0$
6 **return** $k \leftarrow \mathcal{H}_{\mathcal{K}}(m)$

2.4 Symmetric Primitives

SHA512. The FO-Transform and, hence, the hash function are an essential part of all CCA secured lattice-based schemes. As the input to the hash is the decrypted message, even a small error in the decryption (e.g. a chosen ciphertext input or an effective fault attack) will result in a completely randomized hash value and, thus, in a shared key $k = 0$. In the NTTRU case, SHA512 [20] is used. In the presence of quantum computers, the preimage security of hashes is halved. The SHA512 algorithm [20] is part of the SHA2 family and operates on 512-bit blocks. The used functions are defined as

$$Ch(x, y, z) = (x \wedge y) \oplus (\neg x \wedge z) \tag{3}$$

$$Maj(x, y, z) = (x \wedge y) \oplus (x \wedge z) \oplus (y \wedge z) \tag{4}$$

$$\Sigma_0(x) = S^{28}(x) \oplus S^{34}(x) \oplus S^{39}(x) \tag{5}$$

$$\Sigma_1(x) = S^{14}(x) \oplus S^{18}(x) \oplus S^{41}(x) \tag{6}$$

$$\sigma_0(x) = S^1(x) \oplus S^8(x) \oplus R^7(x) \tag{7}$$

$$\sigma_1(x) = S^{19}(x) \oplus S^{61}(x) \oplus R^6(x) \tag{8}$$

In this definition, $S^n(x)$ denotes a shift to the right of x by n bits and R^n denotes a rotation to the right of x by n bits. In contrast to SHA256, for SHA512 the state variables are of size 64-bit. After one block of the message has been processed, the values resulting from the compression function are added to the state variables and reduced modulo 2^{64}. After processing the last block, the hash is obtained by simple concatenation of the eight state variables. The resulting output has a length of 64 bytes.

Keccak. Another symmetric primitive that is frequently used in lattice-based schemes is called Keccak. In 2015, Keccak won the SHA3 competition and became the successor of the SHA2 family. Similar to SHA2, the SHA3 family consists of several functions with different output lengths. The SHA3 standard is derived from special parametrization of the Keccak function. The state size is fixed to 1600 bits and the number of rounds is fixed to 24. Within the function f, the state vector of 1600 bits is processed in several rounds. Within each round of f, several subfunctions are called:

- θ takes two columns in the three-dimensional arranged state and the target bit as input and xor's the parity of the two columns onto the target bit,
- ρ and π rearrange the positions of the bits within the state,
- χ is the non-linear operation that is using the negation function, the boolean and function, and an xor operation, and
- ι which xor's the state vector with a round constant in each round.

Note, that none of these subfunctions requires an arithmetic operation.

2.5   Sampling Algorithms

In some lattice-based schemes, e.g. Kyber and NTRU, the output of the pseudorandom function (PRF) requires additional processing to follow a binomial distribution but the PRF outputs uniformly distributed bits. The uniformly random bitstream can, however, be used as an input to the centered binomial sampler. To obtain such a distribution in the domain $[-\eta, \eta]$, Kyber uses 2η

independent one-bit variables and starts by adding the first η variables and the next η variables. Then one of the two sums is subtracted from the other one. Thus, the coefficient $c \in [-\eta, \eta]$ is calculated as

$$c = \sum_{i=0}^{\eta-1} b_i - \sum_{i=0}^{\eta-1} b_{i+\eta}. \tag{9}$$

NTTRU requires an additional modular reduction to obtain random coefficients in $[-1, 1]$. The NTTRU reference implementation calculates each coefficient by

$$c = (b_1 + b_2) - (b_3 + b_4) \bmod 3. \tag{10}$$

The sampling operation in NTTRU is realized by a lookup table. Both of the sums can take three values, resulting in nine possible outcomes for the coefficient and the table entries. In NTTRU, the authors additionally simplify the approach by directly using the table-based approach on the four input bits. In practice, the table can be realized by a 32-bit variable that stores all the 2^4 possibilities in $\{0, 1, 2\}$ and is shifted by twice the value of the four input bits. Since the distribution is symmetric around zero, it is even possible to only use a 16-bit variable as a lookup table and directly shift by the number obtained from the four concatenated input bits, resulting in

$$c = (L >> (b_1 \| b_2 \| b_3 \| b_4)) \wedge 0x3 - 1 \tag{11}$$

with $L = 0xA815$.

2.6   Side-Channel Attacks and Protection

In recent years methods like Simple Power Analysis (SPA) [21] and Differential Power Analysis (DPA) [11] have seen increased focus for post-quantum schemes. Several attacks on (protected) lattice-based schemes have been proposed using power or timing side-channels [22–26]. The attacks include side-channel assisted CCA attacks where the information from the re-encryption step of the FO-Transform is used for secret recovery [27, 28]. Therefore, it is crucial to protect not only the decryption but also the re-encryption step with appropriate countermeasures.

In practice, the most well-known countermeasure is called masking [29]. Secret variables are split into two or more randomized shares. One can choose between arithmetic masking, where the secret s is split into two shares such that $s = s_1 + s_2 \pmod{q}$ and Boolean masking resulting in a sharing s_1, s_2 such that $s = s_1 \oplus s_2$. In lattice-based cryptography, both possibilities are frequently used in conjunction. Different parts of the decapsulation work more efficiently on either arithmetic or Boolean masking. Therefore, methods to securely convert from one to the other exist [30, 31]. Masked implementations of Saber [15, 16], Kyber [12–14] and, recently, NTTRU-HRSS [17] were proposed. However, no detailed analysis for first-order protection of NTTRU has been performed.

3   Side-Channel Protection of NTTRU

In this section, we will go through the primitives used in NTTRU and provide a first-order masking scheme for each function. This is visualized in Fig. 1. It shows how the two input shares of the secret s_1 and s_2 as well as the unmasked input ciphertext c and public key pk are processed in the algorithm. The masked functions are presented in chronological order from the input secret s_1 and s_2.

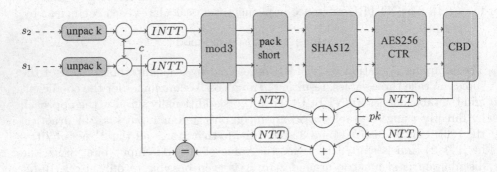

Fig. 1. Masked Decapsulation of NTTRU. Boolean shared data paths in dashed lines. Arithmetically shared data paths in solid lines. Non-linear functions in yellow. (Color figure online)

Masked Unpacking. The first function to encounter that works on secret data is the unpacking function. In our work, we directly store the generated secret key in arithmetic sharing on the device as in most use cases key generation is performed on the same platform. Hence, we do not need a so-called $B2A_q$ conversion. Such a conversion is quite expensive in terms of cycle counts. The approach is possible because the unpacking function does not compress the secret key. Thus, an arithmetic sharing requires the same amount of memory as a "packed" secret key.

3.1   Table-Based Masking of Modulus Conversion

A major challenge in masking NTTRU as well as NTRU is the masking of the modulus conversion. Concretely, it is required to mask the operation

$$(x \bmod {}^{\pm}q) \bmod {}^{\pm}3.$$

The challenge is, that different representatives of $x \bmod q$ lead to different results when reduced modulo 3. In the NTTRU reference implementation [7], the input to the mod 3 function, is an output from the inverse NTT. This means that the coefficients are distributed in $[-(q-1),(q-1)]$ because of the used Barrett reductions.

In the unmasked constant-time implementation, the correct representative of $x \bmod {}^{\pm}q$ is found by first retrieving the most significant bit of x. In case x is negative and, therefore, the most significant bit is 1, x is increased by q. This conditional addition is the most challenging part in the masked implementation. The result is a value in $[0, q-1]$ which is then subtracted by $\frac{q-1}{2}$. The procedure is repeated with the exception of the subtraction of the last constant. With a final subtraction of $\frac{q+1}{2}$ the original value modulo q is restored and the domain of the coefficient is then in $[-\frac{q-1}{2}, \frac{q-1}{2}]$.

We present an approach that incorporates the reduction to the correct representative $\bmod^{\pm}q$ and the reduction modulo 3 in a table-based approach. In our first-order masked approach, we first reduce each share to the domain $[-\frac{q-1}{2}, \frac{q-1}{2}]$ as previously presented, then we compute the A2B conversion of the shared coefficient $a^{(\cdot)}$ as proposed by Debraize [32] and later improved by Van Beirendonck et al. [33] and then extract the most significant bits of both shares. We obtain a boolean sharing $b^{(\cdot)}$ of the most significant bit. We then generate a random input mask bit r_1 and a random output mask r_2 in $[0, q-1]$. Then our lookup table is initialized for $r_1 = 0$:

– The first entry corresponds to the most significant bit being zero. The coefficient a is positive and we require a sharing of zero to be added to a. Consequently, the entry is the inverted output mask r_2.
– The second entry corresponds to the most significant bit being equal to one. The coefficient a is negative and does require the addition of q. Thus, the entry is initialized as $q - r_2$.

Apparently, if $r_1 = 1$ the table entries are initialized the other way around. We present the function in Algorithm 5.

Algorithm 5: Initialization of LUT

Input: Random bit r_1, random output mask $r_2 \in [0, q-1]$
Output: Table $T[2]$
1   $T[0 \oplus r_1] \leftarrow -r_2$
2   $T[1 \oplus r_1] \leftarrow q - r_2$
3   **return** T

After the initialization of the table, both shares are combined carefully with the random bit r_1 by an xor operation. The helper variable with two shares is initialized with $h^{(\cdot)} = (r_2, T[r_1 \oplus b^{(0)} \oplus b^{(1)}])$. Finally, sharewise addition of $a^{(\cdot)} + h^{(\cdot)}$ yields the arithmetically shared value in $[0, q-1]$. We repeat this procedure once after the subtraction of $\frac{q-1}{2}$. Finally, both shares are reduced modulo 3. We show the procedure in Algorithm 6.

Algorithm 6: Masked Conversion to Modulo 3

Input: Shared coefficient $a^{(\cdot)}$ with unmasked coefficients in $[-(q-1), q-1]$
Output: Shared coefficient $a^{(\cdot)} \mod 3$ with unmasked coefficients in $[-1,1]$

1 //Conditionally add q
2 $h^{(\cdot)} \leftarrow A2B(a^{(\cdot)})$
3 $b^{(\cdot)} \leftarrow MSB(h^{(\cdot)})$
4 Sample random bit r_1, random $r_2 \in [0, q-1]$
5 $val \leftarrow r_1 \oplus b^{(0)} \oplus b^{(1)}$
6 $h^{(0)} \leftarrow r2$
7 $h^{(1)} \leftarrow T[val]$
8 $a^{(\cdot)} \leftarrow a^{(\cdot)} + h^{(\cdot)}$
9 //Always subtract
10 $a^{(0)} \leftarrow a^{(0)} - (q-1)/2$
11 //Conditionally add q
12 $h^{(\cdot)} \leftarrow A2B(a^{(\cdot)})$
13 $b^{(\cdot)} \leftarrow MSB(h^{(\cdot)})$
14 Sample random bit r_1, random $r_2 \in [0, q-1]$
15 $val \leftarrow r_1 \oplus b^{(0)} \oplus b^{(1)}$
16 $h^{(0)} \leftarrow r2$
17 $h^{(1)} \leftarrow T[val]$
18 $a^{(\cdot)} \leftarrow a^{(\cdot)} + h^{(\cdot)}$
19 //Always subtract
20 $a^{(0)} \leftarrow a^{(0)} - (q+1)/2$
21 //Now reduce modulo 3 sharewise
22 $a^{(\cdot)} \leftarrow a^{(\cdot)} \mod 3$
23 return $a^{(\cdot)}$

3.2   Masked Packing

To save memory, each coefficient of the message polynomial, which only requires two bits, is not stored in a full 16-bit variable. Instead, each coefficient is concatenated in an array of 96 bytes which is later used as an input for the symmetric primitives. This is the reason why the correct representative of $x \mod 3$ is important. In contrast to the arithmetic modulo 3, for an input to the SHA512 $11_2 = -1 \neq 2 = 10_2$. According to the specification of NTTRU, coefficients of the polynomial are in the domain $[-1, 1]$ whereas the concatenated message is obtained by shifting the interval by one to $[0, 2]$. Consequently, we propose to combine both steps efficiently in one table for the first-order masked approach. Instead of only calculating the entries of the table as a Boolean sharing of the arithmetically shared value a, we provide the Boolean sharing for $a + 1$. In contrast to any higher-order compatible A2B conversion, we do not need a costly Boolean adder on the shares. For each coefficient, we refresh the masking with new random values. Concatenation of the Boolean shared values works sharewise.

3.3   Protected SHA512 and AES256-CTR

In this section, we provide details on how to protect the symmetric primitives from DPA attacks.

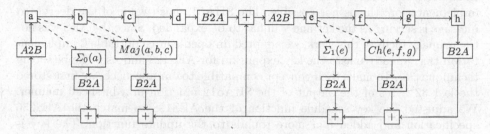

Fig. 2. Masked SHA512 Compression function with conversions in place.

SHA512. In NTTRU, the decrypted message is input to the SHA2-512 hashing function. Due to performance reasons, SHA2 is chosen over SHA3. The drawback of this choice becomes apparent when the masking technique is applied to the hashing algorithm. The SHA2 standard combines arithmetic operations modulo 2^{64} with bitwise Boolean operations. Thus, for masking SHA512, we have two options:

- Usage of A2B conversions: Boolean functions operate on Boolean shares, and arithmetic functions on arithmetic shares. The conversion is performed, if necessary, in between the functions.
- Usage of Boolean Adders: no arithmetic shares are used, and arithmetic additions modulo 2^{64} are performed on boolean shares using specific algorithms.

We evaluated both strategies for the first-order implementation and present the chosen strategy in this section. For the first case, we adapt the compression function to include A2B conversions, as proposed by Debraize [32] and later improved by Van Beirendonck [33], and B2A conversions are realized as presented by Goubin [30]. The performance of this approach (only 7 cycles per B2A conversion) is especially beneficial to the first-order implementation. The resulting flow is shown in Fig. 2. In the latter case, we refer to the control flow of the compression function from Fig. 2 without the conversions. Instead of additions modulo 2^{64}, we use an algorithm based on Goubin's Theorem and in detail analyzed by Coron et al. [34]. Its runtime dependency on the number of bits is rather disadvantageous for SHA512 as it operates on 64 bit variables. For the first-order case, the table-based approach combined with Goubins B2A conversion turns out to be preferable in terms of runtime.

In both cases - using boolean adder or conversions - the only part that remains to be masked is the non-linear AND. This operation cannot be realized sharewise and, thus, is realized as presented in [34].

AES256-CTR. In this work, we additionally adapted an open-source masked implementation of AES, as it is an essential part of the seed generation for the coefficient sampling. For AES128 in counter mode, several masked solutions exist [35–37]. All of these implementations do not mask the key expansion function as the expanded shared key is often assumed to be stored on the chip. In our implementation, this is not possible. The SHA512 hash value of the decrypted message is serving as the key and still has to be expanded. Since the AES was not the primary focus of this work, we adapted an open-source portable C implementation that already masks the key expansion for AES128 and uses the bitslicing technique [35]. To make their concept compatible to our approach, we first stored the last 32 bytes of the output of the SHA512 function in a bitsliced manner. We adjusted the key schedule function of the AES128 to match the AES256 specification and added four more rounds to the update function. The key is updated at the end of each round to obtain the next subkey from the previous subkey. As a message, the increasing nonce for each block combined with a zero-padded IV is used. Finally, the output is restored from the bitsliced variables and used as a pseudorandom input to the polynomial sampler of the NTTRU re-encryption. The results are not particularly optimized concerning cycle counts but still give an upper bound of the cycles needed for symmetric seed expansion. We emphasize that there is still a lot of performance to be gained when applying the several (architecture-specific) optimization techniques as presented, e.g., by Schwabe et al. [36].

3.4   Table-Based Masking of Coefficient Sampling

As described in Sect. 2.5, the sampling in NTTRU is slightly different to Kyber due to the additional modular reduction step. The output of the sampler is in the domain $[-1,1]$ but has to be masked arithmetically mod q. In our masked approach, we first compute the table by computing a masked result for all possible 16 unmasked input values. This is shown in Algorithm 7. The second share of the table is a random value $r_{out} \in R_q$ that is equal for all outcomes. To minimize the size of the table, we additionally assume one share of the input to be random but identical r_{in} for all inputs.

Algorithm 7: Initialization of LUT for first order CBD sampling in the domain $[-1,1]$

Input: Random input mask $r_{in} \in [0,15]$, Random output mask $r_{out} \in [0, q-1]$
Output: Table $T[16]$

1 $val \leftarrow 0$
2 **while** $val < 16$ **do**
3 | $T[val] \leftarrow (0xA815 >> (val \oplus r_{in}) \wedge 0x3) + q - 1 - r_{out} \mod q$
4 | $val \leftarrow val + 1$
5 **end**
6 **return** $T[16]$

During the online phase (Algorithm 8), we remask each coefficient to take r_{in} as one Boolean share. The other share is an input to the lookup table. The table gives a randomized output in R_q that, together with the random but fixed value r_{out}, is equivalent to the arithmetic masking of the sampled value obtained from a centered binomial distribution modulo 3. Note that the sampling technique provides an implicit B2A$_q$ conversion. Finally, we remask the output for each coefficient. This approach does obviously not defend against horizontal attacks. Several other countermeasures, especially table-based approaches, face this issue. Yet, they can be used with additional countermeasures, e.g. shuffling or RNR [38,39], in place. This is out of scope of this paper and is an interesting direction for future work.

Algorithm 8: First order sampling in the domain $[-1, 1]$ based on LUT

Input: Shared buffer $buf^{(\cdot)}[N/2]$
Output: Shared polynomial $a^{(\cdot)}[N]$ with N coefficients

1 generate randomness $r \in [0, q-1]$, $s \in [0, 15]$
2 initialize sampling table with $r_{in} = s$, $r_{out} = r$
3 $i \leftarrow 0$
4 **while** $i < N/2$ **do**
5 $\quad h \leftarrow buf^{(1)}[i] \oplus (s << 4 \lor s)$
6 $\quad h \leftarrow h \oplus buf^{(0)}[i]$
7 $\quad$ generate randomness $rnd \in [0, q-1]$
8 $\quad a^{(0)}[2i] \leftarrow rnd$
9 $\quad a^{(1)}[2i] \leftarrow (T[h \land 0xF] - rnd + r) \bmod q$
10 $\quad$ generate randomness $rnd \in [0, q-1]$
11 $\quad a^{(0)}[2i+1] \leftarrow rnd$
12 $\quad a^{(1)}[2i+1] \leftarrow (T[h >> 4] - rnd + r) \bmod q$
13 $\quad i \leftarrow i+1$
14 **end**
15 **return** $a^{(\cdot)}[N]$

3.5   Masked Comparison

Comparing the original ciphertext to the re-encrypted ciphertext at the end of the FO-Transform (cf. Sect. 2.3) has to be appropriately protected as well because any leakage point in this function can compromise the security of the complete scheme [24,27]. The first approach to do so was proposed by Oder et al. [40]. They separately compare the public input ciphertext parts c_1, c_2 with their re-encrypted counterparts $\tilde{c}_1, \tilde{c}_2$. The methodology requires one randomized share $\tilde{c}_1^{(0)}$ to be subtracted from the public ciphertext c_1 yielding a randomized value. In case that $c_1 = \tilde{c}_1^{(0)} + \tilde{c}_1^{(1)}$ it is also true that $\mathcal{H}(c_1 - \tilde{c}_1^{(0)}) = \mathcal{H}(\tilde{c}_1^{(1)})$. If the re-encrypted ciphertext is different, the hash values yield different results. Thus, the result of $\mathcal{H}(c_1 - \tilde{c}_1^1) \oplus \mathcal{H}(\tilde{c}_1^2)$ does not leak any secret information. It yields zero if the ciphertext parts are equal and a random number if they are not equal. The major drawback of this method is that it can not be used for higher orders. Additionally, this method is susceptible to the same attack vector as the higher-order compatible work by Bache et al. [41] as demonstrated by Bhasin et al. [27] in 2021. The partial unmasking of ciphertexts allows an attacker to distinguish between crafted ciphertexts that are re-encrypted identically or completely different depending on the error that was added to a valid ciphertext. In [15], the hash-based approach is taken and the two ciphertext parts are combined into one hash. Still, internally a Keccak-based hash is split up into multiple parts. The attack by D'Anvers et al. [42] makes use of this property. They propose another fast higher-order compatible comparison algorithm that incorporates the idea of [41] without partially unmasking the ciphertext. The algorithm outperforms the solution by [13], which compares uncompressed coefficients for second and higher orders. In line with the findings of [43] and the previously presented first-order optimized A2B and B2A conversions, we choose the so-called "simple" approach from [43, Algorithm 7] for our masked comparison.

3.6   Keccak (SHA3) as a Speed-Up

In this section, we propose a faster alternative to the presented NTTRU scheme when masking is in place. As described in Sect. 2.4 the SHA3 standard can replace the SHA2 functions without loss of security and offers the advantage of the underlying function Keccak does not need any arithmetic operations to compute the hash value. This is especially beneficial to any masked implementation because any masking conversion, especially at higher orders, requires a large computational overhead. In detail, the runtime is of magnitude $O(n^2 k)$ [34] for a k bit variable in n shares. As SHA512 operates on 64 bit variables, this is a very costly operation that should be avoided if possible. In Keccak, all variables are shared in Boolean domain and the non-linear χ step is very efficient to mask as it includes only one AND operation. Although SHA2 seems to be the faster method of hashing with no side-channel countermeasures in place, as the authors of NTTRU state, it is recommended to use the SHA3 option when side-channel security has to be considered.

4   Evaluation

4.1   Performance Evaluation

In this work, we mostly use adapted code from the reference implementation [7] written in C. We also make use of a masked AES128 [35] in C. It has to be emphasized that most of the base code has a lot of potential in terms of performance. Furthermore, we build some functions on the fixed A2B conversion by Van Beirendonck et al. [33] which is optimized for the Cortex-M4 in terms of side-channel leakage. Additionally, we use the first-order implementation of Keccak for the SHA3 and SHAKE functions presented in [44]. A Cortex-M4 optimized implementation might lead to a faster first-order masked scheme than Kyber on this platform.

We measured the performance of our masked primitives on an ARM Cortex M4 mounted on an STM32F407G-DISC1 board offering up to 192 kByte of RAM. This environment was chosen as it is also the base microcontroller for the PQM4 project [45] for post-quantum algorithms. This is also why a lot of highly optimized code such as the masked assembler SHA3 already exists for this platform. Additionally, many masked implementations,e.g. of Kyber or Saber, exist for the ARM Cortex M4 leading to direct comparability of NTTRU with the NIST finalists. For our benchmarks, we set the clock frequency to 24 MHz. To improve the comparability between platforms we excluded cycle counts required for the randomness generation. For our evaluation, we did not use the onboard TRNG of the STM32F407-DISC1 board and opted for a pseudorandom number generator in software to generate the required masks. This enables easier debugging across several chips. As the development environment, we used the Keil Toolchain MDK Plus 5.29/μ Vision 5.29 with the ARM Compiler Version 5. The code size of our masked NTTRU decapsulation implementation is around 18 kB and the RAM requirement is around 77 kB.

Table 1. CCA2-secure decapsulation cycle counts for different masked lattice-based schemes.

Scheme	CPU	Cycles $\times 10^3$	Cycles $\times 10^3$
		Masked	Unmasked
Saber [15]	Cortex M4	2833	774
Kyber768 [12]	Cortex M4	2978	783
NTRU [17]	Cortex M3	32 472	10 508
NTTRU (This work)	Cortex M4	9448	796
NTTRU-SHA3 (This work)	Cortex M4	3119	

We give a comparison of performance numbers in Table 1. Using a state-of-the-art masked implementation of the SHA3-512 [44] and additionally replacing the non-optimized AES256 with the SHAKE256 option, we achieve a performance number for the first-order implementation of NTTRU that is in the magnitude of the NIST standardization candidate Kyber. We additionally give more in-depth performance numbers in Table 2. Once again, we emphasize that the polynomial arithmetic functions are not optimized for the ARM Cortex M4.

4.2 Side-Channel Evaluation

In this section, we show that our proposed techniques indeed fulfill the requirement of practical first-order security. We used the ChipWhisperer Lite Board with an STM32F303 providing an ARM Cortex M4 core running at 7.37 MHz.

Table 2. Cycle Counts for the masked components of NTTRU

Function	Cycle count		Factor
	Unmasked	1st order	
`poly_unpack_uniform`	(19 396)	0	n.a.
`ntru_decrypt`	241 164	749 966	×3.1
polynomial arithmetic		436 214	
`poly_crepmod3`		313 713	
`poly_pack_short`	4170	96 261	×23
`SHA512`	27 305	4 359 092	×159
`crypto_stream` (AES)	24 028	2 808 228	×116
`ntru_encrypt`	436 570	962 539	×2.2
`poly_short`		106 277	
polynomial arithmetic		856 212	
`comparison`	4998	423 309	×84.7
`crypto_kem_dec`	796 712	9 448 510	×11.9

The sampling rate is four times the clock speed, resulting in 29 MS/s. An advantage of the CWLite board is the synchronized sample and device clock. It is relatively easy to capture small differences in power traces because the traces are perfectly aligned [46]. This lowers the amount of required power traces to detect possible leakage. A disadvantage lies in the small buffer size of around 24, 400 samples. We circumvented this issue by capturing only small building blocks of the algorithm independently. For the ChipWhisperer evaluation, we compiled our code using `arm-none-eabi-gcc` version `10.3.1`. We show that our approaches do not have any obvious leakage points when implemented in practice. We applied the so-called non-specific t-test methodology by Schneider and Moradi [47] to do so. The inputs to the functions are either from a specific fixed ciphertext or a completely randomized ciphertext. We denote the set of traces obtained from function calls with fixed input as $\mathcal{S}_1$ and the set of traces obtained from random inputs as $\mathcal{S}_0$. Sample sizes n_0, n_1, standard deviations s_0, s_1 and sample means μ_0, μ_1 are denoted accordingly. At every point in time, we calculate the t-test statistic

$$t = \frac{\mu_0 - \mu_1}{\sqrt{\frac{s_0^2}{n_0} + \frac{s_1^2}{n_1}}} \tag{12}$$

The methodology by [47] requires a higher t value than 4.5 to correctly reject the hypothesis that both sets are not distinguishable with the confidence of around 99.999%. Thus, in a first-order secure implementation, all absolute values should be smaller than 4.5.

The first target is the table-based modulus conversion (Sect. 3.1). We adjusted our implementation slightly by generating the required random num-

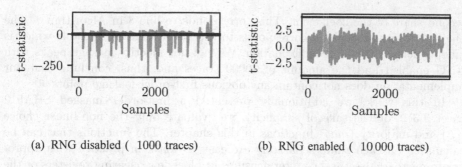

(a) RNG disabled (1000 traces)   (b) RNG enabled (10 000 traces)

Fig. 3. t-statistic of the masked modulus conversion. Red lines indicate the threshold of 4.5. (Color figure online)

bers in advance. The generation is due to the rejection sampling $\bmod q$ not constant time and would make our t-test useless. It is also not necessary to capture the complete conversion of the polynomial. It is sufficient to capture the conversion of only one coefficient as the conversion of all other coefficients is independent and redundant. Our first measurement was taken with the random number generator disabled. Thus, all masks are zero and the values are processed unmasked. In a correct setup of the side-channel setup, one should be able to see a lot of leaking points in this implementation. Therefore, Fig. 3a verifies our correct setup. Even with only 1000 traces several very high t-values can be seen.

We then activated our pseudorandom number generator. The obtained t-test values are visualized in Fig. 3b. We can see that even with 20000 traces and a sampling rate of four times per clock cycle no leakage peaks can be identified. Note that the hardened implementation requires a few minor tweaks and carefully crafted assembly routines to counter microarchitectural leakage.

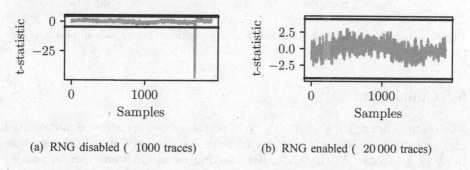

(a) RNG disabled (1000 traces)   (b) RNG enabled (20 000 traces)

Fig. 4. t-statistic of the masked coefficient sampler. Red lines indicate the threshold of 4.5. (Color figure online)

For the sampling technique (Sect. 3.4), we performed a similar evaluation. We obtained the t-statistics visualized in Fig. 4a. The single leakage peak in the unmasked implementation stems from the assignment of the table value to the second share of the coefficient. This corresponds to line 8 in Algorithm 8. The huge part without leakage corresponds to the generation of the table which is independent of the secret information. We can not identify leakage peaks with RNG enabled and the amount of 20000 traces and, thus, conclude that our implementation does not contain any obvious first-order leakage points.

In this work, we additionally presented a first-order masked SHA512 (Sect. 3.3). For the sake of simplicity, we evaluate only the non-linear choice (ch) and majority (maj) functions in this chapter. The functions that can be calculated on each share separately are easy to mask in practice with appropriate microarchitectural countermeasures in place, e.g. clearing registers or the ALU [33]. We show the results in Fig. 5.

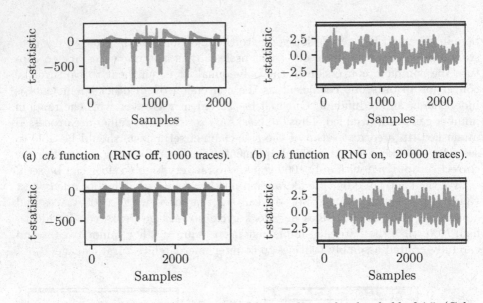

(a) ch function (RNG off, 1000 traces).   (b) ch function (RNG on, 20 000 traces).

Fig. 5. t-statistic of SHA512 functions. Red lines indicate the threshold of 4.5. (Color figure online)

5   Conclusion

The results once again show that a large performance gap between unprotected and protected implementations may more or less strongly impede the applicability of a scheme. As the first-order masking countermeasure can be seen as a minimum requirement nowadays, one should, if possible, aim for the usage of functions with minimal cost when masked. In detail, we strongly encourage the usage of SHA3 functions. As we have shown, their behavior with respect to additive and boolean masking allows NTTRU to be competitive among the first-order masked lattice-based schemes without reducing its security level. A lot of potential is additionally hidden in an optimized version of the NTT for the Cortex M4 which is already available for Kyber. Such further optimizations combined with our proposed NTTRU-SHA3, might outperform masked implementations of the NIST finalists significantly on ARM Cortex-M4.

Acknowledgments. The authors would like to thank Thomas Pöppelmann and Peter Pessl for their valuable feedback and discussions. This work was supported by the German Federal Ministry of Education and Research (BMBF) under the project Aquorypt (16KIS1017). Presented project results were partly supported by the project that has received funding from the European Union's Horizon 2020 research and innovation programme under grant agreement No. 830927.

References

1. Shor, P.W.: Polynomial-time algorithms for prime factorization and discrete logarithms on a quantum computer. SIAM J. Comput. **26**(5), 1484–1509 (1997)
2. National Institute of Standards and Technology. Announcing request for nominations for public-key post-quantum cryptographic algorithms (2016). https://csrc.nist.gov/news/2016/public-key-post-quantum-cryptographic-algorithms
3. Avanzi, R., et al.: Crystals-kyber (version 3.02) - submission to round 3 of the nist post-quantum project (2021). https://pq-crystals.org/kyber/data/kyber-specification-round3-20210804.pdf
4. Basso, A., et al.: SABER: Mod-LWR based KEM (round 3 submission) (2019). https://csrc.nist.gov/CSRC/media/Projects/post-quantum-cryptography/documents/round-3/submissions/SABER-Round3.zip
5. Hoffstein, J., Pipher, J., Silverman, J.H.: NTRU: a ring-based public key cryptosystem. In: Buhler, J.P. (ed.) ANTS 1998. LNCS, vol. 1423, pp. 267–288. Springer, Heidelberg (1998). https://doi.org/10.1007/BFb0054868
6. Chen, C., et al.: Ntru - algorithm specifications and supporting documentation (2019). https://ntru.org/f/ntru-20190330.pdf
7. Lyubashevsky, V., Seiler, G.: NTTRU: truly fast NTRU using NTT. IACR Trans. Cryptogr. Hardw. Embed. Syst. **2019**(3), 180–201 (2019)
8. OpenSSH. Openssh release 9.0. https://www.openssh.com/txt/release-9.0. Accessed 14 Nov 2022
9. ISE Crypto PQC working group. Securing tomorrow today: Why google now protects its internal communications from quantum threats. https://cloud.google.com/blog/products/identity-security/why-google-now-uses-post-quantum-cryptography-for-internal-comms?hl=en. Accessed 21 November 22
10. Albrecht, M.R., Curtis, B.R., Deo, A., Davidson, A., Player, R., Postlethwaite, E.W., Virdia, F., Wunderer, T.: Estimate all the LWE, NTRU schemes! In: Catalano, D., De Prisco, R. (eds.) SCN 2018. LNCS, vol. 11035, pp. 351–367. Springer, Cham (2018). https://doi.org/10.1007/978-3-319-98113-0_19
11. Kocher, P., Jaffe, J., Jun, B.: Differential power analysis. In: Wiener, M. (ed.) CRYPTO 1999. LNCS, vol. 1666, pp. 388–397. Springer, Heidelberg (1999). https://doi.org/10.1007/3-540-48405-1_25
12. Heinz, D., et al.: First-order masked kyber on ARM cortex-m4. IACR Cryptol. ePrint Arch., p. 58 (2022)
13. Bos, J.W., Gourjon, M., Renes, J., Schneider, T., van Vredendaal, C.: Masking kyber: first- and higher-order implementations. IACR Trans. Cryptogr. Hardw. Embed. Syst. **2021**(4), 173–214 (2021)

14. Fritzmann, T., et al.: Masked accelerators and instruction set extensions for post-quantum cryptography. IACR Trans. Cryptogr. Hardw. Embed. Syst. **2022**(1), 414–460 (2022)

15. Van Beirendonck, M., D'Anvers, J.-P., Karmakar, A., Balasch, J., Verbauwhede, I.: A side-channel-resistant implementation of SABER. ACM J. Emerg. Technol. Comput. Syst. **17**(2), 10:1–10:26 (2021)

16. Kundu, S., D'Anvers, J.-P., Van Beirendonck, M., Karmakar, A., Verbauwhede, I.: Higher-order masked saber. IACR Cryptol. ePrint Arch., p. 389 (2022)

17. Coron, J.-S., Gérard, F., Trannoy, M., Zeitoun, R.: High-order masking of NTRU. IACR Cryptol. ePrint Arch., p. 1188 (2022)

18. Bernstein, D.J., Chuengsatiansup, C., Lange, T., van Vredendaal, C.: NTRU prime. IACR Cryptol. ePrint Arch., p. 461 (2016)

19. Fujisaki, E., Okamoto, T.: Secure integration of asymmetric and symmetric encryption schemes. In: Wiener, M. (ed.) CRYPTO 1999. LNCS, vol. 1666, pp. 537–554. Springer, Heidelberg (1999). https://doi.org/10.1007/3-540-48405-1_34

20. National Institute of Standards and Technology. Secure hash standard (2015). https://nvlpubs.nist.gov/nistpubs/FIPS/NIST.FIPS.180-4.pdf

21. Kocher, P.C.: Timing attacks on implementations of Diffie-Hellman, RSA, DSS, and other systems. In: Koblitz, N. (ed.) CRYPTO 1996. LNCS, vol. 1109, pp. 104–113. Springer, Heidelberg (1996). https://doi.org/10.1007/3-540-68697-5_9

22. Hermelink, J., Pessl, P., Pöppelmann, T.: Fault-enabled chosen-ciphertext attacks on kyber. In: Adhikari, A., Küsters, R., Preneel, B. (eds.) INDOCRYPT 2021. LNCS, vol. 13143, pp. 311–334. Springer, Cham (2021). https://doi.org/10.1007/978-3-030-92518-5_15

23. Primas, R., Pessl, P., Mangard, S.: Single-trace side-channel attacks on masked lattice-based encryption. In: Fischer, W., Homma, N. (eds.) CHES 2017. LNCS, vol. 10529, pp. 513–533. Springer, Cham (2017). https://doi.org/10.1007/978-3-319-66787-4_25

24. Guo, Q., Johansson, T., Nilsson, A.: A key-recovery timing attack on post-quantum primitives using the Fujisaki-Okamoto transformation and its application on FrodoKEM. In: Micciancio, D., Ristenpart, T. (eds.) CRYPTO 2020. LNCS, vol. 12171, pp. 359–386. Springer, Cham (2020). https://doi.org/10.1007/978-3-030-56880-1_13

25. Ravi, P., Roy, S.S., Chattopadhyay, A., Bhasin, S.: Generic side-channel attacks on cca-secure lattice-based PKE and kems. IACR Trans. Cryptogr. Hardw. Embed. Syst., **2020**(3), 307–335 (2020)

26. Ravi, P., Bhasin, S., Roy, S.S., Chattopadhyay, A.: Drop by drop you break the rock - exploiting generic vulnerabilities in lattice-based pke/kems using em-based physical attacks. IACR Cryptol. ePrint Arch., p. 549 (2020)

27. Bhasin, S., D'Anvers, J.-P., Heinz, D., Pöppelmann, T., Van Beirendonck, M.: Attacking and defending masked polynomial comparison for lattice-based cryptography. IACR Trans. Cryptogr. Hardw. Embed. Syst. **2021**(3), 334–359 (2021)

28. Hamburg, M., Hermelink, J., Primas, R., Samardjiska, S., Schamberger, T., Streit, S., Strieder, E., van Vredendaal, C.: Chosen ciphertext k-trace attacks on masked CCA2 secure kyber. IACR Trans. Cryptogr. Hardw. Embed. Syst. **2021**(4), 88–113 (2021)

29. Chari, S., Jutla, C.S., Rao, J.R., Rohatgi, P.: Towards sound approaches to counteract power-analysis attacks. In: Wiener, M. (ed.) CRYPTO 1999. LNCS, vol. 1666, pp. 398–412. Springer, Heidelberg (1999). https://doi.org/10.1007/3-540-48405-1_26

30. Goubin, L.: A sound method for switching between boolean and arithmetic masking. In: Koç, Ç.K., Naccache, D., Paar, C. (eds.) CHES 2001. LNCS, vol. 2162, pp. 3–15. Springer, Heidelberg (2001). https://doi.org/10.1007/3-540-44709-1_2

31. Coron, J.-S., Tchulkine, A.: A new algorithm for switching from arithmetic to boolean masking. In: Walter, C.D., Koç, Ç.K., Paar, C. (eds.) CHES 2003. LNCS, vol. 2779, pp. 89–97. Springer, Heidelberg (2003). https://doi.org/10.1007/978-3-540-45238-6_8

32. Debraize, B.: Efficient and provably secure methods for switching from arithmetic to boolean masking. In: Prouff, E., Schaumont, P. (eds.) CHES 2012. LNCS, vol. 7428, pp. 107–121. Springer, Heidelberg (2012). https://doi.org/10.1007/978-3-642-33027-8_7

33. Van Beirendonck, M., D'Anvers, J.-P., Verbauwhede, I.: Analysis and comparison of table-based arithmetic to boolean masking. IACR Trans. Cryptogr. Hardw. Embed. Syst. **2021**(3), 275–297 (2021)

34. Coron, J.-S., Großschädl, J., Vadnala, P.K.: Secure conversion between boolean and arithmetic masking of any order. In: Batina, L., Robshaw, M. (eds.) CHES 2014. LNCS, vol. 8731, pp. 188–205. Springer, Heidelberg (2014). https://doi.org/10.1007/978-3-662-44709-3_11

35. Riou, S.: Masked bitsliced aes128. https://github.com/sebastien-riou/masked-bitsliced-aes-128. Accessed 27 Sept 2022

36. Schwabe, P., Stoffelen, K.: All the AES you need on cortex-M3 and M4. In: Avanzi, R., Heys, H. (eds.) SAC 2016. LNCS, vol. 10532, pp. 180–194. Springer, Cham (2017). https://doi.org/10.1007/978-3-319-69453-5_10

37. ANSSI LSC. Technical analysis of the masked aes implementation. https://github.com/ANSSI-FR/SecAESSTM32/blob/master/doc/technical-report/technical_analysis.pdf. Accessed 21 Nov 2022

38. Zijlstra, T., Bigou, K., Tisserand, A.: FPGA implementation and comparison of protections against SCAs for RLWE. In: Hao, F., Ruj, S., Sen Gupta, S. (eds.) INDOCRYPT 2019. LNCS, vol. 11898, pp. 535–555. Springer, Cham (2019). https://doi.org/10.1007/978-3-030-35423-7_27

39. Heinz, D., Pöppelmann, T.: Combined fault and DPA protection for lattice-based cryptography. IACR Cryptol. ePrint Arch., p. 101 (2021)

40. Oder, T., Schneider, T., Pöppelmann, T., Güneysu, T.: Practical cca2-secure and masked ring-lwe implementation. IACR Trans. Cryptogr. Hardw. Embed. Syst. **2018**(1), 142–174 (2018)

41. Bache, F., Paglialonga, C., Oder, T., Schneider, T., Güneysu, T.: High-speed masking for polynomial comparison in lattice-based kems. IACR Trans. Cryptogr. Hardw. Embed. Syst. **2020**(3), 483–507 (2020)

42. D'Anvers, J.-P., Heinz, D., Pessl, P., Van Beirendonck, M., Verbauwhede, I.: Higher-order masked ciphertext comparison for lattice-based cryptography. IACR Trans. Cryptogr. Hardw. Embed. Syst. **2022**(2), 115–139 (2022)

43. D'Anvers, J.-P., Van Beirendonck, M., Verbauwhede, I.: Revisiting higher-order masked comparison for lattice-based cryptography: Algorithms and bit-sliced implementations. IACR Cryptol. ePrint Arch., p. 110 (2022)

44. Bertoni, G., Daemen, J., Peeters, M., Assche, G.V.: Building power analysis resistant implementations of Keccak (2010)

45. Kannwischer, M.J., Rijneveld, J., Schwabe, P., Stoffelen, K.: pqm4: testing and benchmarking NIST PQC on ARM cortex-m4. IACR Cryptol. ePrint Arch., p. 844 (2019)

46. O'Flynn, C., Chen, Z.D.: ChipWhisperer: an open-source platform for hardware embedded security research. In: Prouff, E. (ed.) COSADE 2014. LNCS, vol. 8622, pp. 243–260. Springer, Cham (2014). https://doi.org/10.1007/978-3-319-10175-0_17

47. Schneider, T., Moradi, A.: Leakage assessment methodology - extended version. J. Cryptogr. Eng. 6(2), 85–99 (2016)

On the Feasibility of Single-Trace Attacks on the Gaussian Sampler Using a CDT

Soundes Marzougui[1]([✉]), Ievgen Kabin[2], Juliane Krämer[3], Thomas Aulbach[3], and Jean-Pierre Seifert[1,4]

[1] Technische Universität Berlin, Berlin, Germany
soundes.marzougui@tu-berlin.de, Jean-Pierre.Seifert@external.telekom.de
[2] IHP - Leibniz-Institut für innovative Mikroelektronik, Frankfurt, Germany
kabin@ihp-microelectronics.com
[3] Universität Regensburg, Regensburg, Germany
{juliane.kraemer,thomas.aulbach}@ur.de
[4] Fraunhofer Institute for Secure Information Technology, Darmstadt, Germany

Abstract. We present a single-trace attack against lattice-based KEMs using the cumulative distribution table for Gaussian sampling and execute it in a real-world environment. Our analysis takes a single power trace of the decapsulation algorithm as input and exploits leakage of the Gaussian sampling subroutine to reveal the session key. We investigated the feasibility of the attack on different boards and proved that the power consumption traces become less informative with higher clock frequencies. Therefore, we introduce a machine-learning denoising technique, which enhances the accuracy of our attack and leverages its success rate to 100%.

We accomplish the attack on FrodoKEM, a lattice-based KEM and third-round alternate candidate. We execute it on a Cortex-M4 board equipped with an STM32F4 micro-controller clocked at different frequencies.

Keywords: FrodoKEM · Gaussian sampler · Machine-learning · Post-quantum cryptography · Power analysis · Side-channel analysis

1 Introduction

Key encapsulation mechanisms (KEM) are widely adopted in Internet protocols to establish a secure communication between two parties through the encryption of the exchanged messages. Classical KEMs - relying on the intractability of factorization or discrete-logarithm problems for large numbers - are considered to be threatened by attacks with quantum computers [31] in the near future [21]. To address the potential threats from quantum attacks, the National Institute of Standards and Technology (NIST) initiated a standardization process for post-quantum schemes in 2016, i.e., for cryptographic schemes which are assumed to be resistant towards attacks with quantum computers [23]. Post-quantum schemes can be categorized in five different families. Of the five, lattice-based cryptography has received significant research traction in recent years. Lattice-based cryptography consists of schemes whose security can be reduced to the hardness of lattice problems, for instance, the shortest vector problem (SVP), the closest vector problem (CVP), and the learning with errors (LWE) problem. Lattice-based schemes have increasingly attracted attention owing to their balanced performance in terms of sizes and speed and have been studied for real-world deployment [8,18,24,34]. In mid-2022, the NIST standardization process reached the end of the third round and both signature schemes and KEMs have been chosen for standardization.

FrodoKEM is a well-known lattice-based key encapsulation mechanism [4]. It was a third-round NIST alternate candidate and recommended by German Federal Office for Information Security (BSI) [9] and the Netherlands National Communications Security Agency (NBV) [1] for achieving quantum-safe communication. Moreover, FrodoKEM was optimized and included in different libraries such as pqm4 [12] and liboqs [33].

Lattice-based KEMs in general and FrodoKEM in specific are considered to be secure against quantum attacks [31]. However, their practical implementations succumb to side-channel analysis where an adversary has access to the victim's device. Regarding this, one might ask whether it will be easier for an attacker with access to a victim's device to directly extract the session key instead of performing a tedious side-channel analysis. For instance, an employee with the knowledge of the device's technical details can easily extract the secret key. Hence, high-end data protection has become a common place standard for every major business entity. Moreover, the session keys generated during cryptographic processes should be secured even against the manufacturer itself, thus deeming such processes 'maker-proof'. Not just that, these session keys are protected by being stored in trusted physical modules [28,35] which are tamper- and intrusion-resistant, highly-trusted, and meet security standards and regulations used, e.g., in banking systems.

Given that, extracting the session key directly from the device is challenging. Hence, most attacks target a vulnerable routine, extract sensitive information via a side-channel analysis, and build the long-term secret key. With the knowledge of the long-term secret key, the session key can be easily calculated by decrypting the exchanged ciphertext.

For example, an attacker having access to a device can retrieve the secret key by observing the power consumption, the drop of voltage, or timing variation.

Related Work: In [26], Ravi et al. identified vulnerabilities in the decapsulation procedure, exploited them to gain information about the decrypted messages, and recovered the long-term secret key within multiple side-channel information. Another attack was proposed by Aysu et al. [3]. The attack targeted the matrix and polynomial schoolbook multiplication used in these protocols. The crux of their attack was to apply a horizontal attack that makes hypotheses on several intermediate values within a single execution, all relating to the same long-term secret, and combine their correlations for estimating the secret key. Despite the fact that their attack needs a single trace, its success highly depends on the accuracy of the used triggering techniques.

In [32], Bo-Yeon Sim et al. analyzed the message encoding operation in the encapsulation phase of different lattice-based KEMs, i.e., CRYSTALS-KYBER, SABER, and FrodoKEM, and obtained the session key with a single power consumption trace [32]. Their experiments show that the success rate of the attack for FrodoKEM can be low to 79%.

In [14], Kim et al. proposed a single trace attack against KEMs employing the cumulative distribution table (CDT) for the error vector sampling. The CDT sampler outputs a sample by sampling first a random value and iterating through the CDT until the entry corresponding to the uniform random value is found. Unlike most of attacks against KEMs in the literature, their attack reveals the session key directly, without the need to obtain the long-term secret key. This attack is convenient tract case ephemeral keys are used and can also be applied to lattice-based encryption algorithms that use CDT for error sampling. The purpose of their attack is to retrieve the sampled error and reduce each LWE instance to a linear relation with the secret information.

In this paper, we investigate the practicability of the attack proposed in [14] in real-world circumstances and provide a proof-of-concept implementation. For that, we use different boards running on different frequencies. We perform our side-channel analysis and show that as compared to the previous work of [14] reading out the samples from a single power consumption trace of the FrodoKEM decapsulation is not feasible. In fact, the measurement gets noisier and less informative with higher frequency and different setup. As a solution, we employ an offline-trained machine-learning classifier on a device similar to the victim's, intended to predict the Gaussian samples during the attack phase. Moreover, we discuss the possible countermeasures to our attack based on literature work.

Contribution: In this paper, we investigate the feasibility of single-trace attacks against KEMs using Gaussian sampling and present a full-key recovery for FrodoKEM. We confirm the practicality of our full-key recovery attack targeting the NIST reference implementation and the optimized code of the pqm4 library for FrodoKEM when executed on a 32-bit Arm Cortex-M4 using machine-learning filtering techniques. We prove that our attack is robust to real-world conditions, such as noisy power measurements and high frequencies. The main contributions of the paper are summarized as follows:

- Evaluation of the feasibility of a single-trace attack against FrodoKEM. Our experimental setup relies on different realistic conditions: different clock frequencies and different target boards.
- Proof-of-concept implementation of a single-trace attack against FrodoKEM.
- Deployment of machine-learning tools to retrieve the sensitive information in case of noisy and/or less informative measurements.
- Discussion of a possible countermeasure implementation of Gaussian sampling as suggested in the literature.

Organization: The remainder of this paper is organized in six sections. In Sect. 2, we give preliminaries on the FrodoKEM scheme and the Gaussian sampling. Then, in Sect. 3, we present our experimental setup and the targeted implementations. In Sect. 4, we present a simple power analysis on the Gaussian sampling routine. Subsequently, we present a detailed mathematical description of our single trace power analysis attack in Sect. 5 and focus on the influence of the introduced noise on the feasibility of our attack. Likewise, in Sect. 6, we describe our machine-learning filtering techniques. We conclude the paper with Sect. 7 where we discuss the possible countermeasure and call attention to the urgent need of further protection against single trace attacks targeting the Gaussian sampler.

2 Background

2.1 Lattices

A *lattice* Λ is a discrete subgroup of $\mathbb{R}^n$. Given $m \leq n$ linearly independent vectors $b_1, ..., b_m \in \mathbb{R}^n$, the lattice $\Lambda(b_1, ..., b_m)$ is the set of all integer linear combinations of the b_i's, i.e.,

$$\Lambda(b_1, ..., b_m) = \Big\{ \sum_{i=1}^m x_i b_i \ \Big| \ x_i \in \mathbb{Z} \Big\},$$

where $b_1, ..., b_m$ form a *basis* of Λ and m is the *rank*. In this paper, we consider full-rank lattices, i.e., with $m = n$. An *integer lattice* is a lattice for which the basis vectors are in $\mathbb{Z}^n$. Usually, we consider elements modulo q, i.e., the basis vectors and coefficients are taken from $\mathbb{Z}_q$.

2.2 Learning with Errors

The Learning with Errors problem (LWE), which is a generalization of the classic Learning Parities with Noise problem, was introduced by Regev [27]. We explain in the following the Learning with Errors problem.

Definition 1. *Let n, q be positive integers, and let χ be a distribution over $\mathbb{Z}$. For $s \in \mathbb{Z}_q^n$, the LWE distribution $A_{s,\chi}$ is the distribution over $\mathbb{Z}_q^n \times \mathbb{Z}_q$ obtained by choosing $a \in \mathbb{Z}_q^n$ uniformly at random and an integer error $e \in \mathbb{Z}$ from χ. The distribution outputs the pair $(a, \langle a, s \rangle + e \bmod q) \in \mathbb{Z}_q^n \times \mathbb{Z}_q$.*

There are two important computational LWE problems:

- The *search problem* is to recover the secret $s \in \mathbb{Z}_q^n$ given a certain number of samples drawn from the LWE distribution $A_{s,\chi}$.
- The *decision problem* is to distinguish a certain number of samples drawn from the LWE distribution from uniformly random samples.

2.3   Gaussian Sampler and CDTs

Several lattice-based schemes use the discrete Gaussian distribution as error distribution χ in Definition 1. A centered discrete Gaussian distribution is used in LWE to ensure that the noise added to the ciphertext is truly random and unbiased, providing a secure and efficient encryption scheme. The discrete Gaussian distribution over a lattice Λ is defined as

$$D_{\Lambda,\sigma}(x) = \frac{\rho_\sigma(x)}{\sum_{y\in\Lambda}\rho_\sigma(y)},\tag{1}$$

where

$$\rho_\sigma(x) = e^{\frac{-x^2}{2\sigma^2}}\tag{2}$$

represents the continuous Gaussian function. When sampling from the positive integers, we simply write D_σ^+, which is defined accordingly by

$$D_\sigma^+(x) = \frac{\rho_\sigma(x)}{\sum_{y=0}^{+\infty}\rho_\sigma(y)}\tag{3}$$

There are different generic ways to sample from a discrete Gaussian distribution. One of the approaches employs the CDT for sampling as in Algorithm 1. First, the CDT ψ is precomputed using the cumulative distribution function of D_σ^+. The idea is that the sampler returns the index i of the table ψ, such that $\psi[i] < x \le \psi[i+1]$, where x is generated uniformly from the interval that is covered by the table. The parameter τ denotes the tail-cut and is chosen such that the probability for drawing from outside the interval is negligible.

Algorithm 1. Gaussian Sampler using CDT

Require: CDT ψ of length l, following a distribution D_σ^+, and having a tailcut τ
Ensure: Sampled value S following the targeted distribution D_σ
 1: $S \leftarrow 0$
 2: $rnd \leftarrow [0,\tau\sigma) \cup \mathbb{Z}$ uniformly at random
 3: $sign \leftarrow [0,1] \cup \mathbb{Z}$ uniformly at random
 4: **for** $(i = 0 \ ; \ i < l - 1; \ i++)$ **do**
 5:     $S \mathrel{+}= (\psi[i] - rnd) >> 15$
 6: **end for**
 7: $S \leftarrow ((-sign) \wedge S) + sign$
 8: **return** S

2.4 Description of FrodoKEM

FrodoKEM is a lattice-based KEM with security based on the standard LWE problem (i.e., not the ring version of the LWE problem). It is a conservative design with security proofs. KEM's are defined as a triple of algorithms (KeyGen, Encaps, Decaps). KeyGen is the algorithm responsible for public and secret key generation. The encapsulation algorithm Encaps generates a random key k and encrypts it using the public key pk to create a ciphertext c and derive a shared secret ss. The decapsulation algorithm Decaps decrypts c using the secret key sk and returns the derived session key ss, or a random output in case the re-encrypted ciphertext does not fully match the previous output of the encapsulation algorithm.

We describe the decapsulation of FrodoKEM as it is the target of our attack, see Algorithm 2. We introduce the following parameters:

- $n, \bar{m}, \bar{n}$ integer matrix dimensions with $n \equiv 0 \pmod 8$
- B is the number of the bits encoded in each matrix entry
- len_{seed_A} the bit length of seeds used for pseudorandom matrix generation
- $len_{seed_{SE}}$ the bit length of seeds used for pseudorandom bit generation for error sampling
- Gen pseudorandom matrix generation algorithm
- T_χ distribution table for sampling
- len_s the length of the bit vector s used for pseudorandom shared secret generation in the event of decapsulation failure
- len_z the bit length of seeds used for pseudorandom generation of $seed_{SE}$
- len_k the bit length of intermediate shared secret k
- len_{pkh} the bit length of the hash of the public key
- len_{ss} the bit length of shared secret ss

The decapsulation starts with the calculation of the matrix M. When simplifying M, we can write it as

$$M = Encode(\mu') + S'E - E'S + E'',$$

where S, S', E, E', and E'' have small entries. Therefore, $S'E - E'S + E''$ will also result in a matrix with small entries, regarded as noise. The $Decode$ (line 4, Algorithm 2) removes this noise and returns the seed μ'. The decapsulation then continues by doing a reencryption and comparing the ciphertexts. If the ciphertexts (line 16, Algorithm 2) are equal, the correct shared key ss is returned.

Algorithm 2. FrodoKEM Key Decapsulation according to [23]

Require: Ciphertext $c_1 \| c_2 \in \{0,1\}^{(\bar{m}.n + \bar{m}.\bar{n})D}$, and secret key $sk' = (s \| seed_A \| b, S^T, pkh) \in \{0,1\}^{len_s + len_{seed_A} + D.n.\bar{n}} \times \mathbb{Z}_q^{\bar{n} \times n} \times \{0,1\}^{len_{pkh}}$

Ensure: Shared secret key $ss \in \{0,1\}^{len_{ss}}$

1: $B' \leftarrow$ Unpack(c_1)
2: $C \leftarrow$ Unpack(c_2)
3: Compute $M \leftarrow C - B'S$
4: Compute $\mu' \leftarrow$ Decode(M)
5: Parse $pk \leftarrow seed_A \| b$
6: Generate pseudorandom values
   $seed_{S'E'} \| k' \leftarrow$ SHAKE$(pkh \| \mu', len_{seed_{SE}} + len_k)$
7: Generate pseudorandom bit string
   $(r^{(0)}, r^{(1)}, \ldots, r^{(2\bar{m}n + \bar{m}\bar{n}-1)}) \leftarrow$ SHAKE $(0x96 \| seed_{SE'}, (2\bar{m}n + \bar{m}\bar{n}).len_\chi)$
8: Sample error matrix $S' \leftarrow$ SampleMatrix$(r^{(0)}, r^{(1)}, \ldots, r^{(\bar{m}n-1)}, \bar{m}, n, T_\chi)$
9: Sample error matrix $E' \leftarrow$ SampleMatrix$(r^{(\bar{m}n)}, r^{(\bar{m}n+1)}, \ldots, r^{(2\bar{m}n-1)}, \bar{m}, n, T_\chi)$
10: Generate $A \leftarrow$ Gen$(seed_A)$
11: Compute $B'' \leftarrow S'A + E'$
12: Sample error matrix $E'' \leftarrow$ SampleMatrix$(r^{(2\bar{m}n)}, \ldots, r^{(2\bar{m}n + \bar{m}\bar{n}-1)}, \bar{m}, \bar{n}, T_\chi)$
13: $B \leftarrow$ Unpack$(b, n, \bar{n})$
14: Compute $V \leftarrow S'B + E''$
15: Compute $C' \leftarrow V +$ Encode(μ')
16: **if** $B' \| C = B'' \| C'$ **then**
17:    **return** shared secret $ss \leftarrow$ SHAKE $(c_1 \| c_2 \| k', len_{ss})$
18: **else**
19:    **return** shared secret $ss \leftarrow$ SHAKE $(c_1 \| c_2 \| s, len_{ss})$
20: **end if**

3 Experimental Setup

In this section, we present the experimental setup used for our side-channel analysis. Our attack targets the implementations taken from the open-source pqm4 library [12], running on the ARM Cortex-M4 and Harvard micro-controllers[1].

3.1 Implementations of FrodoKEM

The FrodoKEM source code [2] was provided as a portable C implementation. The reference implementation of FrodoKEM having the smallest parameter set (frodokem640shake/frodokem640aes) requires almost a megabyte of RAM (including messages and keys). This is mainly due to placing the entire matrix A in RAM. For larger parameter sets, more memory will be required. Therefore, the reference implementations are not suitable for the target platforms considered for this attack (and less interesting as side-channel target anyway). The optimized implementations provided by pqm4 reduce the memory consumption, however,

---

[1] The implementation of our attack can be found at https://github.com/Soundes-M/
   Soundes-M-FrodoKEMSingleTrace-/settings.

the memory footprint remains large, and only the variant of NIST security level I (frodokem640shake) fits on STM32F^2 target platforms consuming 117 KB of RAM (including messages and keys). The larger parameter sets of FrodoKEM consume between 181 KB (frodokem976shake) and 298 KB (frodokem1344aes). This is due to the fact that the implementations of the AES parameter sets of FrodoKEM use more memory than their SHAKE counterparts, and, thus, exceed our memory limits by far [13]. Additionally, pqm4 [12] includes M4-optimized assembly implementations for frodokem640shake and frodokem640aes by [5]. It speeds up the polynomial multiplication and decreases the stack memory consumption [5]. In that context, we mount our attack against the optimized [12] implementation of frodokem640shake.

3.2   Experimental Workbench

To record the traces for the attack, we used two different target boards, i.e., 8-bit Harvard and 32-bit Cortex, mounted on a ChipWhisperer Lite CW308 UFO as in Fig. 1. The ChipWhisperer is equipped with an analog-to-digital (ADC) which converts the voltage input to a digital number representing the magnitude of the voltage.

During recording, the ChipWhisperer and the micro-controller are synchronized. The sampling rate of the analog-to-digital converter (ADC) was set to 4 samples/cycle with 10-bit resolution. We used a Python script running on the PC to collect and store all relevant traces. We also used a high pass filter in the first experiment to remove the low-frequency noise [10]. For higher frequency, we used an external crystal Quarz oscillator.

The reason behind picking the two architectures 8-bit Harvard and 32-bit Cortex is that we wanted to figure out the feasibility of the single trace attack claimed in [14]. The findings in [14] need to be interpreted with cautions. In fact, in [14], the authors used an 8-bit Harvard board equipped with an XMega micro-controller which is especially common in educational embedded applications. In contrast, in real world, Cortex-M boards have been embedded in tens of billions of consumer devices.

Target Boards Setup. Our setup is composed of a CW308 UFO Board which is a board suitable for attacking different sorts of embedded targets. The UFO board has three 20-pin female headers into which the target board fits. They provide both electrical and mechanical connections for the board. The pin 1 in the right of the UFO board (Fig. 1) corresponds to the low-side shunt connection connected to the SMA cable, which is a coaxial cable responsible for transmitting the signal from the target board to the ChipWhisperer. The power consumption measurements are obtained by measuring the voltage drop across the shunt resistor.

---

^{2} We use in our experiments the STM32F4 target board which has 1 MB of Flash memory and 192 KB of RAM.

Fig. 1. Experimental workbench used for our side-channel analysis; it contains two target boards which can be mounted on the UFO board (red), a ChipWhisperer, an external clock oscillator, and a USB cable. (Color figure online)

Clock Frequency Setup. The CW308 has a crystal oscillator driver, which allows the attacker to drive the victim board through the use of an external crystal. In other words, it is possible to generate any frequency by simply putting an appropriate crystal (as shown in Fig. 1) into the socket. This step needs to be followed by adjusting of the baudrate, and routing the specific crystal oscillator to the victim external clock interface (CLKIN) using jumper J3.

4   Simple Side-Channel Analysis

4.1   Threat Model

Our threat model follows the power side-channel model of [19,20,22]. We assume that an attacker has physical access to the victim's device and is equipped with a reasonable measurement setup that can synchronize the sampling rate within the CPU clock period of the victim's device such as the experimental setup described in Sect. 3. The adversary in our model can record the power consumption measurement of the key decapsulation (Algorithm 2).

Although we specify the points for our experiments where the execution of the leaking routine (that is, the Gaussian sampling) starts in the power consumption using triggering techniques, we note that for other devices, the attacker might need engineering aspects of locating these cryptographic routine sub-traces among the whole trace as explained in [6,11,37].

We indicate that our attack is a passive attack; by revealing the session key, the adversary can also see the encrypted messages over a public channel and has the public key of the victim which is stored in his certificate. However, the adversary is not able to modify, drop, replay, or inject messages on the public channel, nor use the retrieved session key to interact with the other party. Basically, the attacker will be able only to decrypt the exchanged encrypted messages between the two parties using the extracted session key.

158   S. Marzougui et al.

4.2   Single-Trace Attack on the Gaussian Sampler

In the FrodoKEM reference and optimized implementation [2,12], the values are expressed in 16-bit integers, and nine bits are used for sampling. When the value is negative and expressed in two's complements, its significant bit is 1.

Listing 1.1. Gaussian Sampler Implementation in the reference and optimized implementation of FrodoKEM [2,12]

```
1  void frodo_sample_n(uint16_t *s, const size_t n) {
2  unsigned int i, j;
3      for (i = 0; i < n; ++i) {
4          uint16_t sample = 0;
5          uint16_t prnd = s[i] >> 1;
6          uint16_t sign = s[i] & 0x1;
7        for (j = 0; j < (unsigned int)(CDF_TABLE_LEN - 1)
8        ; j++) {
9            sample += (uint16_t)(CDF_TABLE[j] - prnd) >> 15;
10       }
11       s[i] = ((-sign) ^ sample) + sign;
12       }
13 }
```

Hence, if the subtraction in line 9, Listing 1.1 yields a negative number, its most significant bit is 1. When this number, expressed in 16 bits, is shifted to the right, one is added to the value *sample*. However, if the subtraction outputs a positive number, its most significant bit is 0. Owing to this, the value of *sample* will not be incremented. By examining the power consumption trace during the iteration through the CDT (Fig. 2(a)), we could distinguish between the addition of *zero* and *one*.

After the iteration through the CDT, the sampler calculates a positive integer called *sample*. Then, a bit-flipping operation is applied (line 11 in Listing 1.1). If the sign bit is flipped and yields zero, then the sample's sign remains the same. Else, the sign is flipped. This can be observed clearly in Fig. 2(b).

Power Consumption Traces with Different Boards. We acknowledge that the observations in Fig. 2 were already investigated by Kim and Hong in [14]. However, they are not always detectable, especially when taking the measurements on boards with different architectures, such as Cortex-M4. We exemplify this through the power consumption trace of one iteration through the CDT on a Cortex-M4 equipped with an STM32F4 Micro-controller in Fig. 3. The results presented in [14] do not apply to our setup. As in Fig. 3(a), one cannot differentiate with the naked eye between the two colors corresponding to the addition of zero and one. Surprisingly, the bit flipping is still vulnerable in this setup as in Fig. 3(b).

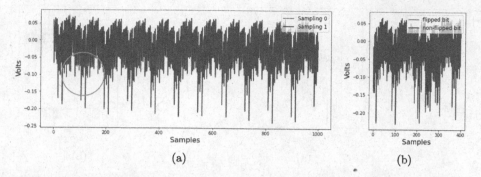

Fig. 2. (a) shows overlapped power consumption measurements during the execution of line 7–10 of Listing 1.1, while (b) shows overlapped power consumption measurements during the sign bit flipping operation (line 11, Listing 1.1). Both measurements are taken on an 8-bit Harvard board equipped with an XMega micro-controller; the red color corresponds to the sampling of the value 0 in (a) and a flipped bit in (b), while the blue color corresponds to the sampling of the value 1 in (a) and a non-flipped bit in (b) (Color figure online)

Explanation. For each target, the C code gets compiled and outputs a binary. The binaries corresponding to the compilation of the C code for different targets are identical, however, they are meant to be executed on targets that are in reality each very different from one another. Each target is a distinct collection of millions of transistors. Hence, this explains the differences in the power consumption traces, which are the measurement of the power consumed by these millions of transistors. The feasibility of side-channel analysis against one board does not imply necessarily its feasibility on other boards. In the following, we present power consumption measurements on different boards having different frequencies, and we show that the results in [14] do neither apply for all types of boards nor for different clock frequencies.

Power Consumption Traces with Different Frequencies. We increased the frequency from 7,327 MHz to 30 MHz and we took the power consumption measurement as in Figs. 4 and 5. The red color corresponds to the power consumption traces taken at a frequency of 7,327 MHz, while the blue color indicates those taken at 30 MHz. When the chip is clocked at 7,327 MHz, we notice (as in the randomly zoomed area in Figs. 4 and 5) that in every clock cycle there are two high peaks. However, at a higher frequency we notice that only one peak is occurring which minimized the fluctuation of the power consumption measurement as compared to those taken at lower frequency.

Explanation: We explain this behaviour based on [17]. There are two peaks (at the low frequency 7,327 MHz). The high peak occurs when the clock edge rises from low to high, smaller peaks take place when the clock signal falls down. At a higher clock frequency, the small peak fades or even vanishes as it overlaps with

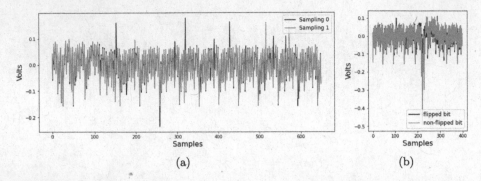

(a)   (b)

Fig. 3. (a) shows overlapped power consumption measurements during the execution of line 7–11 of Listing 1.1, while (b) shows overlapped power consumption measurements during the sign bit flipping operation (line 11, Listing 1.1). Both measurements are taken on a Cortex-M4 equipped with an STM32F4 micro-controller; the red color corresponds to the sampling of the value 0 in (a) and a flipped bit in (b), while the blue color corresponds the sampling of the value 1 in (a) and a non-flipped bit in (b). (Color figure online)

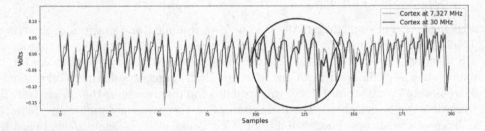

Fig. 4. Overlapped Power consumption measurement during the execution of line 9 of Listing 1.1 on an 32-bit Cortex board equipped with an STM32F4 micro-controller for two different clock frequencies

the highest peak. This yields a less informative measurement as the number of peaks of the power consumption traces decreases with higher frequencies. To this end, we came to the conclusion that single-trace attacks against the CDT Gaussian sampler presented in [14] cannot be generalized to different boards and different frequencies.

5   Description of the Attack and Error Tolerance

Once the victim starts executing the decapsulation algorithm, the attacker records its power consumption. Then, the attacker can locate in the full-trace the power consumption subtrace $T_{S'}$ and $T_{E''}$ corresponding to the sampling of S' and E'' as in Algorithm 2. The experimental setup is detailed in Sect. 3.

The first subtrace of the S' sampling called $T_{S'}$ is itself composed of 5120 subtraces, each corresponding to one iteration through the CDT. We call these

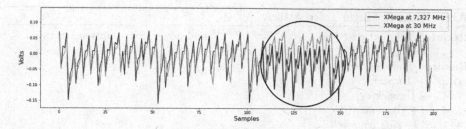

Fig. 5. Overlapped Power consumption measurement during the execution of line 9 of Listing 1.1 on an 8-bit Harvard board equipped with an XMega micro-controller for two different clock frequencies

subtraces $T_{S'_i}$, with $0 \leq i < 5120$. The attacker performs the side-channel analysis (described in Sect. 4) of the collected subtraces to predict the Gaussian samples which are the 5120 entries of the matrix S'. We refer to those side-channel analyses by the function *side_channel* (line 4 and 7, Algorithm 3). Similarly, the attacker gets the subtrace $T_{E''}$ corresponding to the sampling of the 64 entries of the matrix E''. Again, the attacker analyses each subtrace $T_{E''_j}$ to predict the 64 entries of the matrix E'', where $0 \leq j < 64$.

Having the values of S' and E'', the attacker computes the matrix V as in the decapsulation (Algorithm 2) through the following equation:

$$V = S'B + E'' \tag{4}$$

It is known from Algorithm 2 that:

$$C' = V + Encode(\mu') \tag{5}$$

Then, the attacker obtains the matrix $Encode(\mu')$ by plugging Eq. 4 in Eq. 5 as below.

$$C' = S'B + E'' + Encode(\mu') \tag{6}$$

Note that Encode is a function that takes a bit strings of length $l = B \times \bar{m} \times \bar{n}$ as input and encodes it to a matrix of $\bar{m} \times \bar{n}$ entries. We refer to [4] for more details. The Eq. 6 gives the encoding of μ'.

$$Encode(\mu') = C' - S'B - E'' \tag{7}$$

To obtain μ the attacker applies the *Decode* on the right side of the Eq. 7. Note that *Decode* decodes an m-by-n matrix into a bit string of length $B \times m \times n$. This means, it extracts B bits from each entry of the matrix. Hence, μ' can be written as:

$$\mu' = Decode(C' - S'B - E'') \tag{8}$$

The attacker then calculates the session key ss. The attack is summarized in Algorithm 3.

Algorithm 3. Single Trace Attack

Require: Ciphertext $c_1\|c_2 \in \{0,1\}^{(\bar{m}.n+\bar{m}.\bar{n})D}$ and power consumption traces
$\quad T_{S'} = (T_{S'_0},\ldots,T_{S'_{\bar{m}n-1}})$ and $T_{E''} = (T_{E'_0},\ldots,T_{E'_{\bar{m}\bar{n}-1}})$
Ensure: The session key ss
1: $B' \leftarrow$ Unpack(c_1)
2: $C \leftarrow$ Unpack(c_2)
3: **for** $i \in \{0\ldots\bar{m}n\}$ **do**
4: $\quad S'_i \leftarrow side\_channel(T_{S'_i})$
5: **end for**
6: **for** $i \in \{0\ldots\bar{m}\bar{n}\}$ **do**
7: $\quad E''_i \leftarrow side\_channel(T_{E''_i})$
8: **end for**
9: Compute $V = S'B + E''$
10: Compute $Encode(\mu') = C - V$ and get μ' by applying $Decode()$
11: Generate pseudorandom values $seed_{SE'}\|k' \leftarrow$ SHAKE$(pkh\|\mu', len_{SE} + len_k)$
12: shared secret $ss \leftarrow$ SHAKE $(c_1\|c_2\|k', len_{ss})$
13: **return** ss

Noise Tolerance: We notice here that the noise on the samples E'' does not affect the correctness of the attack because the $Decode()$ function rounds the term $C' - S'B - E''$ to the $(32 - B)$ most significant bits. Hence, the B least significant bits -even when guessed wrong- do not have consequences on the value μ' (B is equal to 2 for the first security level of FrodoKEM).

On the other side, having an error on one coefficient of the matrix S' will propagate when this latter is multiplied by B and will result in different erroneous matrix entries. This error can be located in the first bits of the coefficients of the resulting matrix $(S'B)$ which will not be tolerated and result in a wrong value of μ'. We include in the following section, a machine-learning side channel analysis technique that leverage the accuracy of the single trace attack and enhance the attacker capability to retrieve the session key.

6   Machine-Learning Side-Channel Analysis

Side-channel experiments are usually carried out in careful and non-realistic circumstances. For example, the noise is minimized by using noise filtering techniques, or non-commercial prototype boards are targeted. This yields easy-to-analyse power consumption traces. However, in reality the real-world conditions such as noise can prohibit the attack as explained in Sect. 5. To tackle this problem, we write the power consumption[3] at a specific point of time as the following:

$$P = P_{op} + P_{data} + P_{noise} + P_{const} \tag{9}$$

---

[3] We mean here the power consumption of the device while running a cryptographic operation.

The four entities P_{op}, P_{data}, P_{noise}, and P_{const} are functions of time. The entities P_{op} and P_{data} are the power consumption depending on the executed operation and the data, respectively. The entity P_{noise} represents the noise added to the power consumption measurement, and P_{const} refers to constant power consumption that occurs independently of the operation and the data.

Power analysis exploits the dependency between the power consumption and the processed operation and data, i.e., P_{op} and P_{data}. In Sect. 4.2, we figured out two scenarios affecting the ability of an attacker to analyse the power consumption traces. In the first scenario, the noise level is extremely high, i.e., $P_{noise} \gg P_{op} + P_{data}$, which prevents the attacker from detecting the leakage. To characterize the added noise P_{noise}, we recorded the power consumption while running the Gaussian sampling with fixed input, i.e., fixed random numbers. This yields the repeated execution of the same instructions with the same input data. We mounted this experiment with 1000 repetitions on each board. From each of these traces we took always the sample with the same index (i.e., index 120) corresponding to the first point of interest (POI) in the power consumption trace. With these points we computed the two histograms in Figs. 6 and 7.

For a low frequency, we point out that most of the points are concentrated around zero. The shape of the histogram in Fig. 6 indicates that the points in the power traces follow a Gaussian distribution. However, for higher frequency the noise distribution tends to be uniform for a cortex M4 board. For an XMega board, the added noise follows a multidimensional Gaussian distribution.

In the second scenario, the high frequency leads to flattening the power consumption trace, i.e., $P_{op} + P_{data} \sim constant$ (observations in Sect. 4.1 demonstrate that with higher frequencies the power consumption becomes less informative) which can often decrease the capability of an attacker to retrieve the intermediate sensitive data with the naked eye or even with differential power analysis.

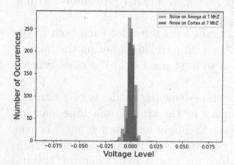
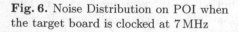
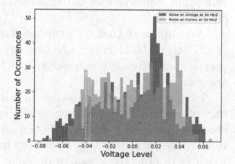

Fig. 6. Noise Distribution on POI when the target board is clocked at 7 MHz

Fig. 7. Noise Distribution on POI when the target board is clocked at 30 MHz

Therefore, in both scenarios, a single-trace attack against FrodoKEM as in [14] could not be mounted in real circumstances. To tackle these challenges, one way is to use a spectrum analyser which displays a spectrum of signal amplitudes on different frequencies and determines the noise added to the signal (power consumption of the device while running the cryptographic operation). In view of the expensive price of a spectrum analyzer, other cheaper ways are considered, e.g., template attacks based on a Gaussian assumption [7]. However, template attacks have been subject to much criticism [16]. First, template attacks hold true only if the assumption on the noise distribution is correct. This is not always fulfilled in a real-world scenario. Moreover, they are useful as long as a limited number of points of interest can be identified in leakage traces and contain most of the information. If the number of useless samples in leakage traces increases and/or the size of the profiling set becomes too limited, the template attacks are useless [16]. Instead, machine-learning side-channel analysis is more powerful in this case.

We propose a machine-learning technique composed of two phases: a profiling phase and an attack phase.

6.1 Profiling Phase

To prepare the profiling, we executed the Gaussian sampling process (Algorithm 1) with random input.

The training of our neural network proceeds as follows. First, we prepare traces of the execution of multiple iterations through the CDT during the Gaussian sampling function with random input (lines 7–13, Listing 1.1). The output of each CDT iteration (i.e., the Gaussian sample) is assigned as the label. With the prepared traces and their corresponding labels, we can build a list of examples $(x, y) \in \mathbb{R}^t \times Y$, where $x \in \mathbb{R}^t$ are the power traces acting as the *features*, and $y \in Y$ are the Gaussian samples acting as the *labels*. We assume that x leaks information about y. The list of these noisy examples (x, y) is split into training, validation, and a test set of the Multi-Layer Perceptron (MLP) machine-learning classifier.

We emphasize that the attacker should train a classifier for each board type (i.e., Cortex-M4, Harvard) and frequency. According to [36], ignoring the board's specifics and diversity can easily lead to an overestimation of the classification accuracy.

Tuning the hyper-parameters of our machine-learning model is of particular importance because it influences the accuracy of the trained machine-learning classifier, hence the practicability of our attack. There are often general heuristics or rules of thumb for configuring hyper-parameters. However, a better approach is to objectively search different values for model hyper-parameters and choose a subset that maximizes the prediction accuracy of our classifier. The so-called hyper-parameter optimization is available in the scikit-learn Python machine-learning library [30]. The result of a hyper-parameter optimization is a single set of well-performing hyper-parameters that is used to configure the MLP classifiers.

We refer to each of our MLP classifiers as *Classifier* which is trained on traces labeled by the output samples. We captured 20,000 power consumption traces. We set 18,000 of them for training and testing and 2,000 for validation.

6.2   Attack Phase

Equipped with the trained MLP classifier, the attacker deduces information about the samples from the power traces.

First, she (the attacker) lets the victim device run the decapsulation process. Then, she extracts from the full power trace the parts of the trace corresponding to the Gaussian sampling of the matrices S' and E''. Each of those traces, i.e., S' and E'' is split itself into snippets corresponding to the sampling of the matrix entries. To this end, the attacker feeds those snippets to the classifier trained in the profiling phase, and obtains a prediction of each entry in the matrices S' and E''.

Once the matrices S' and E'' are predicted by the attacker, this latter plugs this information in Eq. 8 and calculates the value μ' as described in Sect. 5. Therefore, the session key can be calculated by hashing the value of μ' concatenated with the public known values of the ciphertext, k', and len_{ss} as the following: $ss = \text{SHAKE}\,(c_1 \| c_2 \| k', len_{ss})$.

7   Countermeasures and Conclusion

It is important to note that CDT is not the only method of sampling, with binomial sampling being used in modern lattice-based schemes such as Kyber. Our attack may potentially affect the binomial distribution as similar instructions are executed, and we anticipate it to be even more efficient due to the fact that binomial sampling counts the number of positive outcomes in binary experiments, making bitwise operations more susceptible to attack through side-channel analysis. In the following, we discuss the possible countermeasures against the proposed single-trace attack on the CDT sampler.

To avoid the presented single trace attack, the work [38] *might* be a countermeasure. Instead of sampling directly from the target distribution D_σ, they suggest to first start by generating a sample x from the base sampler $D_{\sigma_0}^+$, where $\sigma_0 = \sqrt{1/2 \ln(2)}$.

Then, obtain the value y_u uniformly at random from $[0, \cdots, K-1]$, and compute $z = y_u + Kx$, where $K = \left\lfloor \frac{\sigma}{\sigma_0} + 1 \right\rfloor$ is a constant. Finally, a Bernoulli rejection sampling with acceptance rate

$$p = \exp\left(\frac{-y(y + 2\,Kx)}{2\sigma^2}\right)$$

is applied to ensure that z follows the distribution D_σ^+. In order to obtain also negative samples, one can apply a random sign bit, but has to reject $z = 0$ with probability $1/2$.

This countermeasure *does* protect against the proposed single-trace attack for schemes having relatively high deviation. However, for FrodoKEM the target standard deviation is $\sigma = 2.8$. Therefore, the value of K is small, i.e. $K = 4$. An attacker still can get the samples with a precision K, since she is able to reveal the value of x with the introduced single trace attack. She only misses out on the value $y_u \in \{0, \cdots, K-1\}$, when trying to recover the final sample $z = y_u + Kx$.

One of the common countermeasures is masking. In [29] Schneider et al. presented the first protected (masked) binomial sampler claimed to be secure against side-channel adversaries of arbitrary order. First-order masking countermeasures are not enough to protect against ML attacks. Leveraging the masking order is needed but it yields a performance overhead memory and time-wise. The first-order masking technique has been, however, broken by [22] using machine-learning side-channel analysis.

Another countermeasure was suggested by [14], where a look-up table is used for sampling. One samples a 16-bit integer, and uses it as the index of the look-up table and outputs the corresponding table value (or the sample). However, this countermeasure needs to store a big look-up table. For FrodoKEM-640, the Gaussian sample does not exceed one byte, and the random values are 16-bit precision, where the last significant bit is used for the sign. Hence, a table of size 2^{16} bits is needed.

Additionally, one càn perform the Fisher-Yates random shuffle (or Knuth shuffle) [15] in order to mask the relationship between the side channel and the secret information (the samples). Specifically, after sampling the matrices S' and E'' their samples are shuffled. This countermeasure *might* be robust against our attack, given that each session key is specific to a single session establishment. However, in case the attacker succeeded to force the victim reusing the same session key, the countermeasure of random shuffling is not secure anymore and was proven to leak information [25]. An attacker needs a marginally larger, yet still practical number of samples to rearrange the coordinates and undo the shuffle.

To conclude, KEMs are important cryptographic routines for large-scale communication protocols. As ephemeral secrets are used in these protocols, the risk of being vulnerable to side-channel analysis can be underestimated. This is because the chance of an attack being successful decreases when the same key is used only once in a single execution of the scheme. In this paper, we validate that it is indeed crucial to examine the vulnerability of these schemes against single-trace attacks targeting the session key. As lattice-based key exchange protocols are already deployed in practical applications, their side-channel evaluation should play a role in the decision of their implementation choices. This paper examines the feasibility of side-channel analysis against KEMs using CDT Gaussian sampling and proves that the latter is still vulnerable to machine-learning side-channel attacks even in real-world circumstances. We demonstrate our results using FrodoKEM as an example, which is a NIST alternate candidate from the third round, and has been recommended by the German Federal Office for Information Security (BSI) [9] and the Netherlands National Communications Security Agency (NBV) [1] for achieving quantum-safe communication. Our single-trace attack leads to the recovery of the complete session key.

Acknowledgment. The work described in this paper has been supported by the German Federal Ministry of Education and Research (BMBF) under the project Full Lifecycle Post-Quantum PKI - FLOQI (ID 16KIS1074) and under the project Aquorypt (ID 16KIS1022).

References

1. Netherlands National Communications Security Agency. Prepare for the threat of quantum-computers (2022). https://english.aivd.nl/publications/publications/2022/01/18/prepare-for-the-threat-of-quantumcomputers
2. Alkim, F., et al.: Frodokem: learning with errors key encapsulation. Github. https://github.com/microsoft/PQCrypto-LWEKE
3. Aydin, E., Aysu, A., Tiwari, M., Gerstlauer, A., Orshansky, M.: Horizontal side-channel vulnerabilities of post-quantum key exchange and encapsulation protocols. ACM Trans. Embed. Comput. Syst. **20**(6), October 2021
4. Bos, J., et al.: Take off the ring! practical, quantum-secure key exchange from lwe. In: Proceedings of the 2016 ACM SIGSAC Conference on Computer and Communications Security, pp. 1006–1018 (2016)
5. Bos, J.W., Friedberger, S., Martinoli, M., Oswald, E., Stam, M.: Fly, you fool! faster frodo for the arm cortex-m4. Cryptology ePrint Archive (2018)
6. Castryck, W., Iliashenko, I., Vercauteren, F.: Provably weak instances of ring-lwe revisited, May 2016
7. Chari, S., Rao, J.R., Rohatgi, P.: Template attacks. In: Kaliski, B.S., Koç, K., Paar, C. (eds.) CHES 2002. LNCS, vol. 2523, pp. 13–28. Springer, Heidelberg (2003). https://doi.org/10.1007/3-540-36400-5_3
8. Ducas, L., Durmus, A., Lepoint, T., Lyubashevsky, V.: Bimodal lattice signature scheme (bliss). https://wiki.strongswan.org/projects/strongswan/wiki/BLISS
9. Federal Office for Information Security (BSI). Bsi tr-02102-1: "cryptographic mechanisms: Recommendations and key lengths" version: 2022-1, 2022. https://www.bsi.bund.de/SharedDocs/Downloads/EN/BSI/Publications/TechGuidelines/TG02102/BSI-TR-02102-1.html
10. NewAE Technology Inc. https://www.mouser.com/datasheet/2/894/NAE-CW308-datasheet-1289269.pdf
11. Inci, M.S., Gulmezoglu, B., Irazoqui, G., Eisenbarth, T., Sunar, B.: Cache attacks enable bulk key recovery on the cloud, August 2016
12. Kannwischer, M.J., Rijneveld, J., Schwabe, P., Stoffelen, K.: PQM4: Post-quantum crypto library for the ARM Cortex-M4. https://github.com/mupq/pqm4
13. Kannwischer, M.J., Rijneveld, J., Schwabe, P., Stoffelen, K.: pqm4: testing and benchmarking NIST PQC on ARM cortex-m4. IACR Cryptol. ePrint Arch., p. 844 (2019)
14. Kim, S., Hong, S.: Single trace analysis on constant time cdt sampler and its countermeasure. Appl. Sci. **8**(10) (2018)
15. Knuth, D.E.: Art of computer programming, volume 2: Seminumerical algorithms. Addison-Wesley Professional (2014)

16. Lerman, L., Poussier, R., Bontempi, G., Markowitch, O., Standaert, F.-X.: Template attacks vs. machine learning revisited (and the curse of dimensionality in side-channel analysis). In: Mangard, S., Poschmann, A.Y. (eds.) Constructive Side-Channel Analysis and Secure Design, pp. 20–33. Springer, Cham (2015)

17. Mangard, S., Oswald, E., Popp, T.: Power Analysis Attacks: Revealing the Secrets of Smart Cards (Advances in Information Security). Springer, Heidelberg (2007)

18. Marzougui, S., Krämer, J.: Post-quantum cryptography in embedded systems (2019)

19. Marzougui, S., Ulitzsch, V., Tibouchi, M., Seifert, J.-P.: Profiling side-channel attacks on dilithium: a small bit-fiddling leak breaks it all. Cryptology ePrint Archive, Paper 2022/106, 2022. https://eprint.iacr.org/2022/106

20. Marzougui, S., Wisiol, N., Gersch, P., Krämer, J., Seifert, J.-P.: Machine-learning side-channel attacks on the galactics constant-time implementation of bliss (2021)

21. Mosca, M.: Cybersecurity in an era with quantum computers: will we be ready? IEEE Secur. Privacy 16(5), 38–41 (2018)

22. Ngo, K., Dubrova, E., Guo, Q., Johansson, T.: A side-channel attack on a masked ind-cca secure saber kem implementation. IACR Trans. Cryptographic Hardware Embedded Syst., 676–707 (2021)

23. National Institute of standards and technology. Nist pqc standardization process. https://csrc.nist.gov/Projects/post-quantum-cryptography

24. Paul, S., Schick, F., Seedorf, J.: Tpm-based post-quantum cryptography: a case study on quantum-resistant and mutually authenticated tls for iot environments. In: The 16th International Conference on Availability, Reliability and Security, ARES 2021. Association for Computing Machinery, New York (2021)

25. Pessl, P.: Analyzing the shuffling side-channel countermeasure for lattice-based signatures. In: Dunkelman, O., Sanadhya, S.K. (eds.) INDOCRYPT 2016. LNCS, vol. 10095, pp. 153–170. Springer, Cham (2016). https://doi.org/10.1007/978-3-319-49890-4_9

26. Ravi, P., Roy, S.S., Chattopadhyay, A., Bhasin, S.: Generic side-channel attacks on cca-secure lattice-based pke and kems. IACR Trans. Cryptographic Hardware Embedded Syst. 2020(3), 307–335 (2020)

27. Regev, O.: On lattices, learning with errors, random linear codes, and cryptography. J. ACM 56(6), September 2009

28. Rhode and Schwarz. Kryptogeräte. https://www.rohde-schwarz.com/de/produkte/aerospace-verteidigung-sicherheit/kryptogeraete_230846.html

29. Schneider, T., Paglialonga, C., Oder, T., Güneysu, T.: Efficiently masking binomial sampling at arbitrary orders for lattice-based crypto. In: Lin, D., Sako, K. (eds.) PKC 2019. LNCS, vol. 11443, pp. 534–564. Springer, Cham (2019). https://doi.org/10.1007/978-3-030-17259-6_18

30. Scikit learn. scikit-learn machine learning in python. https://scikit-learn.org/stable/

31. Shor, P.W.: Polynomial-time algorithms for prime factorization and discrete logarithms on a quantum computer. SIAM J. Comput. 26(5), 1484–1509 (1997)

32. Sim, B.-Y., et al.: Single-trace attacks on message encoding in lattice-based kems. IEEE Access 8, 183175–183191 (2020)

33. Stebila, D., Mosca, M.: liboqs is an open source C library for quantum-safe cryptographic algorithms., Cortex-M4. https://github.com/open-quantum-safe/liboqs

34. Ulitzsch, V.Q., Park, S., Marzougui, S., Seifert, J.-P.: A post-quantum secure subscription concealed identifier for 6g. In: Proceedings of the 15th ACM Conference on Security and Privacy in Wireless and Mobile Networks, WiSec 2022, pp. 157–168. Association for Computing Machinery, New York (2022)

35. Utimaco. What is a hardware security module (hsm). https://utimaco.com/de/produkte/technologien/hardware-security-modules/what-hardware-security-module-hsm
36. Wang, H., Brisfors, M., Forsmark, S., Dubrova, E.: How diversity affects deep-learning side-channel attacks. In: 2019 IEEE Nordic Circuits and Systems Conference (NORCAS): NORCHIP and International Symposium of System-on-Chip (SoC), pp. 1–7 (2019)
37. Zhang, Y., Juels, A., Reiter, M.K., Ristenpart, T.: Cross-vm side channels and their use to extract private keys. In Proceedings of the 2012 ACM Conference on Computer and Communications Security, CCS 2012, pp. 305–316. Association for Computing Machinery, New York (2012)
38. Zhao, R.K., Steinfeld, R., Sakzad, A.: Facct: Fast, compact, and constant-time discrete gaussian sampler over integers. IEEE Trans. Comput. **69**(1), 126–137 (2020)

Punctured Syndrome Decoding Problem
Efficient Side-Channel Attacks Against *Classic McEliece*

Vincent Grosso[1]($\boxtimes$) (iD), Pierre-Louis Cayrel[1] (iD), Brice Colombier[1] (iD),
and Vlad-Florin Drăgoi[2,3] (iD)

[1] Université Jean Monnet Saint-Etienne, CNRS, Institut d Optique Graduate School,
Laboratoire Hubert Curien UMR 5516, 42023 Saint-Etienne, France
`vincent.grosso@univ-st-etienne.fr`
[2] Faculty of Exact Sciences, Aurel Vlaicu University, Arad, Romania
[3] LITIS, University of Rouen Normandie, Saint-Etienne du Rouvray, France

Abstract. Among the fourth round finalists of the NIST post-quantum
cryptography standardization process for public-key encryption algorithms and key encapsulation mechanisms, three rely on hard problems
from coding theory. Key encapsulation mechanisms are frequently used
in hybrid cryptographic systems: a public-key algorithm for key exchange
and a secret key algorithm for communication. A major point is thus the
initial key exchange that is performed thanks to a key encapsulation
mechanism. In this paper, we analyze side-channel vulnerabilities of the
key encapsulation mechanism implemented by the *Classic McEliece* cryptosystem, whose security is based on the syndrome decoding problem.
We use side-channel leakages to reduce the complexity of the syndrome
decoding problem by reducing the length of the code considered. The
columns punctured from the original code reduce the complexity of a
hard problem from coding theory. This approach leads to efficient profiled side-channel attacks that recover the session key with high success
rates, even in noisy scenarios.

Keywords: Post-quantum cryptography · Code-based cryptography ·
Side-channel attacks

1 Introduction

Recent developments in quantum computing threaten classical public key cryptography. Indeed, Shor's algorithm [22] could be used to break public key schemes
such as RSA or Diffie-Hellman. Therefore, to prepare security in the quantum
computing era, in 2016, NIST launched a standardization process for post-
quantum cryptography standards to replace current public-key standards which
are vulnerable to quantum computing. In July 2022, the fourth round of the standardization process started. Among the four remaining candidates for public key
encryption algorithms and key encapsulation mechanisms, three are code-based
solutions: *Classic McEliece* [2], BIKE [3], and HQC [1].

   All three proposals implement a solution for IND-CCA secure key exchange
using a Key Encapsulation Mechanism (KEM) [15]. KEMs are used to exchange

private session key over an insecure channel using public cryptography scheme. To avoid short message and padding issues while using public-key encryption . schemes, a key derivation function is used allowing to generate the message sent in the right domain and using most of the time a hash function to derive a uniform random looking secret key, assuming enough entropy in the original message. The security of the private communication relies on the security of the KEM, assuming that secure symmetric algorithms are used. Moreover KEM can be seen as a key-exchange protocol in which only a single message is transmitted, if one of the two parties knows the public key of the second party.

For both *Classic McEliece* and BIKE, the security of the KEM relies on the hardness of the binary Syndrome Decoding Problem (SDP). Conversely, the security of HQC essentially relies on the hardness of decoding a general linear code. The binary SDP is an $\mathcal{NP}$-hard problem stating the following. Knowing a matrix $H \in \mathbb{F}_2^{(n-k) \times n}$, an integer $t \leq n$ and a vector $s^* \in \mathbb{F}_2^{n-k}$, it is difficult to recover $e \in \mathbb{F}_2^n$ such that $He = s^*$ and $\mathrm{HW}(e) = t$. The vector s^* is usually referred to as the *syndrome*. In a KEM, the vector s^* is sent, and the secret data e is reconstructed by the recipient. Thus the encapsulation algorithm consists of a matrix-vector multiplication. The difficulty of the problem depends on the weight t of e. The problem is difficult when e is of sufficiently "low weight".

Some of the best solutions to solve the binary SDP make use of the so-called "information set decoding" strategy (ISD) [4,14,16,19,23]. The key idea is to exploit the "low weight" property of e by selecting a sufficient number of columns that do not operate in the computation of s^*. Afterwards, Gaussian elimination can be performed on the other columns. However, selecting the columns is a challenging phase.

A consequence of the NIST post-quantum cryptography standardization process is to accelerate the development of implementations of code-based cryptography algorithms [7,8,18,21]. In particular, *Classic McEliece* has been implemented on 32-bit microprocessor ARM Cortex-M4 [7], with the limitation that the public key must be stored in the flash memory, and on a Xlilinx Artix-7 FPGA [8]. Implementations on constrained platforms, such as micro-controllers or FPGAs, also lead to physical attacks against different algorithms of code-based cryptography [5,9,12,13]. For example, it has been shown that the session key can be recovered by side-channel attacks with multiple observations during the decapsulation process [13] or with a single observation during the encapsulation process [9]. Colombier *et al.* demonstrated the effectiveness of their method against an implementation on the Chipwhisperer platform, which is known to allow for low-noise side-channel measurements. The efficiency of the proposed method in a more noisy setting was later analyzed in [10].

The focus of this article is on *Classic McEliece*, in particular the matrix-vector multiplication over $\mathbb{F}_2$ used in the syndrome computation. Conversely, BIKE uses polynomial multiplication. Adaptations are needed to apply the attack against other finalists but this is out of the scope of this article.

Contribution. This article exposes in details the inherent limitations of previously proposed side-channel attacks against *Classic McEliece* presented in [9].

In particular, we explain the performance degradation of the existing approach when large noise levels are considered. Besides the intrinsic uncertainty of the Hamming weight classifier, we show that, overall, it is mainly due to an accumulation of errors in the way the integer syndrome is computed, as required by the attack setting and explained below. We then present a new, more efficient method that achieves better resistance against noise present in side-channel traces by resorting to a more traditional divide-and-conquer approach.

This new method is a profiled side-channel attack against Niederreiter-like constructions using packed matrix-vector multiplications, as used in the round four finalist of the NIST standardization process *Classic McEliece*. Moreover, we also study the feasibility of the proposed attacks against implementations that use a larger register size, which is a clear trend in embedded software implementations.

Organization. This article is organized as follows. Section 2 describes existing message-recovery attacks on the packed matrix-vector multiplication as used for the syndrome computation in the *Classic McEliece* cryptosystem. The inherent limitations of these attacks, in particular when it comes to error propagation, are detailed in Sect. 3. In Sect. 4, we introduce a divide-and-conquer strategy that efficiently limits the propagation of errors. Experimental results are given in Sect. 5 and we conclude in Sect. 6.

2   Message-Recovery Attacks on the Packed Matrix-Vector Multiplication

This section introduces code-based KEMs and the target algorithm of the proposed side-channel attack: *Classic McEliece*. In particular, we focus on the matrix-vector multiplication performed during the encapsulation step. We also present previous side-channel attacks that recover the shared session key.

Notations. The following notations are used in this article. A finite field is denoted by $\mathbb{F}$. Matrices and vectors are written in bold capital, respectively small letters, *e.g.* a vector of length n is $c = (c_1, \ldots, c_n)$ and a $k \times n$ matrix is $H = (h_{i,j})_{(i,j) \in \mathbb{N}_k^* \times \mathbb{N}_n^*}$. Let $H_{i,(j-1)w+1:jw}$ be the jth block of size w of the ith row of the H matrix. The concatenation of the vectors a and b is written as $a \parallel b$. The Hamming weight of a binary vector $\mathrm{HW}(e)$ is the number of its non-zero coordinates. The Hamming distance between two vectors a and b is written as $\mathrm{HD}(a, b)$.

2.1   *Classic McEliece* Encapsulation

Like others KEMs, *Classic McEliece* includes three operations: key generation, encapsulation and decapsulation. We focus on the encapsulation step in this work. This is detailed in Algorithm 1, where the target operation of the proposed attack is annotated. This target operation performs a matrix-vector multiplication over $\mathbb{F}_2$ and its implementation is detailed in the next subsection.

Algorithm 1. *Classic McEliece* encapsulation

1: **function** ENCAP($\boldsymbol{H}$)
2:     Generate a uniform random vector $e \in \mathbb{F}_2^n$ with HW(e) = t.
3:     Compute $C \leftarrow \boldsymbol{H}e$ ▷ target operation
4:     Compute $K \leftarrow \mathsf{H}(1 \parallel e \parallel C)$ ▷ session key
5:     **return** (C, K)

2.2 Packed Matrix-Vector Multiplication

Algorithm 2 shows the pseudo code of a software implementation of the matrix-vector multiplication over $\mathbb{F}_2$. This implementation is referred to as "packed" since multiple bits are stored together in the same machine word. The size of the machine word w is a parameter in this algorithm. In the reference implementation of the *Classic McEliece* submission [2], $w = 8$. In the ARM Cortex-M4 implementation by Chen and Chou [7], $w = 32$. In the vectorized implementation of the *Classic McEliece* submission [2], $w = 64$. Boolean instructions then operate over the full machine word to perform operations in parallel. That is the key operation of the encapsulation step in the *Classic McEliece* KEM. As shown in [9], the strongest side-channel leakage occurs for line 5, when the intermediate variable b is updated by repeatedly adding the logical AND of a matrix entry and a vector entry. To be able to refer to specific intermediate values later, we write these intermediate variables as if they were stored in a matrix: $\boldsymbol{b}_{i,j}$. In actual implementations, a single machine word is used.

Algorithm 2. Packed matrix-vector multiplication over $\mathbb{F}_2$

Require: A binary $(n, n-k)$ matrix $\boldsymbol{H}$, and a binary vector e of n elements, the register size w (should be a power of 2)
Ensure: A binary vector $s^* = \boldsymbol{H}e$
1: $s^* \leftarrow 0$
2: **for** $i \leftarrow 1$ to $(n-k)$ **do**
3:     $\boldsymbol{b}_{i,0} \leftarrow 0$
4:     **for** $j \leftarrow 1$ to $\frac{n}{w}$ **do**
5:         $\boldsymbol{b}_{i,j} \leftarrow \boldsymbol{b}_{i,j-1} \oplus \boldsymbol{H}_{i,(j-1)w+1:jw} \wedge e_j$
6:     $t \leftarrow \frac{w}{2}$
7:     **while** $t > 0$ **do**
8:         $\boldsymbol{b}_{i,\frac{n}{w}} \leftarrow \boldsymbol{b}_{i,\frac{n}{w}} \oplus (\boldsymbol{b}_{i,\frac{n}{w}} \gg t)$
9:         $t \leftarrow \frac{t}{2}$
10:    $s^*_{\lfloor \frac{i}{w} \rfloor} \leftarrow s^*_{\lfloor \frac{i}{w} \rfloor} \vee \left(\left(\boldsymbol{b}_{i,\frac{n}{w}} \wedge 1 \right) \ll (i \bmod w) \right)$
11: **return** s^*

2.3   Message Recovery Attack

We describe the method introduced in [9], to recover session keys on cryptosystems based on the binary syndrome decoding problem. This attack uses side-channel information obtained during the encapsulation step. The message recovery attack is composed of four steps, which we describe hereafter.

1. *Side-channel analysis:* the goal of this first step is to estimate the Hamming weight of the successive intermediate values of b during the matrix-vector multiplication, as shown on line 5 in Algorithm 2. For the loop index i, j, we denote by $\widetilde{\mathrm{HW}}(b_{i,j})$ the best guess for the Hamming weight of $b_{i,j}$. In [9], authors use a random-forest classifiers for this step, but other classifiers can be used.
2. *Derivation of the integer syndrome:* with the Hamming weight information obtained in the first step, the attacker may estimate the values of the syndrome s in $\mathbb{N}$, in addition to the binary syndrome s^* which is public. This is done by summing the differences of the maximum of each value found in the previous step, as detailed in Eq. (1).

$$1 \leq i \leq (n-k) \quad \widetilde{s}_i = \sum_{j=1}^{\frac{n}{w}} \left| \widetilde{\mathrm{HW}}(b_{i,j}) - \widetilde{\mathrm{HW}}(b_{i,j-1}) \right| \qquad (1)$$

This computation requires a good estimation of the Hamming weight of the intermediate values. In addition, it only works under additional conditions between $b_{i,j}$ and $b_{i,j-1}$. If those conditions are not met, it can lead to derive an erroneous value for the integer syndrome. We discuss these issues in more details in Sect. 3.
3. *Sort columns:* the next step is to separate the columns into two sets. The first set consists of the columns whose indexes are in the support of e. The second set consists of the other columns. However, this separation is a difficult task. In [9], authors compute a score for each column and sort columns according to this score. The score for the column j, based on the work of Feige and Lellouche [11], is defined in Eq. (2).

$$\forall j \in [\![1, n]\!], \quad \psi_j(\widetilde{s}) = H_{.,j} \cdot \widetilde{s} + \overline{H}_{.,j} \cdot \overline{\widetilde{s}} \qquad (2)$$

where $\overline{H}$ is the complementary of the matrix H and $\overline{\widetilde{s}} = t - \widetilde{s}$, where t is the weight of e as dictated by the security parameters. In [10], the efficiency of this score function is analyzed in the presence of errors.
4. *Information Set Decoding:* as shown in [10] the score function allows to efficiently discriminate most of the columns in the support of e from other columns even in the presence of noise. However, a few columns may still be wrongly classified. In that case, the score function is used to provide a "good" initial permutation for ISD methods.

This method achieves a good success rate in a realistic scenario with measurements on a ChipWhisperer platform [17] for various sets of parameters.

3   Limitation of the CDCG Method

In this section, we present errors that can appear in the method of [9] and reduce the efficiency of the message recovery. We concentrate on side-channel and recombination errors that lead to an incorrect syndrome in $\mathbb{N}$, *i.e.*, the two first steps presented in Sect. 2.3. Eventually, we discuss the impact of such errors on scores output by the ψ score function [11].

3.1   Side-Channel Analysis Error

We first try to identify how side-channel analysis errors alter the estimation of the syndrome s in $\mathbb{N}$. Due to their nature and noise in measurements, side-channel attacks can output guesses that are not the targeted sensitive information used in the implementation.

We say that the side-channel distinguisher makes an error if the highest guess score does not correspond to the Hamming weight of the actual computation: $\widetilde{\mathrm{HW}}(\boldsymbol{b}_{i,j}) \neq \mathrm{HW}(\boldsymbol{b}_{i,j})$. We may rewrite the faulty guess as:

$$\widetilde{\mathrm{HW}}(\boldsymbol{b}_{i,j}) = \mathrm{HW}(\boldsymbol{b}_{i,j}) + \varepsilon_{i,j},$$

with $\varepsilon_{i,j} \neq 0$.

Due to the leakage model, the error is generally small: $\varepsilon_{i,j} \in \{-1, 1\}$ The Hamming weight guess is the real Hamming weight plus or minus one. In practice, we observe on real traces that the error is small for template and random forests when used as side-channel distinguishers.

If the side-channel distinguisher made some errors for the value in row i and column j then the estimated syndrome in $\mathbb{N}$ will be flawed in the ith position. This is clear when considering how the ith component of s is derived from the Hamming weight of the intermediate values:

$$\widetilde{s}_i = \sum_{j=1}^{\frac{n}{w}} |\widetilde{\mathrm{HW}}(\boldsymbol{b}_{i,j-1}) - \widetilde{\mathrm{HW}}(\boldsymbol{b}_{i,j})|$$

$$= \sum_{j=1}^{\frac{n}{w}} |\mathrm{HW}(\boldsymbol{b}_{i,j-1}) - \mathrm{HW}(\boldsymbol{b}_{i,j})| + \varepsilon_{s_i}, \tag{3}$$

where ε_{s_i} comes from the side-channel error on the ith syndrome entry.

This $\varepsilon_{i,j}$ value actually appears in two Hamming distances: for j and $j-1$. As a consequence, the recombination step given in Eq. (3) *amplifies* the side channel noise.

Remark: $\widetilde{s}_i$ corresponds to the number of transitions between $\widetilde{\mathrm{HW}}(\boldsymbol{b}_{i,j-1})$ and $\widetilde{\mathrm{HW}}(\boldsymbol{b}_{i,j})$ for j going from 1 to n/w.

Example 1. For a given row i, let $\mathrm{HW}(\boldsymbol{b}_{i,.}) = (0, 0, 1, 1, 1, 2, 1, 1)$ be the error-free sequence of Hamming weights of the intermediate values. Then, the estimation part should give a guess value of $\widetilde{s}_i = 3$. Indeed, there are 3 transitions $0 \to 1, 1 \to 2$ and $2 \to 1$.

Depending on where the error $\varepsilon_{i,j}$ appears, the consequence on the $\widetilde{s}_i$ value differs.

- Let's assume we observe $\widetilde{HW}(\boldsymbol{b}_{i,.}) = (0,1,1,1,1,2,1,1)$, $\varepsilon_{i,1} = +1$ affects $HW(\boldsymbol{b}_{i,1})$. We derive $\widetilde{s}_i = 3$ and therefore $\varepsilon_{s_i} = 0$
- Let's assume we observe $\widetilde{HW}(\boldsymbol{b}_{i,.}) = (0,0,1,1,1,1,1,1)$, $\varepsilon_{i,5} = -1$ affects $HW(\boldsymbol{b}_{i,5})$. We derive $\widetilde{s}_i = 1$ and therefore $\varepsilon_{s_i} = -2$
- Let's assume we observe $\widetilde{HW}(\boldsymbol{b}_{i,.}) = (0,0,1,1,1,2,1,2)$, $\varepsilon_{i,7} = +1$ affects $HW(\boldsymbol{b}_{i,7})$. We derive $\widetilde{s}_i = 4$ and therefore $\varepsilon_{s_i} = 1$

As shown in the example, a negative or null impact on the estimation of the integer syndrome entry can happen. However, these cases occur with low probability.

The side-channel error is directly linked to the accuracy of the side-channel distinguisher. Indeed, the accuracy corresponds to the probability of a correct guess. We see that, with high probability, any wrong guess of the side-channel distinguisher will lead to an overestimation of the syndrome entry.

3.2 "Double-Cancellation" Error

Another error that can appear, as already discussed in [9], was called the "double cancellation" issue. We recall the problem briefly. We are interested in the successive Hamming weights of the partial matrix-vector product. However, the observations we get are the successive Hamming weight of the $\boldsymbol{b}$ value in line 5 of Algorithm 2. Thus, in the CDCG method, the values we are interested in are estimated with the following approximation of the Hamming distance from the Hamming weight:

$$HD(\boldsymbol{a}, \boldsymbol{b}) \simeq |HW(\boldsymbol{a}) - HW(\boldsymbol{b})|.$$

With this approximation, the $2HW(\boldsymbol{b} \wedge \neg(\boldsymbol{a}))$ part of the Hamming distance computation is omitted. In our case, we know that both vectors $\boldsymbol{a}$ and $\boldsymbol{b}$ are close due to the low weight of the input vector. Indeed, if we look at Line 5 in Algorithm 2, we can notice that in our case, we can consider one vector $\boldsymbol{a}$ to be random, but the second is of the form $\boldsymbol{b} = \boldsymbol{a} \oplus \boldsymbol{c}$, with $\boldsymbol{c}$ of low weight. Indeed $\boldsymbol{c}$ corresponds to the bitwise AND between a vector that looks random, a sub-group of columns of a line of the matrix $\boldsymbol{H}$, that is indistinguishable from a random matrix, and a subpart of the vector $\boldsymbol{e}$ of low weight $\boldsymbol{c} = \boldsymbol{H}_{i,j} \wedge \boldsymbol{e}_j$. In particular, $HW(\boldsymbol{c}) \geq 2$ implies $HW(\boldsymbol{e}) \geq 2$.

The following theorem gives the weight distribution of the blocks.

Theorem 1. *Let n, t, w be strictly positive integers with $t < n$ and w divides n. Let X_i be a discrete random variable denoting the number of blocks of weight i of a binary string of length n and Hamming weight t, where each block has length w. For any $2 \leq j \leq w$ let $\alpha_j \in \{0, \ldots, t\}$ satisfying $\sum_{\ell=1}^{j} \ell \alpha_\ell = t$. Then*

$$\Pr(X_j = \alpha_j, \dots, X_2 = \alpha_2, X_1 = \alpha_1) = \frac{\binom{\frac{n}{w}}{\alpha_1, \dots, \alpha_j}}{\binom{n}{t}} \prod_{\ell=1}^{j} \binom{w}{\ell}^{\alpha_\ell}, \qquad (4)$$

where $\binom{\frac{n}{w}}{\alpha_1, \dots, \alpha_j}$ denotes the multinomial coefficient.

Corollary 1. *The probability that the maximum weight is 1 equals* $\frac{w^t \binom{n/w}{t}}{\binom{n}{t}}$.

Moreover, for $t = o(n)$ *when* $n \to \infty$ *the probability that the weights of the blocks are at most 1 can be approximated by*

$$e^{-\frac{(w-1)t^2}{2n}\left(1 + \frac{(w+1)t}{3n} + \frac{(w^2+w+1)t^2}{6n^2} + O\left(\frac{t^5}{n^4}\right)\right)}.$$

In particular, using only the first term in the exponent for block sizes $w \in \{8, 32, 64\}$ *gives* $e^{-\frac{7t^2}{2n}}$, $e^{-\frac{31t^2}{2n}}$ *and* $e^{-\frac{63t^2}{2n}}$.

Remark 1. In the case of *Classic McEliece*, we have $t = \mathcal{O}(\frac{n}{\log_2 n})$, which implies that the probability of having only weights 0 and 1 blocks is roughly $e^{-c \frac{n}{\log_2^2 n}}$, where c is a constant related to the block size w.

One can deduce that the probability of having at least one block of weight 2 is extremely high. This result implies that the CDCG method has a very high probability of underestimating the Hamming weights. One can notice, as shown in Table 1a, that for block sizes greater or equal to 32, the probability of having only blocks of weight 0 and 1 is extremely small. For $w = 8$ the weight of the blocks is with high probability at most 2. This shows that it is highly probable that at least one word of the e vector will lead to a recombination error, which will affect the estimated syndrome. We also know that in such a case, all wrong estimated values are underestimated.

Having many blocks of weight strictly greater than 1 increases the estimation error. Therefore, determining the expected number of such blocks would be useful.

In Table 1b, we compute a lower bound on the expected value of the number of such blocks. Notice that for $w = 8$ the number of blocks having weight larger than or equal to 2 is indeed, extremely small. Hence in such a scenario, the syndrome estimation should be rather close to the exact value. On the opposite, for $w = 64$ around 30% of the blocks are of Hamming weight greater than or equal to 2. As we shall see, large values of w have a devastating impact on the success probability of the CDCG method.

3.3 Dependent Error

In Sect. 3.2, we showed that it is highly probable that we have a block of the vector with Hamming weight greater than 1. These blocks are problematic since they will impact approximately one-fourth of the Hamming weight estimation for the considered block.

Table 1. Weight of blocks e_j for *Classic McEliece* parameters: probability of the maximum weight and lower bound on the average number of blocks with weights larger than or equal to 2.

		(a) Pr(max(HW(e_j)))			(b) $|\{j \mid \text{HW}(e_j) \geq 2\}|/(n/w)$			
w	max	(3488,64)	(4608,96)	(6688,128)	w	(3488,64)	(4608,96)	(6688, 128)
8	$=1$	0.01378	0.00061	0.00012				
	≤ 2	0.873	0.767	0.739				
	≤ 3	0.997	0.993	0.992	8	3.8/436	6.4/576	7.9/836
	≤ 4	0.999	0.999	0.999				
	≤ 5	0.999	0.999	0.999				
32	$=1$	8.69×10^{-11}	7.59×10^{-19}	3.1×10^{-22}				
	≤ 2	0.0804	0.0077	0.0038				
	≤ 3	0.753	0.543	0.519	32	12.6/109	20.0/144	25.9/209
	≤ 4	0.974	0.936	0.936				
	≤ 5	0.997	0.994	0.994				
64	$=1$	0	0	0				
	≤ 2	5.66×10^{-5}	4.21×10^{-9}	3.80×10^{-10}				
	≤ 3	0.159	0.021	0.015	64	17.1/54.5	24.2/72	31.7/105
	≤ 4	0.715	0.455	0.444				
	≤ 5	0.947	0.865	0.869				

Indeed, if $\text{HW}(e_j) = 2$ and the $H_{i,j}$ are random words, then approximately one-fourth of the product for this word column has weight 2. Among this quarter, half of them are underestimated with the approximation used in the CDCG method if we consider a to be random. Hence, the double cancelation error will impact several results and the error induces by a word of weight higher than 1 will lead to dependent errors on the different syndrome estimations.

3.4   Impact of the Error on the Score Computation

After the estimation step, the side-channel analysis error is increased. This error is then propagated with the evaluation of the column score with the ψ function from [11], as used in [9]. The score for the column j is defined as:

$$\forall j \in [\![1,n]\!], \quad \psi_j(\widetilde{s}) = H_{.,j} \cdot \widetilde{s} + \overline{H}_{.,j} \cdot \overline{\widetilde{s}}. \tag{5}$$

Thus if, the ith coordinate of $\widetilde{s}$ is incorrect, it will modify the score of the whole column. If $H_{i,j} = 1$, then the left part ($H_{.,j} \cdot \widetilde{s}$) is affected. In that case, the score computed by ψ for the column i is the error-free score plus ε_j. If $H_{i,j} = 0$, then the left part ($\overline{H}_{.,j} \cdot \overline{\widetilde{s}}$) is affected. In that case, the score computed by ψ for the column i is the error-free score minus ε_j.

Therefore, any incorrect estimation during the side-channel analysis will influence all the results and affect them differently depending on the value of the bit in the $\boldsymbol{H}$ matrix. On average, half of the columns score will be over-evaluated while the other half will be under-evaluated.

4 Error Propagation Limitation

This section presents a different message recovery attack against Niederreiter-like schemes, that make use of a matrix-vector multiplication in $\mathbb{F}_2$. Our new method does not require estimating the syndrome in $\mathbb{N}$, as previously done in [5,9]. Moreover, it just looks at side-channel results locally and does not propagate the error discussed in Sect. 3.

4.1 Punctured Matrices

In order to cope with the error propagation issue, we propose to use both the incorrect and correct Hamming weight estimations to distinguish between blocks of size w in the error vector where $\boldsymbol{e}_j = \boldsymbol{0}$ and $\boldsymbol{e}_j \neq \boldsymbol{0}$. We recall that the attacker has access to the estimations of the Hamming weight $\widetilde{\mathrm{HW}}(b_{i,j})$.

For simplification, we will denote $w_{i,j} = \widetilde{\mathrm{HW}}(b_{i,j})$ and the matrix of estimated weights $\boldsymbol{W} = (w_{i,j})_{1 \leq i \leq n-k, 1 \leq j \leq \frac{n}{w}}$. The jth column vector of $\boldsymbol{W}$ is $\boldsymbol{w}_j \in \mathbb{N}^{n-k}$, more exactly, $\boldsymbol{w}_j = \left(\widetilde{\mathrm{HW}}(b_{1,j}), \widetilde{\mathrm{HW}}(b_{2,j}), \ldots, \widetilde{\mathrm{HW}}(b_{n-k,j}) \right)$. Algorithm 3 below determines for which index j we have $\boldsymbol{e}_j = 0$.

Algorithm 3. ZERO-DISTINGUISHER

Require: $\boldsymbol{W}$: Hamming weight guess for each intermediate value of the $\boldsymbol{b}$ value in
  Algorithm 2 and a the estimate accuracy computed during profiling phase
Ensure: A set L of blocks to be punctured
1: $L = \{\emptyset\}$
2: $\gamma = (n-k)(1 - a^2 - \frac{(1-a)^2}{2}) + \sqrt{(2a^2 + (1-a)^2)(n-k)\log(n-k)}$
3: **if** $\mathrm{HW}(\boldsymbol{w}_1) \leq (n-k)(1-a) + \sqrt{2a(n-k)\log(n-k)}$ **then**
4:     $L \leftarrow L \cup \{1\}$
5: **for** $j \leftarrow 2$ to $\frac{n}{w}$ **do**
6:     **if** $\mathrm{HW}(\boldsymbol{w}_j - \boldsymbol{w}_{j-1}) \leq \gamma$ **then**
7:         $L \leftarrow L \cup \{j\}$
8: **return** L

If $\boldsymbol{e}_j = 0$ then this implies that, $b_{i,j} = b_{i,j-1}$ for $2 \leq i \leq n-k$. In other words, for the first block, the estimated weight vector $\boldsymbol{w}_1$ should be equal to zero if the estimation is perfect, and if the estimation is not perfect, depending on the accuracy, the value of $\mathrm{HW}(\boldsymbol{w}_1)$ (number of coordinates different from zero) should be rather small. For all the subsequent blocks, the condition $\boldsymbol{e}_j = 0$

Table 2. Distributions of the number of zeros in w_1 and $w_j - w_{j-1}$.

	$\mathrm{HW}(e_j) = 0$	$\mathrm{HW}(e_j) = 1$
$n - k - \mathrm{HW}(w_1)$	$\mathcal{B}(n-k, a)$	$\mathcal{B}\left(n-k, \frac{1+a}{4}\right)$
$n - k - \mathrm{HW}(w_j - w_{j-1})$	$\mathcal{B}\left(n-k, a^2 + \frac{(1-a)^2}{2}\right)$	$\mathcal{B}\left(n-k, \frac{1+a^2}{4}\right)$

implies that there should be no difference between w_j and w_{j-1} if the Hamming weight estimation is perfect. In the non-perfect case, the vector $w_j - w_{j-1}$ should have a small Hamming weight, that depends on the classification accuracy. The following theorem gives the necessary conditions on the accuracy a for Algorithm 3 to successfully output a list of valid zero-weight blocks. In order to distinguish between the case $\mathrm{HW}(e_j) = 0$ and $\mathrm{HW}(e_j) = 1$ we will use the following procedure. Denote the random variable $X_i = n - k - \mathrm{HW}(w_j - w_{j-1})$ given $\mathrm{HW}(e_j) = 0$ and $Y_i = n - k - \mathrm{HW}(w_j - w_{j-1})$ given $\mathrm{HW}(e_j) = 1$ for $j \geq 2$ (for $j = 1$ use $X_1 = n - k - \mathrm{HW}(w_1)$). Then we say that one distinguishes between X_j and Y_j with high probability as long as $\Pr(X_j > Y_j)$ is close to 1. To achieve our goal we will use known results on bounding the tail of binomial distribution and set up a threshold value β^* that acts as an almost perfect separation between the two distributions. More exactly, we will have that $X_j \geq \beta^*$ w.h.p. and $Y_j < \beta^*$ w.h.p. This value β^* will depend on the accuracy parameter a.

Theorem 2. *Assume that the errors are limited to a distance of 1 and overestimation and underestimation are equally probable. Let X_j and Y_j be the random variables as previously defined. Let $a_1 > \frac{1}{3} + \frac{40 \log(n-k)}{9(n-k)} + \frac{8\sqrt{2}\sqrt{8 \log(n-k)^2 + 3(n-k) \log(n-k)}}{9(n-k)}$ and $a_2 \geq 0.5$ be a solution of the equation:*

$$\sqrt{\frac{n-k}{\log(n-k)}} = \frac{4}{5a^2 - 4a + 1}\left(\sqrt{(3a^2 - 2a + 1)} - \sqrt{\frac{1+a^2}{2}}\right).$$

Then $\Pr(X_j > Y_j) > 1 - \frac{1}{(n-k)} - \frac{1}{e^{O((3a-1)(n-k))}}$ as long as $a > a_1$ for $j = 1$ and $a > a_2$ for $j \geq 2$.

Moreover, the threshold separation value between the distributions of $n - k - X_j$ and $n - k - Y_j$ equals $(n-k)(1-a) + \sqrt{2a(n-k)\log(n-k)}$ for $j = 1$ and $(n-k)(1 - a^2 - \frac{(1-a)^2}{2}) + \sqrt{(2a^2 + (1-a)^2)(n-k)\log(n-k)}$ for $j \geq 2$.

The proof of Theorem 2 is provided in the appendix. In Table 2, we illustrate the distributions of X_j and Y_j. Some restrictions on the level of accuracy are to be examined in details. For example if $a = 0.4$ the distribution of $n - k - \mathrm{HW}(w_j - w_{j-1})$ is almost identical when $\mathrm{HW}(e_j) = 0$ and $\mathrm{HW}(e_j) = 1$. The larger the difference between the parameters a (respectively $a^2 + \frac{(1-a)^2}{2}$) and $\frac{1+a}{4}$ (respectively $\frac{1+a^2}{4}$) the better for the distinguisher. The one-distance error assumption is based on Hamming weight leakages with Gaussian noise and assumes univariate attacks. Previous work show that for low-noise setting this assumption can be fulfilled [20,26]

4.2   T-test Based Score

The method presented in the Sect. 4.1 is efficient when considering small registers, or equivalently small sub-matrices. However, as the register size increases, the number of columns kept is too high to perform an efficient ISD. For that, we propose a method to select a permutation for the ISD that can be used on the full matrix or its punctured version. Our method is based on a T-test [24]. The T-test is commonly used for leakage assessment to detect if side-channel traces are dependent on a parameter. The traces are separated into two sets according to the known value of a parameter which may have an influence on them. Here, we use the T-test to identify which columns have an impact on the side-channel traces difference.

To achieve this, for all groups of columns (depending on the implementation and parameter w), we separate the rows into two multisets according to the Hamming distance recovered during the side-channel attack (difference of the Hamming weight), the first one S_0 for Hamming distances equal to 0, the second one S_1 for the other cases. In an error-free scenario, two cases occur:

- All rows are in the same multiset (S_0), which means that none of the columns are used in the computation of the syndrome, and thus, the considered coordinates of the vector e are zero.
- The rows are distributed in the two multisets. Hence some coordinates of e are different from zero. We use a statistical test to determine which columns have a different distribution in the two multisets. If the coordinate of e is null, then the distribution should be similar in the two multisets, whereas if the coordinate of e is not null S_0 should contain rows with 0, and S_1 should contain rows with 1.

In order to deal with errors, either from side-channel analysis or recombination, we use a statistical test to deal with the misplacement of rows in the multisets. The method is described in Algorithm 4. The next step is to use the permutation obtained as an initial permutation for ISD-based methods.

5   Experimental Validation

In this section, we compare our method with the CDCG method in various settings, to evaluate the different approaches in different case studies. In particular, we want to illustrate the limitations of the CDCG method we described before in Sect. 3. Our experimental validation confirms that our T-test-based approach is better suited than the previous method in low and large noise settings. For that, we consider simulation leakages and optimal template attacks [6], *i.e.* with perfect modeling. We consider a leakage of the form $\mathcal{L}_{i,j} = \mathrm{HW}(b_{i,j}) + \mathcal{N}(0, \sigma^2)$,

Algorithm 4. T-test based attacks

Require: W: Hamming weight guesses for each intermediate value of the b value in
Algorithm 2 and a binary $(n, n - k)$ matrix H.
Ensure: A n-permutation ϕ (of the coordinates of the vector e).

```
1: for j ← 1 to n/w do
2:     (S₀, S₁) ← ({∅}, {∅})
3:     for i ← 1 to n − k do   ▷ Separate columns according to side-channel analysis
4:         if w_{i,j} − w_{i,j−1} = 0 then
5:             S₀ ← S₀ ∪ H_{i,(j−1)w+1:jw}
6:         else
7:             S₁ ← S₁ ∪ H_{i,(j−1)w+1:jw}
8:         T-score[(j − 1)w + 1 : jw] ←T-test(S₀ ∼ S₁)   ▷ Perform feature selection
9: return φ ← argsort(T-score)   ▷ Sort in decreasing order
```

where the Hamming weight HW can be on $w = 8$, 32 or 64-bit values and the noise variance σ^2 affects the side-channel distinguisher accuracy. To estimate the accuracy of the template attack, we use the 3-σ rule $a \simeq \mathrm{erf}\left(\frac{1}{2\sqrt{2}\sigma}\right)$, where erf is the Gauss error function [25]. While this estimation may not be true for limit case, $i.e.$ HW($b_{i,j}$) = 0 or HW($b_{i,j}$) = w. We also evaluate the accuracy of the distinguisher and the one observed in experimental results is close to the 3-σ rule one. This is due to the fact that most of the values of HW($b_{i,j}$) are close to $\frac{w}{2}$, and we consider a relatively low-noise case. Experiments confirm that the puncturing methods offer better results than the previous method for large registers and/or high noise.

For reproducibility, the source code of the simulation is given in https://github.com/vingrosso/Side-channel-attacks-Classic-McEliece.git.

5.1 Punctured Matrices

In this experiment, we consider the selection method to reduce the ISD problem via the method presented in Sect. 4.1. We arbitrary set to 2^{40} binary operations the maximum value of a computationally feasible attack. All the lower values are part of the so-called computationally feasible zone.

The idea is to evaluate the resistance to noise of the selection method for different register sizes. We simulate 100 experiments for the first and last set of parameters of *Classic McEliece* $(n, k, t) = (3488, 2720, 64)$ and $(n, k, t) = (8192, 6528, 128)$. The results are plotted in Fig. 1.

As expected for small register size $w = 8$ and high accuracy $a = 0.92$ ($\sigma = 0.26$), the punctured method allows for an effective discrimination of a sufficient number of blocks of columns. Consequently, a simple Gaussian elimination is sufficient to recover the syndrome up to $\sigma < 0.29$. When the noise variance increases, a reduced syndrome decoding problem can be solved. However, the number of columns kept becomes rapidly large, close to all the columns, and requires too much computational power to mount a successful attack.

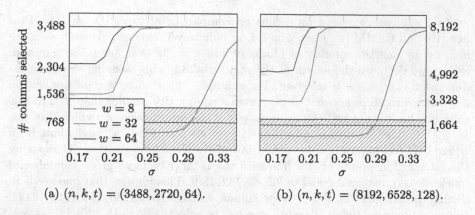

(a) $(n, k, t) = (3488, 2720, 64)$.   (b) $(n, k, t) = (8192, 6528, 128)$.

Fig. 1. Median number of columns selected with the punctured method. The hatching zone corresponds to the computationally feasible zone.

For large registers ($w = 32$ and $w = 64$), each block kept adds 32 or 64 columns for only one or two selected columns. Hence, even for low noise and high accuracy, the number of columns kept is too large and compromises the success of an ISD attack.

For the set of parameters of *Classic McEliece* the length of the codes are divided into a number of blocks n/w equal to $[436, 576, 836, 1024]$ (for $w = 8$), $[109, 144, 209, 256]$ (for $w = 32$) and $[51, 72, 105, 128]$ (for $w = 64$). As for the codimension of the code we obtain a number of blocks $(n - k)/w$ equal to $[96, 156, 208, 208]$ (for $w = 8$), $[24, 39, 52, 52]$ (for $w = 32$) and $[12, 20, 26, 26]$ (for $w = 64$).

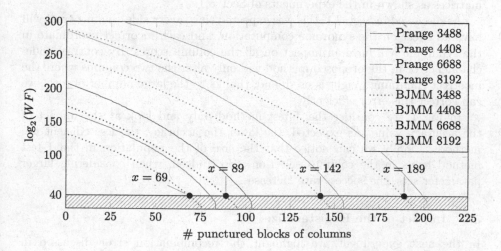

Fig. 2. Two ISD variants on punctured matrices ($w = 32$).

In Fig. 2, we represent an estimated complexity of two ISD variants, Prange [19] and BJMM [4], when applied on punctured matrices. At each step, we increase by one the number of blocks of size $w = 32$ that are to be removed. Hence, we decrease the length of the matrix by 32, while keeping the same codimension, $i.e.$ $n - k$ is constant. For example, the Prange variant applied on $n = 3488$ with 80 punctured blocks, gives a complexity smaller than 2^{30}. In this case, one has to remove 2560 columns out of the information set which is of size $k = 2720$. The horizontal solid line at $y = 40$ points out a rough limit from where ISD techniques become computationally feasible in practice. Computing the intersection points of this line with the BJMM variants gives a number of blocks to be punctured equal to $[69, 89, 142, 189]$. This implies that one needs to distinguish $[2208, 2848, 4544, 6048]$ columns, $i.e.$ to select $[1280, 1760, 2144, 2144]$ columns. Represented as a factor, one has to select $[1.66, 1.41, 1.28, 1.28]$ times $(n - k)$ columns to perform the BJMM attack with a time complexity of 2^{40} binary operations.

5.2   Impact of the Side-Channel Distinguisher Accuracy

In this experiment, we evaluate the impact of the accuracy of the distinguisher on the success of three methods: CDCG punctured, CDCG and T-test. We consider Hamming weight 8-bit leakages, which means $0 \leq \text{HW}(b_{i,j}) \leq 8$, and we consider different values of noise σ to modify the accuracy. We work with the first set of parameters of $Classic McEliece$: $(n, k, t) = (3488, 2720, 64)$. In Fig. 3, we can notice that for every accuracy parameter evaluated, the T-test method achieves a similar success rate, while the success rate of the CDCG method drops rapidly when the accuracy decreases. Applying the score function ψ on the punctured matrix does not help: the limit appears as early as for $\sigma = 0.3$ for punctured matrices as shown in the experiments of Sect. 5.1.

As discussed in Sect. 3.1, this was expected since every side-channel error will have an effect on the syndrome computation, and each incorrect coordinate in the syndrome will have an impact on all the column scores. By contrast, side-channel error in the proposed method will only alter the two columns where the incorrect Hamming weight is used, and, thanks to the large number of rows, we can correct this error efficiently.

In Fig. 4, we consider the T-test method only and look at the impact of the accuracy value. As expected, the lower the accuracy, the less efficient the methods. Finally we can notice that the size of the population in the T-test method helps in the columns selection step. Indeed, when considering larger parameter sets, the success rate increases.

5.3   Impact of the Register Size

In the next experiment, we highlight the recombination error discussed in Sect. 3.2. As discussed in the previous section, the larger the register, the more likely dependent errors are. Hence, we expect the success rate of all methods to drop when larger registers are considered. We fix the accuracy at 0.99822 for a

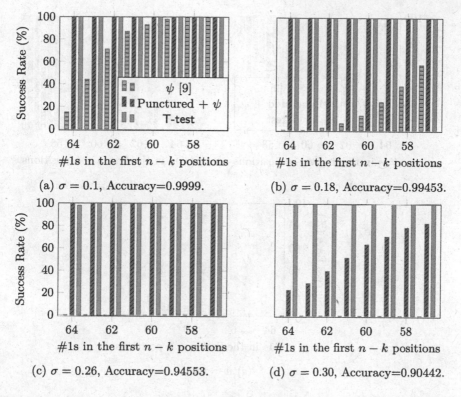

Fig. 3. Success rate of the three methods for 8-bit words and different noise levels.

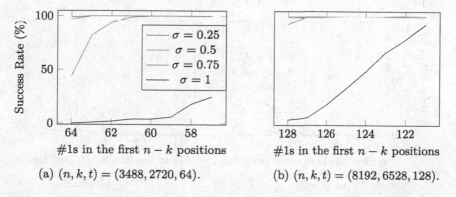

(a) $(n, k, t) = (3488, 2720, 64)$.

(b) $(n, k, t) = (8192, 6528, 128)$.

Fig. 4. Success rate of the T-test method for $w = 8$ and different noise levels for two *Classic McEliece* parameters sets.

noise level of $\sigma = 0.16$ that is close to the accuracy obtained on the real traces used in [9].

In Fig. 5, as expected, the success rate of all three methods decreases when larger registers sizes are considered. However, in all cases, the proposed T-test-

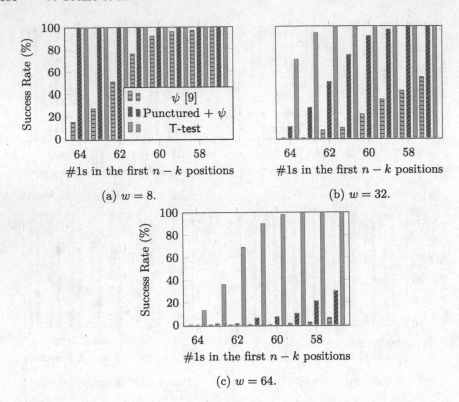

Fig. 5. Comparison of the three methods for different register sizes at noise level $\sigma = 0.16$.

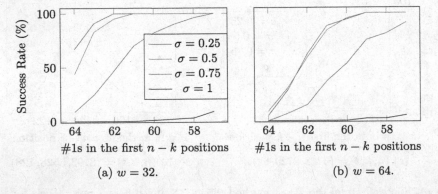

Fig. 6. Success rate of the T-test method for 32-bit and 64-bit words and different noise levels with $(n, k, t) = (3488, 2720, 64)$.

based method shows a better success rate than the CDCG method. We refer to Sect. 3.3 for a more detailed explanation of the impact of the dependent error on the CDCG method. The proposed method is also affected by larger register sizes, especially when noise increase as shown in Fig. 6. For the noise levels considered in this figure, the punctured method does not manage to distinguish blocks with $e_j = 0$ and $e_j \neq 0$. Thus the T-test is the only solution when considering large registers and "high" noise scenarios.

6 Conclusion

In this paper, we analyze and develop techniques to solve the syndrome decoding problem with noisy information. In particular, we analyze some weaknesses of the method proposed in [9]. The weaknesses are due to the redefinition of the classical syndrome decoding problem into the integer syndrome decoding problem. We demonstrate that reformulating to integer syndrome decoding problem propagate errors due to side-channel acquisition.

Next, we present two methods based on a divide-and-conquer approach, to avoid the propagation of the error. The methods presented are based on the fact that the distribution of the side-channel observations are different when a block of the vector e is 0 or not. The first method characterizes the distributions of the estimation according to the accuracy and finds the bound on the number of coordinates equal to 0 to distinguish if the block of the vector e is 0 or not. The second solution separate the rows of the matrix according to the side-channel leakages and evaluate if the rows seems to follow a uniform distribution in the two set or follow different distributions in the two sets. The analysis of the behavior of the two distribution is performed with a T-test. This allows us to discriminate inside the block which coordinate is more likely to follow a different distribution, allowing for an even finer analysis than the first method.

We finally validate our approach with various experiments. Both methods presented offer a better success rate than state-of-the-art attacks and the T-test is generally more efficient when considering larger registers or a higher level of noise. Compared with existing attack paths, this method cannot be used when the attacker obtains an integer syndrome only, without partial information, as done in [5]. In [9], the author suggests using masking as a countermeasure. An interesting research direction would be to evaluate the efficiency of the different approaches when masked implementations are considered.

All presented side-channel attack methods on KEM for code-based cryptography so far exploit profiling. An interesting research direction could be to turn these attacks into a non-profiled attack. Another path could be to adapt the technique to different rings or fields rather than the binary field considered. The specific structure of the public key in the BIKE cryptosystem, a quasi-cyclic moderate density parity check matrix, is not exploited in this work and deserves more investigations.

Acknowledgements. This work was funded by a French national grant managed by the Agence Nationale de la Recherche (ANR): project PQ-TLS reference ANR-22-PETQ-0008 through France 2023 program.

Appendix

Proof of Theorem 1

We deal here with a classical combinatorial urn process. It can be described as follows. We place t balls into $\frac{n}{w}$ urns, where the urns are labeled with respect to the number of balls contained in the urn. Hence, we can have urns labeled with integers from 0 to w. And we are interested in how many urns are labeled with the integer j, where $1 \leq j \leq w$. The number of possible $(i_2, \ldots, i_j)$ urns labeled with $(2, \ldots, j)$ equals

$$\binom{\frac{n}{w}}{i_2}\binom{\frac{n}{w} - i_2}{i_3} \cdots \binom{\frac{n}{w} - i_2 - \cdots - i_{j-1}}{i_j}. \tag{6}$$

As there are $\frac{n}{w} - i_2 - \cdots - i_j$ remaining urns, which are either labeled with 0 or with 1, and since there are a total of t balls from which $2i_2 + \cdots + ji_j$ where already extracted, we can place the remaining balls in the remaining urns in $\binom{\frac{n}{w} - i_2 - \cdots - i_j}{t - 2i_2 \cdots - ji_j}$ possible ways. This makes a total of

$$\binom{\frac{n}{w}}{i_2}\binom{\frac{n}{w} - i_2}{i_3} \cdots \binom{\frac{n}{w} - i_2 - \cdots - i_{j-1}}{i_j}\binom{\frac{n}{w} - i_2 - \cdots - i_j}{t - 2i_2 \cdots - ji_j} = \binom{\frac{n}{w}}{i_1, \ldots, i_j}. \tag{7}$$

with $i_1 = t - 2i_2 - \ldots ji_j$.

Now each urn labeled with j has $\binom{w}{j}$ possible representatives. Thus, we can deduce the number of positive cases which equal

$$\binom{\frac{n}{w}}{i_1, \ldots, i_j} \prod_{l=1}^{j} \binom{w}{l}^{i_l}.$$

Proof of Theorem 2

To prove Theorem 2 we will proceed step by step. We shall assume that errors are limited to a distance of 1 and overestimation and underestimation are equally probable, and the side-channel distinguisher accuracy equal to a.

Lemma 1. *Given $e_j = 0$ we have*

$$\Pr\left(w_{\ell,1} = 0\right) = a, \forall 1 \leq \ell \leq n - k,$$

$$\Pr\left(w_{\ell,j} - w_{\ell,j-1} = 0\right) = a^2 + \frac{(1-a)^2}{2}, \forall 1 \leq \ell \leq n - k, \forall 2 \leq j \leq \frac{n}{w}.$$

Proof. By definition of a we have $\Pr(w_{j,1} = 0) = a, \forall 1 \leq \ell \leq n - k$.

For the intermediate blocks $\Pr\left(w_{\ell,j} - w_{b_\ell,j-1} = 0\right)$ depends on the estimations at step $j-1$ and j. So, either both estimations are correct, with probability a^2, or both estimations are overestimated (resp. underestimates), with probability $\frac{1-a}{2}$.

Corollary 2. *Given $e_j = 0$ we have $HW(w_1) \sim n - k - \mathcal{B}(n - k, a)$ and $HW(w_j - w_{j-1}) \sim n - k - \mathcal{B}\left(n - k, a^2 + \frac{(1-a)^2}{2}\right)$.*

Lemma 2. *Given $HW(e_j) = 1$ we have*

$$\Pr(w_{\ell,1} = 0) = \frac{1+a}{4}, \quad \forall 1 \le \ell \le n - k,$$

$$\Pr(w_{\ell,j} - w_{\ell,j-1} = 0) = \frac{1+a^2}{4}, \quad \forall 1 \le \ell \le n - k, \; \forall 2 \le j \le \frac{n}{w}.$$

Proof. For the first block, without loss of generality, we assume that $e_j(i) = 1$. We have two cases to obtain $w_{\ell,1} = 0$.

1. The ith bit of the word of the matrix is 0, and we correctly estimate $w_{\ell,1}$, the probability is $\frac{a}{2}$.
2. The ith bit of the word of the matrix is 1, and we underestimate $w_{\ell,1}$, probability $\frac{1-a}{4}$.

For the intermediate blocks, without loss of generality, we assume $e_j(i) = 1$. Thus, we have two cases to obtain $w_{\ell,j} - w_{\ell,j-1} = 0$.

1. The ith bit of the word of the matrix is 0, and we made the same error on both evaluations for j and $j - 1$. Both correct, with probability $\frac{a^2}{2}$, both underestimated, with probability $\left(\frac{1-a}{2}\right)^2$, similar for both overestimated, with a probability $\left(\frac{1-a}{2}\right)^2$.
2. The ith bit of the word of the matrix is 1.
   (a) The weight increases (resp. decreases), i.e. $HW(b_{\ell,j}) = HW(b_{\ell,j-1}) + 1$, we correctly estimate $w_{\ell,j}$ but underestimate (resp. overestimate) $w_{\ell,j-1}$ with a probability $\frac{1}{2}\frac{1-a}{2}a$ (resp. $\frac{1}{2}\frac{1-a}{2}a$).
   (b) Similarly, the error can be on $w_{\ell,j}$ overestimation or underestimation, and the difference will be zero depending on the impact on the weight modification, here also, we have two times probability of $\frac{1}{2}\frac{1}{2}\frac{1-a}{2}a$.

By summing all cases, we obtain the following:

$$\Pr(\widetilde{HW}(b_{\ell,j}) - \widetilde{HW}(b_{\ell,j-1}) = 0) = \frac{a^2}{2} + \left(\frac{1-a}{2}\right)^2 + 4\left(\frac{1}{4}\frac{1-a}{2}a\right).$$

Corollary 3. *Given $HW(e_j) = 1$ we have $HW(w_1) \sim n - k - \mathcal{B}(n - k, \frac{1+a}{4})$ and $HW(w_j - w_{j-1}) \sim n - k - \mathcal{B}(n - k, \frac{1+a^2}{4})$.*

Proposition 1. *Let $a > \frac{1}{3} + \frac{40\log(n-k)}{9(n-k)} + \frac{8\sqrt{2}\sqrt{8\log(n-k)^2 + 3(n-k)\log(n-k)}}{9(n-k)}$. Then, $\Pr(X_1 > Y_1) \ge 1 - \frac{1}{(n-k)} - \frac{1}{e^{\mathcal{O}((3a-1)(n-k))}}$.*
Moreover when $e_1 = 0$ we have $HW(w_1) \le (n-k)(1-a) + \sqrt{2a(n-k)\log(n-k)}$.

Proof. Let us first recall that $X_1 = n - k - \mathrm{HW}(\boldsymbol{w}_1)$ given $\boldsymbol{e}_1 = \boldsymbol{0}$ and $Y_1 = n - k - \mathrm{HW}(\boldsymbol{w}_1)$ given $\mathrm{HW}(\boldsymbol{e}_1) = 1$. Also, by Lemma 1 $X_1 \sim \mathcal{B}(n-k, a)$ and by Lemma 2 $Y_1 \sim \mathcal{B}(n-k, \frac{1+a}{4})$. Let $\beta^* = (n-k)\frac{1+a}{4} + \beta$. This value will act as the separation between the distributions. More exactly we will require use the fact that

$$\Pr(X_1 > Y_1) \geq \Pr(X_1 > (n-k)\frac{1+a}{4} + \beta)\Pr(Y_1 < (n-k)\frac{1+a}{4} + \beta). \quad (8)$$

First we need to check the existence of such a value. For that we need to determine if such a positive integer β satisfying $(n-k)\frac{1+a}{4} + \sqrt{(n-k)\frac{1+a}{2}\log(n-k)} \leq (n-k)\frac{1+a}{4} + \beta \leq (n-k)a - \sqrt{2a(n-k)\log(n-k)}$ exists. By making the upper bound and lower bound equal, we obtain the wanted condition on a. This also implies that $\beta < (n-k)\frac{3a-1}{4} - \sqrt{2a(n-k)\log(n-k)}$.

Second, we will determine the probability in (8). Using Chernoff one gets

$$\Pr(Y_1 \geq (n-k)\frac{1+a}{4} + \beta) \leq e^{-\frac{\beta^2}{\frac{1+a}{2}(n-k)+\beta\frac{2}{3}}} \quad (9)$$

$$\Pr(X_1 \leq (n-k)\frac{1+a}{4} + \beta) \leq e^{-\frac{((n-k)a-(n-k)\frac{1+a}{4}-\beta)^2}{2a(n-k)}} \quad (10)$$

$$\Pr(X_1 > Y_1) \geq 1 - e^{-\frac{\beta^2}{\frac{1+a}{2}(n-k)+\beta\frac{2}{3}}} - e^{-\frac{((n-k)\frac{3a-1}{4}-\beta)^2}{2a(n-k)}}. \quad (11)$$

Putting $\beta = \frac{3a-1}{4}(n-k) - \sqrt{2a(n-k)\log(n-k)}$ in the previous equation we deduce $\Pr(X_1 > Y_1) \geq 1 - \frac{1}{e^{\log(n-k)}} - \frac{1}{e^{\mathcal{O}((3a-1)(n-k))}}$. The threshold value equals, $\beta^* = (n-k)a - \sqrt{2a(n-k)\log(n-k)}$.

Proposition 2. *Let* $a \geq 0.5$ *be a solution of the equation*

$$\sqrt{\frac{n-k}{\log(n-k)}} = \frac{4}{5a^2 - 4a + 1}\left(\sqrt{(3a^2 - 2a + 1)} - \sqrt{\frac{1+a^2}{2}}\right).$$

Then, $\Pr(X_1 > Y_1) \geq 1 - \frac{1}{(n-k)} - \frac{1}{e^{\mathcal{O}((3a-1)(n-k))}}$. *Moreover, when* $\boldsymbol{e}_j = \boldsymbol{0}$ *we have* $\mathrm{HW}(\boldsymbol{w}_i - \boldsymbol{w}_{i-1}) \leq (n-k)(1 - a^2 - \frac{(1-a)^2}{2}) + \sqrt{(2a^2 + (1-a)^2)(n-k)\log(n-k)}$.

The proof of this Proposition is identical to the previous one.

References

1. Aguilar Melchor, C., et al.: HQC. Technical report, National Institute of Standards and Technology (2022). https://csrc.nist.gov/Projects/post-quantum-cryptography/round-4-submissions
2. Albrecht, M.R., et al.: Classic McEliece. Technical report, National Institute of Standards and Technology (2022). https://csrc.nist.gov/projects/post-quantum-cryptography/round-4-submissions

3. Aragon, N., et al.: BIKE. Technical report, National Institute of Standards and Technology (2022). https://csrc.nist.gov/Projects/post-quantum-cryptography/round-4-submissions

4. Becker, A., Joux, A., May, A., Meurer, A.: Decoding random binary linear codes in $2n/20$: how $1+1=0$ improves information set decoding. In: Pointcheval, D., Johansson, T. (eds.) EUROCRYPT 2012. LNCS, vol. 7237, pp. 520–536. Springer, Heidelberg (2012). https://doi.org/10.1007/978-3-642-29011-4_31

5. Cayrel, P.-L., Colombier, B., Drăgoi, V.-F., Menu, A., Bossuet, L.: Message-recovery laser fault injection attack on the *Classic McEliece* cryptosystem. In: Canteaut, A., Standaert, F.-X. (eds.) EUROCRYPT 2021. LNCS, vol. 12697, pp. 438–467. Springer, Cham (2021). https://doi.org/10.1007/978-3-030-77886-6_15

6. Chari, S., Rao, J.R., Rohatgi, P.: Template attacks. In: Kaliski, B.S., Koç, K., Paar, C. (eds.) CHES 2002. LNCS, vol. 2523, pp. 13–28. Springer, Heidelberg (2003). https://doi.org/10.1007/3-540-36400-5_3

7. Chen, M., Chou, T.: Classic McEliece on the ARM cortex-M4. IACR Trans. Cryptogr. Hardw. Embed. Syst. **2021**(3), 125–148 (2021). https://doi.org/10.46586/tches.v2021.i3.125-148

8. Chen, P., et al.: Complete and improved FPGA implementation of Classic McEliece. IACR Trans. Cryptogr. Hardw. Embed. Syst. **2022**(3), 71–113 (2022). https://doi.org/10.46586/tches.v2022.i3.71-113

9. Colombier, B., Dragoi, V., Cayrel, P., Grosso, V.: Profiled side-channel attack on cryptosystems based on the binary syndrome decoding problem. IEEE Trans. Inf. Forensics Secur. **17**, 3407–3420 (2022). https://doi.org/10.1109/TIFS.2022.3198277

10. Dragoi, V., Colombier, B., Cayrel, P., Grosso, V.: Integer syndrome decoding in the presence of noise. IACR Cryptol. ePrint Arch, p. 636 (2022). https://eprint.iacr.org/2022/636

11. Feige, U., Lellouche, A.: Quantitative group testing and the rank of random matrices. CoRR abs/2006.09074 (2020). https://arxiv.org/abs/2006.09074

12. Guo, Q., Johansson, A., Johansson, T.: A key-recovery side-channel attack on Classic McEliece implementations. IACR Trans. Cryptogr. Hardw. Embed. Syst. **2022**(4), 800–827 (2022). https://doi.org/10.46586/tches.v2022.i4.800-827

13. Lahr, N., Niederhagen, R., Petri, R., Samardjiska, S.: Side channel information set decoding using iterative chunking. In: Moriai, S., Wang, H. (eds.) ASIACRYPT 2020. LNCS, vol. 12491, pp. 881–910. Springer, Cham (2020). https://doi.org/10.1007/978-3-030-64837-4_29

14. Lee, P.J., Brickell, E.F.: An observation on the security of McEliece's public-key cryptosystem. In: Barstow, D., et al. (eds.) EUROCRYPT 1988. LNCS, vol. 330, pp. 275–280. Springer, Heidelberg (1988). https://doi.org/10.1007/3-540-45961-8_25

15. Lucks, S.: A variant of the cramer-shoup cryptosystem for groups of unknown order. In: Zheng, Y. (ed.) ASIACRYPT 2002. LNCS, vol. 2501, pp. 27–45. Springer, Heidelberg (2002). https://doi.org/10.1007/3-540-36178-2_2

16. May, A., Meurer, A., Thomae, E.: Decoding random linear codes in $\tilde{\mathcal{O}}(2^{0.054n})$. In: Lee, D.H., Wang, X. (eds.) ASIACRYPT 2011. LNCS, vol. 7073, pp. 107–124. Springer, Heidelberg (2011). https://doi.org/10.1007/978-3-642-25385-0_6

17. O'Flynn, C., Chen, Z.D.: ChipWhisperer: an open-source platform for hardware embedded security research. In: Prouff, E. (ed.) COSADE 2014. LNCS, vol. 8622, pp. 243–260. Springer, Cham (2014). https://doi.org/10.1007/978-3-319-10175-0_17

18. Pircher, S., Geier, J., Zeh, A., Mueller-Gritschneder, D.: Exploring the RISC-V vector extension for the Classic McEliece post-quantum cryptosystem. In: 22nd International Symposium on Quality Electronic Design, ISQED 2021, Santa Clara, CA, USA, 7–9 April, 2021, pp. 401–407. IEEE (2021). https://doi.org/10.1109/ISQED51717.2021.9424273
19. Prange, E.: The use of information sets in decoding cyclic codes. IRE Trans. Inf. Theory **8**(5), 5–9 (1962). https://doi.org/10.1109/TIT.1962.1057777
20. Renauld, M., Standaert, F.-X.: Algebraic side-channel attacks. In: Bao, F., Yung, M., Lin, D., Jing, J. (eds.) Inscrypt 2009. LNCS, vol. 6151, pp. 393–410. Springer, Heidelberg (2010). https://doi.org/10.1007/978-3-642-16342-5_29
21. Roth, J., Karatsiolis, E., Krämer, J.: Classic McEliece implementation with low memory footprint. In: Liardet, P.-Y., Mentens, N. (eds.) CARDIS 2020. LNCS, vol. 12609, pp. 34–49. Springer, Cham (2021). https://doi.org/10.1007/978-3-030-68487-7_3
22. Shor, P.W.: Algorithms for quantum computation: Discrete logarithms and factoring. In: 35th Annual Symposium on Foundations of Computer Science, Santa Fe, New Mexico, USA, 20–22 November 1994, pp. 124–134. IEEE Computer Society (1994). https://doi.org/10.1109/SFCS.1994.365700
23. Stern, J.: A method for finding codewords of small weight. In: Cohen, G., Wolfmann, J. (eds.) Coding Theory 1988. LNCS, vol. 388, pp. 106–113. Springer, Heidelberg (1989). https://doi.org/10.1007/BFb0019850
24. Welch, B.L.: The generalization of 'STUDENT'S'problem when several different population variances are involved. Biometrika **34**(1–2), 28–35 (1947)
25. Winters, R.: Practical Predictive Analytics. Packt Publishing, Birmingham, England (2017). http://www.scholarvox.com/book/88842906
26. Zhang, Q., et al.: Side-channel attacks and countermeasures for identity-based cryptographic algorithm SM9. Secur. Commun. Networks **2018**, 9701756:1–9701756:14 (2018). https://doi.org/10.1155/2018/9701756

Analyses and Tools

Energy Consumption of Protected Cryptographic Hardware Cores

An Experimental Study

Aein Rezaei Shahmirzadi[1](✉) [iD], Thorben Moos[2] [iD], and Amir Moradi[1] [iD]

[1] Horst Görtz Institute for IT Security, Ruhr University Bochum, Bochum, Germany
{aein.rezaeishahmirzadi,amir.moradi}@rub.de
[2] Crypto Group, ICTEAM Institute, UCLouvain, Louvain-la-Neuve, Belgium
thorben.moos@uclouvain.be

Abstract. The rapid deployment of the Internet of Things (IoT) brought some interesting topics into the spotlight, one of which is low-power design. IoT devices are usually deployed in environments where access to an electricity network is not feasible and therefore have to be supplied by a battery. Despite the limited energy budget in this setting, many relevant applications require long device runtimes. Additionally, in order to establish secure connections to other IoT devices, cryptographic primitives are required to safely transmit data. Since the devices are physically accessible, enabling adversaries to mount all sorts of physical attacks, physically secure implementations are inevitable.

In this study, we evaluate the energy consumption of cryptographic primitives on a custom 65 nm ASIC with different design architectures ranging from unrolled to serialized implementation. In each design architecture, we compare the consumed energy of different crypto cores. We also examine the energy consumption of different masking schemes up to third-order secure realizations of various block ciphers. Further, in our practical investigations, we explore the energy consumption overhead of countermeasures against fault-injection attacks under different adversary models providing the first practical results on real silicon for protected implementations.

Keywords: Cryptographic implementation · Energy consumption · Masking · Countermeasures · ASIC

1 Introduction

Low energy consumption is one of the key factors when designing battery-powered devices that are expected to operate for months or years without any user intervention. One of the applications for such devices is in the Internet of Things (IoT) where battery lifetime is an important criterion. Using cryptographic primitives became mandatory in such networks to establish secure connections for data transmission. With the increasing number of portable devices which are highly limited with respect to resources, new block ciphers are being

E. B. Kavun and M. Pehl (Eds.): COSADE 2023, LNCS 13979, pp. 195–220, 2023.
https://doi.org/10.1007/978-3-031-29497-6_10

developed to ensure a low area footprint as well as low energy consumption [4]. In addition to the fulfillment of mathematical security requirements, the implementation of corresponding encryption/decryption functions should be physically secure as well since a legitimate user can also play the role of a physical adversary. The crux of the matter is that an attacker can mount all kinds of physical attacks when the device is in hand. This necessitates the use of countermeasures in the implementation of cryptographic primitives to mitigate such a vector of attacks.

There exists a considerable body of work on developing new block ciphers that are optimized with respect to the chip area to fit in small embedded devices. Several new algorithms have been proposed including mCrypton [35], KATAN [20], LED [27], and PRESENT [15]. Other design goals include lower latency in an unrolled architecture targeting applications such as memory encryption. In this architecture, the entire encryption function is realized by a combinational circuit performing the encryption in one clock cycle. Examples include PRINCE [16], PRINCEv2 [17], MANTIS [8], QARMA [3], Orthros [6], and SPEEDY [34]. Several lightweight block ciphers have been proposed considering other implementation aspects. SKINNY [8] offers a balanced performance in software and hardware while GIMLI [10] has been designed to be a cross-platform efficient permutation. CRAFT [9] is efficient when fault protection is desired while MIDORI [4] is optimized with respect to low energy consumption, which is a very important factor in certain applications. MIDORI is the only block cipher designed for applications where energy consumption is the limiting factor. The authors reduced the number of glitches in their construction caused by different delays at the input of a combinational circuit. Based on simulation results, they concluded that a round-based implemented design achieves the best energy performance in MIDORI.

The influence of design architecture has been investigated in several studies [4,5,7,28], where the energy consumption of lightweight ciphers in different architectures was compared. While the outcome of some publications is that the round-based architecture has the best performance, the authors of [5] have shown by simulation that in some cases the optimal solution is achieved when two rounds in the implementation are combined. Moreover, it has been shown that unrolled implementation of some lightweight block ciphers is the most energy-efficient strategy in practice in certain scenarios [42].

With the increasing demand for physically secure implementations, the question arises whether the energy consumption overhead is significant in practice when a countermeasure is employed and how to select the most energy-efficient approach. There are few publications in that regard even in the simulation domain. For example, the masked implementation of several Authenticated Encryption with Associated Data (AEAD) constructions with three and four shares has been studied in [18] by simulation. The authors concluded that energy consumption increases in the number of shares, which is naturally true. However, the study is limited to AEAD designs protected by the Threshold Implementation (TI) strategy with no real data on an Application Specific Integrated Circuit

(ASIC) chip. Therefore, there is a gap in the open literature where only a few countermeasures have been studied with respect to energy efficiency. Moreover, most of the publications presented their result by simulation and no real measurement in practice has been performed. We aim to address this gap in this work by considering a wide range of protected designs including different masking schemes, hiding techniques, and fault countermeasures using a prototype ASIC chip manufactured in 65 nm technology.

Our Contributions. In this paper, we measure the energy consumption of different cryptographic primitives in different architectures and with various countermeasures on a 65 nm prototype ASIC chip. To this end, we investigate two different approaches to perform the measurements and explain the engineering challenges of each method due to small signals and high-frequency components. We first examine unrolled implementations of almost all block ciphers optimized for low latency with regard to their energy consumption. We proceed with measuring the energy consumption of round-based constructions and assess the overhead of using the WDDL logic style [50]. For the first time in the open literature, we compare the energy consumption of first-order secure realizations of different block ciphers where each algorithm is masked by different techniques such as TI [38], CMS [41], etc. Moreover, we report the energy consumption overhead of using the WDDL logic style in addition to masking techniques. We extend our explorations to higher-order masking schemes which are required when a higher level of security is desired. We also measure the energy consumption of code-based fault-protected designs using error-correcting codes and demonstrate that they potentially can outperform the majority voting approach even though they have a higher area overhead. To the best of our knowledge, this work presents the first practical investigation with respect to energy consumption for protected designs using masking schemes, hiding techniques, and fault-protected designs. In fact, the entire state of the art is based on simulations while we measure the power consumption of different designs on real silicon providing more realistic results.

2   Background

2.1   Design Architecture Effect on Energy Consumption

It has been shown that the architecture of an implementation has an impact on its energy and power consumption [4,5,7,28,42]. The reason behind the differences is the depth of the circuit leading to more glitches. Glitches are a known phenomenon in Complementary Metal Oxide Semiconductor (CMOS) circuits, which are undesired signal transitions at the outputs of logic gates due to a mismatch between the arrival time of multiple input signals. This phenomenon in a combinational circuit increases the dynamic power consumption significantly, as the logic gates need to charge and discharge their output capacitances multiple times in each cycle. Since the higher depth of the circuit intensifies the effect of glitches and thus the switching activities, unrolled implementations usually have higher power consumption peaks. However, the output is ready after a short amount of time so the energy consumption can be lower than round-based implementations, which is not always the case as shown in [42]. On the other end, serial implementations have lower depth and lower area overhead but require many more clock cycles to calculate the output. As a result, energy consumption, which is the integral of power consumption over time, can be higher. For instance, the authors of [7] compared serialized implementations with only one S-box instance with round-based implementations in which a round function is executed in one clock cycle. Based on simulation, they naturally concluded that serialized implementations consume more energy.

The round function of a cipher can be instantiated r times and connected sequentially to realize the construction of the cipher, which is called r-round unrolled implementation. Subsequently, the key schedule should be unrolled if necessary. The advantage of this approach is a higher throughput due to faster computation in terms of clock cycles. For example, a block cipher with R rounds provides the result in $\left\lceil \frac{R}{r} \right\rceil$ clock cycles in an r-round unrolled construction. However, as a disadvantage, this leads to higher area overhead and a circuit with larger depth leading to more glitches and thus more significant power peaks. The authors of [5] studied these different implementation strategies by estimating the power consumption of each design using a power compiler after creating the netlist. The authors found that implementing multiple rounds with a combinational circuit, i.e., 2-round unrolled implementation, is the most energy-efficient way for some block ciphers. It has also been demonstrated by simulation that for some full AEAD circuits the optimal number can be even three, i.e., 3-round unrolled implementation [18]. The authors also proposed a formal model for energy consumption in any r-round unrolled block cipher implementation, but it has been never verified in practice. Hence, it would be interesting to examine this trade-off on real silicon. In this work, we take a look at different implementation strategies, including round-based, serialized, and unrolled implementations which are the most common design architectures.

2.2 Masking

It has been shown that having physical access to a target device enables adversaries to recover secret information by monitoring its physical characteristics such as the power consumption. After the seminal work by Kocher et al. [33] known as Differential Power Analysis (DPA), the relevant scientific communities have dedicated a considerable body of research on improving the attack and developing countermeasures. Due to its sound theoretical foundation, masking is among the most commonly employed approaches to prevent Side-Channel Analysis (SCA) attacks in practice. Masking is a technique based on secret-sharing schemes in which the sensitive values in the cipher are randomized to break the relation between key-dependent intermediate values and the physical properties of the underlying device.

In masking schemes, the key-dependent variables are split into several shares and all computations are performed on shared data. Boolean masking is the most popular approach where the XOR result of the shares yields the original data.

TI [38] is the first strategy whose security is not jeopardized by glitches in hardware platforms. Later, the technique has been extended to higher orders in [14] where its limitations have been discussed in [40]. More recently, two separate works [26,41] offered the same level of security with the minimum number of input shares, which is not the case for TI. However, the masked circuit demands for fresh randomness to maintain security. In [47,48] the randomness complexity was reduced to realize the first- and second-order secure hardware implementations using two and three shares.

Due to the high computational complexity of formal verification of masked circuits, several security notions for the secure composition of masked gadgets have been proposed recently [21,29,30,32]. Employing the security notions helps the design and verification of larger circuits usually at the cost of higher implementation costs due to conservative assumptions. The proposed gadgets are optimized under several optimization metrics, e.g., randomness requirements, area overhead, latency, etc. However, there is no investigation of the energy efficiency of the designs in the open literature. We try to cover this gap in this work by investigating the impact of masking schemes on energy consumption, which was measured on a prototype ASIC chip.

2.3 Wave Dynamic Differential Logic (WDDL)

Wave Dynamic Differential Logic (WDDL) has been introduced in [50] to thwart DPA. WDDL cells can be realized by existing standard cell libraries and can be implemented on hardware platforms, including ASICs and FPGAs. This logic style is meant to provide constant power consumption making it independent of the processed data. A WDDL gate consists of a parallel combination of two positive complementary gates. In the precharge phase, all complementary input signals of the combinational WDDL cell are set to 0. Subsequently, the output of every gate is set to 0 automatically. This 0 precharge value ripples through the combinational logic creating a precharge wave. In the evaluation phase, input signals are set to complementary values and the WDDL gate calculates a complementary output.

It has been shown that WDDL does not provide provably-secure SCA protection even though it reduces the leakage [44]. The underlying reason is that the requirements to have constant power consumption are not met in practice. For example, it is essential that the gate always charges ideally a fixed amount of capacitance to make the power consumption input independent. However, it is almost impossible to have the same capacitive load in hardware platforms, even when routing the dual signals identically, due to differences between standard cells and due to process variation. Therefore, it has been used more as a hiding countermeasure to mitigate attacks.

Due to the dual-rail fashion of WDDL, the area overhead is at least doubled compared to a realization with traditional implementation approaches. Moreover, the latency of the design is also doubled in terms of clock cycles due to the fact that the WDDL D-flip-flop consists of two stages of cascaded D-flip-flops. In this work, we investigate the energy consumption overhead of this logic style compared to CMOS circuits with equivalent functionality as well.

2.4   Fault Attacks and Countermeasures

Fault attacks are a type of physical attack in which the attacker forces the target device to operate on a non-regular condition. This can be done by laser beams for more precise fault injections while less accurate ones can be induced by means of clock glitches, voltage glitches, and electromagnetic pulses. Then, the attacker analyzes the faulty or fault-free outcomes to recover the secret key.

Protection against fault attacks has been explored in prior studies by a great number of publications, some focusing on avoiding faulty outputs, others on correcting the induced faults. All proposed countermeasures utilize some sort of redundancy, e.g., time, area, or information redundancy. A naive way to mitigate fault attacks is to calculate the outcome twice followed by checking the consistency of them [36]. More sophisticated approaches have been used in [2] where the authors used code-based Concurrent Error Detection (CED). The authors claim the detection of any bounded number of faults injected in any location of the design implemented in hardware platforms. The crux of the matter is that all detection-based countermeasures cannot provide any security against Statistical Ineffective Fault Attacks (SIFAs) [24]. The authors of [49] addressed the issue and extended the methodology to provide protection against SIFA using Error Correcting Codes (ECCs). More recently, an approach based on both detecting and correcting codes has been presented in [39] combining the principles of [49] and [2]. In fact, depending on the employed code, the constructions guarantee the correction of up to t_c faulty bits and the detection of t_d-bit faults given that $t_d > t_c$.

In this work, we study the methodology presented in [49] and [39] implemented in a prototype ASIC. We report the energy consumption overhead of the countermeasure compared to the unprotected one.

3   Measurement Methods

3.1   Measurement with Differential Oscilloscope Probe

The energy consumption of a circuit is determined by the current draw of the circuit, the operating voltage, and the period of time the circuit is running. One method to measure the energy consumption of an electrical circuit is to measure the voltage V and the current I to estimate the power $P = VI$. The total energy consumption can be straightforwardly computed as it is the integral of the power over time.

$$E = \int_t P(t)dt = \int_t V(t)I(t)dt. \qquad (1)$$

An exemplary circuit for this measurement is demonstrated in Fig. 1. Measuring V_{chip} is straightforward and can be done using a channel of an oscilloscope. We should highlight that measuring V_{chip} is necessary to catch any fluctuation in the actual voltage the chip is running on. Note that, the measurement should be performed with DC coupling since the voltage variations over the shunt resistor are very small compared to V_{DD}. Measuring the current directly is more challenging and needs specific devices. We can use differential probes to estimate the current. Differential probes measure the voltage difference between any two points in the circuit. We can use a differential probe to monitor the voltage drop V_R over a shunt resistor R using the second channel of the oscilloscope. Then, the current can be calculated as $I = \frac{V_R}{R}$.

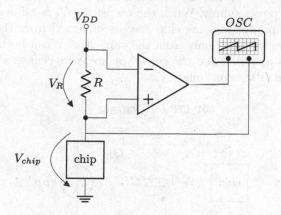

Fig. 1. Schematic of differential probe measurement.

While this method is easy to set up, it demands for high requirements. In small-size technologies, the propagation delay of a node is short leading to high-frequency transitions in the circuit at the clock edges. Hence, the power consumption of a modern ASIC design has short peaks as well as high amplitudes in the high-frequency components. As a result, missing the high-frequency components can lead to an inaccurate measurement. To measure the energy consumption precisely, the operating bandwidth of the differential probe should be high enough to capture all voltage fluctuations over the shunt resistor (V_R in Fig. 1). Since these voltage variations are very small, the differential probe should ideally have an advanced integrated amplifier. Moreover, the sampling frequency of the oscilloscope needs to be very high with enough bandwidth. All in all, a sophisticated oscilloscope with high bandwidth differential probes is required to measure the energy consumption accurately.

3.2 Capacitor Discharge Measurement

In this second method, we use the fact that a capacitor is able to store energy in the electrical field between its plates. The energy remains in the capacitor when the charged capacitor is disconnected from the power supply. The stored energy E in a capacitor with the capacitance C can be calculated by measuring the voltage V from the expression $E = \frac{1}{2}CV^2$. Subsequently, the consumed energy ΔE during encryption in a chip can be obtained by measuring the voltage drop over the capacitor by

$$\Delta E = E_{start} - E_{end} = \frac{1}{2}C(V_{start}^2 - V_{end}^2). \tag{2}$$

We made use of a circuit similar to the one presented in [42] to measure the energy consumption in this work. Borrowed from that, we briefly restate how we use the circuit depicted in Fig. 2 to perform the energy measurement.

The circuit has two transistors to control the setup. Namely, when the transistors Q_1 and Q_2 are on, the capacitor is being charged and the chip is directly supplied by the power supply. When the transistor Q_1 is off and the transistor Q_2 is on, the capacitor and the chip are disconnected from the power supply and the chip gets its power only from the capacitor. When both transistors are off, the chip has no power and the capacitor keeps its charge with no influence through the chip or the controller.

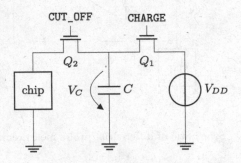

Fig. 2. Schematic of capacitor discharge measurement [42].

To perform an energy measurement, both control signals CHARGE and CUT_OFF are high at the beginning and all inputs are fed to the chip. Meanwhile, the capacitor is being charged. Then, the clock is halted and CHARGE goes low to disconnect the power supply from the capacitor and the chip. After making sure that Q_1 is switched off with enough delay, e.g., 400 ns, we start the encryption by re-supplying the clock of the chip. When the encryption is done, the clock is halted again and CUT_OFF goes low to isolate the capacitor for the measurement. This enables us to measure the capacitor voltage V_C with an oscilloscope more accurately as it is disconnected from the chip and the power supply. We should highlight that all control signals should be synchronized with the chip to exclude the influence of I/O activity. As an advantage, this method is not limited by the bandwidth of the probes or the oscilloscope. We just require to measure the DC level of V_C with high accuracy (see Fig. 2).

4   Setup

The energy consumption measurements have been performed on a prototype ASIC produced in a $65nm$ technology using a commercial standard cell library. It consists of several cryptographic cores of different ciphers, some of which are protected against SCA or fault attacks. There is a general control logic inside the ASIC chip receiving all necessary inputs in a serial fashion and activates the selected core to perform the encryption. Namely, all cores are clock gated and only one core (together with its respective part of the clock tree) is active during the measurement. When the encryption is finished, the control logic observes the ciphertext and sends it back serially as well. The cores and the I/O cells are supplied from different voltages so that the I/O signals have a very low influence on the measurement.

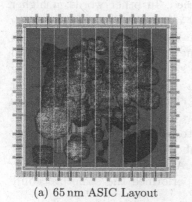

(a) 65 nm ASIC Layout

(b) Custom Measurement Board

Fig. 3. Layout of the 65 nm ASIC and picture of the custom measurement board.

The ASIC is mounted on a custom measurement board where a Xilinx ARTIX-7 FPGA is used for communication and control. Both the layout of the chip and a picture of the measurement board are shown in Fig. 3. The target chip power supply is isolated from the FPGA power supply and different voltage regulators are used to supply the independent power regions on the board. There is a 1Ω shunt resistor in the core power supply with corresponding SMA connectors for measurement. The resistor can be replaced by the capacitor circuit described in Sect. 3.2. The target is clocked at 12 MHz, and we utilized a 12-bit Teledyne LeCroy Waverunner HRO 66Zi at the sampling rate of 2 GS/s in this work.

4.1 Energy Reference

As stated, our prototype ASIC chip contains several cryptographic cores and a general control logic that controls the cores, the Pseudo-Random Number Generator (PRNG) circuit for randomness generation, and the transfer of the plaintexts and ciphertexts. Since a single core is quite small compared to the whole ASIC, the energy consumption of the control logic can be (much) higher and should be excluded. Although all cores and PRNG circuitry are clock gated, they still consume energy due to leakage currents, i.e., static power consumption. We use the same approach presented in [42] to subtract the energy consumed by other components. To this end, we activate no core and measure the energy consumption in the same way as an encryption is measured, in order to achieve the energy reference. In such a manner, we measured a baseline to cancel out the influence of I/O activity, the control logic, and any other component.

The cores in the prototype chip are implemented with various architectures. Hence, different ciphers have different numbers of rounds leading to different numbers of clock cycles required for the round-based implementations. We count the latency of unrolled implementations as two clock cycles here, in the first cycle the inputs are propagated to the combinational circuit and in the second cycle the final result is saved in the output register. As a result, the energy reference (the baseline) of different cores is varied. In other words, a higher number of clock cycles leads to a higher energy overhead. To have an energy reference for unrolled implementations, we measured the energy consumption for two clock cycles exactly the same way that we measure the cores with unrolled implementation. Namely, we follow exactly the same procedure of measuring the core energy consumption, but we select no core (i.e., all clock gates for the individual cores prevent propagation of the clock signal). The same holds for round-based implementations. In this case, we performed the measurement for 100 clock cycles in each round-based design to calculate the average energy consumed per cycle. Then, we multiply the number of clock cycles required for the cipher to compute the energy consumption. Again, to measure the energy reference for round-based implementations, we performed the same procedure while deactivating all cores.

4.2   Static Power and Frequency Impact

It is important to note that the cores being analyzed are clock-gated and not power-gated. This means that even when the clock is off but power is supplied, all cores are consuming energy due to leakage currents, which are a natural occurrence in any active circuit regardless of clock frequency or switching activity. Our energy evaluation process eliminates a significant portion of the power consumption resulting from leakage currents, since both the energy measurement and the energy reference are affected by these currents (only some data-dependent difference remains). This is inevitable for our test chip and the chosen measurement method. However, to not neglect the impact of the static power on the total energy consumption we provide postlayout estimations of the static energy consumed by each crypto core under typical operating conditions in Appendix B. While the contribution of the static power consumption during active computation is barely noteworthy for frequencies in the MHz range and above (less than 1% under typical conditions), it can of course become the dominant source of energy consumption over long time periods when the circuit is very rarely active but always powered.

We would like to highlight that all measurements in this work have been conducted at a constant 12 MHz clock frequency. This might beg the question whether the results would change noticeably for different frequencies. However, due to the fact that our measurement method removes the static power consumption almost entirely and mostly captures the energy consumed through switching activity, we do not anticipate any significant impact of the frequency on the results. The delays, switching times and overall behavior of the gates and circuits are unaffected by the time it takes until the next positive edge arrives. Only when decreasing the clock period below the critical path delay, leading to incorrect operation, the behavior would be affected. Other properties of the clock signal like its transition time, or global factors like the supply voltage or temperature would indeed change the behavior and energy consumption. But if the quality of the clock signal is stable and all outside factors are equal, the frequency is not of primary importance for our measurements. The main factor that changes with different frequencies is the run time of each implementation and therefore the portion of the static power contribution during activity. Yet, if the circuits are not power-gated but only clock-gated, like in our case, leakage currents occur regardless of activity or not.

4.3   Energy Measurement Using Differential Probe

We used a LeCroy AP033 Active Differential Probe with 500 MHz bandwidth to measure the voltage drop over the $1\,\Omega$ shunt resistor enabling us to calculate the current. The chip voltage V_{chip} (shown in Fig. 1) was measured directly by connecting the chip power supply to the oscilloscope with an SMA-BNC coaxial cable. We halted the clock before and after each cipher execution.

In this study, we conducted measurements using our method on two cryptographic cores: unprotected round-based CRAFT [9] and its three-share first-order masked implementation. We collected 10,000 measurements for each core. The fluctuation of V_{chip} and V_R are visible in our measurements, but the difference in energy consumption does not correspond to the size of the circuit. Despite the masked implementation being larger with increased latency compared to the unprotected one, we only observed an 80% increase in energy consumption, which is much lower than expected. This discrepancy may be due to either insufficient bandwidth of the differential probe or low sampling rate leading to undersampling. As a result, we re-conducted the measurements using the capacitor discharge method detailed in Sect. 3.2.

4.4   Energy Measurement Using Capacitor

As mentioned in Sect. 3.2, the circuit has two transistors controlled by the FPGA directly. The FPGA is also controlling the chip. Hence, all control signals are synchronized with the ASIC chip. The clock was halted before and after each cipher call to have a more accurate measurement. After monitoring the voltage drop over the capacitor, we connect the chip to the power supply V_{DD}, so we were able to receive the ciphertext back. It implies that the transistors are fast enough, and the internal state of the ASIC is unchanged during the transistors activity switching between the capacitor and the power supply.

We measured the energy consumption of the two aforementioned implementations with this method. We have observed that the results are more in line with our expectations demonstrating the setup is not limited by the bandwidth/sampling frequency restrictions. Therefore, we used this method to perform the measurements on all cores, reported in the next section.

Table 1. Energy consumption of unrolled cipher implementations.

Design	Block size [bit]	Key size [bit]	Energy/Enc [pJ]	Energy/bit [pJ]
PRINCE [16]	64	128	**361.6**	5.64
PRINCEv2 [17]	64	128	366.4	5.72
PRINCE+v2 [17]	64	128	373.5	5.84
MIDORI [4]	64	128	507.5	7.93
MANTIS [8]	64	128	471.6	7.37
QARMA$_7$-64-σ_0 [3]	64	128	572.1	8.94
QARMA$_7$-64-σ_1 [3]	64	128	593.6	9.27
QARMA$_7$-64-σ_2 [3]	64	128	655.8	10.25
Orthros [6]	128	128	966.4	7.54
SPEEDY-5-192 ENC [34]	192	192	598.4	3.12
SPEEDY-6-192 ENC [34]	192	192	792.0	4.12
SPEEDY-7-192 ENC [34]	192	192	916.2	4.77
SPEEDY-5-192 DEC [34]	192	192	1431.6	7.46
SPEEDY-6-192 DEC [34]	192	192	1910.3	9.95
SPEEDY-7-192 DEC [34]	192	192	2552.1	13.3
GIMLI [10]	384	384	811.1	**2.11**

5   Results

5.1   Unrolled Implementations

As the first case study, we investigate the energy consumption of unrolled implementations of various cryptographic algorithms. Unrolled implementations naturally have a large area footprint and a high power consumption due to the large number of glitches occurring (see [37] for an analysis of the glitching activity of an unrolled PRINCE implementation). However, they should provide a low latency making them a suitable option for high-performance applications like memory encryption.

To perform the measurements, we fixed the key to a random value and selected a plaintext randomly for each cipher call. We collected 10 000 measurements from each core and used the average of the signals to calculate the energy consumption. As stated, we did the same with selecting no core using the same number of measurements to obtain the energy reference. Finally, we calculated the power consumption using Eq. 2. In the following, we briefly introduce each block cipher implemented in our prototype ASIC chip.

PRINCE [16]. PRINCE is optimized with respect to latency in hardware platforms making it suitable for real-time applications. An important feature of the cipher is its minimal additional cost to realize both encryption and decryption in hardware.

PRINCEv2 and PRINCE+v2 [17]. PRINCEv2 is a block cipher based on PRINCE featuring higher security margins without significantly increasing the implementation costs. In our chip, PRINCE and PRINCEv2 are additionally merged into a combined PRINCE+v2 implementation, where a control signal is used to select which cipher should be executed.

MIDORI [4]. MIDORI is a lightweight block cipher optimized with respect to energy efficiency with no claim to provide a low-latency implementation in unrolled fashion. Yet, its S-box is supposed to provide a low gate depth and therefore low latency. Hence, an unrolled implementation of MIDORI-64 is implemented in our prototype ASIC chip.

MANTIS [8]. MANTIS is a lightweight block cipher designed for low-latency applications. Unlike PRINCE, MANTIS is a tweakable block cipher. It uses the same S-box used in MIDORI.

QARMA [3]. QARMA is a family of lightweight tweakable block ciphers targeted at applications with low latency requirements. A variant of QARMA that supports block size of n bits with $2n$ bits of key and $2r + 2$ rounds is denoted by QARMA$_r$-n. QARMA can use three S-Boxes, i.e., σ_0, σ_1, and σ_2, where σ_0 is the lightest one. Qualcomm's product security team designed this block cipher, which is the standard block cipher used in the ARMv8.3-A ISA extensions for pointer authentication [1,19].

Orthros [6]. Orthros is a 128-bit block pseudorandom function with a primary focus on the latency of fully unrolled circuits. The round function is similar to MIDORI with lower latency.

SPEEDY [34]. SPEEDY is a family of low-latency block ciphers with a high-speed 6-bit S-box in contrast to all aforementioned encryption primitives where a 4-bit S-Box is used. An instance of this family with block and key size $6l$ bits iterating over r rounds is denoted by SPEEDY-r-6l. The encryption and decryption functions are different and must be implemented separately.

GIMLI [10]. GIMLI is a 384-bit permutation designed to be a high-performance as well as a high security cryptographic primitive. GIMLI is meant to be efficient across different platforms, including ARM smartphone CPUs, ARM microcontrollers, FPGAs, ASICs, and so forth. The permutation can be used to build tweakable block ciphers, stream ciphers, message-authentication codes, etc. The authors also claimed the energy efficiency of their scheme in hardware platforms.

Table 1 lists all the energy consumption results of ciphers implemented in unrolled fashion. We used the capacitor discharge method to measure the power consumption using 10 000 measurements. As stated, the key is fixed to a random value while the plaintext is selected randomly in each cipher call. The input and output of each implementation are stored in registers and the results in Table 1 include the energy consumption of stores.

PRINCE has the lowest energy consumption per encryption making it suitable for low-latency applications where low amounts of data need to be encrypted once in a while. PRINCEv2 has a slightly larger energy consumption while having higher security margins. It shows that the authors kept their promises and the overhead is not significant. PRINCE+v2 is basically a core containing both PRINCE and PRINCEv2 where the user can choose between either of them to process the given input. As expected, a slightly higher energy usage was measured as it has additional multiplexers. Although MIDORI is not optimized for low latency applications, the energy consumption is competitive compared to other designs. Its S-box is optimized for low depth and energy efficiency making it a good choice to design a low-latency cipher. MANTIS uses the same S-box as MIDORI and is structurally similar to the PRINCE block cipher, but is tweakable. Even though the energy consumption of MANTIS is less than MIDORI, the difference is negligible. Orthros is also based on the MIDORI round function and the designers revised it to achieve lower latency. It has a much higher energy consumption compared to MIDORI and MANTIS but it also deals with larger block size. As a result, energy consumption per bit is a fairer metric. Considering this metric, all three mentioned designs have roughly the same energy consumption.

We measured three different variants of QARMA. Namely, all three S-boxes (σ_0, σ_1, and σ_2) have been used in an unrolled implementation while the number of rounds is fixed to sixteen. This highlights the effect of S-boxes on energy consumption. As demonstrated in the table, σ_0 has the lowest energy consumption at the cost of lower security margins. The other two S-boxes σ_1 and σ_2 have better cryptographic properties with less energy efficiency, demonstrating a trade-off between security and energy consumption. SPEEDY offers different variants with various block and key sizes iterating over several rounds. All implemented designs have 192-bit block size and key size but with a different number of rounds. Since the encryption and decryption functions are not the same, its decryption was also implemented with different rounds. Looking at the encryption function, the variant with the lowest number of rounds has better energy efficiency as expected. As the number of rounds increases, the energy consumption rises but offers better security margins. Even the variant with 7 rounds has the lowest energy consumption per bit compared to all above given cipher cores. The decryption function, however, has a worse performance than the encryption function and consumes more than double the energy. Since the SPEEDY decryption is not nearly as efficient as the encryption, it is advisable to use the encryption function of SPEEDY in modes of operation that require no decryption routine, e.g., CTR, CMAC, and GCM, given that energy efficiency is desired. As the last case study, we take a look at GIMLI. As stated, GIMLI is a cross-platform permutation and has no key. To make an encryption using the primitive, two different keys at the beginning and the end were added to the state using Even-Mansour scheme [25]. As indicated in Table 1, it is the most performant design in terms of energy consumption per bit making it a promising choice in low-latency applications where lower energy consumption is required. Particularly, if a large chunk of data needs to be encrypted. Concrete area and critical path delay values for all implementations analyzed in this work are given in Appendix B. Please note that the targeted clock frequency of the ASIC is below 50 MHz and therefore does not effectively constrain the unrolled circuits, leading to smaller area footprints but larger critical path delays compared to high-performance comparisons presented in [34].

Table 2. Energy consumption of round-based cipher implementations.

Design	Block size [bit]	Key size [bit]	Latency [cycles]	Energy/cycle [pJ]	Energy/Enc [pJ]	Energy/bit [pJ]
AES [23]	128	128	11	3.53	**38.9**	**0.30**
CRAFT [9]	64	128	32	**2.26**	72.5	1.13
CRAFT WDDL [9]	64	128	64	7.32	468.4	7.32

5.2 Non-masked Round-Based Implementations

We proceed with measuring the energy consumption of two different block ciphers, i.e., AES [23] and CRAFT [9], implemented following a round-based architecture. AES is the well-known standardized block cipher, which is widely applied to industrial cryptographic solutions. CRAFT [9] is a tweakable lightweight block cipher primarily focused on efficient protection against fault attacks. It uses the same S-box as MIDORI. Unfortunately, only these two block ciphers were implemented in the prototype ASIC chip. The WDDL realization of the cipher CRAFT is also implemented in the chip.

To measure the energy consumption for each cipher, we performed the measurements 10 000 times for 100 clock cycles while making sure that the cipher is running on the chip. All the unprotected designs needed less than 100 clock cycles to perform the encryption. Therefore, we let the design run for more rounds to have a consistent result. Then, we calculate the average energy consumption per clock cycle for each design. As a result, the energy consumption can be calculated based on the latency of each cipher, i.e., number of required clock cycles. As stated before, we used the same number of measurements to compute the energy reference. We make use of the same fashion for all round-based implementations in the next sections.

The measured energy consumptions are reported in Table 2. AES has better energy efficiency than CRAFT even though it has higher energy consumption per clock cycle. CRAFT has lower area overhead and thus lower energy consumption per cycle. However, it requires more rounds to perform the encryption resulting in higher energy consumption per encryption. Moreover, AES deals with a larger block size resulting in better performance in energy consumption per bit. Based on the results, AES is a better choice for energy consumption efficiency given that the higher area overhead is acceptable. Reducing the side-channel leakage using WDDL method does not come for free; the design consumes roughly 6 times more energy.

5.3 First-Order Secure Masked Implementations

We used the same procedure as in Sect. 5.2 to perform the measurements. All first-order secure designs are fully pipelined, i.e., they can process multiple inputs at each cipher call. To have a fair comparison, we filled the entire pipeline with random inputs to measure the energy consumption. The energy consumption of the different designs is listed in Table 3.

Table 3. Energy consumption of first-order secure masked implementations.

Design	#Block [bit]	#Key [bit]	Latency [cycles]	#P.[a]	Rand. [bit/cycle]	En./Enc[b] [pJ]	En./P.[c] [pJ]	En./bit[d] [pJ]
CRAFT TI[e] [9]	64	128	64	2	0	867.8	433.9	6.8
CRAFT CMS [41]	64	128	128	4	0	2209.3	552.3	8.6
CRAFT NF [47]	64	128	64	2	0	763.3	381.6	6.0
CRAFT TI WDDL[e] [9]	64	128	128	2	0	4748.1	2374.1	37.1
CRAFT CMS WDDL [41]	64	128	256	4	0	12029.0	3007.3	47.0
CRAFT NF WDDL [47]	64	128	128	2	0	5453.3	2727	42.6
SKINNY HPC2 [21]	64	64	160	5	64	6226.8	1245.4	19.5
SKINNY HPC3 [30]	64	64	96	3	128	2596.6	865.5	13.5
SKINNY GHPC [32]	64	64	96	3	64	4654.6	1551.6	24.2
SKINNY GHPC$_{LL}$ [32]	64	64	64	2	1024	1439.7	1439.7	22.5
SKINNY COMAR [29]	64	64	544	17	6	54487.8	3205.2	50.1
PRESENT TI[e] [43]	64	128	64	2	0	1195.7	597.9	9.3
PRESENT NF [47]	64	128	656	1	0	4460.9	4460.9	69.7
AES [45]	128	128	216	1	8	8961.7	8961.7	70.0
KECCAK NF [48]	200	–	72	3	0	1995.3	665.1	10.0

[a]The number of plaintexts that the design can process due to pipeline architecture.
[b]Energy Consumption per Encryption.
[c]Energy Consumption per Plaintext.
[d]Energy Consumption per bit.
[e]With 3 shares.

We should highlight that different cryptographic cores in our prototype chip demand different numbers of fresh masks. Generating fresh randomness is a complex issue in the open literature, as there is no universally accepted method for secure and efficient generation yet. There are many open questions, such as the most efficient True Random Number Generator (TRNG) design, its cost including runtime testing and monitoring, the necessary entropy for an initial seed passed to a PRNG, the concrete security requirements for PRNGs, the potential limitations of Linear Feedback Shift Registers (LFSRs) as PRNGs due to their linear outputs, and the fault or SCA protection of the generators and so on. Hence, we refrain from including the energy consumption associated with concurrent random number generation for masking contexts in our results, as the choices and assumptions we would need to make greatly affect the results. However, we stress that the masked cores which require fresh randomness would cause a larger energy consumption in practice than in our experiments. To provide an intuition for that we give two examples. In [13] a round-based AES-128 in counter mode has been used to generate the required fresh randomness per cycle from an initial seed. In [22] a round-reduced unrolled PRINCE version is employed in output feedback mode for the same purpose. We know from Tables 1 and 2 that round-based AES and unrolled PRINCE consume about 0.3 and 5.6 pJ per output bit produced, which already shows that the cost for generating masking randomness can vary significantly. Yet, there are likely more efficient solutions from an energy efficiency standpoint than using full block ciphers as PRNGs.

We leave the concrete energy cost associated with randomness generation as a topic for future research.

As the first case study in this section, we compare the energy consumption of different first-order secure realizations of CARFT. In CRAFT TI design, the S-box is decomposed into quadratic functions, each of which is masked using TI strategy with three shares. To avoid the propagation of glitches, two register layers are placed in the round function. Similar to CRAFT TI, the S-box is also decomposed in CRAFT CMS design. However, each quadratic function is masked using two shares based on Consolidating Masking Scheme (CMS) [41] forcing four layers of register in the design. As shown in the Table 3, the energy consumption per input of CRAFT TI [47] is lower even though more input shares are used. This highlights that using a larger number of shares not necessarily leads to a higher energy consumption. Following [47], the S-box is not decomposed in CRAFT NF and the design is masked using two shares, which leads to lower energy consumption, outperforming other designs. All three designs were also implemented by WDDL logic style. Theoretically, all these masked WDDL designs are first-order secure with lower higher-order leakage. As expected, the energy consumption is much higher compared to the traditional standard style. However, CRAFT TI WDDL has the best energy efficiency per plaintext even though it is a three-share design using one extra share compared to the other two designs.

The next case study is based on the SKINNY block cipher and composable gadgets are used in all designs. As a matter of fact, all designs were implemented in fully-pipeline round-based architecture. The first SKINNY design is based on the second Hardware Private Circuits multiplication gadget (HPC2) presented in [21]. Recently, the approach was optimized for low-latency application in [30] called HPC3. As shown in Table 3, the design has better latency and also energy consumption at the cost of higher randomness requirements. Generic Hardware Private Circuit (GHPC) [32] is a framework to construct trivially composable and secure hardware gadgets for arbitrary vectorial Boolean functions (not only multiplication). Its low-latency variant $GHPC_{LL}$ has slightly better energy performance than the GHPC. However, its randomness requirement is significantly higher. The authors of [29] presented a methodology for achieving free composition of hardware gadgets to realize a first-order secure masked hardware implementation of arbitrary function utilizing only six random bits in the entire design. However, the cost of area overhead and latency is significantly higher than other methodologies. Looking at Table 3, the energy consumption is also the highest among all compatible cores. All in all, the HPC3 approach appears to be the most energy-efficient, at least as long as the energy cost for randomness generation is not considered (see discussion above).

The PRESENT TI is a fully-pipelined round-based implementation using three shares with no fresh masks [43]. PRESENT NF is a two-share serial implementation that also requires no fresh randomness [47]. Contrary to PRESENT TI, the S-box is not decomposed in PRESENT NF design. As one can see, the energy consumption per plaintext and per bit are significantly higher in serial architecture even though its area footprint is smaller and a lower number of shares is used.

Table 4. Energy consumption of higher-order secure masked implementations.

Design	#d[a]1	#Block [bit]	#Key [bit]	Latency [cycles]	#P.[b]	Rand. [bit/cycle]	En./Enc[c] [pJ]	En./P.[d] [pJ]	En./bit[e] [pJ]
SKINNY NF [48]	2	64	64	128	4	128	4202.2	1050.6	16.4
SKINNY HPC2 [21]	2	64	64	160	5	192	10286.8	2057.4	32.1
SKINNY HPC3 [30]	2	64	64	96	3	384	4613.3	1537.8	24.0
SKINNY HPC2 [21]	3	64	64	160	5	384	15339.3	3067.9	47.9
SKINNY HPC3 [30]	3	64	64	96	3	768	6608.8	2202.9	34.4
PRESENT NF [48]	2	64	128	666	1	8	10546.6	10546.6	164.8
KECCAK NF [48]	2	200	–	72	3	0	3637.9	1212.6	18.2
LED [12]	2	64	128	64	2	384	7502.4	3751.2	117.2

[a]Security order, $d + 1$: number of shares.
[b]The number of plaintexts that the design can process due to pipeline architecture.
[c]Energy Consumption per Encryption.
[d]Energy Consumption per Plaintext.
[e]Energy Consumption per bit.

It clearly highlights the impact of the chosen architecture on the energy consumption. Obviously, round-based architecture should be used in energy-critical applications.

The implemented masked AES in the ASIC chip is based on the technique presented in [46]. The technique primarily focused on optimizing the design on FPGAs using Block RAMs (BRAMs). In the eprint version of the article [45], the authors also provided a two-share byte-serial implementation of the design for ASIC platforms. The energy consumption is high due to its byte-serial architecture. It has almost the same energy consumption per bit as the nibble-serial implementation of PRESENT demonstrating that changing the algorithm and block size did not affect the energy consumption in this case. The last case study is a two-share first-order secure version of KECCAK-200 presented in [48]. The energy consumption of the implementations is not the lowest but outperforms most of the designs. Overall, the CRAFT NF implementation has the best energy performance out of all implemented first-order secure designs.

5.4 Higher-Order Secure Masked Implementations

In this section, we investigate the energy consumption of second- and third-order secure implementations. All round-based designs are fully pipelined as well.

HPC2 [21] and HPC3 [30] are methodologies to achieve composable glitch-robust provably-secure multiplication gadgets at arbitrary order. Thanks to the gadgets' trivial composition property, a complete block cipher can be protected at any security order. Using AGEMA [31], second- and third-order secure SKINNY designs have been constructed and implemented on our prototype ASIC chip where the energy consumption results are listed in Table 4. As expected, second-order secure implementations consume less energy, compared to the corresponding third-order designs. Similar to first-order secure designs, HPC3 has better energy efficiency at the cost of higher randomness requirements. Table 6 in

Table 5. Energy consumption of CRAFT round-based implementations with fault attack countermeasure.

Design	#Red./Nib[a] [bit]	#Correction [bit]	#Detection [bit]	Latency [cycles]	En./Enc[b] [pJ]	En./bit[c] [pJ]
CRAFT [9]	0	0	0	32	72.5	1.13
CRAFT IC II [49]	3	1	0	32	146.4	2.29
CRAFT IC III [39]	4	1	2	32	223.1	3.49
CRAFT IC II [49]	7	2	0	32	464.1	7.25
CRAFT MV[d] [49]	8	1	0	32	217.5	3.39

[a]Redundancy size per nibble.
[b]Energy Consumption per Encryption.
[c]Energy Consumption per bit.
[d]Estimated from CRAFT

Appendix B provides more information about the concrete methods used to verify the security properties of each protected implementation in practice.

We should highlight that trivial composability is not a necessary condition for probing security as shown in [21]. In other words, a masked design can be secure while not following composability notions. Hence, there is a considerable body of work to reduce the implementation cost of masked designs. One of the articles on optimizing the randomness cost of second-order secure implementation is presented in [48]. The authors introduced a methodology to realize a three-share second-order secure masked implementation of quadratic functions with no fresh masks. In this approach, the S-box is decomposed into several quadratic functions and the second-order masked realization only requires fresh masks for the decomposition, i.e., when masked masked quadratic functions are cascaded. The randomness complexity and energy consumption of this approach appear favorable compared to HPC2 and HPC3 methodologies for the SKINNY block cipher (see Table 4).

Since the KECCAK S-box is quadratic, it demands no fresh randomness in the chosen implementation and its energy consumption is 80% higher than the first-order secure one (compare Table 4 and Table 3). PRESENT was also implemented following a nibble-serial architecture similar to the first-order implementation. Its energy consumption is more than double of the first-order secure one.

The next implementation is based on the methodology presented in [12] using seven shares. As an advantage, the required fresh masks can stay fixed during the execution of the cipher. Due to a high number of shares, the energy consumption of the design is considerably high. The methodology was optimized later in [11] but unfortunately, it was not implemented in our ASIC chip.

5.5   Fault Attack Countermeasure Implementations

In this section, we investigate the impact of fault countermeasures on the block cipher CRAFT, which is optimized with respect to protection against Differential Fault Analysis (DFA). While detection-based countermeasures are prone to SIFA [24], correction-based countermeasures provide security at the cost of higher implementation costs. One other solution is to use Majority Voting (MV), where the cipher is instantiated $2t_c + 1$ number of times to correct up to t_c bit faults. Unfortunately, a design equipped with MV was not implemented in the ASIC chip but we can estimate its energy consumption based on the unprotected round-based implementation. To prevent SIFA against a single-bit fault, 3 instances of the cipher and an MV circuitry are required. This is referred to as CRAFT MV in Table 5. Hence, the amount of energy consumption is expected to be tripled at least. Looking at Table 5, the code-based methodology presented in [49], i.e., CRAFT IC II, provides the same level of security as CRAFT MV with less energy consumption even though higher area overhead compared to MV was reported in [49]. This also highlights that the energy consumption of a design with a higher area footprint can be more efficient. Integrating facilities to detect two faulty bits and simultaneously correct one faulty bit at the cost of one more bit redundancy per nibble, i.e., CRAFT IC III, approximately increases the energy consumption by 52%. Protecting the block cipher by correcting two faulty bits comes with significantly more energy consumption due to a higher area overhead and the demand for a larger redundancy, i.e., 7 bits per nibble.

6   Conclusions

In this work, we investigated the energy consumption of various implementations of symmetric cryptographic primitives (mostly block ciphers), ranging from unprotected implementations in round-based and unrolled architecture to designs protected against side-channel analysis and fault-injection attacks. We should highlight that this paper presents a practical energy measurement of protected designs for the first time in the open literature. In almost all previous relevant articles, the exploration was limited to simulation using EDA tools. However, in this study, we presented practical results of measuring the energy consumption on a prototype ASIC chip manufactured in a 65 nm technology.

Our results indicate that unrolled implementation of a block cipher with a higher block size can be beneficial as the energy consumption per bit can be more efficient. We have demonstrated that the number of rounds has a huge impact on the energy consumption in round-based implementations, e.g., AES outperforms CRAFT whose S-box is optimized for lower energy consumption. It has been also shown that WDDL logic style increases energy consumption significantly in practice.

Measuring the energy consumption of first-order masked designs has illustrated that using a higher number of input shares does not necessarily lead to higher energy consumption. Further, serial implementations show a considerably larger energy consumption despite a smaller area footprint. The results for higher-order secure implementations were in line with the expectations. In short, higher orders of security also lead to a larger energy consumption in practice. We also exhibited that manually-crafted optimized designs can outperform the designs constructed by automated tools based on composable gadgets. Moreover, the results revealed that using code-based correction facilities to mitigate fault-injection attacks can outperform the majority voting approach in terms of energy consumption while maintaining the same level of security.

In Appendix A we provide a list of links to repositories published by different authors and corresponding to different academic publications which contain the concrete RTL source code of many of the hardware cores analyzed in this work.

Acknowledgments. The work described in this paper has been supported in part by the Deutsche Forschungsgemeinschaft (DFG, German Research Foundation) under Germany's Excellence Strategy - EXC 2092 CASA - 390781972 and through the project 393207943 GreenSec, and by the European Union (EU) through the ERC project 724725 (acronym SWORD) and the Walloon Region through the FEDER project USERMedia (convention number 501907-379156).

A   List of Links for Open-Source Designs

1. https://github.com/Chair-for-Security-Engineering/SPEEDY: SPEEDY
2. https://github.com/subhadeep-banik/orthros: Orthros
3. https://gimli.cr.yp.to/impl.html: Gimli
4. https://github.com/hadipourh/AES-VHDL/tree/master/AES-ENC/RTL: Unprotected round-based AES
5. https://github.com/emsec/ImpeccableCircuits/tree/master/CRAFT: Unprotected round-based CRAFT and first-order secure CRAFT (CRAFT TI)
6. https://github.com/Chair-for-Security-Engineering/AES_masked_BRAM: First-order Secure AES
7. https://github.com/Chair-for-Security-Engineering/NullFresh: First-order secure CRAFT (CRAFT NF), First-order secure PRESENT (PRESENT NF)
8. https://github.com/Chair-for-Security-Engineering/NullFresh2: First- and second-order secure KECCAK (KECCAK NF), Second-order secure PRESENT (PRESENT NF), Second-order secure SKINNY (SKINNY NF)
9. https://github.com/Chair-for-Security-Engineering/AGEMA: First- and second-order secure SKINNY (SKINNY HPC2, SKINNY HPC3, SKINNY GHPC, SKINNY GHPC$_{LL}$)
10. https://github.com/ChairImpSec/COMAR: SKINNY COMAR
11. https://github.com/emsec/ImpeccableCircuitsII: CRAFT IC II, CRAFT MV

B   Additional Postlayout Details

Table 6. Additional information about all cores.

Design	Area [GE]	Crit. Path [ns]	Stat. En. [nJ/s]	Exp. Ver.[a]	Tool Ver.[b]	Comp. Gadg.[c]
PRINCE [16]	9340.00	11.67	486	–	–	–
PRINCEv2 [17]	9653.50	11.59	1120	–	–	–
PRINCE+v2 [17]	10464.50	11.88	808	–	–	–
MIDORI [4]	11300.25	11.84	1800	–	–	–
MANTIS [8]	13583.75	12.28	1730	–	–	–
QARMA$_7$-64-σ_0 [3]	13772.00	12.17	2150	–	–	–
QARMA$_7$-64-σ_1 [3]	14193.00	12.44	2880	–	–	–
QARMA$_7$-64-σ_2 [3]	15685.75	12.31	3120	–	–	–
Orthros [6]	32342.00	10.80	2160	–	–	–
SPEEDY-5-192 ENC [34]	25632.00	8.24	1750	–	–	–
SPEEDY-6-192 ENC [34]	30676.00	9.88	2040	–	–	–
SPEEDY-7-192 ENC [34]	35788.75	10.40	3770	–	–	–
SPEEDY-5-192 DEC [34]	52548.00	12.10	8530	–	–	–
SPEEDY-6-192 DEC [34]	62986.00	12.69	14500	–	–	–
SPEEDY-7-192 DEC [34]	74331.50	13.21	21000	–	–	–
GIMLI [10]	53829.75	8.85	1080	–	–	–
AES [23]	13939.25	0.58	480	–	–	–
CRAFT [9]	2089.25	0.20	34	–	–	–
CRAFT WDDL [9]	6557.50	0.25	191	–	–	–
CRAFT TI d=1 [9]	8923.25	0.20	280	✓	✗	✗
CRAFT CMS d=1 [41]	8369.50	0.20	237	✓	✗	✗
CRAFT NF d=1 [47]	8015.00	0.20	263	✓	✗	✗
CRAFT TI WDDL d=1 [9]	30419.00	0.24	1070	✗	✗	✗
CRAFT CMS WDDL d=1 [41]	36249.25	0.25	1080	✗	✗	✗
CRAFT NF WDDL d=1 [47]	35283.00	0.25	1350	✗	✗	✗
SKINNY HPC2 d=1 [21]	26128.00	1.41	900	✓	✗	✓
SKINNY HPC3 d=1 [30]	15652.00	0.87	511	✓	✗	✓
SKINNY GHPC d=1 [32]	30316.25	0.87	925	✓	✗	✓
SKINNY GHPC$_{LL}$ d=1 [32]	21660.25	0.88	1010	✓	✗	✓
SKINNY COMAR d=1 [29]	73446.00	1.38	2090	✓	✗	✓
PRESENT TI d=1 [43]	12868.50	0.59	314	✓	✗	✗

(continued)

Table 6. (*continued*)

Design	Area [GE]	Crit. Path [ns]	Stat. En. [nJ/s]	Exp. Ver.[a]	Tool Ver.[b]	Comp. Gadg.[c]
PRESENT NF d=1 [47]	6080.25	0.24	228	✓	✓	✗
AES d=1 [45]	21915.75	1.16	775	✓	✗	✗
KECCAK NF d=1 [48]	21008.00	0.75	694	✓	✓	✗
SKINNY NF d=2 [48]	15648.00	0.45	475	✓	✗	✗
SKINNY HPC2 d=2 [21]	45544.50	0.86	1730	✓	✗	✓
SKINNY HPC3 d=2 [30]	26934.50	1.06	978	✓	✗	✓
SKINNY HPC2 d=3 [21]	69054.00	1.34	2500	✓	✗	✓
SKINNY HPC3 d=3 [30]	40878.25	0.83	1520	✓	✗	✓
PRESENT NF d=2 [48]	11988.75	0.24	506	✓	✓	✗
KECCAK NF d=2 [48]	35919.00	0.75	1430	✓	✓	✗
LED d=2 [12]	37923.75	0.59	1600	✗	✗	✗
CRAFT IC II r=3 [49]	6080.25	0.59	164	✗	✓	✗
CRAFT IC III r=4 [39]	9278.25	0.20	397	✗	✓	✗
CRAFT IC II r=7 [49]	22599.75	0.23	573	✗	✓	✗

[a]The conceptual security properties of the full implementation (i.e., the concrete RTL code used) have been experimentally verified in a published article.
[b]The conceptual security properties of the full implementation (i.e., the concrete RTL code used) have been verified using a tool in a published article.
[c]The implementation is composed entirely of provably composable gadgets and the security properties of the individual gadgets have been exhaustively verified using a tool in a published article.

References

1. Qualcomm Product Security. Pointer Authentication on ARMv8.3 - Design and Analysis of the New Software Security Instructions. Technical report, January 2017. https://www.qualcomm.com/documents/whitepaper-pointer-authentication-arm v83
2. Aghaie, A., Moradi, A., Rasoolzadeh, S., Shahmirzadi, A.R., Schellenberg, F., Schneider, T.: Impeccable circuits. IEEE Trans. Comput. **69**(3), 361–376 (2020)
3. Avanzi, R.: The QARMA block cipher family. Almost MDS matrices over rings with zero divisors, nearly symmetric even-mansour constructions with non-involutory central rounds, and search heuristics for low-latency s-boxes. IACR Trans. Symmetric Cryptol. **2017**(1), 4–44 (2017)
4. Banik, S., et al.: Midori: a block cipher for low energy. In: Iwata, T., Cheon, J.H. (eds.) ASIACRYPT 2015. LNCS, vol. 9453, pp. 411–436. Springer, Heidelberg (2015). https://doi.org/10.1007/978-3-662-48800-3_17
5. Banik, S., Bogdanov, A., Regazzoni, F.: Exploring energy efficiency of lightweight block ciphers. In: Dunkelman, O., Keliher, L. (eds.) SAC 2015. LNCS, vol. 9566, pp. 178–194. Springer, Cham (2016). https://doi.org/10.1007/978-3-319-31301-6_10

6. Banik, S., Isobe, T., Liu, F., Minematsu, K., Sakamoto, K.: Orthros: a low-latency PRF. IACR Trans. Symmetric Cryptol. **2021**(1), 37–77 (2021)
7. Batina, L., et al.: Dietary recommendations for lightweight block ciphers: power, energy and area analysis of recently developed architectures. In: Hutter, M., Schmidt, J.-M. (eds.) RFIDSec 2013. LNCS, vol. 8262, pp. 103–112. Springer, Heidelberg (2013). https://doi.org/10.1007/978-3-642-41332-2_7
8. Beierle, C., et al.: The SKINNY family of block ciphers and its low-latency variant MANTIS. In: Robshaw, M., Katz, J. (eds.) CRYPTO 2016. LNCS, vol. 9815, pp. 123–153. Springer, Heidelberg (2016). https://doi.org/10.1007/978-3-662-53008-5_5
9. Beierle, C., Leander, G., Moradi, A., Rasoolzadeh, S.: CRAFT: lightweight tweakable block cipher with efficient protection against DFA attacks. IACR Trans. Symmetric Cryptol. **2019**(1), 5–45 (2019)
10. Bernstein, D.J., et al.: GIMLI?: a cross-platform permutation. In: Fischer, W., Homma, N. (eds.) CHES 2017. LNCS, vol. 10529, pp. 299–320. Springer, Cham (2017). https://doi.org/10.1007/978-3-319-66787-4_15
11. Beyne, T., Dhooghe, S., Moradi, A., Shahmirzadi, A.R.: Cryptanalysis of efficient masked ciphers: applications to low latency. IACR Trans. Cryptogr. Hardw. Embed. Syst. **2022**(1), 679–721 (2022)
12. Beyne, T., Dhooghe, S., Zhang, Z.: Cryptanalysis of masked ciphers: a not so random idea. In: Moriai, S., Wang, H. (eds.) ASIACRYPT 2020. LNCS, vol. 12491, pp. 817–850. Springer, Cham (2020). https://doi.org/10.1007/978-3-030-64837-4_27
13. Bilgin, B., Gierlichs, B., Nikova, S., Nikov, V., Rijmen, V.: A more efficient AES threshold implementation. In: Pointcheval, D., Vergnaud, D. (eds.) AFRICACRYPT 2014. LNCS, vol. 8469, pp. 267–284. Springer, Cham (2014). https://doi.org/10.1007/978-3-319-06734-6_17
14. Bilgin, B., Gierlichs, B., Nikova, S., Nikov, V., Rijmen, V.: Higher-order threshold implementations. In: Sarkar, P., Iwata, T. (eds.) ASIACRYPT 2014. LNCS, vol. 8874, pp. 326–343. Springer, Heidelberg (2014). https://doi.org/10.1007/978-3-662-45608-8_18
15. Bogdanov, A., et al.: PRESENT: an ultra-lightweight block cipher. In: Paillier, P., Verbauwhede, I. (eds.) CHES 2007. LNCS, vol. 4727, pp. 450–466. Springer, Heidelberg (2007). https://doi.org/10.1007/978-3-540-74735-2_31
16. Borghoff, J., et al.: PRINCE – a low-latency block cipher for pervasive computing applications - extended abstract. In: Wang, X., Sako, K. (eds.) ASIACRYPT 2012. LNCS, vol. 7658, pp. 208–225. Springer, Heidelberg (2012). https://doi.org/10.1007/978-3-642-34961-4_14
17. Božilov, D., et al.: PRINCEv2 - more security for (almost) no overhead. In: Dunkelman, O., Jacobson, Jr., M.J., O'Flynn, C. (eds.) SAC 2020. LNCS, vol. 12804, pp. 483–511. Springer, Cham (2021). https://doi.org/10.1007/978-3-030-81652-0_19
18. Caforio, A., Balli, F., Banik, S.: Energy analysis of lightweight AEAD circuits. In: Krenn, S., Shulman, H., Vaudenay, S. (eds.) CANS 2020. LNCS, vol. 12579, pp. 23–42. Springer, Cham (2020). https://doi.org/10.1007/978-3-030-65411-5_2
19. Can, A., Krishnaswamy, A., Turner, R.: Code pointer authentication for hardware flow control, uS Patent 9,514,305 (6 December2016)
20. De Cannière, C., Dunkelman, O., Knežević, M.: KATAN and KTANTAN—a family of small and efficient hardware-oriented block ciphers. In: Clavier, C., Gaj, K. (eds.) CHES 2009. LNCS, vol. 5747, pp. 272–288. Springer, Heidelberg (2009). https://doi.org/10.1007/978-3-642-04138-9_20

21. Cassiers, G., Grégoire, B., Levi, I., Standaert, F.: Hardware private circuits: from trivial composition to full verification. IEEE Trans. Comput. **70**(10), 1677–1690 (2021)

22. De Cnudde, T., Reparaz, O., Bilgin, B., Nikova, S., Nikov, V., Rijmen, V.: Masking AES with $d+1$ shares in hardware. In: Gierlichs, B., Poschmann, A.Y. (eds.) CHES 2016. LNCS, vol. 9813, pp. 194–212. Springer, Heidelberg (2016). https://doi.org/10.1007/978-3-662-53140-2_10

23. Daemen, J., Rijmen, V.: The Design of Rijndael: AES - The Advanced Encryption Standard. Information Security and Cryptography, Springer, Heidelberg (2002). https://doi.org/10.1007/978-3-662-04722-4

24. Dobraunig, C., Eichlseder, M., Korak, T., Mangard, S., Mendel, F., Primas, R.: SIFA: exploiting ineffective fault inductions on symmetric cryptography. IACR Trans. Cryptogr. Hardw. Embed. Syst. **2018**(3), 547–572 (2018)

25. Even, S., Mansour, Y.: A construction of a cipher from a single pseudorandom permutation. J. Cryptol. **10**(3), 151–161 (1997). https://doi.org/10.1007/s001459900025

26. Groß, H., Mangard, S., Korak, T.: Domain-oriented masking: compact masked hardware implementations with arbitrary protection order. In: Theory of Implementation Security - TIS@CCS 2016, p. 3. ACM (2016)

27. Guo, J., Peyrin, T., Poschmann, A., Robshaw, M.: The LED block cipher. In: Preneel, B., Takagi, T. (eds.) CHES 2011. LNCS, vol. 6917, pp. 326–341. Springer, Heidelberg (2011). https://doi.org/10.1007/978-3-642-23951-9_22

28. Kerckhof, S., Durvaux, F., Hocquet, C., Bol, D., Standaert, F.-X.: Towards green cryptography: a comparison of lightweight ciphers from the energy viewpoint. In: Prouff, E., Schaumont, P. (eds.) CHES 2012. LNCS, vol. 7428, pp. 390–407. Springer, Heidelberg (2012). https://doi.org/10.1007/978-3-642-33027-8_23

29. Knichel, D., Moradi, A.: Composable gadgets with reused fresh masks first-order probing-secure hardware circuits with only 6 fresh masks. IACR Trans. Cryptogr. Hardw. Embed. Syst. **2022**(3), 114–140 (2022)

30. Knichel, D., Moradi, A.: Low-latency hardware private circuits. In: Proceedings of the 2022 ACM SIGSAC Conference on Computer and Communications Security, CCS 2022, Los Angeles, CA, USA, 7–11 November 2022, pp. 1799–1812. ACM (2022)

31. Knichel, D., Moradi, A., Müller, N., Sasdrich, P.: Automated generation of masked hardware. IACR Trans. Cryptogr. Hardw. Embed. Syst. **2022**(1), 589–629 (2022)

32. Knichel, D., Sasdrich, P., Moradi, A.: Generic hardware private circuits towards automated generation of composable secure gadgets. IACR Trans. Cryptogr. Hardw. Embed. Syst. **2022**(1), 323–344 (2022)

33. Kocher, P., Jaffe, J., Jun, B.: Differential power analysis. In: Wiener, M. (ed.) CRYPTO 1999. LNCS, vol. 1666, pp. 388–397. Springer, Heidelberg (1999). https://doi.org/10.1007/3-540-48405-1_25

34. Leander, G., Moos, T., Moradi, A., Rasoolzadeh, S.: The SPEEDY family of block ciphers engineering an ultra low-latency cipher from gate level for secure processor architectures. IACR Trans. Cryptogr. Hardw. Embed. Syst. **2021**(4), 510–545 (2021)

35. Lim, C.H., Korkishko, T.: mCrypton – a lightweight block cipher for security of low-cost RFID tags and sensors. In: Song, J.-S., Kwon, T., Yung, M. (eds.) WISA 2005. LNCS, vol. 3786, pp. 243–258. Springer, Heidelberg (2006). https://doi.org/10.1007/11604938_19

36. Malkin, T.G., Standaert, F.-X., Yung, M.: A comparative cost/security analysis of fault attack countermeasures. In: Breveglieri, L., Koren, I., Naccache, D., Seifert, J.-P. (eds.) FDTC 2006. LNCS, vol. 4236, pp. 159–172. Springer, Heidelberg (2006). https://doi.org/10.1007/11889700_15

37. Moos, T.: Unrolled cryptography on silicon: a physical security analysis. IACR Trans. Cryptogr. Hardw. Embed. Syst. **2020**(4), 416–442 (2020)

38. Nikova, S., Rechberger, C., Rijmen, V.: Threshold implementations against side-channel attacks and glitches. In: Ning, P., Qing, S., Li, N. (eds.) ICICS 2006. LNCS, vol. 4307, pp. 529–545. Springer, Heidelberg (2006). https://doi.org/10.1007/11935308_38

39. Rasoolzadeh, S., Shahmirzadi, A.R., Moradi, A.: Impeccable circuits III. In: IEEE International Test Conference, ITC 2021, Anaheim, CA, USA, 10–15 October 2021, pp. 163–169. IEEE (2021)

40. Reparaz, O.: A note on the security of higher-order threshold implementations. IACR Cryptology ePrint Archive, vol. 2015, p. 1 (2015)

41. Reparaz, O., Bilgin, B., Nikova, S., Gierlichs, B., Verbauwhede, I.: Consolidating masking schemes. In: Gennaro, R., Robshaw, M. (eds.) CRYPTO 2015. LNCS, vol. 9215, pp. 764–783. Springer, Heidelberg (2015). https://doi.org/10.1007/978-3-662-47989-6_37

42. Richter, B., Moradi, A.: Lightweight ciphers on a 65 nm ASIC A comparative study on energy consumption. In: 2020 IEEE Computer Society Annual Symposium on VLSI, ISVLSI 2020, Limassol, Cyprus, 6–8 July 2020, pp. 530–535. IEEE (2020)

43. Sasdrich, P., Moradi, A., Güneysu, T.: Affine equivalence and its application to tightening threshold implementations. In: Dunkelman, O., Keliher, L. (eds.) SAC 2015. LNCS, vol. 9566, pp. 263–276. Springer, Cham (2016). https://doi.org/10.1007/978-3-319-31301-6_16

44. Selmane, N., Bhasin, S., Guilley, S., Graba, T., Danger, J.: WDDL is protected against setup time violation attacks. In: Sixth International Workshop on Fault Diagnosis and Tolerance in Cryptography, FDTC 2009, Lausanne, Switzerland, 6 September 2009, pp. 73–83. IEEE Computer Society (2009)

45. Shahmirzadi, A.R., Bozilov, D., Moradi, A.: New first-order secure AES performance records. IACR Cryptology ePrint Archive, p. 37 (2021)

46. Shahmirzadi, A.R., Bozilov, D., Moradi, A.: New first-order secure AES performance records. IACR Trans. Cryptogr. Hardw. Embed. Syst. **2021**(2), 304–327 (2021)

47. Shahmirzadi, A.R., Moradi, A.: Re-consolidating first-order masking schemes - nullifying fresh randomness. IACR Trans. Cryptogr. Hardw. Embed. Syst. **2021**(1), 305–342 (2020)

48. Shahmirzadi, A.R., Moradi, A.: Second-order SCA security with almost no fresh randomness. IACR Trans. Cryptogr. Hardw. Embed. Syst. **2021**(3), 708–755 (2021)

49. Shahmirzadi, A.R., Rasoolzadeh, S., Moradi, A.: Impeccable circuits II. In: DAC 2020, pp. 1–6. IEEE (2020)

50. Tiri, K., Verbauwhede, I.: A logic level design methodology for a secure DPA resistant ASIC or FPGA implementation. In: 2004 Design, Automation and Test in Europe Conference and Exposition (DATE 2004), 16–20 February 2004, Paris, France, pp. 246–251. IEEE Computer Society (2004)

Whiteboxgrind – Automated Analysis of Whitebox Cryptography

Tobias Holl[1], Katharina Bogad[2], and Michael Gruber[3(✉)]

[1] Ruhr-Universität Bochum, Bochum, Germany
tobias.holl@rub.de
[2] Fraunhofer Institute for Applied and Integrated Security, Garching, Germany
katharina.bogad@aisec.fraunhofer.de
[3] Chair of Security in Information Technology,
Technical University of Munich, Munich, Germany
m.gruber@tum.de

Abstract. Digital intellectual property is often protected by encrypting the data up to the point of use. Whitebox cryptography is an attempt to provide users with the ability to decrypt that data without actually revealing the key by embedding the key inside a cryptographic implementation. In this work, we design and implement WHITEBOXGRIND, a fast, fully automated toolchain that obtains execution traces from whitebox implementations and applies DCA to recover the hidden embedded keys. To evaluate WHITEBOXGRIND, we analysed whiteboxes of the CHES WhibOx 2019 competition, and found WHITEBOXGRIND to provide a significant performance improvement over the state-of-the-art tooling, enabling attacks that were previously infeasible due to memory constraints. Furthermore, we provide WHITEBOXGRIND's source code.

Keywords: Whitebox · Differential Computation Analysis · Side Channel Analysis · CHES WhibOx

1 Introduction

When modern software needs to protect data from unauthorized access, cryptography is the only feasible solution. While encrypted communications generally allow for some form of key exchange or agreement, protecting data at rest requires storing an encryption key somewhere. This is easy if the software runs in a trusted environment (e.g. in a Trusted Platform Module (TPM) or on a corporate server), but not so straightforward in other cases (e.g. on devices controlled by end users).

So-called *whitebox* implementations combine a cryptographic algorithm with a fixed key, and add additional layers of obfuscation to hide the key from the user. Therefore, *whitebox* implementations violate Kerckhoffs's principle by design. Usually, these "whiteboxes" are used when the goal is to shield data or code from inspection by a potential adversary in an untrusted ecosystem (i.e. the user and their device respectively). This includes Digital Rights Management (DRM), but is also found as a hardening mechanism against manipulation in other software that deals with confidential information (e.g. banking apps) [14].

© The Author(s), under exclusive license to Springer Nature Switzerland AG 2023
E. B. Kavun and M. Pehl (Eds.): COSADE 2023, LNCS 13979, pp. 221–240, 2023.
https://doi.org/10.1007/978-3-031-29497-6_11

The name *whitebox cryptography* already betrays that such a system is inherently insecure: Since all internal details are observable, it is always theoretically possible (though not always practically feasible) to reconstruct both the secret key and the cryptographic algorithm. Instead of preventing decryption entirely, whitebox cryptography can only serve as an obfuscation mechanism that discourages or delays a potential attacker by increasing the cost of an attack.

The straightforward approach to extract the key from a whitebox is direct reverse engineering. However, modern whiteboxes are sufficiently obfuscated to make this an extremely tedious and challenging task: Layers of obfuscation can be applied automatically, inflating the amount of code and data a reverse engineer needs to examine, while an attacker must manually understand and deobfuscate each layer.

Apart from glaring vulnerabilities in the cryptography itself, it is also essentially impossible to successfully attack such a system by merely observing and controlling its inputs and outputs, as modern cryptosystems are highly resistant to such attacks by design: For a cryptosystem to be considered even adequate, we generally require them to be resistant against both chosen-plaintext and (adaptive) chosen-ciphertext attacks [17], where attackers are able to make arbitrary queries to an *encryption* and *decryption oracle*—much like an attacker that only uses a whitebox implementation, but does not analyze its internals.

However, implementations of cryptosystems can still leak information due to a *side-channel*. By analyzing the time taken for a cryptographic operation (a *timing attack*), or the power consumed by the device during that time (e.g. via Differential Power Analysis (DPA) [19]), it can sometimes be possible to extract the key from a whitebox system. An active attacker that is able to manipulate the internal state of the cryptosystem while it is running has even more options (e.g. Fault Injection Analysis (FIA), where deviations in the output caused by a manipulation of internal state are analyzed).

In embedded systems, hardware protection mechanisms can require attackers who try to mount such an attack to make a significant upfront investment into specialized equipment. Software-only whiteboxes cannot rely on such hardening approaches: Since we can fully control the environment in which they are executed, it becomes much easier to isolate the whitebox implementation from the rest of the system. Sources of randomness which would ordinarily be used to hide internal values from an observer can easily be replaced with a deterministic stream of numbers. Here, hardware implementations can rely on a Cryptographically secure Random Number Generator (CSRNG) that is much harder to manipulate or replace. For software, we additionally have access to a large set of introspection tools such as debuggers and emulators that can be used to examine the internal workings of the whitebox in detail. This also means that side-channel attacks can be mounted not just on physical observations such as time and power consumption, but also on the internal behavior of the program during execution. The state-of-the-art equivalent to DPA for such whiteboxes is Differential Computation Analysis (DCA), which instead of deriving leakage information from the power consumption directly uses values extracted from traces of the program's execution [3,4]. Because these types of attacks require large amounts of data obtained by continuously observating the whitebox implementation, they generally require some level of automation to be feasible.

Contribution. In this work, we propose an automatic approach to efficiently collect and filter execution traces of whitebox implementations. In particular, we make the following contributions: We construct a fast tracer using Valgrind's [24] just-in-time-compilation abilities. We design a novel trace storage format that enables both fast processing and space-efficient storage. We implement our approach in WHITEBOXGRIND, a fully automated parallel DCA attack toolchain (trace collection, filtering, and the DCA), and benchmark it on several submissions to the 2019 *CHES WhibOx* contest [7]. While we target AES in this paper, the tracing and filtering stages of WHITEBOXGRIND generalize to arbitrary whitebox implementations; only the implementation of the attack itself needs to be adapted to the targeted cryptosystem. Also, we provide WHITEBOXGRIND's source code[1].

2   Related Work

There are several other tools that attempt to perform side-channel attacks on whitebox cryptography:

Frameworks. Bos et al. [4], and Bock et al. [3] propose similar instrumentation-based approaches for tracing and applying Differential Computation Analysis (DCA), but without discussing any strategies to handle the vast amounts of data generated by their approaches. Both approaches are based on the idea of instrumenting the implementation with Valgrind [24] and recording the execution. Additionally, the same tooling can be used to perform FIA, though there is some difficulty in identifying the correct time and place at which a fault should be injected.

Sample Reduction. In order to reduce the amount of data that needs to be processed, Breunesse et al. introduced Conditional Sample Reduction (CSR) [5]. Our solution is less aggressive in discarding samples and cannot remove "superfluous" traces. We instead opt for an approach with much lower memory requirements that also requires less knowledge about the target implementation. We discuss the differences in more detail in Sect. 4.4.

Attack Tools. Finally, there are generic side-channel attack tools that process traces from arbitrary sources (if they can be brought into the right format). Examples include *LASCAR* [20] and *QSCAT* [13].

3   Background

We focus mainly on attacks against whitebox implementations of the Advanced Encryption Standard (AES). In the following, we briefly introduce the structure of AES and the main concepts behind DCA, including its application to AES, and discuss various ways to obtain program traces.

---

[1] https://gitlab.lrz.de/tueisec/whiteboxgrind.

3.1   Advanced Encryption Standard

The AES [12] is a 128-bit block cipher based on a substitution-permutation network (SPN). Like most block ciphers, it is composed of several near-identical rounds which consist from the following functions:

AddRoundKey adds the current round key $k^{(i)}$ to the state by a simple bit-wise XOR ($\oplus$). This is equivalent to an element-wise addition in $GF(2^8)$.

SubBytes is a nonlinear byte-wise substitution where each byte a_i of the state is substituted via a constant look-up table to the output byte $b_i = S[a_i]$. The S-Box is carefully designed to make AES more resistant against various kinds of attacks [9], including differential and linear cryptanalysis [2, 22].

ShiftRows is a simple permutation of the bytes. When considering the state's 16 bytes as elements of a matrix in $GF(2^8)^{4 \times 4}$ (stored in column-major order), each row is rotated to the left one element further than the previous row, with the first row not being modified at all. This ensures that localized state changes propagate quickly to all state bytes (a desirable property for ciphers known as *diffusion*) [9, 10, 25].

MixColumns has a similar purpose by applying a linear transformation in $GF(2^8)$ to the individual *columns* of the same matrix.

3.2   Whitebox Cryptography

Cryptographic implementations where the key is configurable first derive the round keys $k^{(i)}$ from the cipher key k using the AES *key schedule*. In whitebox implementations, on the other hand, the key schedule is usually done in advance (since the key is already known at compile time) and is not present in the final implementation. Since the keys are fixed, the individual components of each round can be combined into a single table lookup (known as a T-box) [9]. If this lookup also includes the key addition, the values stored in the table can reveal the round key. To avoid this, *internal encodings* apply transformations to the input and output of such a table (or more generally of any internal operation). *External encodings* are similar, except that the transformations are applied to the plaintexts and ciphertexts outside the encryption algorithm [8, 21]. Usually, additional obfuscation is then applied to further hide the round keys from an observer.

3.3   Correlation Power Analysis

Differential Power Analysis (DPA) is a type of power analysis based on partitioning which was proposed in 1999 by Kocher et al. [19]. Brier et al. proposed a similar approach called Correlation Power Analysis (CPA) which uses correlation as a distinguisher in 2004 [6]. For a CPA attack, the power profile of a cryptographic operation is measured multiple times, e.g., in the context of AES different plaintexts with the same key. Subsequently, an intermediate value t, which depends on known values, and an unknown part (a single byte) of the key is chosen. A possible intermediate value t during the AES-*encryption* is the output of a first round's S-box. The intermediate value t is calculated as $t = S(k_0^{(0)} \oplus p_0)$ for all key hypotheses of the key byte $k_0^{(0)}$ The correlation of all key hypotheses with the measured power traces can be calculated after the application of a power model to the intermediate value. For the CPA of AES the intermediate value's Hamming Weight (HW) is commonly used as power model as it requires no prior knowledge about the state. The correct key byte is then determined by the hypothesis that yields the highest absolute correlation value. The principles of DPA were applied to whitebox cryptography by Bos et al. [4]. In the context of whitebox cryptography, DPA is referred to as DCA.

3.4   Program Tracing

Program traces are a useful tool in software analysis that allow us to draw conclusions about the underlying software's behavior (even if not much about the program is known, e.g. [11]). This means that there are quite a few different approaches by which we can obtain them:

Full Emulation. The idea behind fully emulating software is simple: we model hardware behavior as accurately as possible, and then simply run the software under analysis in the emulator. This allows us to observe all the internals of a program without having to understand it before. Constructing the emulator is a painstaking process, but only needs to be done once for a specific piece of hardware, and while the result is usually quite slow in terms of real-time performance, the data obtained is as close to the ground truth as one can get if the emulator is constructed accurately. Unfortunately, the performance penalty is usually quite severe, which is a problem for analyses like DCA that require *multiple* execution traces.

Hooking. A much faster approach is to identify locations of interest in the program and modify the code at those locations to emit tracing events. However, accurately modifying the program without accidentally damaging functionality or missing out on some events can be difficult (especially if the implementation is one that hardened against reverse-engineering, like the ones we are dealing with in this work).

Debugger-Based Tracing. Another common way to follow the execution of a program is to use a debugger's single-step feature: The debugger repeatedly signals the operating system to execute a single instruction at a time, after which control returns to the debugger, which can then inspect registers and memory. Here, we run into the opposite problem of the emulator: After an instruction has been executed, we need to understand *which* changes it made. Additionally, the frequent context switches between debugger and target come with a significant performance penalty.

Hardware-Based Tracing. Some modern processors have features that allow constructing execution traces directly in the CPU. These features generally have low runtime overhead and access to ground-truth information, which are particularly desirable features for a program tracer. Unfortunately, they are often limited in scope (e.g. Intel's *processor trace* feature [15] only records control flow events, so the exact execution flow needs to be reconstructed after-the-fact, and information on memory accesses is missing entirely). Additionally, hardware-based tracing cannot usually intercept sources of nondeterminism (e.g. system calls), so elements from other tracing methods (debugging or hooking) will need to be borrowed—alongside their disadvantages.

Lifting and JIT. A good compromise between the previous approaches is based on just-in-time compilation (JIT). The idea is to analyze a chunk of code that is about to be executed, *lift* it to an intermediate representation (IR) by carefully breaking down the CPU instructions into smaller operations, insert the code that logs the appropriate events, and then compile it back down to native code that is then executed. This lifting operation can be slow, but if pieces of code are executed multiple times, the results can be cached. Because the event logging is embedded directly into the native code, no expensive callbacks or context switches are necessary while the code is executing.

4   Whiteboxgrind

In the following, we describe our approach to efficiently trace and attack whitebox implementations, which we implemented in our WHITEBOXGRIND toolchain.

4.1   Trace Acquisition

We use a custom tool for the Valgrind framework [24] in order to obtain execution traces of a target whitebox when invoked with different inputs. It records every instruction executed during the cryptographic operation alongside all memory accesses.

We chose to base our tracer on Valgrind instead of one of the other approaches described in Sect. 3.4 for performance reasons: For every original instruction, at least one of our hooks is called to generate the instruction trace, plus hooks for every memory access. If the hooks are not implemented natively or not embedded directly into the execution stream, each hook invocation comes with a significant performance penalty.

Valgrind also uses a JIT-based approach, but allows us to manipulate the generated code on a lower level: When a basic block starts executing, Valgrind lifts it to its VEX IR by representing each instruction as a series of IR instructions, with particularly complex operations represented by calls to helper functions. Figure 1 shows how an example function is translated to VEX. On this intermediate representation, the active tool can perform arbitrary transformations. In WHITEBOXGRIND, we use this to insert our own instrumentation steps. Once control returns to Valgrind, the IR is compiled back down to native code and executed.

```
1 uint8_t Sbox[256];
2 uint8_t Shift[16] = /* ... */;
3 void last_round(uint8_t state[16],
4                 uint8_t k[16]) {
5   uint8_t t[16];
6   for (int i = 0; i < 16; ++i)
7     t[Shift[i]] = Sbox[state[i]];
8   for (int i = 0; i < 16; ++i)
9     state[i] = t[i] ^ k[i];
10 }
```

```
1 mov    r9, &Shift
2 mov    r8, &Sbox
3 xor    eax, eax
4 movzx  ecx, byte [&state+rax]
5 movzx  edx, byte [rax+r9]
6 inc    rax
7 mov    cl, byte [r8+rcx]
8 mov    byte [&t+rdx], cl
9 cmp    rax, 0x10
10 jne    to line 4
```

```
1 ---- IMark(Address of movzx, 5, 0) ----
2 t18 = GET:I64(r9)
3 t16 = Add64(t11,t18)
4 t22 = LDle:I8(t16)
5    ≡ Ist_WrTmp(t22, Iex_Load(t16, 8bit,
         LE))
6 t48 = 8Uto32(t22)
7 t21 = t48
8 t49 = 32Uto64(t21)
9 t20 = t49
10 PUT(rdx) = t20
```

(a) Source Code   (b) Assembly Code

(c) VEX IR

Fig. 1. Example of the translation between source code, AMD64 assembly code, and the VEX IR

During instrumentation, we insert code to emit a program counter trace event on every Ist_IMark statement (which marks the start of a new instruction, hence the name), and a memory access event whenever the statement type or the type of a subexpression indicates that a memory access will take place. Within subexpressions, only memory reads can occur (Iex_Load). An example of this is the statement in Fig. 1c that is highlighted in green. We also log a memory read on Ist_LoadG statements if the associated guard condition is satisfied. Memory writes (Ist_Store or Ist_StoreG with a guard condition) and compare-and-swap instructions (Ist_CAS) are tracked separately. Beyond that, we need to handle calls to external helper functions that VEX inserts for more complicated instructions (Ist_Dirty) and load-linked/store-conditional (LLSC) statements (Ist_LLSC), both of which helpfully track their memory side effects in the VEX statement structure.

For all events, we store the value of the current instruction pointer or program counter. For memory accesses, we additionally store the target memory address, the value that is read or written, and the size or "width" of that value. Valgrind additionally provides us with the endianness of the access, though on most architectures this value is a constant. For compare-and-swap instructions, we store both the old value that is read for the comparison and the new value which is written if the comparison succeeds. Because we may later want to synchronize between the different types of events, each event is accompanied by an index that counts up as events are emitted, regardless of type.

In order to avoid tracing *all* of the target binary, we support isolating the encryption or decryption function. Depending on the scenario, this is done either using Valgrind's *client requests*, which allow the program under analysis to indicate to the tracer to start and stop tracing[2], or by starting and stopping tracing at user-provided addresses.

Between these points, the tracer ensures that execution of the traced binary is deterministic: System calls and other non-deterministic instructions such as rdtsc (returning the current processor timestamp) and rdrand (returning a random value) are reported to the user for manual patching, and can generally be replaced with "normal" instructions that return a constant value instead.

---

[2] We use this feature in combination with a custom harness for our evaluation in Sect. 5, where the encryption function is provided directly.

This means that the resulting traces can be compared across executions: The only reason why traces can differ from each other is that each run of the whitebox is provided with different inputs.

For convenience, WHITEBOXGRIND comes with a wrapper tool that manages the individual runs of the tracer. In particular, it takes care of input generation, configuring the tracer appropriately, collecting the trace events (via a Unix domain socket connected to the tracer), and finally storing the results.

4.2 Trace Storage

The traces generated in the previous step can be quite large (cf. Section 5). In order to perform further processing within reasonable limits on runtime and memory use, we need to store traces in a compressed format that still allows fast parallel access.

Unfortunately, existing formats either do not fully meet these requirements (e.g. the default implementation of HDF5 requires high-overhead locking to operate in a threadsafe manner, and the ParallelHDF5 variant only supports multi-*processing* rather than multithreading [26]), or are not designed with multidimensional data in mind (libraries such as *fst* [18] focus explicitly on two-dimensional data, while our traces—a matrix[3] of structured trace events with multiple attributes as described in Sect. 4.1—are essentially three-dimensional).

Therefore, we designed the y5 file format to address these shortcomings and enable efficient processing of our traces. Below, we briefly explain each of the design goals we considered during the development of the y5 file format, and how we achieved them.

Support for Trace Transposition. Throughout our pipeline, we want to be able to process traces in parallel. Both during sample reduction (cf. Sect. 4.4) and in the actual attack (cf. Sect. 4.6), operations work on a set of matching samples, one from each trace. In a traditional storage format, this would mean storing the matrix of traces in column-major order (so that we can sequentially read columns of matching samples from the file). However, to create such a file, we would need to produce *all* traces at the same time, and ensure that all tracers generate events in a synchronized fashion, because it is impossible to know ahead of time how large each trace will be. This would significantly impact tracer performance and resource usage. Instead, our tracing framework stores one trace after the other (with traces as rows), and we transpose the matrix during the first sample reduction step in order to then be able to write processed columns of matching samples (turning traces into columns). Figure 2 shows how the dimensions of the data in a y5 file change during processing. The file format needs to accommodate this matrix transposition.

Compression. Memory and control flow traces both contain highly redundant information. Values may be read multiple times, loops mean the same instructions occur repeatedly, and because Valgrind does not implement Address Space

---

[3] Initially, each row of the matrix contains a full trace of the program.

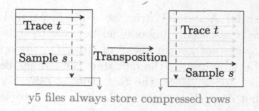

Fig. 2. Transposition of traces during processing.

Layout Randomization (ASLR), memory addresses all share similar prefixes and remain the same across traces. To reduce the size of our traces while stored on disk, we need to compress the data in a way that ensures fast compression and decompression as well as significant size reduction. We use Google's *Brotli* compression algorithm [1] at a medium compression level to achieve a trade-off between these two goals. Each row, regardless of whether that represents a full trace or an aligned set of samples across all traces, is compressed separately to allow independent decompression without having to first process additional rows.

Fast Seeking. While it is useful to be able to decompress each row separately, we still need to locate the start of the row in the file. To do this, we prefix each row with its compressed size. This means we can easily skip each row during processing. However, this still makes seeking to the nth row a slow operation on larger trace files with many rows. In addition to the row headers, we maintain a fixed-size Table of Contents (TOC) at the start of the file[4]. Initially (while the number of rows r is less than the number of entries t in the table), each row has its own TOC entry. As more rows are added, entry t starts representing row $2r$, then $4r$ and so on. This allows us to fairly swiftly skip a large part of the file before following the row headers to finally locate a target row.

Low Memory Footprint. Most software relies on a common file processing paradigm: read the compressed data into a buffer, decompress it into another buffer, and then process the data in that buffer. Because the operating system already caches the compressed file contents in memory, this pairing of reading and decompressing essentially stores the file contents in memory twice. We instead rely on a streaming approach: We directly map a segment[5] of the compressed file into memory. Then, as data is requested for processing, we extend that segment at the end (to be able to decompress more of the file), while shrinking it from the front to remove already-decompressed parts from memory. Because of this, we only keep a fixed amount of compressed data in RAM, and the user can manage how much of the decompressed data they want to request at any given time.

---

[4] In our implementation, the size is configurable, but only at the time the file is created.

[5] The size of this segment is configurable to make parallel processing less memory-intensive, while optimizing single-threaded performance by reducing the number of mapping requests that need to be made.

Support for Parallel Access. Writing to a file in parallel without knowing the size in advance is essentially impossible, because the offsets at which each thread should write are not known ahead of time. On the other hand, *reading* files in parallel is only limited by the fact that the storage device usually does not support parallel access. Here, the fact that we also need to decompress the data means that even though the device may need to serialize our access requests, the subsequent decompression of different rows can be performed in parallel, which significantly improves read speeds. Using memory-mapped IO is very helpful here, because this allows us to maintain multiple windows into the file at different offsets, while normal file descriptor-based APIs expect there to be a single canonical offset into a file at which reading is performed.

Figure 3 shows the layout of a y5 file. Fields that are fixed at file creation time are hatched, the others can change as more data is added to the file. Each row represents eight bytes of data; multi-byte fields are packed in little-endian format for faster processing on x86 CPUs (i.e. most commonly available hardware). We provide a C++ library for UNIX-like systems[6] as well as low-level Python bindings using *pybind11* [16] in order to interface with existing software.

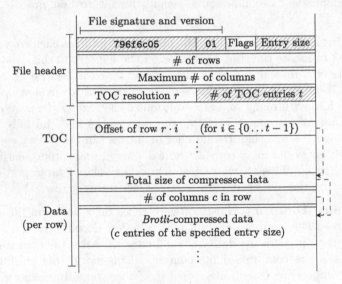

Fig. 3. Structure of a y5 file.

4.3 Parallel Architecture

Each of our tools consumes a y5 file. Depending on the input format and use case, we read either chunks of rows or chunks of columns in parallel by distributing the individual compressed rows into a thread pool. The task scheduler in charge of reading collects the decompressed data and passes it along to a processing pipeline.

---

[6] We are not aware of any constraints that would make a native Windows implementation impossible, but do not currently support Windows' memory-mapped IO functions.

Each pipeline step takes place in a separate thread, optionally distributing parallel implementations of "slow" tasks (including any processing step that needs to iterate over the individual trace events in the data) to a thread pool that can scale to an arbitrary number of CPUs. By transferring data ownership directly, we can avoid expensive locking operations.

Finally, any output chunks are written back to a y5 file. To ensure proper ordering, each chunk is accompanied by its index. In the (rare) case that chunks do arrive out of order, later chunks are held back until the missing chunk arrives. To limit total memory consumption caused by uneven processing speeds (e.g. if reading is faster than the processing, the chunks would "pile up" while waiting for that stage of the pipeline to clear up), we restrict the total number of chunks in processing at any given point in time.

4.4   Sample Reduction

Obfuscation measures in whitebox implementations can inflate the total number of instructions and memory accesses significantly, especially if—as in [7]—it is specifically designed to resist analysis. This intentionally added complexity helps defend against manual reverse-engineering efforts and seriously harms the ability of automated tooling to process the entire implementation, both in terms of code analysis (e.g. for decompilation) and with regards to the traces that we use. In essence, we have *too much* data to efficiently perform the attacks described in Sect. 3.3. To reduce the size of the traces that we analyze, we can rely on two observations:

Non-data-dependent Events. First, trace events that remain the same (including the value that is read or written in a memory access) along all recorded traces usually do not depend on the input data[7]. We can discard these events.

Repeated Events. Second, repeated occurrences of the same set of trace events across all traces (e.g. repeated memory reads from the same address without the value being modified inbetween) can be deduplicated, since the attacks do not take structures across multiple trace events into account. This is equivalent to the *duplicate column removal* described in [5].

If the traces are properly aligned (i.e. there is no data-dependent execution that causes the same part of the cryptographic algorithm to yield a variable number of trace events depending on the input), both of these cases can be filtered out[8]. For non-aligned traces (e.g. where the length of the trace depends on the input), more sophisticated filtering approaches are needed. We do not currently handle non-aligned traces.

WHITEBOXGRIND uses separate tools to remove events that match either of the two criteria described above.

---

[7] Assuming a random distribution of inputs, the probability of this not being the case is generally low in terms of the number of traces.

[8] This is not always the case. However, data-dependent execution that depends on intermediate values directly leaks information about those values, which can then be used for similar attacks. WHITEBOXGRIND does not currently implement this.

To reduce the number of passes over the raw data, we first remove non-data-dependent events during the initial transposition step described in Sect. 4.2. Unlike Conditional Sample Reduction (CSR) [5], we do not attempt to remove "superfluous" traces that will not yield additional information during the attack stage: CSR partitions the trace matrix into groups depending on which input values can result in the value found in a specific observation. Then, samples that observe inconsistent (i.e. different) values for the same partial input can be discarded. Similarly, traces with inputs in the same partition can be deduplicated. However, this requires the user to select a partitioning function/bit mask to choose relevant input bits, and has a $\mathcal{O}(n)$ memory requirement (linear in the trace size), which can become prohibitive for the lengths involved in our evaluation (see Sect. 5). Instead, we filter out samples where the value does not depend on *any* of the input bits. Problems with random masking can be avoided by substituting random sources with constant values (by intercepting system calls and relevant machine code instructions such as rdrand in the tracer).

Perfectly identifying repeated events for deduplication in theory requires us to keep the entire set of known events in memory (which is infeasible given the size of some of our traces) or to repeatedly search the events we have already emitted (at an unacceptable $\mathcal{O}(n^2)$ complexity). Instead, we use a hash-table-based least-recently used (LRU) cache that can grow up to a fixed size, letting us efficiently identify duplicates that are "close enough" to each other in time[9]. Because the attacks implemented by WHITEBOXGRIND act on individual samples, non-removed duplicates increase the execution time of the subsequent steps, but do not impact the final result [5].

4.5   Visualization

Understanding the internal structure of a whitebox implementation from a program trace by hand is difficult without some form of visualization. Plotting the program counter over time in a scatter plot reveals how the code is structured, and doing the same for memory accesses reveals the layout of the data (both of the intermediate values and of constants such as S- or T-boxes).

During our research, we observed that the traces generated by WHITEBOX-GRIND can be too large to comfortably load into RAM and visualize even after sample reduction[10]. To remedy the situation, we implemented a *renderer on steroids* that uses the DirectX Direct2D API [23] to draw the trace diagram.

Further than using a GPU to render the plot, we also introduced algorithmic optimizations. Traditional rendering programs usually scale the data in a lossless way to the screen, compressing neighbouring points together until all data fits into the available space. This results in a high-quality, high-accuraccy plot of

---

[9] A randomized cache eviction policy would allow us to remove further events without increasing the cache size, but the added reduction in event count we observed during our evaluation using this policy (even repeatedly) was marginal.

[10] Existing tools generally insist on doing this; we can only speculate as to why this is the case.

the data, that retains the full shape even if scaled down. For our use case, we are only interested in the macro shape of the collected traces—consequently, we can skip the expensive compression step under the assumption that trace entries are indicative of their neighbours. Intutively, this is at least the case for the program counter plot: While our data is in no form steady, we argue that within basic execution blocks some properties of steadiness are retained (mainly, that if no jump instruction is encountered the next instruction is neighbouring the currently executed instruction).

Then, we can restrict loading to a subset of the whole data and assume that the general shape of the plot remains unchanged. Implementation-wise, we realize this by pre-computing the available space of the plot in pixels, and distributing these pixels evenly across the time axis of the plot. We then use a windowing approach to pan, zoom and scale the displayed data.

A drawback of this method is its inherent loss of some data. Unlike algorithms based on compression, our plotter may miss spikes in execution, giving a false impression of the overall shape if these spikes are small enough.

However, we argue that this is not a problem for our use-case. Our down-sampling approach suppresses noise spikes if they are sufficiently small, but in general preserves the overall shape of the plot. Barring sudden jumps, we intu-itively compare our algorithm to audio recording with varying sample rates, where sample rate reductions are audible, but even very low sample rates retain enough information that a human can recognize a recording.

Furthermore, in our testing we found that while the plot-invisible noise might be the parts we are interested in to recover the key, the plot is more meaningful when applied to filtered data. With the accompanying reduction in overall plot size, less down-sampling needs to be done for low zoom levels, which improves the plots accuracy. Concerning the larger structures we are interested in (e.g. to identify the different rounds in an AES implementation). We can see in Fig. 4 the internal structure of the `distracted_leavitt` whitebox from [7]: there, six separate loops (easily discernible from the image) of nine iterations each (note the slightly larger distance between these iterations) process the current state in four 32-bit blocks in a T-box-esque implementation.

4.6   Attack

Once the traces are pruned to a manageable size, WHITEBOXGRIND applies a standard DCA approach to recover the key. We apply a leakage model (by default, we use the HW, though this is easily replaced if desired) to the values read from or written to memory by the whitebox and use the results as our side-channel leakages.

Using a user-configurable selection function on either the plain- or cipher-text of the values recorded alongside the traces (cf. Sect. 3.3), we compute the hypothesis values $\mathbf{H} \in \mathbb{R}^{256 \times t}$ (one value for each possible key byte and each of the t program traces), and center the values around the origin $\mathbf{h}_k = \mathbf{H}_k - \overline{\mathbf{H}_k}$ for each of the key byte values $k = 0 \ldots 255$. This processing only needs to be performed once for each attack run and can be done ahead of time.

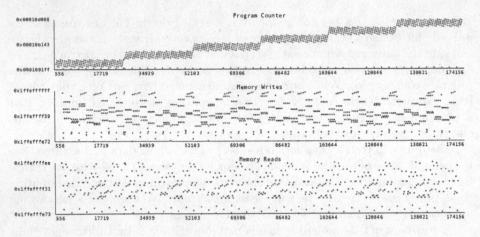

Fig. 4. Access patterns of the `distracted_leavitt` whitebox from [7]

As chunks of traces arrive (cf. Sect. 4.3), we normalize each set of events in parallel. Given our leakage matrix $\mathbf{T} \in \mathbb{R}^{s \times t}$ consisting of s samples across t separate program traces[11], we compute the centered values $\mathbf{t}_i = \mathbf{T}_i - \overline{\mathbf{T}_i}$ for each sample, and the Euclidean norm $\|\mathbf{t}_i\|$.

Now, computing the Pearson correlation coefficient between the hypotheses obtained from the selection function and the leakage values from each of the trace events is simple:

$$r_{i,k} = \frac{\mathbf{t}_i \cdot \mathbf{h}_k}{\|\mathbf{t}_i\| \|\mathbf{h}_k\|}$$

It is sufficient to store $\operatorname{argmax}_k |r_{i,k}| \, \forall i \in \{0 \dots s\}$ in order to obtain the final key (of course, to compute the argmax value, we also need to store the corresponding maximal $|r_{i,k}|$). Because we want to allow for *some* visualization of the correlation we instead store $\max_i |r_{i,k}| \, \forall i \in \{0 \dots s\}, k \in \{0 \dots 256\}$ (at processing-block-level resolution). If the attack is successful, the correct key byte value should show a peak when plotting the 256 resulting correlation values. Figure 5a shows such a case. Similarly, plotting the maximum correlation against the index of the sample where it is obtained (Fig. 5b) shows where that key byte is processed. In this case, we are targeting the first round.

Note that this deviates from the behavior of tools such as *LASCAR* [20], which attempt to store the full matrix of *all* $r_{i,k}$ (which is, of course, suboptimal given the amount of data that needs to be processed). The impact of this optimization is examined further in Sect. 5.

---

[11] In practice, elements of $\mathbf{T}$ are of course not from $\mathbb{R}$; rather, common Hamming weight leakages are in $\mathbb{Z}/256\mathbb{Z}$, i.e. a single byte value—but after normalization, they are treated as floating-point values. Mathematically, we assume they are in $\mathbb{R}$, and simply accept some small level of error in the practical computations.

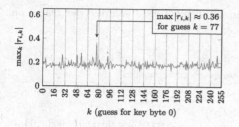
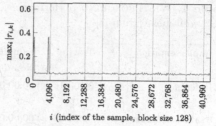

(a) Peak correlation $\max_k |r_{i,k}|$ for each k (across guesses)

(b) Peak correlation $\max_i |r_{i,k}|$ for each i (across samples)

Fig. 5. Correlation for key byte 0 of `peaceful_williams` [7]

5   Evaluation

We evaluated WHITEBOXGRIND on a set of 7 whiteboxes with no data-dependent execution from the 2019 *CHES WhibOx* contest [7] and a "textbook" reference AES implementation with a hard-coded key that was not hardened against side-channel attacks. For each implementation, we collected execution traces for the same set of plaintexts that was randomly selected prior to the evaluation. For this evaluation, we used the values that are read from memory (as opposed to values written to memory or those involved in compare-and-swap operations, for which we obtain separate traces) as our side-channel.

Table 1 shows the time taken by each of WHITEBOXGRIND's individual tools on the traces generated by the first 100 inputs to each of the targets alongside the number of samples per trace in the resulting outputs. Note that this is generally insufficient to perform a successful attack, but serves nicely to illustrate the performance differences between approaches. We should note that while it is possible to obtain traces in parallel and concatenate the y5 files afterwards, we did not do this for this evaluation. All performance measurements were taken on a machine with an AMD EPYC 7552 CPU with 96 threads and 1TB of total RAM (at 3200 MT/s and CL22). To avoid high IO latencies on physical disk accesses, we stored all data on a 300 GB RAM disk.

The time taken for any operation generally scales with the size of the traces, but the correlation is not fully linear. Besides the amount of data involved, performance can also depend on other implementation characteristics (e.g. for the tracer, some instructions are far less efficient after VEX translation than others).

The initial 100 traces collected for our evaluation were sufficient to recover the correct key from the unprotected reference implementation, but not from any of the other implementations. For those implementations where collecting traces was reasonably fast, we collected additional traces to prove the correctness of our implementation. At 500 traces, we were also able to recover the key from the (obfuscated) `peaceful_williams` whitebox.

Additionally, we compared WHITEBOXGRIND's runtime performance (again at 100 traces) to that of the CPA implemented in *LASCAR* [20]. Figure 6 shows the performance improvements we achieve over *LASCAR*'s implementation.

Table 1. WHITEBOXGRIND performance (time and number of samples per trace) on AES whiteboxes from [7]

Implementation	Tracing	Sample reduction		Leakage	Attack
		Non-data-dependent	Repeated		
Reference	00:00:16	00:00:00	00:00:00	00:00:00	00:00:00
	1191	992	992		
distracted_leavitt	00:00:36	00:00:02	00:00:02	00:00:01	00:00:03
	26020	14113	13951		
elegant_turing	06:54:14	01:14:21	00:42:49	00:17:09	01:04:58
	72928481	27971488	17215702		
flamboyant_engelbart	01:19:22	00:16:49	00:06:29	00:02:52	00:10:46
	17232291	5733448	2981379		
friendly_edison	13:13:53	05:01:08	04:02:02	01:30:41	05:45:18
	214383342	141535907	91556105		
goofy_archimedes	00:00:18	00:00:00	00:00:00	00:00:00	00:00:00
	4412	2413	2386		
goofy_lichterman	05:56:55	00:55:13	00:35:22	00:13:27	00:52:04
	53746357	21207273	12968282		
peaceful_williams	00:01:13	00:00:07	00:00:05	00:00:02	00:00:10
	241761	57645	42525		

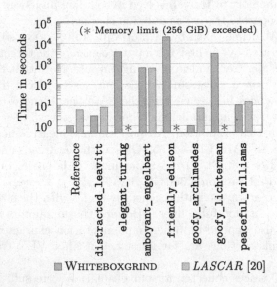

Fig. 6. Performance of WHITEBOXGRIND's CPA compared to *LASCAR* [20]

Finally, we analyzed the impact of our sample reduction strategies (cf. Section 4.4) and of the data compression in the y5 file format (cf. Section 4.2):

On the WhibOx implementations [7], we observed a reduction in size of between 29.27% (for friendly_edison) and 76.16% (for peaceful_williams) by removing samples that do not differ between inputs, and up to 48.00% (for `flamboyant_engelbart`) by removing recurring samples. As an example, Fig. 7 shows how the two sample reduction steps affect the traces obtained from the `peaceful_williams` whitebox. `peaceful_williams` implements AES by means of a virtual machine that processes a hardcoded instruction stream. This is the steadily rising line in Fig. 7a. Together with the line at the bottom (accesses to a compiler-generated jump table), these accesses do not depend on the input, and are filtered out.

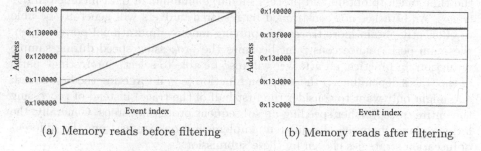

(a) Memory reads before filtering   (b) Memory reads after filtering

Fig. 7. Sample reduction for `peaceful_williams` [7]

Because the trace data is highly structured, y5's compression was able to reduce the total file size of all eight memory read traces from Table 1 before sample reduction by 91.88% (from 2137 GiB to 174 GiB). On the transposed traces after filtering, the compression ratio is similar (91.92%, from 123 GiB to 99 GiB). Only after the leakage is computed (where only a single byte is stored per entry) does the average compression ratio drop below 90% (however, at that point the amount of data is already significantly lower than at the start). Figure 8 shows the compression ratios after each processing step.

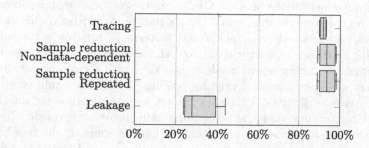

Fig. 8. Compression ratios using y5 on traced memory reads from Table 1.

6   Discussion

We believe that WHITEBOXGRIND proves that a fully automated analysis of many whitebox implementations is feasible given sufficient computing resources. Unless an implementation is specifically hardened to avoid side-channel attacks based on memory values (e.g. by relying on register values only, which can easily be countered by adjusting our instrumentation strategy), it will usually be possible to use the intermediate values observed to draw conclusions about the key that is used. During our evaluation, we found that we were mostly constrained by the time taken to obtain and process the large amounts of data included in our traces. An attacker not constrained by research budgets will generally be able to efficiently obtain more traces by applying more computational power—then, the main performance constraint becomes the processing speed during sample reduction. In practice, an attacker will also be able to select "interesting" parts of the traces depending on the selection function (e.g. if targeting the first round, one might only want to consider the first half of the trace) instead of processing the entire trace, further speeding up subsequent processing steps. Generally, the large variance between the different implementations stems from the different obfuscation strategies chosen by these submissions.

One possible way to defeat the approach described in this work is to introduce data-dependent execution that causes a misalignment between different traces (if possible, without leaking intermediate values). This can be achieved by explicit dependencies on the original plaintext, which does not need to be kept secret. A more sophisticated approach to re-aligning the traces—perhaps based on algorithms normally used for line-based text diffing, or those used for other side-channel attacks (e.g. [27])—might enable successful attacks on those obfuscation schemes.

7   Conclusion

In this work we examined whether it is possible to fully automate DCA against whitebox implementations of AES. Of course, this involves making some trade-offs with regard to performance and attack results. Notwithstanding these particularities, we achieved an attack speed increase of roughly a magnitude on commodity hardware against a reference AES implementation. We stress that this performance measurement needs to be taken with a grain of salt: for about half of our whitebox samples, existing tooling yielded no result at all due to practical space constraints. This work should be considered as yet another sign that whitebox cryptography is a fundamentally broken approach: Given that it is possible to fully automate key extraction for some of the less hardened approaches, most implementations will not hold up to a dedicated attacker with reverse engineering skills. We suspect that it will be possible to apply sufficient obfuscation to make a fully automated approach infeasible to the point where the tools need to be adjusted to the specific target by hand. However, real-world implementations usually have to conform to more requirements than such theoretical designs, which means that the automated analysis approach presented in this work will still hold value for many such implementations. This also applies to non-AES whiteboxes which are vulnerable to DCA-style attacks. Our method of obtaining and filtering instruction traces does not assume any specifics about the implementation under test, so that only minor modifications to the attack code are required for WHITEBOXGRIND to support attacks on other cryptosystems.

Acknowledgments. We would like to thank the anonymous reviewers for their valuable comments and suggestions on the paper, as these helped us to improve it. This work was partially funded by the German Federal Ministry of Education and Research (BMBF) in the SIPSENSIN project under grant number 16KIS1663 and by the German Research Foundation (DFG) under the Excellence Strategy - EXC 2092 CASA - 390781972. This work was done while Tobias Holl and Katharina Bogad were at the Technical University of Munich.

References

1. Alakuijala, J., Szabadka, Z.: Brotli compressed data format. RFC 7932, July 2016
2. Biham, E., Shamir, A.: Differential cryptanalysis of DES-like cryptosystems. J. Cryptol. **4**(1), 3–72 (1991)
3. Bock, E.A., et al.: White-box cryptography: don't forget about grey-box attacks. J. Cryptol. **32**(4), 1095–1143 (2019)
4. Bos, J.W., Hubain, C., Michiels, W., Teuwen, P.: Differential computation analysis: hiding your white-box designs is not enough. In: Gierlichs, B., Poschmann, A.Y. (eds.) CHES 2016. LNCS, vol. 9813, pp. 215–236. Springer, Heidelberg (2016). https://doi.org/10.1007/978-3-662-53140-2_11
5. Breunesse, C.-B., Kizhvatov, I., Muijrers, R., Spruyt, A.: Towards fully automated analysis of whiteboxes: perfect dimensionality reduction for perfect leakage. Cryptology ePrint Archive, Report 2018/095 (2018). https://ia.cr/2018/095
6. Brier, E., Clavier, C., Olivier, F.: Correlation power analysis with a leakage model. In: Joye, M., Quisquater, J.-J. (eds.) CHES 2004. LNCS, vol. 3156, pp. 16–29. Springer, Heidelberg (2004). https://doi.org/10.1007/978-3-540-28632-5_2
7. CHES 2019. WhibOx contest, August 2019
8. Chow, S., Eisen, P., Johnson, H., Van Oorschot, P.C.: White-box cryptography and an AES implementation. In: Nyberg, K., Heys, H. (eds.) SAC 2002. LNCS, vol. 2595, pp. 250–270. Springer, Heidelberg (2003). https://doi.org/10.1007/3-540-36492-7_17
9. Daemen, J., Rijmen, V.: The Rijndael Block Cipher. AES Proposal, March 1999
10. Daemen, J., Rijmen, V.: The wide trail design strategy. In: Honary, B. (ed.) Cryptography and Coding 2001. LNCS, vol. 2260, pp. 222–238. Springer, Heidelberg (2001). https://doi.org/10.1007/3-540-45325-3_20
11. Dolan-Gavitt, B., Leek, T., Hodosh, J., Lee, W.: Tappan Zee (North) bridge: mining memory accesses for introspection. In: Proceedings of the 2013 ACM SIGSAC Conference on Computer and Communications Security - CCS 2013. ACM Press, November 2013
12. Dworkin, M., et al.: Federal Information Processing Standards Publication 197: Advanced Encryption Standard (AES), 2001-11-26 (2001)
13. "FdLSifu". QSCAT – Qt Side Channel Analysis Tool. Online [retrieved 2022-04-28] (2017–2021)

14. Haupert, V., Maier, D., Schneider, N., Kirsch, J., Müller, T.: Honey, I shrunk your app security: the state of android app hardening. In: Giuffrida, C., Bardin, S., Blanc, G. (eds.) DIMVA 2018. LNCS, vol. 10885, pp. 69–91. Springer, Cham (2018). https://doi.org/10.1007/978-3-319-93411-2_4

15. Intel Corporation: Intel®Architecture Instruction Set Extensions Programming Reference. Intel (2021)

16. Jakob, W., Rhinelander, J., Moldovan, D.: pybind11 - Seamless operability between C++11 and Python (2017). https://github.com/pybind/pybind11

17. Katz, J., Lindell, Y.: Introduction to Modern Cryptography, 1st edn. Chapman & Hall/CRC, Boca Raton (2008)

18. Klik, M., et al.: The FST format and FSTLIB library. [retrieved 2022-04-21], April 2019

19. Kocher, P., Jaffe, J., Jun, B.: Differential power analysis. In: Wiener, M. (ed.) CRYPTO 1999. LNCS, vol. 1666, pp. 388–397. Springer, Heidelberg (1999). https://doi.org/10.1007/3-540-48405-1_25

20. Donjon, L.: Lascar: donjon side channel library. [retrieved 2022–04-21], February 2019–2022

21. Lepoint, T., Rivain, M.: Another nail in the coffin of white-box AES implementations. Cryptology ePrint Archive, Report 2013/455 (2013). https://ia.cr/2013/455

22. Matsui, M., Yamagishi, A.: A new method for known plaintext attack of FEAL cipher. In: Rueppel, R.A. (ed.) EUROCRYPT 1992. LNCS, vol. 658, pp. 81–91. Springer, Heidelberg (1993). https://doi.org/10.1007/3-540-47555-9_7

23. Microsoft: Direct2d API. https://docs.microsoft.com/en-us/windows/win32/direct2d/direct2d-portal

24. Nethercote, N., Seward, J.: Valgrind: a framework for heavyweight dynamic binary instrumentation. ACM SIGPLAN Not. **42**(6), 89–100 (2007)

25. Shannon, C.: A Mathematical Theory of Cryptography. Memorandum, Bell Laboratories, Murray Hill (1945)

26. The HDF Group: HDF5 Application Developer's Guide. [retrieved 2021-10-07], September 2019

27. Weiser, S., Zankl, A., Spreitzer, R., Miller, K., Mangard, S., Sigl, G.: DATA - differential address trace analysis: finding address-based Side-Channels in binaries. In 27th USENIX Security Symposium (USENIX Security 2018), Baltimore, MD, August 2018, pp. 603–620. USENIX Association (2018)

White-Box Cryptography with Global Device Binding from Message-Recoverable Signatures and Token-Based Obfuscation

Shashank Agrawal[1], Alpírez Bock Estuardo[2(✉)], Yilei Chen[3],
and Gaven Watson[4]

[1] Coinbase, San Francisco, USA
[2] Xiphera LTD, Espoo, Finland
estuardo.alpirezbock@xiphera.com
[3] Tsinghua University, Beijing, China
[4] Meta, Menlo Park, USA

Abstract. Device binding for white-box cryptography ensures that a white-box program is only executable on one specific device and is unusable elsewhere. In this paper we ask the following: is it possible to design a *global* white-box program which is compiled once, but can be securely shared with multiple users and bound to each of their devices? Acknowledging this question, we define different flavours of security for such global white-boxes and provide corresponding constructions.

We first consider families of *strong* global white-boxes which can be securely distributed and bound to users' devices without the need of sharing secrets between compiling entities and users. We then show how such strong global white-boxes can be constructed based on message recoverable signatures (MRS). To this end, we introduce *puncturable* MRS which we build based on puncturable pseudorandom functions and indistinguishability obfuscation. We later consider the use of Token-Based Obfuscation for constructing a simpler family of global white-boxes, and show new ways of building white-box crypto, from more accepted assumptions as previously considered in the literature.

Keywords: White-box crypto · Mobile payments · Device binding · Puncturable signatures with message recovery

1 Introduction

The white-box attack model considers adversaries with complete access to the implementation code of a cryptographic program and with control of its execution environment. White-box cryptography was introduced in 2002 [11,12] and finds its main use cases in Digital-Rights Management (DRM) and

This work was conducted while all authors were at VISA Research.

mobile-payment applications [15, 30].[1] In both cases, standard symmetric encryption ciphers are implemented in a white-box fashion. However, it is not publicly known how exactly the ciphers are implemented and which level of security they actually achieve. The scientific community has proposed white-box designs for DES [12, 23] and AES [4, 10, 11, 21, 33], but all of these approaches have been subject to key-extraction attacks (cf. [18, 20, 32] and [9, 14, 22, 26, 27]).

It remains an open question, whether one can construct a white-box implementation of DES or AES which remains secure against key-extraction attacks. In practice, white-box designs remain robust for a certain period of time, and key extraction is mitigated by periodically rotating the embedded keys and updating the white-box obfuscation. However, we should note that in the application scenarios discussed above, white-box programs also implement countermeasures against so called *code-lifting* attacks.

Code-Lifting Attacks and Device Binding. White-box programs may be susceptible to code-lifting attacks, where, an adversary simply copies the execution code of the program with its embedded secret key [31]. The adversary can then run the code for his own purposes on any device or environment of his choice, without needing to perform a key-extraction or reverse-engineering attack.

One approach to mitigate code-lifting attacks is to implement *device binding* operations [5, 15, 29]. That is, the white-box programs are configured such that they can only be executed on one specific device. In practice, device binding plays an important role in combination with white-box cryptography for protecting mobile payment applications, as recommended by EMVCo [15]. Device binding can be implemented by having the white-box program verify a specific signature provided by some trusted component or party. Alternatively, one can design a white-box program which does not compute directly on raw inputs, but rather on *encoded* inputs. The corresponding encoding algorithm can be extracted from the secure hardware of a device. This encoding forces us thus to run our white-box program in combination with that device.

It may seem counterintuitive to combine white-box cryptography with dependency on some trusted hardware. However, in many environments the availability of specific secure hardware and what algorithms they support may be somewhat limited. For example, payment processes rely heavily on 3DES which has only been supported in Android Keystore recently (since v9) and is not supported by many secure elements. This is clearly an example where a device may have trusted hardware available but it cannot provide the required cryptographic functionality. One can view our approach of using both a trusted component and a white-box obfuscation scheme as a means to bootstrap the limited functionality of the trusted component to facilitate the secure computation of a complex functionality. In addition it facilitates added *crypto-agility*, once secure hardware is deployed it can be relatively hard to update with newer algorithms. By bootstrapping with a white-box obfuscation scheme we can enable a secure hardware deployment to support new and needed cryptographic schemes.

---

[1] The extended version of this paper [1] provides a broad discussion on the role of white-box cryptography in mobile payments.

Security definitions for white-box cryptography with device binding have been presented in recent years [2,3]. The definitions in these works capture the property that the corresponding programs only execute correctly in combination with *one* specific device and are otherwise useless, while preserving their corresponding security properties. In the second work [3], the authors provide feasibility results for white-boxed payment applications. Their constructions are based on puncturable pseudorandom functions (PPRF) and indistinguishability obfuscation (iO) [6].

1.1 Our Contributions

In this paper, we first make the observation that previous constructions for device binding [2,3] necessitate that a unique white-box program is created for each device. In this line, we ask the following question: is it possible to create a single *global white-box* which can be distributed to multiple users and securely bound to each user's device? With such a construction, we aim to take further steps towards more practical white-box approaches. Namely with a global white-box, our compiler needs to generate only one white-box application and place it directly in the cloud available for download (avoiding multiple expensive obfuscation operations). Such a setting stands in-line with traditional app stores and does not necessitate any additional side-loading when downloading the program.

At a high-level we consider a global white-box compiler which will obfuscate some function F. Generally, the function F corresponds to the description of a program we wish to combine with a white-box decryption program. Our schemes must satisfy two important properties: ensure the confidentiality of inputs to the white-box (e.g. an encrypted stream in the case of DRM or a bank provided key in the case of payments-also known as LUKs: *limited use keys*) and ensure that the white-box can only be evaluated on inputs which have been *"bound"* to a device's trusted component. To capture these properties we introduce corresponding notions of security for two classes of global white-box programs. On this line, we give examples of how each class of global white-box can be constructed by providing corresponding provably secure constructions.

1.2 Global White-Boxes

Ideally, we would like a software provider (or server) to compile a single white-box program and upload it to the cloud. Any user who wants to acquire the program can download it to their device. However upon download, the white-box program should not (yet) be functional. Instead, the program should first be properly enrolled and bound to a user's device. This way we ensure that the program is not subject to code-lifting attacks. Below we introduce two possible ways of constructing global white-boxes with their corresponding enrollment processes.

244   S. Agrawal et al.

Simple Case. First we consider a white-box which is compiled to only work on inputs which are encoded using some secret key material. This key material is generated by the server such that the corresponding *decoding* key can be embedded when creating the white-box. A user can only run this white-box if he obtains the corresponding encoding key from the server. By securely storing this key in the hardware of a user's device, we ensure that use of the white-box is bound to that device. The pseudocode on the right describes how such a white-box program would work in collaboration with the secure hardware, denoted here as HW. The secure hardware takes as input a ciphertext that we wish to later decrypt with our white-box program. HW encodes the ciphertext with the key it obtained from the server, e_s, and obtains $\tilde{c}$. The white-box program has a decoding and a decryption key embedded (d_s and k) and it takes as input the encoded ciphertext $\tilde{c}$. The white-box first decodes a ciphertext and then decrypts it.

$$\frac{\mathsf{HW}(c)}{\tilde{c} \leftarrow \mathsf{Encode}(e_s, c)}$$
return $\tilde{c}$

$$\frac{\mathsf{WB}(\tilde{c})}{c \leftarrow \mathsf{Decode}(d_s, \tilde{c})}$$
$m \leftarrow \mathsf{Dec}(k, c)$
return m

Note that the white-box program needs to be obfuscated such that an adversary is unable to separate the decoding and the decryption operations. This makes it impossible for an adversary to run the white-box without access to a hardware device with the corresponding encoding key. The scenario described above achieves our initial goal of a *global white-box* as long as the encoding key can be securely shared between the server and the devices.

Strong Case. A stronger approach is if each user makes use of their own (unique) key for encoding inputs to the white-box. Here we additionally ensure that even if a device's trusted hardware is compromised this only affects the binding of that device and no others, thus providing a stronger level of security. To implement this approach we need a white-box which takes two encoded inputs. One input is the ciphertext encoded via the secret key of the user's hardware. The other input is the corresponding decoding key of the user's hardware, but encoded via the server's secret key. The white-box should first recover the decoding key of the user and then use the recovered key to decode the encoded ciphertext, as shown in the pseudocode below. Here d_h is the decoding key of the user's hardware. The server encodes d_h via the server's secret key e_s. The hardware encodes a ciphertext via the hardware's secret key and returns $\tilde{c}$.

$$\frac{\mathsf{Server}(d_h)}{\tilde{d}_h \leftarrow \mathsf{Encode}(e_s, d_h)}$$
return $\tilde{d}_h$

$$\frac{\mathsf{HW}(c)}{\tilde{c} \leftarrow \mathsf{Encode}(e_h, c)}$$
return $\tilde{c}$

$$\frac{\mathsf{WB}(\tilde{d}_h, \tilde{c})}{d_h \leftarrow \mathsf{Decode}(d_s, \tilde{d}_h)}$$
$c \leftarrow \mathsf{Decode}(d_h, \tilde{c})$
$m \leftarrow \mathsf{Dec}(k, c)$
return m

Here as before, the white-box program should be obfuscated such that an adversary is unable to separate the decode and decryption algorithms. Note that if an adversary copies the white-box, a ciphertext *and* the encoded key $\tilde{d}_h$ (or even gains knowledge of the decoding keys d_s and d_h), the adversary is still unable to correctly perform a decryption, unless he can access the corresponding hardware in order to correctly encode the ciphertext.

We refer to the scenario described above as a *strong global white-box*. The idea is that the white-box program will only output correct values if both its inputs are provided consistently, i.e. if the encoded key $\tilde{d}_h$ is used in combination with inputs encoded via the device holding d_h. In what follows we explain how we can construct white-boxes used in both global settings, starting with the stronger one.

Message-Recoverable Signatures for Strong Global White-Boxes. Message-recoverable signatures (MRS) were introduced by Bellare and Rogaway [7]. Unlike traditional signature schemes, whose signing algorithm generates a signature for a particular message, an MRS signing algorithm *embeds* the signature within the message. Additionally, an MRS scheme consists of a *recover* algorithm which verifies the signature and returns the original message. Security of MRS holds as long as an adversary is unable to forge a valid signed message. The original benefit of using MRS as opposed to a traditional signature is that it reduces the amount of data that must be sent between the signing and the verifying entity. In [7], the authors show how MRS schemes can be derived from RSA-based schemes.

As of today, MRS-inspired approaches are used in practice for implementing device binding for white-box programs running on mobile phones with trusted components [24]. In such approaches, the trusted component on a user's phone generates an RSA key pair and securely stores the secret key. The public key is shared with the entity compiling the white-box program and the white-box is compiled such that it has the public key embedded in it, together with a symmetric decryption key. Whenever we want to decrypt a ciphertext, we first sign it via the secret key stored in the trusted component. We then give this signed ciphertext as input to the white-box, which first uses the public key to recover the ciphertext before the final decryption with the symmetric key. Note that given such a white-box program, it should be difficult for an adversary to separate the message recovery from the decryption algorithm. Thus, the white-box program (with the embedded public key) can only be used in the presence of the trusted component which generates the signed ciphertexts.

By extending this approach, we can build a compiler which creates a single white-box program that may be used by all legitimate users. This approach would use two layers of message-recoverable signatures and the white-box program would have the public key of the server and a symmetric decryption key embedded. The first layer will use the embedded public key to recover the unique public key of the user. The second layer will use that user's public key to decode the ciphertext. Thus ensuring the stricter requirement of per-device binding of a strong global white-box. The use of MRS makes the enrollment process described in the previous section easier, since no secrets need to be shared between the server and the user.

In this paper we will build strong global white-boxes exactly as described above. Our MRS scheme will be a puncturable MRS which we build based on puncturable PRFs and iO. Our construction can then simply take the form of

$\mathrm{Dec}(k^*, \mathrm{Rcvr}(\mathrm{Rcvr}(.,.)))$, with a layer of obfuscation around it. Our construction can be seen as a design outline for implementing such strong global white-boxes in practice. Note however that in practice, we'd need to substitute the puncturable primitives and iO with more efficient, implementation-friendly primitives and obfuscation schemes.

MRS vs Traditional Signatures. We note that device binding for white-box programs could also be implemented using a traditional signature scheme. In this case instead of encoding the message we wish to compute via an MRS scheme, the trusted component generates a separate signature for that specific message. The white-box program would verify the signature and only proceed if the signature was valid. In this paper we choose to focus on the use of MRS in order to validate and extend approaches used in practice [24]. Why such MRS-inspired approaches are used in practice instead of traditional signature schemes is not completely clear. In early white-box related works, it was proposed to make use of *external encodings* for protecting white-box AES designs against code-lifting attacks [11,25]. Here, external encodings refer to encodings provided by an external source (e.g. a secure hardware), and the white-box program is designed such that it computes correctly only on values encoded via that external source. The approach of using MRS correlates with this proposal since we are using the secret signing key as our encoding function and the public key embedded in the white-box as a decoding function. Note that for such a design, the recover algorithm can be simplified and does not really need to check for the validity of the signature. Instead, it can directly perform the decoding using the embedded public key. If the input was not encoded or encoded using the wrong secret key, then the output of the white-box will be anyway faulty (see Sect. 1.2). It is an interesting question whether it is easier to obfuscate (in practice) a program which checks for the validity of a signature (and then decrypts) or a program which decrypts directly on encoded inputs.

Token-Based Obfuscation for (Simple) Global White-Boxes. TBO allows to obfuscate any circuit (or program) and its security is achieved under the restriction that the obfuscated circuit can only be executed for specific inputs: the inputs for which a user obtains a token (see [17] for the definition of TBO). A token-based obfuscation scheme is therefore defined in combination with a token-generation algorithm, where the token generation key is created together with the obfuscated program. We recall now that for achieving device-binding, we want to generate a white-box program which can only be correctly executed in combination with a specific trusted component. Here, token-based obfuscation directly gives us the functionality and security we desire for our complete white-box scheme when we place our token input generator directly on the trusted component.

For context, consider the following simplified example. Let F be a pseudorandom permutation with an embedded secret key, such that $F(c) = x$. Furthermore, assume that we want to use this pseudorandom permutation as a decryption function. That is, the input c corresponds to a ciphertext which was generated for some message x via the inverse of F. We now obfuscate F via token-based obfuscation: $(O[F], \mathsf{MSK}) \leftarrow\!\!\$ \ \mathsf{TBO.Obf}(F)$. We obtain thus a program $O[F]$ which alone reveals nothing about F. $O[F]$ can be used for recovering x only when we can obtain a valid token for the corresponding c value: $\tilde{c} \leftarrow\!\!\$ \ \mathsf{TBO.InpGen}(\mathsf{MSK}, c)$. Upon receiving $\tilde{c}$, a user can recover x via $O[F](\tilde{c})$. Thus, if we implement the token-generation algorithm within the trusted component of a device, the obfuscated program becomes useful only if it has access to that device, achieving thus the property of device binding. In the extended version of this paper [1] we provide security notions for simple global white-boxes and present provable secure constructions from TBO.

2 Preliminaries and Notation

$a \leftarrow b$ denotes the assignment of a value b to a variable a. We denote by $a \leftarrow A(b)$ the execution of a deterministic algorithm A on input b to produce an output a. $a \leftarrow\!\!\$ \ A(b)$ denotes the execution of a probabilistic algorithm A. We use square brackets to denote a fixed value hard-coded into an algorithm, e.g. $A[k]$ denotes that the value k is hard-coded in the algorithm A. $a\|b$ denotes the concatenation of two values a and b, while $|a|$ denotes the length of a value a. $q \leftarrow\!\!\$ \ Q$ denotes the process of randomly sampling an element q from a set (or distribution) Q.

By 1^λ we denote (the unary representation of) the security parameter, which all algorithms receive as input. We write it explicitly for the algorithms which only take the security parameter as input and leave it implicit for the rest. The subscript to an adversary $\mathcal{A}$ denotes the class of oracles the adversary gets access to in our security definitions. With $\approx_c$ we denote computationally indistinguishability.

Definition 1 (Obfuscation [6,19]). *A probabilistic algorithm O is an obfuscator for a class of circuit $\mathcal{C}$ if the following conditions hold:*

- *(Preservation of the function) For all inputs x, $\Pr[C(x) = O(C(x))] > 1 - \mathsf{negl}(\lambda)$.*
- *(Polynomially slowdown) There is a polynomial p s.t. $|O(C)| < p(|C|)$.*
- *(Strong virtual black-box obfuscation) For any PPT adversary $\mathcal{A}$, there is a PPT simulator Sim s.t. for all C, $\left\{ \mathcal{A}(1^\lambda, O(C)) \right\} \approx_c \left\{ \mathsf{Sim}^{C(\cdot)}(1^\lambda, |C|) \right\}$.*
- *(Indistinguishability obfuscation) For functionally equivalent circuits C_0, C_1, with $|C_0| = |C_1|$, $O(C_0) \approx_c O(C_1)$.*

Let us recall the definition of puncturable PRFs.

Definition 2 (Puncturable PRF [28]). *Let $l(\lambda)$ and $m(\lambda)$ be the input and output lengths. A family of puncturable pseudorandom functions $\mathsf{G} = \{\mathsf{PPRF}\}$ is given by a triple of efficient functions (Setup, Eval, Punc), where $\mathsf{Setup}(1^\lambda)$ generates the key K, such that PPRF maps from $\{0,1\}^{l(\lambda)}$ to $\{0,1\}^{m(\lambda)}$; $\mathsf{Eval}(K, x)$ takes a key K, an input x, outputs $\mathsf{PPRF}(K, x)$; $\mathsf{Punc}(K, x^*)$ takes a key K and an input x^*, outputs a punctured key $K\{x^*\}$.*

It satisfies the following conditions:

Functionality Preserved over Unpunctured Points: *For all x^* and keys K, if $K\{x^*\} = \mathsf{Punc}(K, x^*)$, then for all $x \neq x^*$, $\mathsf{PPRF}(K,x) = \mathsf{PPRF}(K\{x^*\}, x)$.*

Pseudorandom on the Punctured Points: *For every input x^*, the value of F on x^* is indistinguishable from random in the presence of the key punctured at x^*. That is, the following two distributions are indistinguishable for every x^*:*

$$(x^*, K\{x^*\}, G_K(x^*)) \text{ and } (x^*, K\{x^*\}, r^*),$$

where K is output by $\mathsf{Setup}(1^\lambda)$, $K\{x^*\}$ is output by $\mathsf{Punc}(K, x^*)$, and r^* is uniform in $\{0,1\}^{m(\lambda)}$.

Theorem [28]. *If one-way function exists, then for all length parameters $l(\lambda)$, $m(\lambda)$, there is a puncturable PRF family that maps from $l(\lambda)$ bits to $m(\lambda)$ bits.*

Definition 3 (Message recoverable signatures). *A message-recoverable signature (MRS) scheme is a tuple of three algorithms $(\mathsf{KGen}, \mathsf{Sig}, \mathsf{Rcvr})$ such that KGen and Sig are probabilistic polynomial-time algorithms (PPT) and Rcvr is a deterministic polynomial-time algorithm and have the following syntax:*

$$\mathsf{sk}, \mathsf{pk} \leftarrow_\$ \mathsf{KGen}(1^\lambda), \quad \tilde{m} \leftarrow_\$ \mathsf{Sig}(\mathsf{sk}, m), \quad m|\bot \leftarrow \mathsf{Rcvr}(\mathsf{pk}, \tilde{m}).$$

Moreover, this scheme is correct, *if for all messages $m \in \{0,1\}^*$,*

$$\Pr[\mathsf{Rcvr}(\mathsf{pk}, \mathsf{Sig}(\mathsf{sk}, m)) = m] = 1$$

where the probability is over the randomness of $\mathsf{sk}, \mathsf{pk} \leftarrow_\$ \mathsf{KGen}(1^\lambda)$ and Sig.

For the security of MRS we consider a selective security definition where the adversary is tasked with forging a valid signature for a randomly chosen message. This notion aligns well with the use we want to give to MRS in this paper, since we will use MRS to encode ciphertexts, which correspond to the encryption of some content or randomly generated secret keys (see Sect. 1.2).

Definition 4. *An MRS scheme is secure if for all PPT adversaries $\mathcal{A}$, their advantage $\left|\Pr\left[\mathsf{Exp}^{\mathsf{unf}}_{\mathcal{A},\mathsf{MRS}}(1^\lambda) = 1\right]\right|$ is negligible.*

$\mathsf{Exp}^{\mathsf{unf}}_{\mathcal{A},\mathsf{MRS}}(1^\lambda)$	$\mathcal{O}_{\mathsf{Sig}}(m)$
$\mathsf{sk}, \mathsf{pk} \leftarrow_\$ \mathsf{KGen}(1^\lambda)$	if $m \neq m^*$
$m^* \leftarrow_\$ \{0,1\}^\lambda$	$\tilde{m} \leftarrow_\$ \mathsf{Sig}(\mathsf{sk}, m)$
$\tilde{m} \leftarrow_\$ \mathcal{A}^{\mathcal{O}_{\mathsf{Sig}}}(\mathsf{pk}, m^*)$	return $\tilde{m}$
if $m^* = \mathsf{Rcvr}(\mathsf{pk}, \tilde{m})$ win $\leftarrow 1$	
return win	

3 Strong Global White-Boxes

We next explain our setting where we consider a provider which creates an obfuscated program (for some functionality F) which will be distributed to a collection of devices (also see Sects. 1.2 and 4 for more context). A user *enrolls* his device by calling the trusted component and generating a secret-public key pair and some ID value. The user then shares the public key and the ID with the server. The server will generate a certificate based on this public key via an MRS scheme: the server uses its secret key for signing the user's public key. Thus, we obtain a *signed* (or encoded) version of the user's public key, denoted cert, which is sent back to the user.

The provider generates and encrypts the inputs of the white-box program (e.g. the DRM content or the limited use keys (LUKs) for payment) and sends the corresponding ciphertexts to the user. For decrypting the ciphertexts, the user first encodes them via his trusted component. The trusted component encodes the ciphertexts via MRS, i.e. it signs them. The user now gives the encoded ciphertext and the cert as inputs to the white-box program. The white-box program will first *recover* (or decode) the user's public key from the cert and then use that public key to recover the original ciphertext, which afterwards will be decrypted.

Note that a user is only able to correctly run the white-box program if he (1) obtains a legitimate cert and (2) encodes the input ciphertexts via the secret key of its trusted component. Moreover the cert used must be an encoding, under the secret key of the server, of the public key corresponding to the secret key used to encode inputs to the white-box. Below we define the syntax of each algorithm.

Definition 5. *A Strong Global White-box scheme* sGW-Scheme *consists of the following algorithms*

- *A randomized compiler* Comp *which takes as input a function $F \in \mathcal{F}$, with syntax $z \leftarrow F(x, y)$. The compiler returns a program* WB *and two randomly generated keys* rk *and* ek*, i.e. $(\mathsf{rk}, \mathsf{ek}, \mathsf{WB}) \leftarrow\!\!\$ \; \mathsf{Comp}(F)$.*
- *A probabilistic algorithm* Init*, which on input the security parameter, outputs the following values: a secret key* sk*, an associated public key* pk *and an identifier* ID*, i.e. $(\mathsf{sk}, \mathsf{pk}, \mathsf{ID}) \leftarrow\!\!\$ \; \mathsf{Init}(1^n)$.*
- *A probabilistic algorithm* Enroll *which takes as input a secret (registration) key* rk *and a request message* pk*, and outputs an authenticated badge* cert*, i.e. $(\mathsf{cert}) \leftarrow\!\!\$ \; \mathsf{Enroll}(\mathsf{rk}, \mathsf{pk})$.*
- *A probabilistic algorithm* Encrypt *which takes as input a secret (encryption) key* ek*, a value x, and an identifier* ID*, and outputs an encrypted message c, i.e. $c \leftarrow\!\!\$ \; \mathsf{Encrypt}(\mathsf{ek}, x, \mathsf{ID})$.*
- *A probabilistic algorithm* Encode *which on input of a secret (binding/encoding) key* sk *and a value c, and an identifier* ID *returns a value $\tilde{c}$, i.e. $\tilde{c} \leftarrow\!\!\$ \; \mathsf{Encode}(\mathsf{sk}, c, \mathsf{ID})$.*

Correctness states that for every genuine rk *and* pk*, such that* cert $\leftarrow\!\!\$$ Enroll $(\mathsf{rk}, \mathsf{pk})$, *for every function $F : \mathcal{X} \times \mathcal{Y} \to \mathcal{Z}$, for all $x \in \mathcal{X}$, all $y \in \mathcal{Y}$, we have*

$$\Pr[\mathsf{WB}(\mathsf{Encode}(\mathsf{sk}, \mathsf{Encrypt}(\mathsf{ek}, x, \mathsf{ID})), \mathsf{cert}, y) = F(x, y)] = 1,$$

where the probability is over the randomness of all algorithms and the corresponding secret keys sk, ek, rk*.*

Security Definitions. We first formalize the privacy property of an sGW-scheme via the game depicted in Fig. 1. We recall that we could have two different types of global white-boxes depending on the application we are considering. If the global white-box is meant to decrypt broadcasted data, e.g. as in DRM applications, then *all* global white-boxes should be able to decrypt *all* values. In turn if the white-boxes are used for payment applications, the inputs to the white-boxes are user specific and the ciphertexts sent should only be decrypted by one specific user. For our privacy game, we consider the case where information is broadcast to all owners of white-boxes. Thus, we remark that one white-box allows an adversary to decrypt any broadcasted value as long as he has access to a registered hardware. This also implies that the encryptions are not user specific. For this reason, we do not consider the ID values in this game (they will become relevant for a later model). We now describe the security experiment.

The adversary is given access to several oracles which permit him to enroll devices, receive encrypted inputs from the provider, and bind these to a legitimately enrolled device. For the purposes of the experiment, we assume that the trusted component cannot be impersonated (i.e. some secure attestation process ensures the validity of pk submitted to the Enroll oracle). Note that the adversary can run the white-box on any value c encoded via any device which has been properly enrolled, and can enroll as many devices as he wants.[2] The adversary encodes values via the Encode oracle, which he queries with c and a public key value pk which indicates which device he will use for encoding. Additionally, the adversary is given access to a challenge oracle, to which he submits an input x. As output, this oracle returns either the encryption of x or the encryption of a random value r. The adversary wins the security experiment if he can distinguish between these values. Note that to prevent trivial attacks the adversary cannot query the Encode oracle for values which were output by the challenge oracle unless the encoding is meant to be done with a device which has not yet been enrolled. This captures the property that the white-box program should only work properly on inputs encoded via enrolled devices.

Definition 6 (Privacy). *We say that a sGW-scheme is private if for all PPT adversaries $\mathcal{A}$ playing the privacy game described in Fig. 1, the distinguishing advantage $\Pr[\mathsf{Exp}_{\mathcal{A}}^{\mathsf{priv}}(1^n) = 1] - \frac{1}{2}$ is negligible.*

An obfuscation scheme which satisfies the privacy notion above ensures that an adversary cannot deduce the private input x shared by the provider. When obfuscating a specific function F, what we actually wish to guarantee is that the adversary cannot evaluate the function F on secret input x without using a legitimate device enrolled with the provider. For instance when considering a

---

[2] This capability is somewhat similar to the capability an adversary might have to obtain re-compiled versions of a white-box program, introduced by Delerablée et al. in [13] with respect to notions such as security against key extraction, one-wayness, incompressibility and traceability. Each new white-box program is compiled based on different randomness, but on the same secret key, allowing thus to decrypt or encrypt the same values.

$\mathsf{Exp}_{\mathcal{A}}^{\mathsf{priv}}(1^n)$	$\mathcal{O}_{\mathsf{Enroll}}(\mathsf{pk})$	$\mathcal{O}_{\mathsf{Chall}}(x)$
$b \leftarrow_\$ \{0,1\}$	**if** $\mathsf{SK}[\mathsf{pk}] \neq \perp$ **and** $\mathsf{pk} \notin \mathcal{P}$	$r \leftarrow_\$ \mathcal{X}$
$F \leftarrow_\$ \mathcal{A}(1^n)$	$\quad$ cert $\leftarrow_\$ \mathsf{Enroll}(\mathsf{rk}, \mathsf{pk})$	**if** $b = 1$
$\mathcal{C}, \mathcal{P} \leftarrow \emptyset$	$\quad$ $\mathsf{E}[\mathsf{pk}] \leftarrow 1$	$\quad c \leftarrow_\$ \mathsf{Encrypt}(\mathsf{ek}, x)$
$(\mathsf{rk}, \mathsf{ek}, \mathsf{WB}) \leftarrow_\$ \mathsf{Comp}(F)$	$\quad$ **return** cert	**else**
$b^* \leftarrow_\$ \mathcal{A}^{\mathcal{O}}(F, \mathsf{WB})$		$\quad c \leftarrow_\$ \mathsf{Encrypt}(\mathsf{ek}, r)$
return $(b^* = b)$	$\mathcal{O}_{\mathsf{Encrypt}}(x)$	$\mathcal{C} := \mathcal{C} \cup c$
	$c \leftarrow_\$ \mathsf{Encrypt}(\mathsf{ek}, x)$	**return** c
$\mathcal{O}_{\mathsf{Init}}()$	**return** c	
$(\mathsf{sk}, \mathsf{pk}) \leftarrow_\$ \mathsf{Init}(1^n)$	$\mathcal{O}_{\mathsf{Encode}}(c, \mathsf{pk})$	
$\mathsf{SK}[\mathsf{pk}] \leftarrow \mathsf{sk}$	**if** $c \notin \mathcal{C}$ **or** $\perp \leftarrow \mathsf{E}[\mathsf{pk}]$	
return pk	$\quad \mathsf{sk} \leftarrow \mathsf{SK}[\mathsf{pk}]$	
	$\quad \tilde{c} \leftarrow_\$ \mathsf{Encode}(\mathsf{sk}, c)$	
	$\quad \mathcal{P} := \mathcal{P} \cup \mathsf{pk}$	
	$\quad$ **return** $\tilde{c}$	

Fig. 1. Privacy $\mathsf{Exp}_{\mathcal{A}}^{\mathsf{priv}}(1^n)$ security game.

mobile payment application, the function F we obfuscate is a message authentication code (MAC). Specifically, $F(x, y) = \mathrm{MAC}(x, y)$, where x is a limited-use key (LUK) for the MAC, and y is the transaction data to be authenticated. Just like for DRM, the Enroll process ensures that only legitimate users who have registered their device are able to run WB correctly. Therefore, for use case such as payments what we ultimately wish to ensure is that an adversary in unable to *forge* the output of an obfuscated program.

An additional difference for mobile payments use case is that the generated ciphertexts should only be decrypted by one specific user. Otherwise, an adversary could download the global white-box, enroll it, and then steal the ciphertexts corresponding to some other user. Thus, the ciphertexts given to a user need to somehow be linked with the user's device, in such way that they can only be decrypted if the white-box program is run on that one device. Below we introduce our forgery security definition for strong global white-boxes. This definition captures the property that an adversary should not be able to forge valid outputs of the function F for ciphertexts which correspond to some other user's device.

The forgery security experiment and corresponding oracles are depicted in Fig. 2. Unlike the privacy experiment, this notion is now parameterized by a specific F. We need this restriction since otherwise, the adversary could choose an F which computes values which are trivial to forge. An additional difference is that we do not let the adversary choose the values to be encrypted by the encryption oracle. This is because knowing a value x would trivially allow the adversary to compute a valid output $F(x, y) = z$. Instead when the adversary queries an encryption oracle, a value is generated at random, encrypted and then the ciphertext is given to the adversary. We note that this restriction seems fair in this model. Namely in this use case, the encrypted values correspond to key material which will later be used for authentication. Therefore, it is normal to assume that these values will be generated at random and will initially be unknown to a user or an adversary. Below we explain how the oracles are defined.

The Init oracle generates key material for a specific device. It also generates an ID value which identifies the device (or the owner of that device). The Enroll oracle is queried via a public key and its corresponding ID. This corresponds to the device for which we wish to obtain a valid certificate in order to run the white-box program on that device. The oracle returns a certificate specific for that device. The Encrypt oracle is queried via a public key and its corresponding ID. The oracle encrypts a randomly generated value according to the specific ID provided by the adversary and keeps track of a list for the plaintext-ciphertext pairs. Note that this ciphertext should only be decrypted correctly via the device corresponding to the given ID.

The Encode oracle is queried by providing a ciphertext (together with its corresponding ID) and a public key (together with its corresponding ID). That is, when querying this oracle, we indicate which device we wish to use for encoding the given ciphertext. If the device we mean to use has the same ID as the ciphertext, then we store this ciphertext-public key pair in a set. Namely for this pair, we know that the resulting encoding should be properly *decoded* by the global white-box. Thus having such an encoded value would let the adversary trivially generate a valid value z.

We now explain the winning conditions. The adversary outputs two tuples, each relevant to one different winning condition. For the first tuple $(z^*, c, y, \overline{\mathsf{pk}})$, the adversary wins if his given values compute to $F(\mathsf{Dec}(\mathsf{ek}, c, \mathsf{ID}), y) = z^*$, as long as one of the following holds: (1) The public key ID provided for the decryption of c, and c, were not used together for querying the Encode oracle; or, (2) the device public key ID provided for the decryption of c has not been enrolled yet. This captures the general property of device enrollment mentioned above. For the second tuple (c^*, x^*), the adversary wins if the provided value c^* corresponds to a ciphertext encrypting x^*.

Alternative Winning Condition. With the second winning condition we wish to capture that a value x is never leaked during its decryption and computation with the white-box program. In practice, we usually obfuscate the complete white-box program including function F and we wish to ensure the privacy of such values x. Namely, if such values x are leaked, an adversary would have an easier way of attacking a user's application by simply observing how they are once computed by the white-box, bypassing an adversary's need to perform a code-lifting attack. Note that without this second winning condition, a white-box program which does not obfuscate F would be secure in the model.

Definition 7 (Forgery). *We say that an* sGW-*scheme in combination with some function* $F \in \mathcal{F}$ *is unforgeable if all PPT adversaries* $\mathcal{A}$ *have a negligible probability of winning the* $\mathsf{Exp}^{\mathsf{forgery}}_{\mathcal{A}, F}(1^n)$ *game in Fig. 2.*

$\mathsf{Exp}_{F,\mathcal{A}}^{\mathsf{unf}}(1^n)$	$\mathcal{O}_{\mathsf{Enroll}}(\overline{\mathsf{pk}})$	$\mathcal{O}_{\mathsf{Encode}}(\tilde{c},\overline{\mathsf{pk}})$
$\mathcal{C} \leftarrow \emptyset$	if $\mathsf{SK}[\mathsf{pk}] \neq \bot$	$c\|\mathsf{ID}^* \leftarrow \tilde{c}$
$(\mathsf{rk},\mathsf{ek},\mathsf{WB}) \leftarrow_\$ \mathsf{Comp}(F)$	$\mathsf{pk}\|\mathsf{ID} \leftarrow \overline{\mathsf{pk}}$	$\mathsf{pk}\|\mathsf{ID} \leftarrow \overline{\mathsf{pk}}$
$(c,y,z^*,\overline{\mathsf{pk}}),(x^*,c^*) \leftarrow_\$ \mathcal{A}^{\mathcal{O}}(F,\mathsf{WB})$	$\mathsf{cert} \leftarrow_\$ \mathsf{Enroll}(\mathsf{rk},\mathsf{pk})$	if $\mathsf{ID} = \mathsf{ID}^*$
$\mathsf{pk}\|\mathsf{ID} \leftarrow \overline{\mathsf{pk}}$	$E[\overline{\mathsf{pk}}] \leftarrow 1$	$\mathcal{C} := \mathcal{C} \cup (c,\overline{\mathsf{pk}})$
$x \leftarrow \mathsf{Dec}(\mathsf{ek},c,\mathsf{ID})$	return cert	$\mathsf{sk} \leftarrow \mathsf{SK}[\overline{\mathsf{pk}}]$
if $((c,\overline{\mathsf{pk}}) \notin \mathcal{C}$ or $\bot \leftarrow E[\overline{\mathsf{pk}}])$		$\tilde{c} \leftarrow_\$ \mathsf{Encode}(\mathsf{sk},c,\mathsf{ID})$
and $F(x,y) = z^*$	$\mathcal{O}_{\mathsf{Encrypt}}(\overline{\mathsf{pk}})$	return $\tilde{c}$
return 1	$x \leftarrow_\$ \mathcal{X}$	
or if $\mathsf{X}[c^*] \to x^*$	$\mathsf{pk}\|\mathsf{ID} \leftarrow \overline{\mathsf{pk}}$	$\mathcal{O}_{\mathsf{Ver}}(c,y,z,\overline{\mathsf{pk}})$
return 1	$c \leftarrow_\$ \mathsf{Encrypt}(\mathsf{ek},x,\mathsf{ID})$	$\mathsf{pk}\|\mathsf{ID} \leftarrow \overline{\mathsf{pk}}$
else return 0	$\mathsf{X}[c] \leftarrow x$	$x \leftarrow \mathsf{Dec}(\mathsf{ek},c,\mathsf{ID})$
	$\tilde{c} \leftarrow c\|\mathsf{ID}$	if $F(x,y) = z$
$\mathcal{O}_{\mathsf{Init}}()$	return $\tilde{c}$	return 1
$(\mathsf{sk},\mathsf{pk},\mathsf{ID}) \leftarrow_\$ \mathsf{Init}(1^n)$		else return $\bot$
$\overline{\mathsf{pk}} \leftarrow \mathsf{pk}\|\mathsf{ID}$		
$\mathsf{SK}[\overline{\mathsf{pk}}] \leftarrow \mathsf{sk}$		
return $\overline{\mathsf{pk}}$		

Fig. 2. Forgery security game.

4 Message-Recoverable Signatures for sGW-Schemes

Our idea for constructing strong global white-boxes via MRS consists on using two layers of recover algorithms within our white-box program. The first layer will recover the user's public key, which has been signed by the provider as a method of enrolling this device within the system. The second recover algorithm uses the recovered public key to recover the input which was signed by the trusted component. Below we provide a pseudocode description of the algorithms for the case that WB is a white-box decryption program. Here, WB is bound to the Encode component and can only be used correctly if the corresponding pk_2 has been signed by the Enroll algorithm.

$\mathsf{Enroll}(\mathsf{sk}_1,\mathsf{pk}_2)$
$\mathsf{cert} \leftarrow_\$ \mathsf{Sig}(\mathsf{sk}_1,\mathsf{pk}_2)$
return cert

$\mathsf{Encode}[\mathsf{sk}_2](c)$
$\tilde{c} \leftarrow_\$ \mathsf{Sig}(\mathsf{sk}_2,c)$
return $\tilde{c}$

$\mathsf{WB}(\mathsf{cert},\tilde{c})$
$\mathsf{pk}_2 \leftarrow \mathsf{Rcvr}(\mathsf{pk}_1,\mathsf{cert})$
$c \leftarrow \mathsf{Rcvr}(\mathsf{pk}_2,\tilde{c})$
$m \leftarrow \mathsf{Dec}(k,c)$
return m

In practice, we would instantiate such a construction with, for instance, RSA for the public-key operations and AES-based schemes for symmetric-key decryption. On top of that, we would apply some efficient form of obfuscation to the circuit describing WB to hide the symmetric key k and to stop an adversary from separating the decryption program from the recover algorithms. For our formal constructions, we use indistinguishability obfuscation together with iO-friendly, puncturable pseudorandom functions and puncturable message recoverable signatures, which we introduce below. Let us remark that we can also view the construction as using general-purpose obfuscation together with normal signature with message recovery (such as RSA), since all the existing iO candidates can be viewed as candidate VBB obfuscators except for the "self-referring" programs used as the counterexamples of VBB [6]. Such a view is also used in other works [16]. The use of puncturable signature and other iO-friendly primitives is for achieving a feasibility result with provable security guarantee.

Instantiating Our Construction via Puncturable MRS. We apply indistinguishability obfuscation to our circuit in order to achieve the desired security. Recall that for iO, we need two circuits which are functional equivalent but differ in their description. Specifically for a white-box design, our functional equivalent circuits should differ on their sensitive information, ensuring that an adversary is not able to extract that sensitive information from the obfuscated program. Thus, we construct our circuit using puncturable primitives.

Puncturable signature schemes have been presented by both Bellare et al. [8], and by Sahai and Waters [28] for short signatures. Both the schemes are based on PPRFs and provide a public verification algorithm which lets a user verify the validity of a signature. We next introduce puncturable message recovery signature schemes, which we construct via PPRFs and indistinguishability obfuscation. Our construction is inspired by the CCA-secure public-key encryption scheme presented by Sahai and Waters [28, Section 5.3], but we swap the roles of the encryption and decryption functions. That is, we use the secret keys of PPRFs for signing messages and we create an obfuscated program, embedding those keys, and treat it as the public key used for recovering the messages. With our puncturable recover algorithms, we can construct our strong white-box program of the form $\mathsf{Dec}(k^*, \mathsf{Rcvr}_2(\mathsf{Rcvr}_1(\mathsf{pk}^*, \cdot)))$, resembling the pseudocode above, and obfuscate it via iO.

Construction 1. *Let* PPRF *be a secure puncturable PRF, let* Setup *denote an algorithm choosing a punctured key, let* G *be a PRG and iO be an (indistinguishability) obfuscator. Then a signature scheme with message recovery* MRS *can be constructed as follows:*

$C[K_1, K_2](\tilde{m})$	$\mathsf{KGen}(1^\lambda)$	$\mathsf{Sig}(\mathsf{sk}, m)$	$\mathsf{Rcvr}(\tilde{m})$
$(t, c_1, c_2) \leftarrow \tilde{m}$	$K_1 \leftarrow_\$ \mathsf{Setup}_{g1}(1^\lambda)$	$K_1, K_2 \leftarrow \mathsf{sk}$	$m \leftarrow \mathsf{pk}(\tilde{m})$
if $G(c_2) = G(\mathsf{PPRF}_2(K_2, t\|c_1))$	$K_2 \leftarrow_\$ \mathsf{Setup}_{g2}(1^\lambda)$	$r \leftarrow_\$ \{0,1\}^\lambda$	return m
$w \leftarrow \mathsf{PPRF}_1(K_1, t)$	$\mathsf{sk} \leftarrow (K_1, K_2)$	$t \leftarrow G(r)$	
$m \leftarrow c_1 \oplus w$	$\mathsf{pk} \leftarrow_\$ iO(C[K_1, K_2])$	$w \leftarrow \mathsf{PPRF}_1(K_1, t)$	
return m	return sk, pk	$c_1 \leftarrow m \oplus w$	
else return $\perp$		$c_2 \leftarrow \mathsf{PPRF}_2(K_2, t\|c_1)$	
		$\tilde{m} \leftarrow (t, c_1, c_2)$	
		return $\tilde{m}$	

Theorem 1. *If iO is a secure indistinguishability obfuscator, PRG is a pseudorandom generator and* PPRF *is a secure PPRF, then* MRS *is a secure signature scheme with message recovery.*

Proof. We first prove via a series of hybrids that this construction is a secure MRS. We will go via a sequence of hybrids where we will show that an adversary cannot forge a valid encoding for a randomly chosen message, even if the adversary has access to the public (recovery) key.

Hybrid 0: The first hybrid corresponds to the unf security game described in Definition 4. The keys sk, pk are generated according to the KGen algorithm. A challenge oracle generates the challenge message m^* at random.

Hybrid 1: The same as Hybrid 0 with the following changes: for some point z, we generate the PRF value $\tau \leftarrow \mathsf{PPRF}(K_2, z)$. Then we puncture K_2 on z and obtain K_2^z. We then consider the following C_2 described below. C and C_2 are functional equivalent. This game hop reduces to iO security.

$C_2[K_1, K_2^z, z, \tau](\tilde{m})$	$C_3[K_1, K_2^z, z, y](\tilde{m})$	$C_4[K_1^{t*}, K_2^z, z, w^*, y](\tilde{m})$
$(t, c_1, c_2) \leftarrow \tilde{m}$	$(t, c_1, c_2) \leftarrow \tilde{m}$	$(t, c_1, c_2) \leftarrow \tilde{m}$
if $t\|c_1 = z$ **and** $G(c_2) = G(\tau)$	**if** $t\|c_1 = z$ **and** $G(c_2) = y$	**if** $t\|c_1 = z$ **and** $G(c_2) = y$
or if $G(c_2) = G(\mathsf{PPRF}_2(K_2^z, t\|c_1))$	**or if** $G(c_2) = G(\mathsf{PPRF}_2(K_2^z, t\|c_1))$	$\quad m \leftarrow w^* \oplus c_1$
$\quad w \leftarrow \mathsf{PPRF}_1(K_1, t)$	$\quad w \leftarrow \mathsf{PPRF}_1(K_1, t)$	$\quad$ return m
$\quad m \leftarrow c_1 \oplus w$	$\quad m \leftarrow c_1 \oplus w$	**if** $G(c_2) = G(\mathsf{PPRF}_2(K_2^z, t\|c_1))$
$\quad$ return m	$\quad$ return m	$\quad w \leftarrow \mathsf{PPRF}_1(K_1^{t*}, t)$
else return $\perp$	**else return** $\perp$	$\quad m \leftarrow c_1 \oplus w$
		$\quad$ return m
		else return $\perp$

Hybrid 2: same as hybrid 3, but we substitute τ by a random value. Then we query $y \leftarrow G(\tau)$ and we consider the circuit C_3 described above. It is clear that C_2 and C_3 are functional equivalent. This game hop reduces to the PPRF security and iO security.

Hybrid 3: same as Hybrid 2, but we sample y at random: $y \leftarrow_\$ \{0,1\}^{2n}$. Then we take the first bits of the value z which correspond to the value t used for querying PPRF_1. So we take $t^* \leftarrow z[t]$, and we puncture K_1 on t^*, obtaining K_1^{t*}. And now we compute $w^* \leftarrow \mathsf{PPRF}_1(K_1, t^*)$. Now we consider the circuit C_4. It is clear that $C_3 \approx C_4$. This gamehop reduces to PRG- and iO security.

Finally, we can argue that with high probability the value y is outside of the image of the PRG and we can substitute the output on the third line by an all 0 string. Thus showing that the adversary has no advantage of forging a valid message. $\square$

Remark: We could consider a security model specifying the *puncturing security* of our MRS. The model would be the same as in Definition 4, but we would additionally give the adversary the punctured signing key sk^{m^*}. Such a model is analogous to the *selective unforgeability of puncturable digital signatures* model from [8]. In our case, the PPRF security ensures that the punctured signing key does not give any additional advantage to the adversary. *Note:* for puncturing we don't only need to consider the challenge message, but also the randomness used when signing that massage. To make the steps in the proof more smooth, we could adapt our construction of the signing algorithm such that the random value t is explicitly provided as input. In the security game, we would thus have a value $m^*||t^* \leftarrow_\$ \{0,1\}^{2n}$ used as a challenge message and we would puncture the signing key on it. Below we elaborate on the puncturing property of our scheme.

Puncturing the MRS Scheme. We now explain how we puncture our MRS scheme on some input message m. Let us assume that t^* is the random value generated when signing the message m^*. We calculate $w^* \leftarrow \mathsf{PPRF}(K_1, t^*)$, then calculate $c_1^* \leftarrow m^* \oplus w^*$. Now, we can say that when we puncture MRS on the input message m^*, we puncture Sig by puncturing the PPRF keys K_1 on the point t^* and K_2 on the input $t^*||c_1^*$ respectively. As a consequence, the Recover algorithm is punctured on the input $\tilde{m} = t^*, c_1^*, c_2^*$, with $c_2^* = \mathsf{PPRF}(K_2, t^*||c_1^*)$. That is, the recover algorithm cannot verify and recover such a message since the PPRF on its second line cannot

$$\Gamma'[\tilde{c}^*, \mathsf{pk}_1^{c^*}, \mathsf{cert}^*, \mathsf{pk}_2^{*,\mathsf{pk}1}, c^*, v^*, \mathsf{ek}^{r^*}, F](\mathsf{cert}, \tilde{c}, y)$$

1 : $\mathsf{cert}||\mathsf{pk}_1 \leftarrow \mathsf{cert}$
2 : $\tilde{c}||c \leftarrow \tilde{c}$
3 : **if** $\mathsf{cert} = \mathsf{cert}^*$ **and** $G(\mathsf{pk}_1) = G(\mathsf{pk}_1^*)$
4 : $\mathsf{pk}_1 \leftarrow \mathsf{pk}_1^{c^*}$
5 : **else if** $G(\mathsf{pk}_1) \neq G(\mathsf{Rcvr}(\mathsf{pk}_2^{*,\mathsf{pk}1}, \mathsf{cert}^*))$
6 :   **return** $\bot$
7 : **if** $\tilde{c} = \tilde{c}^*$ **and** $G(c) = G(c^*)$
8 : $c \leftarrow c^*$
9 : **else if** $G(c) \neq G(\mathsf{Rcvr}(\mathsf{pk}_1, \tilde{c}))$
10 :   **return** $\bot$
11 : **else**
12 : $t, r \leftarrow c$
13 : **if** $r = r^*$
14 : $v \leftarrow v^*$
15 : **else**
16 : $v \leftarrow \mathsf{PPRF}(\mathsf{ek}^{r^*}, r)$
17 : $x \leftarrow t \oplus v$
18 :   **return** $F(x, y)$
19 : **else return** $\bot$

calculate $\mathsf{PPRF}(K_2, t^*||c_1^*)$. We need to keep this observation in mind when proving security of our strong global white-boxes built from puncturable MRS. In the construction, our white-boxes will use the puncturable recover algorithms. We will argue that we puncture a specific input to the signing algorithm and we will use its corresponding output in the hybrids.

Strong Global White-Box from Puncturable MRS. We now use our MRS constructed in the previous section for constructing strong global white-boxes. The puncturing property of the MRS will allow us to use it in combination of iO and prove its security. We first construct a strong global white-box which should be secure in our privacy model.

Construction 2. *Let* $(\mathsf{KGen}, \mathsf{Sig}, \mathsf{Rcvr})$ *be a puncturable MRS, let* PPRF *be a secure puncturable PRF, let* G *be a PRG and let* $i\mathsf{O}$ *be an indistinguishability obfuscator.*

$\Gamma[\mathsf{pk}_2, \mathsf{ek}, F](\mathsf{cert}, \tilde{c}, y)$	$\mathsf{Comp}(F)$	$\mathsf{Encrypt}(\mathsf{ek}, (x))$
$\mathsf{cert}\|\|\mathsf{pk}_1 \leftarrow \mathsf{cert}$	*1*: $\quad \mathsf{sk}_2, \mathsf{pk}_2 \leftarrow_\$ \mathsf{MRS.KGen}(1^\lambda)$	*1*: $\quad r \leftarrow_\$ \{0,1\}^n$
$\tilde{c}\|\|c \leftarrow \tilde{c}$	*2*: $\quad \mathsf{rk} \leftarrow \mathsf{sk}_2$	*2*: $\quad v \leftarrow \mathsf{PPRF}(\mathsf{ek}, r)$
if $G(\mathsf{pk}_1) \neq G(\mathsf{Rcvr}(\mathsf{pk}_2, \mathsf{cert}))$	*3*: $\quad \mathsf{ek} \leftarrow_\$ \{0,1\}^\lambda$	*3*: $\quad t \leftarrow x \oplus v$
$\quad$ return $\perp$	*4*: $\quad \mathsf{WB} \leftarrow_\$ i\mathsf{O}(\Gamma[\mathsf{pk}_2, \mathsf{ek}, F])$	*4*: $\quad c \leftarrow (t, r)$
else if $G(c) \neq G(\mathsf{Rcvr}(\mathsf{pk}_1, \tilde{c}))$	*5*: $\quad$ *return* $\mathsf{rk}, \mathsf{ek}, \mathsf{WB}$	*5*: $\quad$ *return* c
$\quad$ return $\perp$		
else		
$\quad t, r \leftarrow c$		
$\quad v \leftarrow \mathsf{PPRF}(\mathsf{ek}, r)$		
$\quad x \leftarrow t \oplus v$		
$\quad$ return $F(x, y)$		
else return $\perp$		

$\mathsf{Enroll}(\mathsf{rk}, (\mathsf{pk}_1))$	$\mathsf{Encode}(\mathsf{sk}_1, c))$	$\mathsf{Init}(1^\lambda)$
1: $\quad \mathsf{cert} \leftarrow_\$ \mathsf{MRS.Sig}(\mathsf{rk}, \mathsf{pk}_1)$	*1*: $\quad \tilde{c} \leftarrow_\$ \mathsf{MRS.Sig}(\mathsf{sk}_1, c)$	*1*: $\quad \mathsf{sk}, \mathsf{pk} \leftarrow_\$ \mathsf{MRS.KGen}(1^\lambda)$
2: $\quad \mathsf{cert} \leftarrow \mathsf{cert}\|\|\mathsf{pk}_1$	*2*: $\quad \tilde{c} \leftarrow \tilde{c}\|\|c$	*2*: $\quad$ *return* $(\mathsf{sk}_1, \mathsf{pk}_1)$
3: $\quad$ *return* cert	*3*: $\quad$ *return* $\tilde{c}$	

Theorem 2. *Let* $i\mathsf{O}$ *be a an indistinguishability obfuscator and let* MRS *be a puncturable MRS scheme. Let* PRG *be a pseudorandom generator, and* PPRF *a secure puncturable pseudorandom function. Then Construction 2 is a privacy-secure* sGW *scheme.*

Proof. We now go through a series of hybrids, where the first one corresponds to our privacy game in Fig. 1. We recall that in this game, we care that the adversary does not learn anything about the value x unless he has access to an enrolled hardware device.

Hybrid 0: The keys $\mathsf{ek}, \mathsf{sk}_1, pk_1, \mathsf{sk}_2$ and pk_2 are generated at random. Recall that the keys $(\mathsf{sk}_2, \mathsf{pk}_2), \mathsf{ek}$ will be used for compiling the program. The outputs of the Enroll, Init, Encrypt and Encode oracles are obtained in the same way as described for the algorithms in Construction 2 with the corresponding names. The challenge oracle generates the ciphertext z^* by encrypting either a value x

or r (depending on the bit value of b). The encryption is performed in the same way as described for the Encrypt algorithm in Construction 2 and b is chosen at random.

Hybrid 1: this hybrid is the same as Hybrid 0 except that we will puncture the programs on the points defined as follows.

1. Let (sk_1, pk_1) be the secret-public key pair of the protected user and let $\tilde{c}^* \leftarrow\$ \mathsf{Sig}(sk_1, c^*)$ be the value generated by the Encode oracle when our user queries it on c^*. We puncture sk_1 on c^* to get $\mathsf{sk}_1^{c^*}$; as a consequence our recover algorithm is punctured on $\tilde{c}^*$ and we refer to the punctured public key as $\mathsf{pk}_1^{c^*}$
2. Let cert^* be the value generated by our Enroll oracle when the user calls it on pk_1^*. Let us thus puncture Sig on the input pk_1^*, obtaining thus the punctured signing key $\mathsf{rk}_{\mathsf{pk}_1}^*$. As a consequence, our Recover program pk_2 is punctured on cert^*: $\mathsf{pk}_2^{*,\mathsf{pk1}}$
3. Let r^* denote the value of r used when generating the challenge ciphertext c^* and let v^* be $\mathsf{PPRF}(\mathsf{ek}, r^*)$.
4. Let c^* be $(x \oplus v^*, r^*)$ and puncture ek on r^* and get ek^{r^*}.
5. Finally, generate the circuit Γ' as described above.

The circuits Γ and Γ' in Hybrids 0 and 1 are functionally equivalent and this game hop reduces to iO security.

Remark: Note that in the circuit description of Γ^*, the Recover algorithm on line 9 is not using a punctured key. This has the following reasoning: if pk_1 is defined as in line 4, then the Recover algorithm in line 9 uses a punctured key. In all other cases, the Recover algorithm uses a non-punctured key.

Hybrid 2: the same as Hybrid 1 with the following exceptions. We first replace pk_1^* with $\mathsf{pk}_1^* \leftarrow\$ \{0,1\}^\lambda$. Then, we calculate $h \leftarrow\$ G(\mathsf{pk}_1^*)$. We hardcode h in Γ' and replace $G(\mathsf{pk}_1^*)$ by h on line 3. This game hop reduces to PPRF and iO-security.

Hybrid 3: the same as Hybrid 2 with the following exceptions. We first replace c^* with $c^* \leftarrow\$ \{0,1\}^\lambda$. Then, we calculate $h' \leftarrow\$ G(c^*)$. We hardcode h' in Γ' and replace $G(c^*)$ by h' on line 7. This game hop reduces to PPRF and iO-security.

Hybrid 4: the same as Hybrid 3 with the following exceptions. We sample $h' \leftarrow\$ \{0,1\}^{2\lambda}$. Now note that with high probability h' is outside of the image of the PRG G. Thus, line 8 is no longer needed, since the check in line 7 will only be satisfied with negligible probability. This game hop reduces to PRG and iO-security.

Hybrid 5: the same as hybrid 4 with the following exception: we replace v^* by $v^* \leftarrow\$ \{0,1\}^\lambda$. This game hop reduces to PPRF security.

    The fact that v^* is random lets us x^* is random for both cases $b = 0$ and $b = 1$, and thus the adversary only has negligible probability of winning the privacy game. $\square$

Note that this construction can be easily extended for user specific encryptions, where the values c are only meant to be decrypted by one specific user. We can prove the security of such a construction in the Forgery game from Definition 7.

References

1. Agrawal, S., Bock, E.A., Chen, Y., Watson, G.: White-box cryptography with global device binding from message-recoverable signatures and token-based obfuscation. Cryptology ePrint Archive, Paper 2021/767 (2021). https://eprint.iacr.org/2021/767

2. Bock, E.A., Amadori, A., Brzuska, C., Michiels, W.: On the security goals of white-box cryptography. IACR Trans. Cryptogr. Hardw. Embed. Syst. **2020**(2), 327–357 (2020)

3. Alpirez Bock, E., Brzuska, C., Fischlin, M., Janson, C., Michiels, W.: Security reductions for white-box key-storage in mobile payments. In: Moriai, S., Wang, H. (eds.) ASIACRYPT 2020. LNCS, vol. 12491, pp. 221–252. Springer, Cham (2020). https://doi.org/10.1007/978-3-030-64837-4_8

4. Baek, C.H., Cheon, J.H., Hong, H.: White-box AES implementation revisited. J. Commun. Netw. **18**(3), 273–287 (2016)

5. Banik, S., Bogdanov, A., Isobe, T., Jepsen, M.B.: Analysis of software countermeasures for whitebox encryption. IACR Trans. Symmetric Cryptol. **2017**(1), 307–328 (2017)

6. Barak, B., et al.: On the (im)possibility of obfuscating programs. In: Kilian, J. (ed.) CRYPTO 2001. LNCS, vol. 2139, pp. 1–18. Springer, Heidelberg (2001). https://doi.org/10.1007/3-540-44647-8_1

7. Bellare, M., Rogaway, P.: The exact security of digital signatures-how to sign with RSA and Rabin. In: Maurer, U. (ed.) EUROCRYPT 1996. LNCS, vol. 1070, pp. 399–416. Springer, Heidelberg (1996). https://doi.org/10.1007/3-540-68339-9_34

8. Bellare, M., Stepanovs, I., Waters, B.: New negative results on differing-inputs obfuscation. In: Fischlin, M., Coron, J.-S. (eds.) EUROCRYPT 2016. LNCS, vol. 9666, pp. 792–821. Springer, Heidelberg (2016). https://doi.org/10.1007/978-3-662-49896-5_28

9. Billet, O., Gilbert, H., Ech-Chatbi, C.: Cryptanalysis of a white box AES implementation. In: Handschuh, H., Hasan, M.A. (eds.) SAC 2004. LNCS, vol. 3357, pp. 227–240. Springer, Heidelberg (2004). https://doi.org/10.1007/978-3-540-30564-4_16

10. Bringer, J., Chabanne, H., Dottax, E.: White box cryptography: another attempt. Cryptology ePrint Archive, Report 2006/468 (2006). http://eprint.iacr.org/2006/468

11. Chow, S., Eisen, P.A., Johnson, H., van Oorschot, P.C.: White-box cryptography and an AES implementation. In: Nyberg, K., Heys, H.M. (eds.) SAC 2002. LNCS, vol. 2595, pp. 250–270. Springer, Heidelberg (2003)

12. Chow, S., Eisen, P., Johnson, H., van Oorschot, P.C.: A white-box DES implementation for DRM applications. In: Feigenbaum, J. (ed.) DRM 2002. LNCS, vol. 2696, pp. 1–15. Springer, Heidelberg (2003). https://doi.org/10.1007/978-3-540-44993-5_1

13. Delerablée, C., Lepoint, T., Paillier, P., Rivain, M.: White-box security notions for symmetric encryption schemes. In: Lange, T., Lauter, K., Lisoněk, P. (eds.) SAC 2013. LNCS, vol. 8282, pp. 247–264. Springer, Heidelberg (2014). https://doi.org/10.1007/978-3-662-43414-7_13

14. Derbez, P., Fouque, P.-A., Lambin, B., Minaud, B.: On recovering affine encodings in white-box implementations. IACR Trans. Cryptogr. Hardw. Embed. Syst. **2018**(3), 121–149 (2018)

15. EMVCo: EMV mobile payment: software-based mobile payment security requirements (2019). https://www.emvco.com/wp-content/uploads/documents/EMVCo-SBMP-16-G01-V1.2_SBMP_Security_Requirements.pdf

16. Gentry, C., Halevi, S., Raykova, M., Wichs, D.: Outsourcing private RAM computation. In: FOCS, pp. 404–413. IEEE Computer Society (2014)

17. Goldwasser, S., Kalai, Y., Popa, R.A., Vaikuntanathan, V., Zeldovich, N.: Reusable garbled circuits and succinct functional encryption. In Proceedings of the forty-fifth annual ACM symposium on Theory of computing, pp. 555–564. ACM (2013)

18. Goubin, L., Masereel, J.-M., Quisquater, M.: Cryptanalysis of white box DES implementations. In: Adams, C., Miri, A., Wiener, M. (eds.) SAC 2007. LNCS, vol. 4876, pp. 278–295. Springer, Heidelberg (2007). https://doi.org/10.1007/978-3-540-77360-3_18

19. Hada, S.: Zero-knowledge and code obfuscation. In: Okamoto, T. (ed.) ASIACRYPT 2000. LNCS, vol. 1976, pp. 443–457. Springer, Heidelberg (2000). https://doi.org/10.1007/3-540-44448-3_34

20. Jacob, M., Boneh, D., Felten, E.: Attacking an obfuscated cipher by injecting faults. In: Feigenbaum, J. (ed.) DRM 2002. LNCS, vol. 2696, pp. 16–31. Springer, Heidelberg (2003). https://doi.org/10.1007/978-3-540-44993-5_2

21. Karroumi, M.: Protecting white-box AES with dual ciphers. In: Rhee, K.-H., Nyang, D.H. (eds.) ICISC 2010. LNCS, vol. 6829, pp. 278–291. Springer, Heidelberg (2011). https://doi.org/10.1007/978-3-642-24209-0_19

22. Lepoint, T., Rivain, M., De Mulder, Y., Roelse, P., Preneel, B.: Two attacks on a white-box AES implementation. In: Lange, T., Lauter, K., Lisoněk, P. (eds.) SAC 2013. LNCS, vol. 8282, pp. 265–285. Springer, Heidelberg (2014). https://doi.org/10.1007/978-3-662-43414-7_14

23. Link, H.E., Neumann, W.D.: Clarifying obfuscation: improving the security of white-box encoding. Cryptology ePrint Archive, Report 2004/025 (2004). http://eprint.iacr.org/2004/025

24. Michiels, W.: Device binding from digital signatures. Personal Communication

25. Muir, J.A.: A tutorial on white-box AES. Cryptology ePrint Archive, Report 2013/104 (2013). http://eprint.iacr.org/2013/104

26. De Mulder, Y., Roelse, P., Preneel, B.: Cryptanalysis of the Xiao – Lai white-box AES implementation. In: Knudsen, L.R., Wu, H. (eds.) SAC 2012. LNCS, vol. 7707, pp. 34–49. Springer, Heidelberg (2013). https://doi.org/10.1007/978-3-642-35999-6_3

27. De Mulder, Y., Wyseur, B., Preneel, B.: Cryptanalysis of a perturbated white-box AES implementation. In: Gong, G., Gupta, K.C. (eds.) INDOCRYPT 2010. LNCS, vol. 6498, pp. 292–310. Springer, Heidelberg (2010). https://doi.org/10.1007/978-3-642-17401-8_21

28. Sahai, A., Waters, B.: How to use indistinguishability obfuscation: deniable encryption, and more. In: Shmoys, D.B. (ed.) 46th ACM STOC, pp. 475–484. ACM Press, May/June 2014

29. Sanfelix, E., de Haas, J., Mune, C.: Unboxing the white-box: practical attacks against obfuscated ciphers. Presentation at BlackHat Europe 2015 (2015). https://www.blackhat.com/eu-15/briefings.html
30. Smart Card Alliance Mobile and NFC Council: Host card emulation 101. In: White paper (2014). https://www.securetechalliance.org/wp-content/uploads/HCE-101-WP-FINAL-081114-clean.pdf
31. Wyseur, B.: White-box cryptography. In: van Tilborg, H.C.A., Jajodia, S. (eds.) Encyclopedia of Cryptography and Security, 2nd edn, pp. 1386–1387. Springer, Boston (2011). https://doi.org/10.1007/978-1-4419-5906-5_627
32. Wyseur, B., Michiels, W., Gorissen, P., Preneel, B.: Cryptanalysis of white-box DES implementations with arbitrary external encodings. In: Adams, C., Miri, A., Wiener, M. (eds.) SAC 2007. LNCS, vol. 4876, pp. 264–277. Springer, Heidelberg (2007). https://doi.org/10.1007/978-3-540-77360-3_17
33. Xiao, Y., Lai, X.: A secure implementation of white-box AES. In: 2009 2nd International Conference on Computer Science and Its Applications, pp. 1–6. IEEE Computer Society (2009)

Author Index

E. B. Kavun and M. Pehl (Eds.): COSADE 2023, LNCS 13979, p. 263, 2023.
https://doi.org/10.1007/978-3-031-29497-6

Printed in the United States
by Baker & Taylor Publisher Services

Printed in the United States
by Baker & Taylor Publisher Services